Slavery Obscured

THE BLACK ATLANTIC

General Editor: Polly Rewt, The Open University and University of Stirling

Series Advisers: Caryl Phillips, novelist; David Dabydeen, Centre for Caribbean Studies, University of Warwick; Vincent Carretta, Professor of English, University of Maryland; Angus Calder, writer.

The cultural and theoretical parameters of the Black Atlantic world are explored and treated critically in this timely series. It offers students, scholars and general readers essential texts which focus on the international black experience. The broad scope of the series is innovative and ambitious, treating literary, historical, biographical, musical and visual arts subjects from an interdisciplinary and cross-cultural perspective.

The books address current debates on what constitutes the Black Atlantic, both geographically and theoretically. They include anthologized primary material and collections of seminal critical value to courses on the African diaspora and related subjects. They will also appeal more widely to a readership interested in biographical and other material that presents scholarship accessibly.

Also in the series:
Paul E. Lovejoy (editor), *Identity in the Shadow of Slavery*
Nancy Priscilla Naro, *A Slave's Place, a Master's World: Fashioning Dependency in Rural Brazil*
Alasdair Pettinger (editor), *Always Elsewhere: Travels of the Black Atlantic*
James Walvin, *An African's Life: The Life and Times of Olaudah Equiano, 1745–1797*
James Walvin, *Making the Black Atlantic: Britain and the African Diaspora*

SLAVERY OBSCURED

The Social History of the Slave Trade
in an English Provincial Port

MADGE DRESSER

CONTINUUM
London and New York

Continuum

The Tower Building, 11 York Road, London SE1 7NX
370 Lexington Avenue, New York, NY 10017–6503

First published 2001

British Library Cataloguing-in-Publication Data

A catalogue record for this book is available from the British Library.

ISBN   0–8264–4875–5 (hardback)
             0–8264–4876–3 (paperback)

Library of Congress Cataloging-in-Publication Data

Dresser, Madge.
    Slavery obscured: the social history of the slave trade in an English provincial port/ Madge Dresser.
      p.   cm. — (The Black Atlantic)
    Includes bibliographical references and index.
    ISBN 0–8264–4875–5 (hb.). — ISBN 0–8264–4876–3 (pbk.)
    1. Slave-trade—England—Bristol—History. 2. Slavery—England—Bristol—History.
3 Bristol (England)—Social conditions. I. Title. II. Series.

HT1164.B74 D74 2001
382'.44'0942393—dc21   00–052344

Designed and typeset by Ben Cracknell Studios
Printed and bound in Great Britain

CONTENTS

ILLUSTRATIONS

TABLES

ABBREVIATIONS

BBCL	Bristol Baptist College Library
BCRL	Bristol Central Reference Library
BGPA	*Bristol Gazette and Public Advertiser*
BL	British Library, London
BM	*Bristol Mercury*
BMBJ	*Bonner and Middleton's Bristol Journal*
BQ	*Baptist Quarterly*
BRO	Bristol Record Office
BSMV	Bristol Society of Merchant Venturers
BULSC	University of Bristol Library, Special Collections
BWI	*Bristol Weekly Intelligencer*
CalSPCol	*Calendar of State Papers Colonial*
CalSPDom	*Calendar of State Papers Domestic*
FFBJ	*Felix Farley's Bristol Journal*
GRO	Gloucestershire County Record Office, Gloucester
HL	Huntington Library, California
HMC	Historical Manuscripts Commission (of the British Library)
JBMHS	*Journal of the Barbados Museum and Historical Society*
JCTP	*Journal of the Commissioners for Trade and Plantations*
JRL	John Rylands University Library of Manchester
PRO	Public Record Office, Kew, nr. London
SA	*Slavery and Abolition*
SMV	Society of Merchant Venturers of Bristol Archives
SRO	Somerset County Record Office, Taunton
TBGAS	*Transactions of the Bristol and Gloucestershire Archaeological Society*
WMQ	*William and Mary Quarterly*
WRO	Wiltshire County Record Office, Trowbridge

Richard Jeffreys Lewis, *The Death of Colston*, c. 1844. Bristol City Museum and Art Gallery

ACKNOWLEDGEMENTS

Books, like films, depend on the help and support of many people. The production of this one was made possible by the generous award of a year's research leave funded by the Arts and Humanities Research Board, and by my own university, the University of the West of England, Bristol. The Faculty of Humanities and the Vice-Chancellor there also provided me with further financial assistance.

Particular thanks go to Professors William Beinart of St Antony's College, Oxford, and Ronald Hutton of the University of Bristol for supporting my grant application, to Dr Pamela Sharpe, currently Queen's Fellow at the University of Western Australia, for her wise advice, and to Marika Sherwood, Research Fellow at the Institute of Commonwealth Studies, for her inspiration and example. I am also grateful to Sir George White for his help with sources on the history of Barbados.

I should also like to express my heartfelt gratitude to those who were kind enough to take the time to read preliminary drafts of some of the chapters in this book, especially Angus Calder, Carol Dyhouse, Polly Rewt, Wilf Summerbell and Nick von Tunzelman. They all offered truly constructive criticism, and though the faults that remain are mine alone, any strengths that this book may have owes much to them. Carol's warm encouragement and sensible advice helped me make the difficult transition from research to writing.

The School of History of the University of the West of England (UWE) is staffed by fine historians who are also excellent colleagues. My particular thanks go to Peter Fleming, June Hannam, Katherine Holden, Diana Jeater, Moira Martin, Steve Poole, Geoffrey Swain and Glyn Stone, whose ideas and enthusiasm for this project were very much appreciated, as was the help and advice offered by Geoffrey Channon, until recently the Dean of Humanities, and by James Gibbs and Robin Jarvis of the School of English, and Bill Evans of the Directorate. I am grateful also to Linda Skinner and her staff at UWE's Centre for Research, Industry and Innovation, to David Bruce of the School of Business Studies and to Stuart Taylor of the Faculty of Engineering. Thanks also to Tina Shortman for her secretarial assistance.

This book grew out of a paper I gave in 1996 to the African Studies Association (UK), and I should like to thank those present, including Robin Law and David

Richardson, for their perceptive comments. Much of the initial research was done whilst I served as historical consultant to the Exhibition on Bristol and the Transatlantic Slave Trade organized by the Bristol City Museum and Art Gallery. It was a real pleasure and privilege to work with the museum staff. Stephen Price, the Director, has shared my love of this subject, as has Sue Giles, the exhibition's curator. I am grateful to Sheena Stoddard, fine arts curator, to Jeremy Dixon for his invaluable help with the illustrations, maps and the design of two of the figures in this book, and to Christine Jackson and John Bryant and the exhibition team.

Another source of guidance and help was the librarians and archivists whose collections I consulted. Michael Richardson and Hannah Lowery of the University of Bristol Library's Special Collections, Jane Bradley and Dawn Dyer of Bristol Central Reference Library and Pat Denney of the Society of Merchant Venturers of the City of Bristol went well beyond the call of duty to put sources my way and make my research a real pleasure. Thanks to the staff of the St Matthias branch of the University of the West of England Library for help with inter-library loans and to John Williams, Richard Burley and the staff of the Bristol Record Office for their efficiency and dispatch, to Guy Grannum of the Public Record Office for his extremely useful guidance and to Jeffrey Spittal of John Wesley's New Rooms for his continuing kindness and erudition. I am grateful also to Mary Robinson for making my time at the Huntington Library so worthwhile, to the staff of the University of Melbourne, Australia, for microfilming some of the Bright Family Collection for me, and to Susan Mills of the Angus Library, Regent's College, Oxford, for helping me find my way through her excellent collection. The staff of the British Library, the Baptist College Library in Bristol, the Institute of Commonwealth Studies, the John Rylands University Library in Manchester, the Rhodes House Library and the Bodleian Library in Oxford, the Woodbrook College Library in Birmingham, and the archivists of the Leeds District Archives and the County Record Offices of Gloucestershire, Somerset and Wiltshire were all helpful. I am also grateful to the Society of Merchant Venturers for allowing me free access to their wonderful collection. Permission for the reproduction of the illustrations in this book has been most generously given by the Bristol City Museum and Art Gallery, Bristol Central Library and the family of Eric Fraser.

I have thanked all those individuals who have given me particular references in the endnotes, but would also like to thank here Peter Alexander, Jonathan Barry, Edward Beaumont, Steve Behrendt, Joseph Bettey, Jim Brennan, Sue Brittain, Muriel Mitcheson Brown, Mary Campbell, Christine Chivallon, Suzanne Clarke, Tom Duckenfield, Christine Eickelmann, Martin Crossley Evans, Peter Fryer, Gad Heuman, Harry Goulbourne, John Gunnery, Derrick Hunt, Ronald Hughes, Mark Horton, Raj Lalla, Doreen Lindegaard, Ken Morgan, Jim MacNeill, Melanie Newton, Ruth Paley, Anthony Phillips, Mansell Protheroe, Ron Ramdin, Tatiana Rees, David Richardson, David Small, Jeffrey Spittal, Helen Taylor, Hugh Thomas and Mary Waldron for the insights and expertise they were generous enough to share.

My publisher Janet Joyce of Continuum has been an exemplar of patience and forbearance, as have Sandra Margolies and Peter Harrison. Polly Rewt has been a most supportive and approachable editor.

Books are very disruptive of family life and my family has had to suffer a distracted member of the household for far too long. So thanks to all my family, especially Helen Dresser and Lilian Summerbell for their understanding, Wilf for his perceptive advice and unfailing support, and Daniel, whose encouragement, cajoling and sacrifice of computer time have meant more to me than he knows.

To the memory of my father Leonard Dresser,
to my mother Helen Dresser,
and to Wilf and Daniel Summerbell

Forgetting
sometimes
vanishes into oblivion
it's the threshold of recollection
on the edge
of absence

Memory
you fashion yourself
with dabs
of oblivion . . .

(from Patrick Chamoiseau,
School Days, translated by
Linda Coverdale, London, 1998)

INTRODUCTION

'Bristol, Britannia's second mart and eye!'

James Grainger, *The Sugar-Cane* (1746)

'Ship-shape and Bristol fashion', proclaims a 1954 bank advertisement, featuring John and Sebastian Cabot (Figure 1). Looking sternly heroic, these icons of Atlantic exploration have been co-opted to promote the cause of an English provincial bank.[1] The advertisement trumpets the proud seafaring legacy of Bristol, England, and is typically upbeat in its assessment of that city's past. It describes Bristol as a city made famous by the voyages of the Cabots and prosperous by the city's Society of Merchant Venturers. It celebrates the city's foreign trade: 'wine from Spain, gold and ivory from Africa, sugar from the West Indies'. Asserting that 'ship-shape and Bristol fashion' referred to the city's reputation for fine seamanship, it is less than frank about Bristol's major role in the Atlantic slave trade, saying only:

> Its merchants were quick to replace by some new industry any part of their trade which showed signs of diminution, as a result either of changing world conditions, or, as was once the case, of Government action spurred on by a developing social conscience.[2]

This veiled reference to the city's slaving past is typical of many of the pronouncements made about the city in the immediate post-war period. Yet it was enslaved Africans, far more than gold or ivory, who constituted the crucial element in the city's trade with Africa. And it was the forced labour of these Africans on West Indian plantations which underwrote the city's prosperity throughout the eighteenth and early nineteenth centuries.

There were those in the late nineteenth and early twentieth centuries who did write about the city's slaving past. Yet despite this, and despite a widespread popular fascination with the subject, there has been until very recently little official recognition of its existence, let alone its significance.[3]

'Ship-shape and Bristol fashion'

IF THE voyages of John and Sebastian Cabot made Bristol famous, the Society of Merchant Venturers made it prosperous. By the year 1500 the Society controlled all the city's foreign trade and there came to its quays and warehouses, in steady stream, wine from Spain, gold and ivory from Africa, sugar from the West Indies. The fame of its navigators became such that, even now, 'ship-shape and Bristol fashion' expresses, on sailing vessels, high praise of seamanship; its merchants were quick to replace by some new industry any part of their trade which showed signs of diminution, as a result either of changing world conditions or, as was once the case, of Government action spurred on by a developing social conscience. The tide of fortune continued to flow, and Bristol, though perhaps less colourful than of old, is still one of our great seaports, with extensive manufacturing and industrial resources.

WESTMINSTER ✦ BANK LIMITED

Figure 1   Advertisement for Westminster Bank Ltd, 'Ship-shape and Bristol fashion', illustration by Eric Fraser, c. 1954. Reproduced with kind permission of the Fraser family

The legacy of Edward Colston is a case in point. Colston (1636–1721) was an English merchant whose hugely generous legacies to his native city, Bristol, made him the Getty of his day. His statue still presides over the city centre, a number of schools and buildings still bear his name and his birthday is still celebrated in Bristol's oldest church every November. His name continues to command loyalty, respect and gratitude from many Bristolians.

The painting of Edward Colston's deathbed by Richard Jeffreys Lewis, which is reproduced as the frontispiece to this book, was first unearthed from the stores of Bristol's City Museum and Art Gallery in 1998, where it had languished for at least a century, and would no doubt have languished for some time to come had it not been for the staging in 1999 of the city's first ever exhibition on the transatlantic slave trade.

At first it was thought that this oddly stylized portrayal of Bristol's most generous benefactor was an irrelevance to the exhibition, painted as it was in 1844, more than a hundred years after Colston's death. It was then discovered that it had been painted the year after Colston's intact body had been exhumed during the renovation of the church in which it had been interred. Newspaper reports of the exhumation made much of the fact that the body and head of the great man had not decayed and indeed were, for some brief moments after their uncovering, miraculously well preserved.[4]

Aside from its grisly provenance, there was another disturbing feature in the painting itself. For amidst the usual emblems of philanthropy – the weeping mourners, the Anglican cleric, the almoner at the door – was a kneeling woman. She is centre stage and holds Colston's hand, and she is undeniably of African origin. Could this lady be the 'black Mary' named as a servant in Colston's will? Or did 'black Mary' allude, as some have maintained, merely to a brunette of Welsh or English origin? The positioning of the maidservant in relation to Colston is suggestive. Does it imply a more complicated personal attachment between the bachelor philanthropist and his maid? Or does the artist mean it to represent, along with the clasped hand, a posthumous plea for reconciliation between the slaver and the enslaved?[5] Whatever the answers to these questions, the picture's content and history aptly symbolize the way slave-trading activities have been both obscured and revealed in Bristol's collective civic consciousness.

For the truth is that Edward Colston was directly involved in the slave trade. He was an official in the Royal African Company, the company which until 1698 possessed the British monopoly on the slave trade. This fact was established by H. J. Wilkins, a Bristol vicar who wrote a well-documented study of Colston in the 1920s.[6] Indeed, the company minutes show that Colston was present at meetings which organized and approved the sale and transport of Africans to the Caribbean. Some subsequent scholars have preferred to stress, along with his undoubted generosity to charitable causes, his other commercial involvements – in fruit and wines and cloth, and in West Indian sugar.[7] Nevertheless, it is this last commercial interest which further confirms that a significant part of his wealth was derived from the labour of slaves.

There has long been reluctance in some quarters to acknowledge Colston's participation in the slave trade. According to one contemporary source, he was represented shortly after his death as a great East India merchant with no mention made of his Caribbean or African interests.[8] Nor is there, in the fine Victorian statue of him bestriding the city centre, any hint of his trafficking in human cargo. Indeed, recent suggestions that the plinth should be reworked to include a less hagiographic description of the great man's past, or indeed, that the statue itself should be removed, unleashed a furious controversy in the local press in 1998, a controversy which uncannily recalled the debate over the slave trade itself waged in the papers two centuries before. The correspondent who wrote angrily as follows typifies the defensiveness of many: 'Here we go again! Once more the activist diggers of the past want to make us feel guilty for the actions of our forefathers.'[9]

The aim of my study is not to assign guilt, but to flesh out some of the questions left unaddressed by the economic and political historians who have approached this subject before. In so doing, I wish to incorporate some of the theoretical insights proffered by recent writers on race, popular culture and gender. Though its focus is local, the concerns of this study have demanded I explore beyond the boundaries of Bristol and Britain into aspects of Caribbean and West African history.

The first chapter, on the development of the slave trade in Bristol, seeks to set it in its colonial context and to update our understanding of how it operated in one particular city. This chapter utilizes the recent work of David Richardson and other economic historians of Bristol along with my own original research in order to locate some of the social and business networks which connected people of virtually all ranks to the 'African trade'.

In Chapter 2 we shall seek to consider how white Bristolians regarded people of African origin in the first three-quarters of the eighteenth century. This is the first sustained examination of the representation of black people in the Bristol press and the first to evaluate what can be distilled about contemporary racial attitudes from Bristol seamen's accounts. It discusses what we know about the black and mixed-race presence in Bristol and asks if the close personal connections obtaining between the city's residents and Caribbean plantocracies hardened anti-black prejudices.

We shall go on in Chapter 3 to assess, in the light of original research, the connections between Bristol's 'urban renaissance' in the Georgian era and slave-produced wealth. Excavating the links between housebuilding and slave-trading, this chapter examines the pedigree of some stately homes in the city's vicinity, and notes the rise of refinement and gentility made possible by the city's participation in the Atlantic economy.

The evolution of attitudes towards slavery and race during the long Parliamentary campaign against the slave trade is the subject of Chapters 4 and 5. Here the role of women, hitherto neglected by historians of Georgian Bristol, is examined. Chapter 6 investigates such attitudes during the campaign to emancipate slaves in the British colonies until its formal parliamentary success in 1833. Was anti-slavery simply the concern of a middle-class minority? Or did it strike a chord with other social groups? What motivated anti-slavery campaigners? And how did local members of the pro-slavery lobby organize themselves and articulate their concerns? The last three chapters seek to extend the discussion beyond a consideration of the parliamentary campaigns to one of the city's changing political culture. Finally, the Conclusion briefly considers, in a more discursive way, some aspects of the legacy of Bristol's slaving past for the nineteenth and twentieth centuries.

Although this study makes no claims to have exhausted the primary sources relevant to the subject under study, it has tried to consider a wide range of disparate, often fragmentary material in relationship to the questions raised above. It has followed through the careers of individuals and examined the links between them and the cultural milieu in which they operated. It has used literary ephemera alongside wills, depositions, diaries and business accounts in an attempt to unpack the mentality of those who had few qualms about trading in slaves, those who agonized about it and those who opposed it. Where possible I have incorporated the voices of Africans themselves, citing, for example, the correspondence of the Efik traders of the Niger Delta, the letter of an unemployed black servant, and the remarks of black seamen quoted in white sources. Throughout this book, the emphasis has been on trying to recover the sense people made of their own situations and to attempt, as far as possible, to 'research local [and] think global'.

Notes

1 The print commissioned by the Westminster Bank is by Eric Fraser (1901–83) and is probably part of a series of historic scenes commissioned by the bank around 1954. I am grateful to the Fraser family for this information and for their generous permission to reproduce the print here. The Westminster Bank, which grew out of smaller banks, including the Bristol or 'Old' Bank, became part of the National Westminster group in the 1970s, which itself has since been taken over by the Royal Bank of Scotland.

2 *Ibid.*

3 John Latimer's *Annals of Bristol in the Seventeenth Century* (Bristol: William George, 1900), *Annals of Bristol in the Eighteenth Century* (Bristol: privately printed, 1893) and *Annals of Bristol in the Nineteenth Century* (Bristol: privately printed, 1893) establish him as the most notable chronicler of the slave trade, trawling the city's old newspapers and other documents and talking extensively to the families of slave-traders and planters, and evidently a few surviving slave-owners and traders as well, according to his friend and contemporary Henry W. Case:

the kind temperament of several of these persons was known to me in my boyhood, and also to my old friend . . . Mr. John Latimer. Some of the persons (or their immediate descendants) lived near us and near the late George Muller at Paul Street in Kingsdown; while others resided at Berkeley Square and Queen Square; and were amiable people. Henry W. Case, *On Sea and Land On Creek and River: Being an Account of Experiences in the Visitation of Assemblies of Christians in the West Indies and British Guiana; With reminiscences of Pioneer Missionaries and of the Slave Trade Formerly Carried on From Bristol* (London, 1910), pp. 1–3.

4 A direct descendant of Colston, Frederick Colston, and possibly the artist himself were present at the exhumation; *Felix Farley's Bristol Journal*, 9 and 16 September 1843.

5 By 1843, of course, the slaves were emancipated, but underinvestment and falling sugar prices meant poverty and unrest in the Caribbean, so the picture might also be alluding to the need for better relations between planters and their formally free but largely discontented workforce. See Abigail Bakan, *Ideology and Class Conflict in Jamaica: The Politics of Rebellion* (Montreal, Kingston, London and Buffalo, 1990), pp. 26–35.

6 H. J. Wilkins, *Edward Colston (1636–1721): A Chronological Account of His Life and Work Together with an Account of the Colston Societies and Memorials in Bristol* (Bristol and London, 1920).

7 See Ken Morgan for the latest assessment of Edward Colston in his *Edward Colston and Bristol* (Bristol: Bristol Historical Association, 1999).

8 Silas Told, *An Account of the Life and Dealings of God with Silas Told, late preacher of the Gospel* . . . (London, 1786), pp. 19–25.

9 *Evening Post* (Bristol, England), 29 January 1998. My thanks to Matthew Shelley and David Harrison of the *Evening Post* for affording me access to the unpublished letters and calls made during this time.

= 1 =

BRISTOL AND THE TRANSATLANTIC SLAVE TRADE

Bristol . . . is a maritime trading city, with a small cathedral. It is remarkable there, that all men that are dealers, even in ship trades, launch into adventures by sea, chiefly to the West India plantations and Spain. A poor shopkeeper, that sells candles, will have a bale of stockings, or a piece of stuff for Nevis or Virginia etc., and rather than fail, they trade in men. (Roger North, Recorder of Bristol in the late seventeenth century, cited in J. H. Bettey, *Bristol Observed: Visitors' Impressions of the City from Domesday to the Blitz* (Bristol, 1989), p. 59)

The moral atmosphere of the British West Indies in the first thirty years after sugar cane was introduced, was that of a gold rush. (Richard Pares, *A West India Fortune* (London, 1950), p. 25)

'Negroes', wrote the late-Victorian scholar George Saintsbury, were by the late seventeenth century seen 'to be the strength and sinews of the Western World'.[1] He was of course referring to those Africans whose enslavement provided the labour power so needed on the colonial plantations of the Americas and the Caribbean. The question we shall examine in this chapter is the relation between this slave labour and the port of Bristol, England's second city for much of the late seventeenth and eighteenth centuries.

How were the foundations for Bristol's involvement in the transatlantic slave trade first established? Most discussions of the subject begin at 1698. This was the year in which the Royal African Company, formed in 1672, lost its monopoly of 'the Guinea trade' or 'African trade'. Ships from ports other than London could, after years of lobbying, now legally participate in the enslavement of Africans. Bristol had in the early Middle Ages been a centre for the trafficking of English slaves.[2]

However, it is generally assumed that the city did not resume slaving until 1698, when Bristol's 'Guinea trade' sprang up nearly fully grown, like the goddess of trade herself.

Yet the Port of Bristol and individual Bristolians were involved in the earliest days of Atlantic exploration and American colonization. And since the activities of exploration, colonization and slaving were inextricably linked, we must question anew the length and nature of the city's association with the Atlantic slave trade. The first part of this chapter, then, reconsiders the period before 1698, one usually glossed over in most conventional histories. It aims to show that Bristol's growing prosperity after 1660 was to a significant degree dependent on African slave labour in the Caribbean and American colonies. It will argue that Bristolians had personal experience as slave-owners and as illegal slave-traders well before 1698.[3] The focus will be on a sample of Bristol-born merchants active in the Caribbean and North America.

We will then turn to consider the legal slave trade in the city, paying particular attention to what recent scholarly work has established about it, especially regarding the first half of the eighteenth century. In this early period, Bristol was a more important slaving port than Liverpool and even, for a brief time, surpassed London, to become the nation's number one slaving port. David Richardson has already offered a 'collective portrait' of the city's major slave-traders and an impressively thorough compendium of their participation in the African trade in this early period.[4] But what more can we learn about some of these men? And who else besides them in Bristol profited from slaving voyages? Building on recent scholarship, this chapter aims to exploit a disparate range of primary sources, including indentures, wills, business records, private correspondence and various papers of state, in the service of new questions about Bristol's slaving past.

Bristol and the trade in Africans before 1698

Bristol in the age of exploration

According to one contemporary Spanish source, Bristol ships, inspired by John Cabot, had begun to ply the Atlantic in search of the 'island of Brazil and the seven cities' a year before Columbus made his historic voyage.[5] In 1497 John Cabot (Giovanni Caboto), a Genoese by birth but a naturalized citizen of Venice, set sail from Bristol for what was to be known as Newfoundland. His son Sebastian, long claimed to be a native son of Bristol, has also been celebrated for his contributions to Atlantic exploration. Both are popularly assumed to pre-date any associations with the slave trade, which with some justice is seen, so far as Britain is concerned, as an eighteenth-century phenomenon.

Yet Sebastian, who worked for the Spanish government for many years, travelled to the La Plata estuary in Latin America with a contingent of African slaves and was said to have enslaved a small party of Amerindians whom he kept with him at his house in Seville. Cabot knew a number of Bristol merchants resident in Seville during this time and is said to have been a particular friend of the former mayor of Bristol, the merchant Robert Thorne (the younger) (*c.* 1492–1532), who invested in Cabot's voyage to La Plata.[6]

Thorne, along with his brother Nicholas (1496–1546), owned a soap factory in Seville in partnership with some Genoese. The Thorne brothers, later revered in their native city as the founders of its venerable grammar school, were by all accounts immensely rich. They are credited by Sacks and other historians for being amongst the earliest English merchants to trade directly to the West Indies, their wealth being said to have come from soap, leather, wine and other trades typically associated with Spain.[7] But Seville was also the centre of a flourishing slave trade in 'blacks, Muslims and Canary Islanders'. Though the slave trade in Seville was mainly dominated by Genoese, Hugh Thomas lists Robert Thorne as one of the city's 'major slave traders'.[8] Further research is needed to determine the extent of Thorne's involvement in the trade, but Thorne's close association with Genoese merchants is suggestive. Might Bristol's earliest-endowed school, which survives today, have been financed in part by slavery?

More significantly, Thorne's putative involvement casts Bristol's long-standing links with Spain and Portugal into a new light since it may have helped to generate the city's interest not only in colonization and exploration,[9] but in the slave trade itself. In the context of the sixteenth century, when Portuguese *conversos* (Jews forcibly converted to Christianity by the Inquisition) and the Genoese were visibly involved in the beginnings of the Atlantic slave trade, an old English proverb, 'one Jew is equal to two Genoese, one Bristolian to two Jews', begins to make new sense.[10]

There seem to have been English merchants in Seville interested in Guinea as early as 1480, and Portuguese discoveries of the islands off the Guinea coast were talked about in Bristol that same year.[11] Fragmentary evidence suggests that the interest of Bristol mariners in Guinea may go back as far as 1501, and that there were English interlopers in Guinea from the 1540s. Certainly, the King of Spain complained about English incursions into the Guinea waters from the late 1550s. Evidently the Portuguese, who had the right to supply the Spanish colonies in America with slaves, could sub-let their privileges to others, even Englishmen, and the Spanish authorities were worried about informal collaboration between English 'pirates' and unofficial Spanish and Portuguese slaving interests.[12] In this context, we see that Bristol merchants resident in the Iberian Peninsula were well placed to learn about the profits to be derived from the slave trade and to make personal contacts with traders directly involved in it.[13]

By the second half of the sixteenth century, merchants in London and Bristol had begun to explore possible commercial links with West Africa. In 1552, the very year Bristol's Society of Merchant Venturers was founded, Captain Thomas Wyndham sailed out of Bristol with some Bristol merchandise on board to the Barbary or North African coast. Four years later, William Towerson, in search of African gold, brought his ships safely back from Guinea to Bristol's 'Hungroad'.[14] More research is needed to determine whether Bristol men were amongst the 400 crew who sailed with John Hawkins on his slaving adventures off what is now Sierra Leone in the 1560s, but the exploits of Hawkins, as a West Country man, would undoubtedly have been of particular interest to his contemporaries in Bristol.[15] By the 1570s, Bristol merchants petitioning for the restoration of trade to Portugal complained that some of their number had antagonized the Portuguese by trading in Guinea.[16] But Portugal's claim to exclusive trading rights in the area seems later to have been withdrawn, since by 1593 'thee coast of Geney' was listed as one of the 'places of trade' which Bristol merchants were officially allowed to visit.[17]

This early Bristol trade to Africa was occasional and was primarily interested in not slaves, but gold and other goods. Nevertheless, the trading contacts and capital links were being developed which would facilitate the development of the so-called triangular trade from England to Africa to the Caribbean and the Americas. What Robin Blackburn said about John Hawkins applies equally well to Bristol merchants acting as privateers and legitimate merchants during this time:

> John Hawkins acquired his slave trading contacts and know-how in the Canaries and the Azores, and many lesser privateers not only traded with the Spanish or Portuguese colonists but also learnt from them the unfamiliar customs of the New World, including smoking tobacco, drinking chocolate . . . and holding slaves.[18]

Though English involvement in African slaving was not to be in earnest until the 1640s, by the early seventeenth century there are already indications that African slaves would soon be part of the trading pattern. Consider, for example, that Robert John and Thomas Aldworth owned the *Gabriel* of Bristol, which made a voyage to buy hides, salt and ivory from Guinea. The Aldworths are famous for their promotion of the exploration and the colonization of North America, most notably Virginia. But they had also, by 1618, established Bristol's first sugar refinery and possessed a plantation in Jamaica later in the century.[19] Though the sugar they first refined in Bristol probably came from Portuguese colonies, notably the Azores, Madeira and Brazil, it would have been slave produced.[20]

Sir Ferdinando Gorges (1565–1647), another Bristolian celebrated for his visionary role in the colonization of North America, was Lord Proprietor of Maine and a founding member of the Virginia Company. Less well known are his investments in the Bermuda (or Somers Islands) Company, founded in 1612, and in the Guinea Company, established six years later. Gorges was a patentee of the Guinea Company, an early precursor of the Royal African Company, which was concerned with the gold and ivory trade on the West African coast. Though Gorges's participation seems to pre-date any formal English involvement in the slave trade per se, it helped, as we shall see, to lay the foundation for it. We have no direct evidence that Gorges himself owned African slaves, though he did briefly host captive Native Americans from Virginia. African slaves, however, were present in small numbers in both Bermuda and Virginia as early as the 1620s when he was still actively involved in both companies.[21]

Intriguingly, the African presence in Bristol coincides with this opening up of the African trade. The first surviving reference to a 'blackamore' in Bristol dates from the last quarter of the sixteenth century, and relates to a gardener employed in the merchant Sir John Young's 'Great House', which backed onto the city's quayside.[22] The existence of only nine other Africans has so far been uncovered by local researchers for the period up to 1651 (Table 1).

Table 1 Bristol residents of African origin, 1603–98

Date	Name given	Description
1603	Joan Smyth	'A blackamore', buried St Philip and St Jacob's Church
1610	Peter	'Blackamoore', buried St Philip and St Jacob's Church
1612	Katherine	'A black negra', buried Christchurch parish
1625	Cattelena	'Single negro woman', died in Almondsbury
1631	Solomon	Baptized St Augustine's Church, 'a black belonging to William Hayman'
1632	Marye	Buried(?) St Philip and St Jacob's, 'a servant to William Edmonds'
1640	Francis	Buried Broadmead Baptist church, a 'blackamore or eithiopian' servant to a merchant
1651	Two unnamed men	Captured from a Portuguese ship by a Bristol privateer and purchased by Robert Yeamans
1667	Dinah Black	Servant in Bristol to Dorothy Smith, forcibly transported to West Indies. A baptized Christian
1677	Titus Blackmore	Owned by Humphrey Hooke, a man reputed to have property in Barbados
1684	William	'Son of a black', baptized St Augustine's Church
1692	G. Blackmore	Buried St James's
1693	William Bristoll	'A Black' of Mr Alderman Swimmers, baptized St Augustine's Church
1694	George Quillo	Baptized Mangotsfield Church (north of Bristol)
1697	Mary and Sarah	Mary, 'base child of Sarah a negro' baptized 1697 at St Philip and St Jacob's
1698	'Negro boy'	'Of Major Yates', buried St Werburgh's Church

Sources: D. P. Lindegaard, *Black Bristolians of the Seventeenth, Eighteenth and Nineteenth Centuries*, (Bristol: privately printed, n.d.); Pip Jones and Rita Youseph, *The Black Population of Bristol in the Eighteenth Century*; BCRL, Braikenridge Collection.

The laconic entries in church records, though an invaluable source in the days before provincial newspapers, tell us little about these individuals. We do know that 'Katherine' had worked at the Horsehead Tavern in Christmas Street, again near the quay. We know too that 'Catellena' was a single 'Negro' woman who had lived in Almondsbury, a village just to the north of the city. Catellena, whose name suggests some connection with Spain or Portugal, was said to have left an estate of over £6, a modest enough amount even for those days, but one which indicates she was not a slave.[23] Three of the people recorded in the city before 1640 had a connection with St Philip and St Jacob's Church, which was sited near the 'Old Market' area of the city, a commercial and manufacturing area. This in itself suggests a link between merchants and African servants which pre-dates any formal entry of Bristol into the African trade.

By the beginning of the seventeenth century, Bristol's Society of Merchant Venturers, first established in 1552, had re-formed and consolidated its position as the most exclusive voice of the city's overseas merchants.[24] This was the very time which saw the establishment of a British presence in the Caribbean and the mainland colonies. Wars were fought with the French, Dutch and Spanish with alarming regularity throughout the seventeenth and eighteenth centuries to establish British hegemony in these regions. Bristolians were involved in this process as military men, merchants, mariners and settlers right from the beginning.

Trade with Barbados (settled in 1627) and the Leeward Islands – St Christopher (1624), Nevis (1628) and Montserrat and Antigua (1632) – early engaged the interest of Bristol merchants. By the time Jamaica was wrested from Spain in 1655, the West Indian trade was well on its way to becoming a major sector in Bristol's economy. Labour was a crucial factor in exploiting the potential wealth of the Caribbean and the mainland colonies. In the decade after 1645 alone, some 10,000 white voluntary servants and some 3000 'convicts rogues and political prisoners' were shipped from Britain to Barbados.[25] Bristol was a major exit point for such servants and much has been made of the 10,000 or so who passed through the port en route to the colonies between 1654 and 1685.[26]

A number of prominent Bristol merchants gained lucrative contracts shipping Irish rebels to the West Indies in the 1650s.[27] Conditions aboard these ships must have been grim, and conditions in the Caribbean were especially harsh for the 'papist' Irish, whom planters considered refractory and alien.[28] There was also, from the early 1650s, a scandalous trade of 'spiriting' or kidnapping of English children to serve on the plantations by unscrupulous captains, and Bristol MP Sir John Knight was the first to put his name to an abortive bill in the early 1660s to stop this practice. Apparently, Bristol's mayor of 1663, Sir Robert Cann, asked the government for powers to inspect ships in order to root out this same abuse.[29] It was also reportedly common for petty criminals to be 'advised' to ask to be transported to the Caribbean to labour on the plantations in order to avoid a death sentence. They were then sent to the West Indies, where they were sold as convict labour, some apparently serving on the plantations owned by members of Bristol's oligarchic corporation.

English political dissidents were also used as forced plantation labour. At least one member of an eminent West Indian family began as a Bristol merchant transporting Monmouth rebels to the Caribbean.[30] Shortly after the Monmouth rebellion in 1685, when the notoriously vindictive Chief Justice Jeffreys swept into the city to ensure that the rebels were severely punished, he unexpectedly rounded on members of Bristol's corporation for 'kidnapping' people for the plantations. Jeffreys fined Bristol's mayor, William Hayman, £1000 and threatened court action against some of his aldermen, including William Swymmer, John Napper and Sir Robert Cann.

Historians of Bristol have understandably focused on the colourful history of the city's white transportees. The hard lives and undoubted mistreatment of many of the white servants have passed into local folklore.[31] As a result, it becomes all the more important to turn to historians of the Caribbean to remind ourselves that African slaves hugely outnumbered white labour in the islands as early, in some cases, as the early 1660s. Unlike their white counterparts, they and their offspring were condemned to slavery in perpetuity.

It was of course the conversion of the Caribbean islands to sugar production from the 1640s onwards which guaranteed the eventual predominance of African labour in the British Caribbean. Thus Barbados, which in the 1640s had relied on a racially mixed labour force to work its plantations of tobacco, cotton, ginger and indigo, had by 1680 become a sugar island of large plantations, dependent on a mainly African workforce.[32] Many ordinary Bristolians had to leave Barbados, forced out by this Caribbean version of the enclosure movement. They left to seek their fortune in Jamaica or the mainland American colonies, a few remaining as part of a residual population of poor whites or 'redlegs'.[33] This conversion to large sugar estates replicated itself throughout the British Caribbean as the seventeenth century progressed. Along with it, as Richard Sheridan explains, went 'the re-emigration of small proprietors and indentured servants, and the introduction of Negro slaves'.[34]

Bristol merchants had helped to effect this transition to sugar, but what precisely was the link between them and specifically slave-generated wealth in this period? What evidence survives to indicate that Bristol ships were involved in the illegal slave trade servicing the Caribbean and mainland colonies before 1698? How else might Bristol merchants be linked to the provision and exploitation of African labour?

Bristol and the illegal slave trade

The supply of slaves to the British Caribbean was originally dominated by Dutch traders, though British traders were active at least as early as the 1640s and some of them had Bristol connections. For example, the Bristol-born William Pennoyer organized a series of voyages to Guinea between 1645 and 1647. William and his brother Thomas Pennoyer were important colonial traders who were based in London but maintained links via the tobacco trade with Bristol.[35] The Pennoyers were linked through business and possibly religious affiliation to the London slave-traders Maurice Thomson and Rowland Wilson. By the early 1650s Thomson and Wilson used one James Pope as their agent for several slaving voyages to the Gambia. Pope, sailing aboard their ship the *Friendship*, was instructed on one voyage to 'find 15 or 20 many lusty young Negers and bring them home with you for London' (presumably to work as page-boys) as well as packing the ships full of Africans for Barbados.[36] He seems almost certainly to have been linked with the Bristol Popes, whose family would by the 1660s be engaged in the sugar-refining industry.[37]

One early instance of a slave being supplied to one Englishman by another comes in a document signed on 23 February 1655 by Samuel Drew, an inhabitant of Barbados. In it, Drew formally gave notice that he would free one of his African slaves on the condition that he receive another: 'release by Samuel Drew . . . of his nigger called Anthony who seemed to have a desire to become a Christian, in lieu of another nigger called Sampson delivered him by General Penn'.[38] The 'General Penn' referred to is none other than Vice-Admiral William Penn, whose maritime skills would help secure Jamaica from the Spanish later that same year. This is the same Penn who would, in 1660, stand unsuccessfully for a Bristol parliamentary seat and soon after represent the West Country port of Weymouth. Penn was a native of Bristol and his memorial can still be seen in the city's cathedral. His son was the Quaker William Penn, who would go on to found the colony of Pennsylvania.[39]

What was General Penn doing supplying one slave 'in lieu of' another? The fact that Samuel Drew sent notice of this 'swap' to Penn implies that Penn had been contracted to supply a slave to Drew in the first place. Was Penn augmenting his naval salary with a bit of private slaving on the side? No historians of Bristol have ever associated either Penn with the business of slavery, though both father and son apparently owned slaves.[40] In any case, the whole exchange between Drew and Penn Sr pre-dates Bristol's official entry into the Atlantic slave trade.

By 1660 the lucrative trade in supplying black labour was declared to be the exclusive privilege of the Royal Company of Adventurers, which gained its charter in 1663. The company's claims led to a war with the Dutch, who conceded to the company by 1667.[41] From 1672 the Adventurers' successor, the Royal African Company, arrogated the exclusive right to supply the British colonies with slaves. In fact, British private traders or 'interlopers' illegally plied the Caribbean and Virginian coasts with boatloads of slaves throughout this period.[42] In 1679, Jamaican agents of the Royal African Company complained of 'the Interlopers who . . . sculke only in Creekes and Bayes about the remote ports of the Islands'. Although the officials reassured their London bosses that the profits of the interlopers were not as grand as their bravado might indicate, the fact remains that interlopers found appreciative buyers. So although the interlopers undercut the RAC, it was still well worth their while to take the risks they did.[43] Interlopers were not prone to documenting their illegal voyages, being, according to one source, 'treated worse than Turks' if caught, so hard evidence is scarce. Occasionally, oblique indications of involvement in the covert African trade come to light, such as the parcel of '13 Elephants Teeth' left by a Bristol mariner, John Teague, who died in Jamaica around 1695.[44]

In Barbados the smuggling of slaves was said to be rampant. Usually slaves were landed on the windward coast, the ships departing before the company's agent could take effective action.[45] Given that the northern settlement of Speightstown was known as 'Little Bristol' because of the preponderance of Bristol ships trading there,[46] it seems reasonable to suppose that some Bristolians were involved in this illicit commerce. The Governor of Barbados was reprimanded by the British government for countenancing the smuggling. In 1676, for example, the British government learned from a Royal African Company official that

> several ships have lately arrived, at our Island of Barbados, from those parts of Africa with Negros and other goods and several others are now on the said coast: all which are set out by privat Traders. And that the said African Companys agents seising about 80 Negros, part of 150 negros soe imported . . . in the Ship *Providence* [a London ship]; the same were violently taken away from them, and they are those who assisted them, beaten and wounded.[47]

London was 'very much unsatisfied' with the derisory fines the Governor of Barbados had imposed on the interlopers and warned him in no uncertain terms to ensure that interloping ships were seized and smugglers duly punished. A Bristol ship was recorded as having been seized in Barbados in 1686.[48]

A similar state of affairs existed in the island of Nevis, where resident planters, including the Bristol-born merchant Richard Cary, violently prevented the company agent from seizing an interloper's ship in 1680. But the next year, the company agent successfully seized the *Isabella* of Bristol for illegally trading to Guinea.[49] The *Calendar of State Papers* mentions another Bristol ship seized in Bristol itself for breaking the monopoly.[50] Patrick McGrath provides evidence for only two Bristol ships involved in the illegal trade before 1690, concluding from this that such traffic was probably not too significant before 1698.[51] Be that as it may, McGrath fails to consider that it was a common fiction for ships going to Africa to slave to state their destination as Madeira or the Cape Verde Islands.[52] McGrath himself, in his edited collection of documents pertaining to Bristol merchants, cites papers relating to three Madeira-bound ships, all dating from 1679. Circumstantial evidence from the three suggests that they were intending to trade in Guinea. The name of one such ship, the *Blackamore*, is suggestive in itself, but when we consider that it was provisioned by such men as John Cary, and sugar merchants Thomas Deane and James Pope, the connection with the Africa trade is further indicated. The cargo of the other two ships, the *Hopewell* and the *Mary*, included not only the various types of cloth popular with West Africans, but the felt hats which were an indispensable commodity on slaving ships after 1698.[53]

Bristol in the Caribbean

If we take the careers of a few Bristol men who were resident in the Caribbean in this period, we can better see how the links between colonization, trade and slavery manifested themselves. Bristol merchants, it is true, were busy supplying essential goods to Caribbean settlers – shoes, horses, farming implements and clothes, goods which have little if anything to do with slavery[54] (though one of these merchants is known to have purchased two Africans captured from a Portuguese ship and sent them to work on properties he held in Spain).[55] But Bristol merchants could also be asked to supply their planter-customers with labour and it is this function which renders the connection between slaving and mercantile activity more visible.

Samuel Farmer (1613–78), a Bristol merchant active in Barbados during the years of Cromwell's rule, is a living embodiment of such a connection. In 1645 Farmer bought over 500 acres of two estates belonging to one William Hilliard. In return, not only was Farmer obliged to live on the larger of the estates in St John's and to oversee its management, but he was also to supply the estate with 90 African slaves. By the time he died, he appears also to have owned a 300-acre plantation in the parish of St Thomas (reportedly still called 'Farmers'), although he may well have died heavily indebted. As Richard Pares observed, it was slavery, above all, which necessitated heavy capital investment in the sugar industry, and this in turn resulted in the ever-increasing dependence of the planter upon the merchant who advanced this capital.[56] As planters defaulted on their debts, merchants took over ownership of the plantations, and became planters themselves. By the time Farmer was imprisoned for seditious behaviour towards the Governor of Barbados in 1660, he had served as Speaker of the Barbados Assembly and owned an estate which employed some 200 slaves.[57]

Another early example of the way mercantile activity overlapped with slave-owning before the 1680s is that of Lieutenant Colonel George Standfast and his heirs. George Standfast was a Bristol merchant with property in both Bristol and Barbados. His will of 1657 shows him to be a very wealthy man, bequeathing to his daughter Mary some £5000 worth of goods, and similar amounts to his sons George and John, including £2000 worth of sugar. In addition, John was assigned all his father's interests in sugar-refining, and both sons inherited their father's sugar plantation. African slaves are not explicitly mentioned in his will, but it is more than likely they were employed there. By 1679 John Standfast was listed as the proprietor of a 351-acre plantation in St James parish, a plantation which employed 10 white servants and 238 'negroes'. Standfast died a year later, at which time the Mount Standfast plantation passed to his maternal uncle Thomas Spiar. Spiar, who himself owned property in Bristol as well as the Fontabelle plantation in Barbados, bequeathed on his death in 1682 no fewer than '16 negroes' to his wife Mary in addition to those on his plantations. The wealth generated by his plantations is indicated by the fact that Spiar also left £3500 to each of his two daughters.[58]

Sir John Yeamans's career demonstrates perfectly the way politics and the development of slavery were linked in this period. The scion of a prosperous family of Bristol brewers, Yeamans, whose cousin was executed in the city for his royalist sympathies, found himself on Barbados in the 1650s, where his family held some property and where he soon gained influence.[59] Sacks's rather sanitized description of Yeamans mentions him as a planter in Barbados who went on to be knighted and then to become an early governor of South Carolina (1672–74). Historians of Bristol make no explicit comment on his role as a slave-owner, though the will he made in 1671 before embarking for South Carolina explicitly states that he left his wife 30,000 lb. of sugar, a house with 45 acres and a number of named 'Negro' slaves. By contrast, historians of Barbados see him as instrumental to the foundation of a particularly draconian slave regime in South Carolina. Beckles states that the arrival of Yeamans and other Barbadians in South Carolina helped to ensure the colony's rapid development of 'the largest slave population in North America during the seventeenth century'.[60] Not only did Yeamans bring a gang of his slaves with him to Carolina, but he later told the Lords Proprietors that slave labour was essential to the future success of the new settlement: 'least wee should presume to far wee shall only say that this settlement has been made and upheld by negroes and without constant supplies of them cannot subsist'.[61] It was such people, Dunn tells us, who 'helped to shape South Carolina into a slave-based society, closer in character to the West Indian sugar islands than any other mainland colony'.[62]

Once secured by the British, Jamaica attracted an increasing proportion of Bristol merchants. In the 1660s Anthony Swymmer I was active in Port Royal, the early capital of the island, where he was an official representative of Bristol's Society of Merchant Venturers. Either he or his son and namesake Anthony II commanded a company of the infantry regiment in Port Royal. Certainly Anthony II, who had been born in Bristol, was listed as owning land in Jamaica in 1694.[63] His business partner was his brother William, who remained in Bristol, serving as alderman and, in 1679, as the city's sheriff. William and Anthony II traded in sugar, and William seems to have had a share in a Barbados sugar plantation, possibly inherited from his father.[64] It seems to have been this generation of Swymmers who, along with Bristol merchants John Napper and their uncle William Hayman, supplied, or at least attempted to supply, black slaves to William Helyar's Bybrook Plantation in Jamaica in 1684 and 1686. The involvement of the Swymmers and Napper with the Helyars is of interest to our discussion for a number of reasons. For a start, readers will recall that around this very time, William Swymmer, Napper and Hayman had been among those 'named and shamed' in Bristol for 'kidnapping' white labourers and selling them in the West Indies.[65] What is more, the correspondence concerning the provision of black labour to Helyar's Bybrook Plantation pre-dates any dispensations allowing Bristol merchants to supply 'negro' slaves.

It is possible that the Swymmers were merely buying slaves from Royal African agents in Nevis, or they may have mixed legitimate factoring with illegal trading.[66] In either case, they were involved in supplying Africans to the plantations. From these beginnings the family later found a prominent role in both Bristol and Jamaica.[67]

William Helyar was a West Country landowner. Living in East Coker, Somerset, he had many commercial contacts in nearby Bristol, and his family was linked with the Cary family.[68] His sugar was handled by Bristol merchants and he ordered other supplies from them for his estate.

In one deal, the Swymmer brothers, along with their uncle, seem to have attempted to supply Bybrook Plantation[69] with illegally procured slaves. In January 1684 William Swymmer and William Hayman of Bristol wrote to Squire Helyar in Somerset to explain why the cargo of 'tenn Negrs Slaves' Helyar had ordered from them was never delivered. The very fact that the money was to be paid in Bristol rather than Nevis or even Jamaica indicates that this was not part of Royal African Company business:

> In January last we covenanted with you to deliver you tenn Negres Slaves to say five men and five women in the Island of Jamaica at £17 sterling p head to be pd. In this citty and according to the covenant with you we forthwith gave order to our factor Mr. Robert Legg in Jamaica to deliver to you sd tenn negros to you. . . . Now we understand that Robert Legg did not deliver you sd Negroes but for what reason we know not, and have sold them for lesse moneys than you were to pay for them and have also acted many other things to our own prejudice and losse.[70]

Swymmer and his uncle, anxious not to lose such a high-status customer as Helyar, attempt to persuade him that no harm had been done by their failure to complete their side of the contract. The merchants argued that the slaves Helyar was to have received had arrived in Jamaica in a such a poor state of health that the Helyars were better off without them. In the passage extracted below, Swymmer and Hayman allude to having lost a high proportion of the slaves before their arrival on the island. They also refer to the slaves as 'our negroes'. Both phrases suggest that the slaves fell ill whilst being transported from Africa on a Bristol-owned ship:

> Sir, we are much conserned that you[r] order was not completed. . . . considering we were connected [?] with so worthy a Gent. as you[r] selfe though we believe [it] noe ways prejudicial to you notwithstanding that Mr. Hellyar your overseer of your plantations writes you; *for our negroes proved very sicke and dyseased this yeare, and [we] lost forty of 120 and the rest were landed very much out of order* and would have been capable but of very little service thise yeare if they had lived which is much to be feared.[71] [emphasis added]

Their letter closes with an offer to instruct Anthony Swymmer in Jamaica to buy slaves on Helyar's behalf for the original price quoted 'from the first ship that arrives whatever they cost'.[72]

By today's standards the letter would seem laughably crude were its subtext not so chillingly brutal. Even by the standards of the day it was transparently self-serving and Helyar, unmollified, threatened the merchants with legal action.[73]

In what seems to be a separate deal in 1686, William Swymmer writes to William Helyar about some apparent delay in the delivery of another consignment of African slaves. In the following letter, it is clear that Swymmer's wife, Elizabeth, is operating as an active partner in the business negotiations over the slaves:

> I rec'd yours by the hands of Mr. John Napper some time ago at which tyme I Imformed him yt yor sonn and my wife agreed to Deliver the negros montyoned [mentioned] in your letter . . . I montyond [mentioned] though I susayned [sustained] loss before by Mr. Hilliard's [the former overseer] ill management in Jamaica, your sonn and my wife agreed for one halfe males and the other half ffemales, which will playnlye appear by your sonns owne testymonye.

This is the only case I have come across where a Bristol woman is mentioned as participating in her husband's slave-factoring/trading business. Elizabeth Swymmer's role underlines the importance that personal contacts and trust played in commerce during that time, and it is possibly implied that Elizabeth herself may have been in Jamaica to deal with William Helyar's son. For unspecified reasons the deal seems to have fallen through, and it is not clear whether the original intention had been to ship slaves directly from Africa (Figure 2) to Jamaica or to buy from the Royal African Company and sell them on to Helyar. In any case, no slaves appear to have been supplied, and Anthony Swymmer offers to provide cash to Helyar's son John to enable him to buy direct from illegal traders, rather than commission Swymmer to buy them from the Royal African Company.[74]

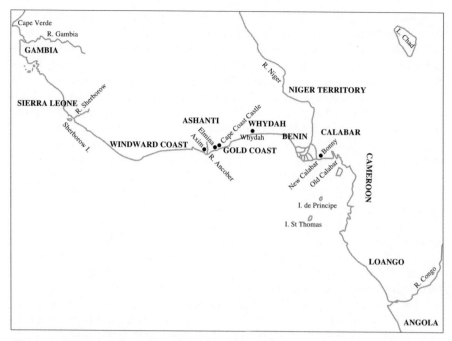

Figure 2   The Guinea coast, showing principal slave centres
Source: C. M. MacInnes, *England and Slavery* (Bristol: Arrowsmith, 1934)

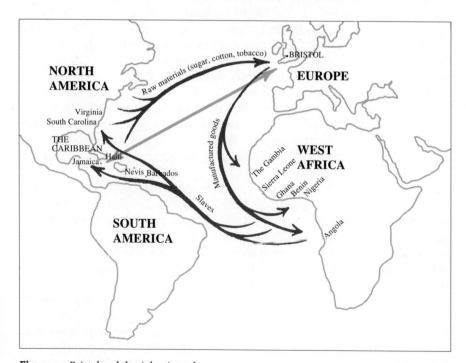

Figure 3   Bristol and the Atlantic trade

Similar configurations of colonizers, merchants, agents and planters from Bristol can be found on other Caribbean islands.[75] The fortunes of Nevis seem particularly intertwined with that of Bristol in this period. Sir James Russell, buried in Bristol's St James's Church, first secured Nevis for the British and became its Governor. He owned a slave plantation in Nevis and one in St Christophers which originally belonged to his wife.[76] The Bristol merchant Thomas Woodward left a slave estate in Nevis to his heirs as early as 1678.[77] Richard Pares has immortalized the Pinney family, whose patriarch, Azariah, was sent to the island after the Monmouth rebellion and whose descendants went on to become influential in both Bristol and Nevis.[78] The Bristol merchant John Combes served on the island's council.[79] And John Knight Jr (1616–79), who founded Bristol's second sugar refinery, which was the first to use Caribbean sugar, had a plantation in Nevis.

In Bristol, Knight's sugar house used as its premises the by now somewhat decayed Great House of Sir John Young, where an African gardener had laboured nearly a century earlier. By Knight's day, the house had passed from Sir Ferdinando Gorges to his widow Elizabeth. A cousin of Sir Ferdinando introduced Knight to Elizabeth Gorges, and she and her sister-in-law, Helena Smyth, were the first to assist Knight in setting up his refining business. Smyth lent him money, as did Elizabeth Appleton Challoner, and Elizabeth Gorges rented the Great House to him. Knight also drew upon loans from family members, but it is worth noting the role female patrons played in this enterprise.

Elizabeth's step-grandson, Ferdinando Gorges, the wealthy Barbadian sugar planter and agent to the Governor of the Leeward Islands, and later a substantial shareholder in the Royal African Company, provided invaluable patronage for Knight's new venture.[80] But by 1654, a need for more cash drove Knight to seek formal partners in his enterprise. One was his irascible older cousin, the MP John Knight (later Sir John Knight of Temple), a High Tory merchant with Caribbean connections who hated Quakers so much that he attempted to ship some to the Caribbean as convict labour. Sir John Knight would soon break with his cousin, partly because of the latter's Puritan leanings.[81] Knight's other early partner was Shershaw Cary, a wealthy linen draper with myriad family and business connections in Virginia and the West Indies who had lived in Barbados for three years in the 1650s.[82]

John Knight's son, heir and namesake (later Sir John Knight of the Hill) spent his youth as a factor on his father's plantation and wanted to play a political role in the Caribbean. In 1684, this younger Knight lobbied hard for the governorship of the Leeward Islands after Sir William Stapleton's retirement from the post. His mercantile background was to count against him, for he was judged by the Council of Nevis to be unsuitable 'in time of war, owing to his want of experience, and in time of peace, owing to his interest in trade'.[83]

Despite such snubs, Bristol merchants were at the hub of a plantation economy as early as the 1650s. It was an economy that was increasingly slave dependent (Figure 3). Bristol merchants had close, often first-hand knowledge of the slave regimes, not the least because an increasing number had plantations themselves. By the 1680s there were four main sugar-refining partnerships in the city involving some of Bristol's most influential merchants, including Edward Colston, who was a partner in the St Peter's Sugar House. This had been started by the Aldworths and a coterie of Baptist merchants led by Thomas Ellis, but by the 1690s it had become part of the Pope enterprise.[84]

Sir John Knight of Temple, like his contemporary Edward Colston (who as we have seen was himself a Caribbean sugar merchant and official of the Royal African Company), represented a particularly authoritarian and rigidly traditional mode of political thinking. Sir John Knight and Edward Colston were High Tory and High Church, and rigidly against any democratic leanings in either religion or politics. This may tempt us, in the light of the Bristol royalists in Barbados, to associate the sugar and slave trades with a particularly reactionary brand of politics. A reverence for hierarchy and unquestioning obedience certainly does seem to characterize the world-view of many slave-holders. Traditional Tory thinking held that a few men were born to rule and the rest born to obey.

But John Knight Jr and Shershaw Cary were of the opposite stamp, with decidedly republican leanings. Their ideological forebear was Samuel Farmer, that 'Magna Carta man', who owned slaves but resisted fiercely the power of the Crown over colonial settlements. Religious Dissenters – Puritans and their Presbyterian, Baptist, Quaker and Independent descendants – resisted the idea of the king as their spiritual superior. To varying degrees, they held to the notion of the spiritual equality of all who accepted Christ as their saviour. The most extreme adherents to this doctrine, Quakers such as George Fox and Puritans such as Thomas Tryon, did indeed speak out in the seventeenth century against the evils of enslaving other Christians. The mistreatment and degradation of Africans was, in their view, bad enough, but the real evil was that such treatment prevented the conversion of Africans to Christianity and thereby delayed the redemption of the world. Fox and Tryon, however, were voices in the wilderness.

Even that father of democratic thinking, the political philosopher John Locke, who gave us the notion that government must rest on the consent of the governed, was himself a member of the Royal African Company. For Locke and his Whig allies it was the ownership of property, and not the mere fact of his humanity, which made man truly rational and fitted for self-government. (Since few Englishwomen of any station owned property, their political status was as problematic as that of the English pauper or the African slave. What distinguished them from the African slave was their religion, their nationality and their colour.) Significantly, one of the most impassioned published indictments against the cruelty of a Caribbean slave regime (though not against the institution of slavery itself) came from the pen of Locke's female contemporary, the royalist spy and playwright Aphra Behn. Slave-holding was generally acceptable to both Tory and Whig, Anglican and Dissenter, though for somewhat different reasons.

It was because slave labour afforded such visions of prosperity and advancement that the consciences of all but a few were silenced. Richard Pares likened the moral atmosphere of the West Indies in the late seventeenth century to that of a gold rush.[85] If Bristol seemed more pious and sedate, that was in part because the 'gold' that was to be mined could be safely, if brutally, extracted abroad. No one better illustrates this attitude than Shershaw Cary's son John. John Cary knew the slave and sugar trade at first hand, having spent time in the West Indies during his apprenticeship as a sugar merchant and having lent money to planters.[86] His democratic leanings led him to advocate giving the vote to all Bristol's taxpayers and to argue that aldermen should be elected rather than appointed. By the same token, he also chafed against the restrictive and elitist structures which excluded the outports like Bristol from sharing fully in the profits of the 'triangular trade'. Cary's heart rested with the men of business. Like Locke, he regarded those who had no property at all, such as paupers or slaves, as in a different political category. Cary, like a number of fellow Whigs in Bristol, *was* concerned with what he saw as the proper management of pauperism. Cary and other Bristol Whigs were involved in the establishment in 1696 of the 'Bristol Incorporation of the Poor', an attempt to rationalize Poor Law provision in the city. But as Sacks has pointed out, Cary believed that the economy was driven by its own laws, and that neither indiscriminate charity nor royal patronage was in tune with the economy's natural mechanism. It was free trade (within certain prescribed limits) rather than free men which most seemed to exercise Cary's enthusiasm.[87] Impatient with the aristocrats who dominated colonial policy, Cary wanted men with practical business experience to be consulted, quite a radical view in those days, given aristocrats' contempt for most traders and merchants.

In 1690 John Cary acted as an agent for the Merchant Venturers in London and was appointed, along with William Swymmer, William Hayman, Robert Yate and others, to draw up a petition to Parliament for 'letting the merchants of this Citty to a share of the African Trade'.[88] That same year, special dispensation was granted to a limited number of Bristol's ships to make the journey from Bristol to Africa and on to the Americas and back again.[89]

Although no stranger to the slave markets of the Caribbean, Cary seems to have been more of an idealist than his fellow Whigs Swymmer and Hayman. A correspondent with John Locke, Cary saw free trade and commerce as a civilizing force which stimulated arts and manufactures. His vision was a world opened up to trade and thence to the values of prudent Christianity. It was this, as well as a hope of riches, which motivated John Cary to challenge the Royal African Company's monopoly, to urge the expansion of Britain's colonial ventures and thereby to become nationally prominent as a writer on economic issues.[90] As early as 1695, Cary argues that the African trade, as he calls it, is more central to national prosperity than any other trade.[91]

> The African Trade is a Trade of the most Advantage to this Kingdom of any we drive, and as it were all Profit, the first Cost being little more than small Matters of our own Manufactures, for which we have in Return, *Gold, Teeth* [ivory], *Wax and Negroes*, the last whereof are much better than the first, being indeed the best Traffick the Kingdom hath.[92]

It is the 'Negroes', Cary argues, who are the linchpin of the whole economy, for it is by their

Hands by which our Plantations are improved; and tis by their Labours such great Quantities of *Sugar, Tobacco, Cotton, Ginger* and *Indigo* are raised, which being bulky Commodities imploy great Numbers of our Ships for their Transporting hither, and the greater number of Ships employs the greater number of Handicraft Trades at home, spends more of our Product and Manufactures, and makes more Sailors, who are maintained by a separate Employ.[93]

It was arguments such as Cary's which enabled the Merchant Venturers to enlist the support of Bristol's two Whig MPs on behalf of a freer trade to Africa – that is, freer trade in slaves. By 1695 these MPs, Thomas Day and Robert Yate, had agreed to support the campaign.[94] It seems perverse to modern sensibilities that the campaign to 'free up' the trade in slaves was in any sense allied with a modernizing call for reform. Yet that is how contemporary Whigs must have seen it. Of course, the Society of Merchant Venturers was itself a restrictive organization, but it lobbied on behalf of both its members and other traders in the city in 1694 against the imposition of any tax on Bristol's trade with Africa.[95] Bristol's Merchant Venturers, with Cary as their propagandist, wanted liberty to trade with Africa and equality in the trading arena. The pursuit of profit in this context was seen as a necessary and honourable activity which would contribute to the happiness of the nation at large. The liberty and happiness of Africans was, by this view, a complete irrelevance.

Once the monopoly of the Royal African Company had been broken, Bristol's civic and mercantile elite resisted any attempt of chartered companies to reimpose a monopoly on the African trade. For over the next half century the Society of Merchant Venturers in particular lobbied the Board of Trade as well as Parliament to oppose duties on West Indian produce and import taxes on slaves (which some American colonies such as Virginia introduced), and worked for the ending of the 10 per cent duty which outports had to pay in order to participate in the African trade. In most of these activities they were supported by the city's MPs, the overwhelming majority of whom had some vested interests in the African or West Indian trade (Table 2). In this sense at least, slavery had helped to shape the political life of Bristol.

Bristol and the African trade, 1698–1750

The most exciting recent scholarship on Bristol's slave trade has been by economic historians. In the decades after the Second World War, Walter Minchinton wrote a series of articles on the port and its merchants, including one on the 1767 voyage of the slaver *Africa*.[96] More recently, Kenneth Morgan has written authoritatively about Bristol's place in the Atlantic economy in the eighteenth century and about some of the city's merchants.[97] The most important work has been by David Richardson, who has written extensively on the subject of the slave trade and those involved in it. His monumental work *Bristol, Africa and the Eighteenth-Century Slave Trade to America* is a four-volume compendium which attempts to list in chronological order every voyage made from Bristol to Africa

Table 2 Bristol MPs and their interests in slave plantations and/or the slave trade,
1679–1754

Dates in Parliament	Name	Party allegiance	Slave-related interests
1679	John Knight	Tory	Merchant, investor in sugar firm
1679	Sir Robert Cann		West Indian sugar plantation owner
1681	Thomas Earle	Whig	None known
1681	Sir Richard Hart	Tory	
1685	Sir Richard Crumpe		Leading West India merchant in Bristol
1685	Sir Jonathan Churchill, died and replaced by Sir Richard Hart in December	Tory	None known
1689 and 1690	Sir John Knight	Whig	Nevis plantation owner, son of the owner of Bristol's first sugar refinery processing Caribbean sugar
1689 and 1690	Sir Richard Hart	Tory	Involved in sugar trade
1695, 1698 and 1701	Robert Yate	Whig	Maternal grandfather Sir Thomas Cann, proprietor of Jamaican plantation; father Robert Yate, himself West Indian merchant
1695 and 1698	Sir Thomas Daye	Whig	West Indian plantation owner
1701–10	Sir William Daines		Son of Virginia planter, himself a Virginia and Maryland merchant; son-in-law of William Swymmer
1710	Edward Colston	Tory	Spanish and West Indian merchant, member of the Court of Assistants of the Royal African Company. Partner in Bristol's oldest sugar refinery, St Peter's Sugar House
1710 and 1713	Joseph Earle	Tory (but later changes allegiance)	Son-in-law of Sir Robert Cann, invested in slaving voyage; privateer
1713	Thomas Edwards Jr	Tory with Whiggish sympathies	Married to daughter and heir of Sir William Hayman, who was also Edward Colston's niece and heir; in 1729 listed as part-owner of a Bristol slave ship

Table 2 – *continued*

Dates in Parliament	Name	Party allegiance	Slave-related interests
1715	Joseph Earle	Whig	Known to have invested in one slave ship
1715	Sir W. Daines	Whig	See earlier entry
1722	Joseph Earle	Whig	See earlier entry
1722	Sir A. Elton	Whig	Invested in slave ships; merchant partner in copper, glass, iron works; shipowner; invested in some African ships
1727	Abraham Elton II	Whig	African merchant, had had South Sea shares till 1720
1727	John Scrope	Whig	Commissioner for colonizing Georgia; lauded in Bristol for his 'grand services to the African trade'
1734	Thomas Coster	Tory	Slave ship owner, part-owner of copper works
1734	Sir A. Elton II	Whig	African merchant
1739	Edward Southwell	Tory	Involved in West Indian adminstration; second wife daughter of West Indian heiress and Wm Blathwaite
1741	Sir Abraham Elton II	Whig	See earlier entry
1741	Edward Southwell	Tory	See earlier entry
1742	Robert Hoblyn	Tory	Brass interests – husband of Thomas Coster's daughter and sole heir
1747	Edward Southwell	Tory	See earlier entry
1747	Robert Hoblyn	Tory	See earlier entry
1754	Robert Nugent	Whig	Advocate of free trade to Africa
1754	Richard Beckford	Tory	Son of Peter Beckford; planter and Speaker of the House of Assembly in Jamaica

Sources: W. R. Williams, *Parliamentary History of the County of Gloucestershire including the Cities of Bristol and Gloucester* (Hereford: privately printed, 1898); J. Latimer, *Annals of Bristol in the Seventeenth Century* and *Annals of Bristol in the Eighteenth Century*; W. E. Minchinton, *The Trade of Bristol in the Eighteenth Century*; P. McGrath, *Merchants and Merchandise*; C. Whitworth, *The Succession of Parliament* (London, 1764); Leslie Stephen (ed.), *The Dictionary of National Biography* (London, 1885); B. D. Henning, *The House of Commons, 1660–1690*, vol. 2 (London, 1983); Romney Sedgwick (ed.), *The House of Commons, 1715–1754*, vol. 2 (London, 1970); Margaret Elton, *Annals of the Elton Family: Bristol Merchants and Somerset Landowners* (Dover, 1984); Andrew Hanham, MSS on Sir William Daines and Sir Robert Yate (London, 2000); reference to Thomas Edward's investment in a slave ship in PRO, Petition of James and Peter Day, owners of the ship *Ferret* of Bristol, 1729, SP36/14 pt. 2.

Table 3 Leading agents of Bristol slaving voyages, 1698–1807 (qualification = 10 voyages)

Agents	Voyages managed	Period of management
Anderson, né Young, Charles	16	1797–1805
Anderson, John	66	1764–97
Becher, John	28	1711–32
Becher, Michael	25	1727–32
Bright, Henry	21	1749–66
Challoner, William	13	1714–26
Chilcott, John	12	1770–7
Coghlan, John	10	1759–81
Cross, John	16	1737–47
Dampier, Henry	34	1727–44
Day, James	56	1711–42
Day, Peter	20	1711–34
Deane, Thomas	40	1747–64
Dolman, Thomas	11	1711–30
Duckinfield, John	23	1714–30
Farr, Richard	37	1726–45
Farr, Richard Jr	20	1747–72
Fowler, John	77	1758–77
Freke, Thomas	14	1716–31
Gordon, Robert	14	1751–67
Gordon, William	25	1729–57
Grant, Abel	14	1721–43
Hamilton, David	28	1766–78
Hare, William	38	1729–52
Harris, Philip	16	1715–26
Henvill, Richard	30	1709–44
Hobhouse, Isaac	44	1722–47
Hooke, Abraham	23	1702–27
Iles, Joseph	19	1720–50
Jacob, Samuel	40	1716–47
Jefferis, Joseph	12	1717–34
Jefferis, William	34	1713–47
Jenkins, Walter	11	1732–41
Jones, James	68	1783–95
Jones, Thomas	34	1767–94
Laroche, James	132	1728–69
Lougher, Richard and Walter (R. Lougher also managed eight voyages on his own between 1722 and 1728)	15	1725–45
Lougher, Walter	34	1732–60

Table 3 – *continued*

Agents	Voyages managed	Period of management
McTaggart, James	14	1771–87
Pennington, Thomas	13	1734–49
Powell, John	58	1755–76
Power, Thomas	13	1734–48
Rogers, Francis	10	1700–14
Rogers, James	51	1783–92
Ruddock, Noblett	30	1712–25
Rumsey, James	20	1753–62
Saunders, Edmund	32	1723–39
Scandret, Charles and Christopher (Charles Scandret also managed six voyages with John Scandret between 1721 and 1728)	10	1721–8
Sims, Thomas	25	1763–72
Tonge, Henry	42	1730–53
Tunbridge, Robert	18	1708–21
Way, Joseph	17	1702–20

Source: David Richardson, *The Bristol Slave Traders: A Collective Portrait* (Bristol, 1985)

between 1698 and 1807.[98] The overwhelming majority of these ships went on from Africa to America or the Caribbean with a cargo of enslaved Africans in their holds. In other words, the 'African trade', though it sometimes involved the trade in other commodities, was almost always primarily focused on the trade in slaves. These ships sold their human cargo at varying rates of profit before returning to their home port. They were often laden with raw materials such as sugar, cotton, rice, indigo, coffee or cocoa which they had obtained in the Caribbean or, in the case of dyewood, gum and ivory, in Africa.[99]

Based on many years of research, Richardson's work provides us with the names of the shipowners and merchants who financed and provisioned each voyage, the masters who sailed each ship, and the number of slaves transported per voyage from Africa to markets in the New World. Where the evidence permits, Richardson notes from which areas of Africa slaves were taken, incidences of mortality amongst both the crew and its captive passengers, as well as slave revolts and mutinies. His work enables us to discern, with unprecedented precision, just how important a role the African trade played in both the national and the local economy.[100]

At first sight, Richardson's findings indicate that Bristol's role in the British slave trade was a modest one. Something less than 20 per cent of all overseas voyages made from Bristol between 1698 and 1807 have been estimated to have been slaving voyages.[101] Though Bristol was briefly the nation's premier slaving port, the 'African trade' was never the city's biggest trade sector. Indeed, we are told that it constituted only between 4 and 9 per cent of all ships leaving the port in the eighteenth century. But this modest percentage, as Richardson himself points out, is misleading. Slave ships absorbed a larger capital investment than, say, ships sailing directly to America or to Europe, and they tied up that capital for a longer time. Slaving voyages averaged between a year and eighteen months in duration.

Compared to the numbers of Africans transported from London and Liverpool over the century, Bristol's national role in the trade may also at first sight seem minor. According to the latest figures available, during the period between 1698 and 1807, there were 2008 slaving voyages from Bristol, and they delivered some 486,059 enslaved Africans to the New World. Liverpool delivered over twice that number, 1,154,457, during the same period.[102] Yet Richardson reminds us that Bristol nevertheless played a crucial role in the trade's early development:

> Bristol merchants responded with greater alacrity than their rivals in other outports to the opportunities offered by the Act of 1698, and . . . in general it was Bristol merchants more than those of either London or Liverpool that provided most of the impetus behind the substantial expansion of British trade with Africa that occurred between 1713 and 1730.[103]

Few today realize that for a brief period, from around 1723 to around 1743, Bristol was the nation's number one slaving port, eclipsing London as well as its newer rival, Liverpool. Thus by the mid-1740s, when the city's role as a slaving port was overtaken by that of Liverpool, Bristol had already helped to establish an effective trading and political infrastructure to support the trade.

What is more, Bristol may have transported significantly more slaves than Richardson's figures indicate. By his own admission, not all the Bristol ships which slaved in Africa are included in his survey. Richardson relied primarily on the port books which recorded ships leaving or coming into English ports, and supplemented this information with data from other official government and trading sources. As he himself cautions, the surviving evidence is sometimes patchy.[104] One contemporary document purporting to list 'Ships now on the African trade belonging to the Port of Bristol' for January 1729 surfaced during the course of this research, and names seven slaving ships which are not cited at all in Richardson's massive survey. Three additional ships which Richardson has named only in relation to much earlier or later voyages are also reported as active around the year or so prior to 1729. These ten Bristol-owned vessels evidently carried 3300 slaves over and above the 10,872 people reportedly delivered to the Americas between 1728 and 1732.[105]

Richardson's work also enables scholars to trace the wider impact African merchants made on the city's development. Richardson himself has written an additional 'collective portrait' of the city's leading slave traders.[106] Here he shows that the leading slaving agents in Bristol in the period 1698–1807 (listed in Table 3) founded few dynasties and tended not to be the leading figures in the sugar and tobacco industry. However, his other research reveals that many eminent

Bristol merchants who did not specialize in slaving nevertheless made investments in slaving voyages. In this way, Richardson's work exposes the wider role which slave-trading played in the city's economic life.

Making money from the slave trade

Even the men named in Richardson's table had investments aside from the African trade itself. Noblett Ruddock traded directly to Ireland and America;[107] his brother-in-law, Philip Harris, owned East India goods and a sugar house, both of which enhanced his African trading.[108] Edmund Saunders dabbled in property development.[109] There were also a good number of other men, not included in Richardson's list, like Joseph Swayne,[110] who only occasionally invested in a slave ship and who owned extensive properties throughout Gloucestershire and Herefordshire or who, like Thomas Coster (Figure 4) manufactured goods which were sold elsewhere as well as to Guinea. Coster, who invested in some slaving ventures to Africa, also had a share in the *Prince William* of Bristol, which in 1738 delivered two slaves from Jamaica to New York along with other cargo. A number of Bristol merchants had investments in similar voyages.[111]

Who else besides the shipowners and merchants directly involved in the slaving voyages stood to make money out of Bristol's African trade?

There were of course the captains, surgeons and mariners who served aboard slave ships. Sometimes the captains were relatives of the merchants involved. William Swymmer, probably the grandson of Alderman William Swymmer, was one of eleven out of the 252 slaving captains sailing between 1730 and 1745 who managed to invest in at least one of his ship's voyages.[112]

There were also those who invested in companies which engaged in slaving. The shareholders and office-holders in the Royal African Company, including William and Edward Colston, are obvious candidates, but so too are the many investors in the East India Company and the South Sea Company. Elizabeth Skrine, a devout Bristol Anglican who turned to Moravianism in the 1750s, may not have realized that the East India Company, in which she had shares,[113] had had a short-lived but profitable interest in a slave trade conducted between Madagascar and the Caribbean. Also, many of the textiles exported to the West African coast in return for slaves were of East Indian origin and as such were imported to England exclusively by the company. The South Sea Company was very much involved in the provision of slaves to Spanish America until 1750. Mary Baker of Bristol, for example, owned £300 worth of South Sea shares when she died in 1739, and despite the opposition of the Merchant Venturers to its African ambitions, some eminent local merchants such as Abraham Elton II owned shares in it too.[114]

There were also the various Bristol postholders, ranging from the Collector of Customs to the more mysterious tidewaiter, who benefited from the increased trade to Africa and the colonies. If fees for unloading cargo (wharfage) went directly to the Society of Merchant Venturers, which built the quays, other emoluments went to the various carters and porters who shifted the goods from the wharf and to the ships' pilots who guided the ships along the treacherous course of the Avon. Shipbuilders, manufacturers and importers of trade goods also profited from the

Figure 4 Thomas Gardner after J. De Groot, *Thomas Coster* (detail), *c.* 1734. Mezzotint. Bristol City Museum and Art Gallery

African trade. After 1713, when the British won the exclusive right to supply slaves to Spanish colonies, Bristol's craftsmen and labourers were increasingly employed in the city's shipyards building Africa snows and brigantines. The builder James Hilhouse made both his name and his fortune in the early eighteenth century. Hilhouse, who also invested in some slaving voyages, died in 1754, leaving £30,000 to his son, who carried on the business.[115] The array of names given to the slavers which issued from the yards of James Hilhouse and Sydenham Teast and others proclaimed romance and local pride despite their actual purpose. The usual *Bettys*, *Anns* and *Rubys*, *Mercurys*, *Georges* and *Dreadnoughts* were joined by vessels named after local notables – the *Colston*, the *Hayman*, the *Freke*. The *Mary Redcliffe* bore the name of Bristol's most famous parish church, whilst the *Oldbury*'s name was that of a nearby village. Some like the *Serleon*, the *Bonny*, the *Angola* and the *Calabar Merchant*, referred to West Africa. The *Blackmore*, which made a number of voyages in the early eighteenth century, unselfconsciously proclaimed its commercial intentions. Some names were aspirational, such as the *Commerce*, the *Expectation*, and even the *Content*, the *Happy* and the marvellously misnamed *Mercy*. It was aboard such ships that over 90,000 Africans perished through sickness, fear, mistreatment, violent suppression and the occasional shipwreck.

Textiles constituted the largest element of merchandise loaded aboard the Guinea-bound ships. Baffts, brawles and romallos from India, serviceable serges and perpets from Devon and increasingly, as the century wore on, stripped and coloured cottons from Lancashire were purchased by Bristol merchants, who knew that each type of cloth would be carefully examined and possibly rejected by their West African customers according to the particular fashion of the time or region.[116] Prestige goods from the locality included Bristol glassware, umbrellas and 'negro hats' edged in gold, silver or copper, or beads imported from India or Venice. These luxury items were used by leading African traders to display their wealth and thus confirm their social and political standing. Such goods vied for space with more utilitarian items such as locally manufactured brass 'guinea pots' or 'neptunes' employed by West Africans for the distillation of salt from sea water and for cooking. Brass bangles or manillas, which served, along with iron and copper rods, as currency were particularly favoured by traders in the Bight of Benin.[117] (By the late 1730s many of Bristol's prominent traders had shares in a local brass battery, including William Swymmer Jr.[118]) Brandy and gin cordial oiled (or inflamed) the negotiations with West African traders as they haggled over the goods on offer. Guns, cutlasses, knives and a dedicated blend of 'guinea gunpowder' constituted an increasingly important element of most slaving cargoes. So too did specially manufactured 'guinea guns', notorious for their propensity to blow up in the hands of their new owners. In 1728 over 21,000 small arms had been delivered to West African traders by Bristol-owned ships. Most of these guns were manufactured locally, though Bristol gunsmiths were increasingly edged out by the metal goods manufacturers in the Midlands as the century progressed.[119] By 1750 it was said that Bristol vessels shipped gunpowder, India goods (textiles and trinkets), cowries (shells from the Maldives used as currency) and slezias (fine linens from Silesia, which is now in Poland) to the slaving port of Whydah.[120]

Of course, it was not only providers of trade goods who benefited from slaving ships. These ships needed to be sheathed with copper to provide protection from the teredo worm which lurked in the warm waters off the West African coast, thus boosting the nascent copper-smelting industry in the region. The value of the cargo and ship needed to be protected against the perils of the voyage, and the insuring of African ships both spurred on the early development of the insurance industry and drew in a wide range of investors in Bristol who were otherwise uninvolved in the African trade.[121] At a more prosaic level, sailmakers, makers of navigational instruments, ship's chandlers, coopers, apothecaries and the various small retailers who provided meat and bread to feed the crew and the horsebeans to feed the slaves all stood to make some money from the African trade.[122] So too did the clerks employed in the merchants' counting houses, the labourers in their warehouses, the women who did the captain's laundry and the men who cleaned the ships on their return – all had a vested interest in the trade.[123] As the city council put it in a petition to the Commons in 1713:

Bristolians depended for their subsistence on their West Indies and Africa Trade which employed greater numbers of people in shipyards and in the manufacture of wool, iron, tin, copper, brass etc. a considerable part whereof is exported to Africa for the buying of Negroes.[124]

In addition to such local employments, we know that a number of Bristol men gained their livelihoods as officials at the various forts established along the West African coast or as slaving agents in America and the Caribbean. William Whetstone Rogers, the son of the famous sailor and slaver Woodes Rogers, was, for example, an employee of the Royal African Company before his death in 1735. In the 1750s Charles Bell appears to have risen from being master of a Bristol slaving ship to Governor of Cape Coast Castle (in what is now Ghana) via a succession of company posts, illegally augmenting his income with private slave-trading.[125] John Hippisley, the son and namesake of Bristol's first theatre impresario, served as a fort administrator before his early death on the coast in 1766.[126] The young merchants who gained their experience in Charleston, South Carolina, or Kingston, Jamaica, before returning to Bristol included Henry Bright and John Pinney amongst others. The Bristol merchant William Raymond, for example, was an agent in Barbados to slavers from Bristol and elsewhere in the early part of the eighteenth century, whilst slave factors in Jamaica included the firms of Tyndall & Assheton and Watson & Swymmer.[127]

It was customary for Bristol slavers, like their continental European counterparts, to purchase slaves. Although there were cases, particularly early on, of captains kidnapping Africans, these were the exception to the rule. As Herbert Klein points out,

> European buyers were totally dependent on African sellers for the delivery of slaves. European traders never seriously penetrated beyond the coast before the late nineteenth century because of the military power of the African states and the threat of disease. . . . Slaves in numbers sufficient to fill the holds of the slave ships only arrived to the coast via African merchants willing to bring them from the interior.[128]

When Bristol slavers arrived on the West African coast, they might stop at one of the established forts or factories, or they might cast their anchor offshore and wait for canoemen to make contact with them. The routine varied, and sometimes, as in Old Calabar on the Niger Delta, it was customary for the slavers to give the 'cabouceers' or local headmen the goods on 'trust' and wait for them to return with slaves. Such 'trust' was reinforced by the practice of 'pawning', whereby relatives of the African traders were left on board English ships until the promised slaves were provided. The understanding was that if the traders did not return by the agreed time, the English were entitled to sell their relatives into bondage. Sometimes the ships' captains broke their contract, turning their voluntary guests into unwilling slaves, but the actions of such rogue captains disrupted established trading patterns, and in at least one case, the Bristol press waxed indignant over the kidnapping of the son of the King of Popo, and complaints were made to the Commissioners of Trade.[129]

Ships had at times to pay bribes or 'customs', as the King of Dahomey put it, to local rulers, and when Bristol merchants balked at paying such to the King of Barra, they were reprimanded by the Commissioners of Trade and told to make the required payment. Competition for slaves from other European ships meant that Bristol slavers might wait off the coast for many weeks for slaves, increasing the risk to both the crew and those slaves already purchased as conditions on board deteriorated. Isaac Hobhouse was relieved to learn that the 'cargo of Negroes' transported aboard his ship the *Rainbow* in 1737 fetched a good price 'considering the condition and state they were carried in'.[130]

Because the supply and prices of slaves were so variable, other goods were often bought, including dyewood, wax and ivory, to diffuse the risk. The difficulties in procuring saleable slaves and ensuring that they and the crew survived the voyage have been well documented by previous writers. Suffice it to say that attacks by pirates, competition from other English and European traders, slave revolts, suicides, crew mutinies, and above all illness made the African trade a particularly uncertain one for its Bristol merchants. A letter reprinted in the London press in 1737 from the Bristol ship the *Princess of Orange* reported that a hundred men-slaves had jumped overboard, but that all but 33 were retrieved from the sea and successfully sold 'before any discovery was made of the injury the salt water had done them'.[131]

Once a cargo had arrived in the Caribbean or the mainland colonies, there was no guarantee that the slaves could be sold quickly. If sales were slow, conditions on board the ships could deteriorate badly and so, of course, could the profits. In 1736, for example, it was reported that seven Bristol ships with a mixture of Gold Coast and Windward slaves went out to Jamaica, but 'Could not sell them, lay there for several months; obliged to go to Hispaniola, and sell them to great disadvantage.'[132] Twenty years later, a merchant wrote to his Bristol associates that it took a month for the Bristol snow *Africa* to sell all her slaves in the Caribbean, despite its being 'a most butifull [sic] Cargo of . . . chiefly young People from 15–20 [years of age] which are not accustomed to destroy themselves like those who are older'.[133]

Slave deaths aboard Bristol ships averaged just over 14 per cent per voyage between 1698 and 1807. However, mortality during the period up to 1750 was much higher, with over a quarter of all slaves dying before they reached the Americas. Ships with inexperienced captains tended to have the highest mortalities, as this letter from a new slave ship captain to the Bristol merchant Isaac Hobhouse illustrates:

> I arrived at Mounserratt the 22d of January with 239 slaves which are now all sold better than expectation so that I am in opes to make a tolerable good voage notwithstanding I've had the misforturn of beuring seventy odd slaves; as good as any now sold I am somewhat dissatisfied that it should happen to a young begginer but thank God it can't be said its owing to Niglect for sir I Can asure you that it have been the Constant Care and endeavor for me for your Interests and of the Gentlemen that have Imployed mee.[134]

Despite this, though, profits were still attractive enough to encourage Bristol merchants to continue with the trade. As Francis Bright urged his brother and business partner in Bristol, Henry Bright, beef and candles were selling slowly in Jamaica in 1747, and if they had invested 'that sum in fitt[ing] up of a Guinea ship for the Bight [of Benin] or Angola we should have got more money by it'.[135]

Although not every slaver which discharged its traumatized human cargo in the Caribbean or American mainland returned laden with raw materials, many did. Those returning from the Caribbean brought back cotton, ginger, tobacco, cocoa and, increasingly, sugar. Those returning from Virginia brought tobacco; those from South Carolina, mainly indigo and rice. As the American merchant Henry Laurens wrote to Richard Farr in Bristol in 1748,

> I can venture to assure you there is a pretty good prospect for the Sale of Negroes in that Colony as Rice promises to be a good commodity,. . . and . . . we expect it will for the future make a very considerable addition to our remittances to Britain.[136]

The refining industries which processed the tobacco, chocolate and sugar were, as we shall later see, crucial to Bristol's eighteenth-century prosperity.

Their voyage completed, returning captains and surgeons and first mates might bring with them a 'privilege negro' awarded as a bonus for a successful journey. Yet contrary to popular belief, slavers do not seem to have brought large numbers of Africans to the city en masse; most were sold in Jamaica, Barbados or Virginia. What Bristol crews and merchants did bring back with them, from both Africa and the New World, were their experiences of slavery and new attitudes towards the Africans they had helped to enslave.

John Duckinfield and other slave traders

A small number of men dominated the Bristol African trade until 1807. Richardson lists nineteen men, who came from a range of social backgrounds. There were sons of mariners, yeomen and tradesmen as well as those from established mercantile and landed families. Apprenticeship and marriage were sometimes the ways by which men of modest means achieved entry into merchant families and thereby the African trade. Merchants in Bristol tended to own rather than hire their ships, and each voyage was a venture, the risks of which were often shared with other partners. Some of these partners were seasoned slaving merchants; others were businessmen and gentlemen who only occasionally invested in the African trade.

John Duckinfield (also spelt Duckenfield) was a middle-ranking slaving agent. He was the son of a Cheshire man and was apprenticed to the Bristol merchant William Andrews, a close associate of William Swymmer, in 1695. By 1701 he had become a burgess of the city by marrying his master's daughter.[137] In all but two years between 1712 and 1725, Duckinfield sent out at least one of his six ships to make the triangular voyage. In some respects his progress was typical of this early period. He had a range of business interests sending ships direct to America and the West Indies as well as making the triangular circuit to Africa and

America.[138] On occasion Duckinfield would co-partner a slaving voyage with other merchants, but appears more often to have financed the venture on his own. A captain of two of his earlier voyages was Edmund Saunders, who would himself go on to eclipse his former employer as a leading slaving merchant in the city.

In most instances Duckinfield followed a conventional route, taking slaves from the West African coast to deliver them on one occasion to Barbados, but more often to Jamaica or Virginia, two favourite destinations of Bristol merchants. Sometimes his returning ships would deliver African products back to Bristol, including ivory and redwood, 'Guinea grains' (pepper) or hides.

Like others in his trade, he faced risk. Once his captain had to return from Virginia with no less than 7 tons of Swedish bar iron and 728 lb. of beads which the traders in Calabar had refused to purchase. Three times, pirates had interfered with his ships. On one voyage, pirates in the Caribbean plundered over a thousand pounds of goods from his ship before letting it proceed back to Bristol.[139] On another, pirates off the African coast had captured his ship for their own use.[140] On the final occasion, corsairs off the Barbary coast not only captured the ship the *Little Bristol* (which Duckinfield co-owned with Warren Carey and John Scandret) but imprisoned the crew. An anguished letter from the ship's master, John Normanton, complained that when the English ambassador intervened on the crew's behalf, he so abruptly turned down the King of Morocco's offer to recompense him for the seizure of the ship that the King rescinded the offer and enslaved the crew: '[the] loss of ship and cargo [and] our slavery is only attributed to his [the ambassador's] haughtiness pride and ambition to stand upon his Majesty's [?] Honour in a country where neither Honour, Christianity nor Justice is to be had.'[141] The fate of the captain and his crew is not known, but this particular venture also illustrates one of the insurance scams that tempted slaving merchants. For the London merchants who insured the *Little Bristol*, thinking it already safely departed, were later angered to discover (as they alleged) that they had in fact pledged their money *after* the ship had been seized.[142]

What distinguishes Duckinfield from most other African merchants in Bristol, however, was that on at least two occasions he traded in slaves from Madagascar.[143] This was a controversial route for a number of reasons. The voyage to the Indian Ocean was longer, but the slaves, who tended to be people of mixed African and Malay heritage, were evidently cheaper and easier to purchase than those from West Africa. However, only members of the East India Company had the legal right to trade with Madagascar. There had been interlopers on this trade in the 1690s, possibly including Duckinfield himself, and only three British traders briefly managed to secure permission to trade there for a short period in 1717. Two were from Liverpool, and the other, from Bristol, was John Duckinfield himself. That year Duckinfield loaded some 540 Malagasy slaves onto his ship the *Prince Eugene*. Later Duckinfield pleaded in vain for a renewal of his licence to recoup the losses made on that voyage, losses due largely to the death of nearly half of the Malagasy on board. This high rate was due, he argued, mainly to 'the inadvertency of our master in purchasing boys and girls instead of men'.[144] Duckinfield hoped to excite the compassion of the East India Company not on behalf of the children who died, but on his own, since the deaths of these children had occasioned him financial loss. He promised that if granted the licence, he would get his master to report to the company on the activities of the European pirates infesting the Madagascar coast. Despite the fact that his plea was accompanied by a petition signed by no fewer than 30 MPs, the East India Company refused it. It evidently suspected that Duckinfield had already colluded with the pirates in question by permitting his ship to sell them provisions. Undeterred, Duckinfield seems to have gone to Madagascar anyway the following year, but his ship's cargo was impounded in Virginia and his captain sent back home in a man-of-war to face trial, all because East India goods were found on board his ship.[145]

Despite such setbacks, Duckinfield did well. He was probably a sugar merchant, and though he never held civic office, he did become Master of the Merchant Venturers in 1736.[146] He died a wealthy man in 1745, leaving £3000 to be divided between his three daughters and an undisclosed, though reportedly 'considerable', amount in England and Jamaica to be administered by his eldest son, William. His second son, Robert, is listed as the owner of a sizeable Jamaican plantation in the year of his father's death and possessed no less than 5000 acres by 1750, a legacy he must have owed largely to his father's endeavours.[147]

Like most leading Bristol slaving agents, Duckinfield does not seem to have founded a slaving dynasty. Indeed, most of the men listed by Richardson do not appear to have children. The Swymmers, however, were a modest exception to the rule. No fewer than four generations of William Swymmers appear to have had investments in Bristol's African trade, the youngest of them having invested in slaving vessels as late as 1751.[148]

Bristol as a slaving port

In 1750, just as Bristol's predominance as a slaving port was beginning to wane, a new body which included representatives from both London and the outports was established to supervise the African trade. The Company of Merchants Trading to Africa represented a new era in the regulation of the slave trade.[149] Of its 475 members, 236 came from Bristol, 147 from London and 92 from Liverpool.

By 1750, increasing numbers of Bristol merchants were shifting their attentions from the African to the less risky West Indian and American trades. Of the 134 British ships said to be trading to Africa that year it was reported that 75 ships were from Liverpool, 47 from Bristol, 6 from Chester, Lancaster or Plymouth, and 6 were presumed to be from London.[150] Bristol remained a significant slaving port right up to the end of the eighteenth century, but the trade became concentrated in fewer hands, and by the 1780s fewer leading African traders were from established Bristol families.[151] This did not, however, mean that Bristol was becoming less dependent on the institution of slave labour. For in the words of one contemporary, 'if the negro trade was lost, the colonies must be lost'.[152] Echoing the words of John Cary over half a century earlier, the editor of Bristol's *Felix Farley's Bristol Journal* grasped the ecology of the transatlantic slave trade well when he concluded that

Commerce is a Circle. Whatever improves one Part affects all. The African, more especially the Slave Trade, depends on the prosperity of our West Indian Islands. Both these take off an immense Quantity of British commodities and manufactures, employ a vast number of ships, encourage our Seamen, consume great Quantities of provisions and are in many other respects, useful to Great Britain.[153]

Notes

1 W. Noel Saintsbury (ed.), *Calendar of State Papers Colonial: America and West Indies, 1661–1668* (London: HMSO, 1880, reprinted Vaduz, 1964), p. lxxxviii.

2 C. M. MacInnes, *England and Slavery* (Bristol, 1934), p. 14.

3 David Harris Sacks, *The Widening Gate: Bristol and the Atlantic Economy, 1450–1700* (Berkeley, California, 1991); C. M. MacInnes, *Bristol: A Gateway of Empire* (Bristol, 1939, reprinted Newton Abbot, 1969) and his 'Bristol and the Slave Trade', in Patrick McGrath (ed.), *Bristol in the Eighteenth Century* (Bristol: Bristol Historical Association, 1972), pp. 162–3; Patrick McGrath, *The Merchant Venturers of Bristol: A History of the Society of Merchant Venturers of the City of Bristol from its Origin to the Present Day* (Bristol: Society of Merchant Venturers of the City of Bristol, 1975) and his *Merchants and Merchandise in Seventeenth-Century Bristol* (Bristol: Bristol Record Society, 1955), and I. U. Hall, 'Whitson Sugar House, Bristol, 1665–1824', *Transactions of the Bristol and Gloucester Archaeological Society*, vol. 65 (1944), pp. 7–10, all mention in passing the importance of the West India trade at this date, and MacInnes briefly acknowledges, as did J. Latimer, *Annals of Bristol in the Seventeenth Century* (Bristol: William Georges, 1900), the probability of a flourishing contraband trade in slaves. James A. Rawley, in *The Transatlantic Slave Trade: A History* (New York, London, 1981), stresses more than the others Bristol's participation in the trade before 1698.

4 David Richardson, *Bristol, Africa and the Eighteenth-Century Slave Trade to America*, 4 vols (vols 37, 39, 42 and 47) (Bristol: Bristol Record Society, 1986, 1987, 1991 and 1996) and his *The Bristol Slave Traders: A Collective Portrait* (Bristol: Bristol Historical Association, 1985).

5 Don Pedro de Ayala, Spanish ambassador to England, to Ferdinand and Isabella, King and Queen of Spain, 25 July 1498, *Calendar of State Papers, Spanish Series*, vol. 1, pp. 168–79, in Eric Williams (ed.), *Documents of West Indian History* (New York: A and B Books Publishers, 1967, reprinted 1994), p. 206.

6 James A. Williamson, *Maritime Enterprise, 1485–1558* (Oxford, 1913), pp. 260–2; H. R. Fox Bourne, *English Merchants: Memoirs in Illustration of the Progress of British Commerce*, 2 vols (London: Richard Bentley, 1866), vol. 1, p. 156; MacInnes, *Bristol: A Gateway of Empire*, pp. 34–6, 44–8; Hugh Thomas, *The Slave Trade: The History of the Atlantic Slave Trade, 1440–1870* (London, 1997), pp. 96–105; Ruth Pike, *Enterprise and Adventure: The Genoese in Seville and the Opening up of the New World* (Ithaca, NY, and London, 1966), pp. 105, 195n. For Seville's slave trade at this time, see Ruth Pike, *Aristocrats and Traders: Sevillian Society in the Sixteenth Century* (Ithaca, NY, and London, 1972), pp. 175–81. For Thorne's involvement as a Seville merchant in the West India trade and his association with Cabot, see Gordon Connell-Smith, 'English Merchants Trading to the New World in the Early Sixteenth Century', *Bulletin of the Institute of Historical Research*, vol. 23 (1950), p. 58.

6 Jean Vanes (ed.), *Documents Illustrating the Overseas Trade of Bristol in the Sixteenth Century* (Bristol: Bristol Record Society, 1979), p. 21; Fox Bourne, *English Merchants*, vol. 1, pp. 153–7. According to Bourne, their father, Robert Thorne the elder (d. 1526),

had also lived in Seville, probably on account of his involvement in the soap trade, and was reportedly honoured by King Ferdinand of Spain, though for what services is not made clear. He was also appointed in 1510 to 'hold in commission of office of Admiral of England in Bristol', and was the city's mayor in 1515.

7 Sacks, *The Widening Gate*, pp. 30–1; MacInnes, *Bristol: A Gateway of Empire*, pp. 35–48. MacInnes does speak about Thorne the younger's close association with three Portuguese merchants from the Azores.

8 Thomas, *The Slave Trade: The History of the Atlantic Slave Trade, 1440–1870* (London, 1997), p. 84. I am indebted to Lord Thomas for a list of English merchants in sixteenth-century Seville which includes the names of Thorne and several other Bristol merchants. Though Lord Thomas asserts that it was the Florentines who dominated the slave trade in Seville, Ruth Pike argues convincingly that it was the Genoese in her *Enterprise and Adventure*, pp. 55–6.

9 As G. D. Ramsay points out in his *English Overseas Trade during the Centuries of Emergence* (London, 1957), p. 134.

10 This proverb was cited by Samuel Curwen, who visited Bristol in 1778; see G. A. Ward (ed.), *Samuel Curwen, Journals and Letters* (London, 1842) cited in Peter T. Marcy, 'Eighteenth Century Views of Bristol and Bristolians', in McGrath (ed.), *Bristol in the Eighteenth Century*, p. 36. Though Curwen said the proverb denoted the sharp practice of Bristol traders, the saying seems oddly anachronistic. It seems unlikely that the Genoese would be referred to by eighteenth-century pundits since trade to Italy had been long eclipsed by trade to the Americas. The saying makes much more sense as an early modern survival.

11 Robin Law and P. E. H. Hair, 'The English in West Africa', in Nicholas Canny (ed.), *The Origins of Empire: British Overseas Enterprise to the Close of the Seventeenth Century* (Oxford, 1998), vol. 1, p. 244, note that English merchants seeking pilots for Guinea were expelled from Seville, probably at the behest of the Portuguese.

12 John Blake, *European Beginnings in West Africa 1454–1578: A Survey of the First Century of White Enterprise in West Africa, with Special Emphasis upon the Rivalry of the Great Powers* (London, 1937), pp. 71, 144–5, and Fox Bourne, *English Merchants*, vol. 1, p. 151. Bourne names Richard Warde, Thomas Ashehurst and John Thomas, all of Bristol, together with three Portuguese, as receiving a licence to explore, at their own expense, unknown territories, but Blake notes that these men were expressly forbidden to sail to lands already known to any Christian – a provision which would exclude Guinea. He does name Thomas Ashurst (*sic*), Hugh Elliot (also of Bristol) and two Portuguese merchants as those allowed by Henry VII to make discoveries in this period. Perhaps the most important point for our purposes is that collaboration between Bristol merchants and Portuguese merchants did occur. MacInnes, *Bristol: A Gateway to Empire*, pp. 34–5, also stresses the close relationships between Bristol merchants and the Spanish. William Hawkins the elder may possibly have traded in Guinea in 1530, according to A. N. Porter (ed.), *Atlas of British Overseas Expansion* (New York and London, 1991), pp. 18–19, and Fox Bourne, *English Merchants*, vol. 1, p. 198. Regarding English incursions into Guinea in the 1550s and possible collusion between English and Iberian unofficial slaving interests, see P. E. H. Hair, 'Protestants as Pirates, Slavers and Proto-missionaries: Sierra Leone, 1568 and 1582', *Journal of Ecclesiastical History*, vol. 21, no. 3 (July 1970), p. 205n. Hair's article indicates the need for scholars of Bristol's early modern history to trawl the archives of Lisbon and Seville.

13 McGrath, in *The Merchant Venturers of Bristol*, pp. 10–23, notes that the Spanish Company (chartered by the Crown in 1577) was more active and powerful in late sixteenth-century Bristol than the Society of Merchant Venturers although the business of the Spanish Company (which retained a monopoly of all English trade to Spain and Portugal) was disrupted by war with Spain between 1585 and 1604. When the monopoly

was reinstated and the patent renewed in 1605, 97 of the 577 merchants named in the patent were Bristolians.

14 John William Blake (ed.), *Europeans in West Africa, 1450–1560* (London: Hakluyt Society, 1942), vol. 2, pp. 251–4, 271; Elizabeth Donnan, *Documents Illustrative of the Slave Trade to America*, 4 vols (Washington, DC: Carnegie Institution of America, 1930–5), vol. 1, pp. 42–4. It does not seem that this early incarnation of the Society of Merchant Venturers of Bristol was involved in these ventures.

15 Hair, 'Protestants as Pirates', p. 213 notes that in 1568 some 500 Africans were taken by Hawkins's expedition. In 1972, when I first came to Bristol, Hawkins's coat of arms, which includes the enchained head of an African, was displayed in the verger's room of the Lord Mayor's Chapel.

16 J. Vanes (ed.), *The Overseas Trade of Bristol*, pp. 24, 157n; Porter (ed.), *Atlas of British Overseas Expansion*, p. 18, claims that falling profits 'caused the English effectively to abandon the Guinea trade after 1571', a claim that seems at odds with the evidence cited in the text. It is interesting that Hawkins began his ventures in Africa after experience of trading with the Canaries, thus pointing again to the way Iberian trade served as a staging post in the development of the English slave trade.

17 Vanes (ed.), *The Overseas Trade of Bristol*, p. 163.

18 Robin Blackburn, *The Making of New World Slavery: From the Baroque to the Modern, 1492–1800* (London, 1997), p. 220.

19 See Trevor Burnard, 'Who Bought Slaves in Early America? Purchasers of Slaves from the Royal African Company in Jamaica, 1674–1708', *Slavery and Abolition*, vol. 17, no. 2 (August 1996), p. 83 regarding the Jamaican plantation.

20 Ramsay, *English Overseas Trade*, pp. 136–8.

21 Raymond Gorges, *The Story of a Family through Eleven Centuries . . . being a History of the Family of Gorges* (Boston: privately printed, 1944), p. 135. Raymond Gorges seems to conflate the original Guinea Company with its successor, which was reconstituted *c.* 1631 and which was involved in slaving. According to Theodore K. Rabb, *Enterprise and Empire: Merchant and Gentry Investment in the Expansion of England, 1575–1630* (Cambridge, MA, 1967), pp. 300, 232, 245n, 193–4, Sir Ferdinando Gorges was a charter member of the original Guinea Company founded in 1618. See also MacInnes, *Bristol: A Gateway of Empire*, pp. 71, 96–106, 126, 152–3, and Robert Brenner, *Merchants and Revolution: Commercial Change, Political Conflict, and London's Overseas Traders, 1550–1653* (Cambridge: 1993), pp. 163–4, for later history of the Guinea Company after 1631 and its involvement in the slave trade. For the Bermuda Company, see Richard Pares, *Merchants and Planters* (Cambridge, Economic History Review, 1960), vol. 2, appendix I. For the early presence of African slaves in Viriginia and Bermuda, see Thomas, *The Slave Trade*, pp. 174–6, and J. Henry Lefroy (ed.), *The Historye of the Bermudaes or Summer Island* (London: Hakluyt Society, 1882), pp. 243–4.

22 Pip Jones and Rita Youseph, in *The Black Population of Bristol in the Eighteenth Century* (Bristol: Bristol Historical Association, 1994), p. 2, indicate that the gardener was employed *c.* 1560. However, property deeds in Merchant Venturers archives in Bristol relating to Young's estate (Box 1, bundle 1, part 1) suggest that the Great House was built between *c.* 1575 and 1599. I am grateful to Nicholas A. D. Molyneax for this information. We do not know enough about Young's trading activities to link him with the Africa or the Iberian trades.

23 The reference of the burial of 'Katherine a blacke negra servante' at the Horsehead Tavern in Christmas Street was taken from the Christ Church parish register and cited in BRL, Braikenridge Collection, Inns and Taverns, p. 42. Catellena lived in Almondsbury, now a suburb of Bristol; Jones and Youseph, *The Black Population of Bristol*, p. 2. The landed magnate Thomas Chester had his great house in Almondsbury, so there may be a connection.

24 It re-formed in 1601, according to McGrath in *The Merchant Venturers of Bristol*, pp. 12, 23–38.
25 Hilary McD. Beckles, 'The Economic Origins of Black Slavery in the British West Indies, 1640–1680: A Tentative Analysis of the Barbados Model', *Journal of Caribbean History*, vol. 16 (1982), pp. 42–3.
26 McGrath, *The Merchant Venturers of Bristol*, p. 59; Beckles, 'The Economic Origins of Black Slavery', p. 42.
27 Take the case of Robert Yate, a Bristol merchant and father of the MP of the same name. The older Yate was a Royalist sympathizer during the Civil War but stayed on to serve Cromwell. Henry Hazard and Robert Immans were two Bristol merchants licensed to 'carry 200 Irishmen to the Caribbee islands from Ireland'. I am grateful to Andrew Hannam for the information on Robert Yate, which is currently in preparation for publication as part of the History of Parliament Trust Series on the history of the House of Commons. The item on Hazard and Immans is from *CalSPCol, 1574–1660*, p. 387. According to 'P.H.B. an amateur historian working in the archives of the Bristol Society of Merchant Venturers', Robert Cann and the Quaker Thomas Speed, both, like Yate, members of the society, transported Irish rebels from Ireland to Barbados. See, too, Society of Merchant Venturers of Bristol Archives (henceforth SMV), P.H.B., 'The Business of Adventuring and Slave Trading and Members of the Society of Merchant Venturers Concerned, 1569–1833' (unpublished typescript, March 1974).
28 Hilary McD. Beckles, 'Rebels and Reactionaries: The Political Responses of White Labourers to Planter Class Hegemony in Seventeenth Century Barbados', *Journal of Caribbean History*, vol. 15 (1981), p. 15.
29 B. D. Henning, *The House of Commons, 1660–1690*, 3 vols (London, 1983), vol. 2, p. 693, for Knight, and *CalSPCol, 1661–1668*, p. 98. Regarding the corporate ordinance of September 1652 against the 'inveighing, purloining and stealing away of boys, maids and others' to be sold 'across the seas', see Jones and Youseph, *Black Population*, p. 21.
30 See, for example, Daniel Pym of Bristol, who in 1685 transported 100 prisoners from Wells in Somerset after the Monmouth rising. His brother, Col. Charles Pym, who as shown below was implicated in the smuggling of black slaves, became Chief Justice of Nevis. A dynasty of these Bristol Pyms figured among the elite of Nevis's plantocracy for the next century; Vere Langford Olivier (ed.), *Caribbeana: Being Miscellaneous Papers relating to the History, Genealogy, Topography and Antiquities of the British West Indies*, 6 vols (London, 1910), vol. 3, pp. 50–1.
31 Sacks, in *The Widening Gate*, pp. 252–64, offers the most up-to-date analysis of the white servants bound for the colonies, but is not interested in the racial dimension of the plantation workforce. In 1685 Judge Jeffreys came to Bristol as part of the notorious 'Bloody Assizes' ordered after the abortive Monmouth rebellion. According to Latimer, Jeffreys took this opportunity of accusing Bristol's mayor and aldermen of corruptly kidnapping petty criminals in order to use them on their plantations. Again according to Latimer, Jeffreys was a corrupt drunk who used this accusation in order to punish those corporation members whom he suspected of being sympathetic to the Monmouth rebels. In contrast, MacInnes, somewhat less convincingly, portrays Jeffreys as righting a wrong in the interests of justice. As we shall later see, a number of those so accused, namely John Napper and William Swymmer, had supplied black labour (probably illegally) to Jamaican planters – see Latimer, *Annals of Bristol in the Seventeenth Century*, pp. 433–8; MacInnes, *Bristol: A Gateway of Empire*, pp. 156–71; MacInnes, 'Bristol and the Slave Trade', pp. 162–3; and Frances Bickely (ed.), *CalSPDom, February–December 1685*, pp. 335–6 for Lord Chief Justice Jeffreys's letter of 22 September 1685 to the Earl of Sunderland regarding the Bristol mayor Sir William Hayman, and others involved in the 'villainy' of kidnapping. Richard Pares, in his wonderful study of the Pinney

family of Bristol, *A West India Fortune* (London, 1950), pp. 7–8, says that crimping or kidnapping was largely suppressed in Bristol by 1682.

32 Hilary McD. Beckles, 'The "Hub of Empire": The Caribbean and Britain in the Seventeenth Century', in Canny (ed.), *The Origins of Empire*, p. 224; Richard S. Dunn, 'The Barbados Census of 1680: Profile of the Richest Colony in English America', *William and Mary Quarterly*, vol. 26 (October 1969), p. 7, working from previously unexploited census data from 1680, is keen to show that the white population as a whole was still some 20,000 in 1680 and that earlier historians had exaggerated white depopulation for this period. The point of interest to us here is that African slaves were on the island in numbers which outstripped those of white indentured servants. The 10,000 servants who cleared from Bristol between 1654 and 1685 were predominantly literate and often of yeoman stock. Pares, in *Merchants and Planters*, pp. 18–19, points out that by 1650, though white tradesmen refiners and other specialist workers were still sent out to Barbados, 'the English peasant' had been 'taken over by an African'. See also Richard Sheridan, *The Development of the Plantations to 1750, an Era of West Indian Prosperity, 1750–1775* (Barbados and London, 1970), pp. 27–8. In Virginia, black : white ratios were not so extreme, thanks to the preponderance of tobacco, initially associated with small farms and a free or racially mixed workforce, but even here, an early eighteenth-century commentator remarked that white servants made up 'but an insignificant number when compared with the vast shoals of Negroes'; Hugh James, *The Present State of Virginia (1724)*, in John Andrew Doyle, *English in America: Virginia, Maryland and the Carolinas*, 5 vols (London: Longman Green, 1882), p. 516n.

33 By the 1690s, white servants were increasingly difficult to find in Barbados, since the incessant wars in the region afforded them more lucrative employment and planters' representatives complained that 'that sorte of peple that did use to goe to the Plantations goe now into the Armyes'; PRO, Barbados Correspondence, 7 September 1692, CO28/1.

34 Sheridan, *The Development of the Plantations*, pp. 27–8. Hilary McD. Beckles, *White Servitude and Black Slavery in Barbados, 1627–1715* (Knoxville, TN, 1989), pp. 152–61, looks at the displacement of some small white freeholders (including some from Bristol) by the sugar barons of Barbados.

35 Pennoyer's continuing contact with Bristol had to do with the importation of tobacco 'from the plantations in the Cairribbee Islands', i.e. St Christophers; PRO, 'Miles Lavington . . . of the Custom House of the port of Bristol. V. Brian Rogers, merchant, William Pennoyer merchant, and others', E134/17Chas1/Hil21 and E134/18Chas1Trin1.

36 Donnan, *Documents*, vol. 1, pp. 125–33.

37 For the Pennoyer brothers, see Brenner, *Merchants and Revolution*, pp. 165–76, 193–4, and Kenneth R. Andrews, *Ships, Money and Politics: Seafaring and Naval Enterprise in the Reign of Charles I* (Cambridge, 1991), pp. 57–8, 201. We know that Thomson had been directed to go to Bristol in order to provision a ship for the slave colony of Providence in 1641, so he must have had contacts, and as a religious Dissenter, he was likely to have liaised with other Dissenters there. Andrews lists the Pennoyers and James Russell (possibly the James Russell of Bristol and Nevis) as amongst Thomson's fellow radicals and business associates. The James Pope listed was an agent supervising the slaving voyage of the *Friendship* to the River Gambia in Guinea, 'touching on the way, at the Cape Verde Islands and such other places as Mr. James Pope should desire'. It is not unreasonable to suppose that the Pope he employed was one of the Bristol Popes, who under John Pope became involved as sugar traders in the 1650s. A James Pope is listed as a merchant involved in 1679 with a Madeira-bound ship, the *Blackamore*, which, as I argue below, probably traded in slaves. A James Pope is also listed as a sugar importer in 1684 and as a member of Bristol's Common Council as late as 1695. But this James Pope would have had to be in his sixties or seventies by then to have been the man who

worked for Pennoyer in the 1650s; or it could have been an older relation, as first names often ran in families in this period. The Popes were eminent sugar-refiners by the end of the seventeenth century. See W. Noel Saintsbury (ed.), *CalSPCol, 1574–1660* (London: HMSO, 1860, reprinted 1964), p. 317; BL, Historical Manuscripts Commission, *Portland Manuscripts* (London: HMSO, 1893), vol. 2, p. 29; Society of Merchant Venturers Library, *Wharfage Book*, 30 November 1684; V. T. Harlow, *A History of Barbados, 1635–1685* (Oxford, 1926), p. 310 and p. 310n; Brenner, *Merchants and Revolution*, pp. 164–5, 174–5, 192, 417; Alfred Beaven, *Bristol Lists: Municipal and Miscellaneous* (Bristol: T. D. Taylor, 1899), pp. 206–9; Donald Jones, *Bristol's Sugar Trade and Refining Industry* (Bristol: Bristol Branch of the Historical Association, 1996), p. 6.

38 BL, HMC, *Portland Manuscripts*, vol. 2, p. 90. The document was dated according to the pre-reform calendar as 23 February 1654/5. From the context of the calendared extract it is clear that the 'General' referred to was one William Penn who served with Admiral Venables in securing Jamaica for the British in 1655. Admiral Penn, variously described elsewhere as a 'gallant tar' and a 'rogue and a rascal', unsuccessfully contested a Bristol parliamentary seat in 1660, but was returned that same year for Weymouth. It is significant that Drew released one slave because of the slave's wish to become a Christian, suggesting an unease with enslaving a baptized man; W. R. Williams, *Parliamentary History of the County of Gloucestershire including the Cities of Bristol and Gloucester* (Hereford: privately printed, 1898), p. 117; Latimer, *Annals of Bristol in the Seventeenth Century*, pp. 292–3.

39 William Penn Jr was also a slave-owner, though on a modest scale. Recent investigations into the letters, and the record and cash books he kept at his plantation in Pennsylvania – Pennsbury Manor – document his sale of a 'black fisherman' in 1685 and his ownership of five slaves between 1699 and 1701. My thanks to Lara Murphy, Head of Interpretive Research at Pennsbury Manor, Pennsylvania, for this information and to Jim McNeill of Easton's Living History in Bristol for putting me in touch with her. See also Nigel Tattersfield, *The Forgotten Trade: Comprising the Log of the Daniel and Henry of 1700 and Accounts of the Slave Trade from the Minor Ports of England, 1698–1725* (London, 1991), p. 32.

40 For William Penn Jr, see Tattersfield, *The Forgotten Trade*, p. 32.

41 Ferdinando Gorges, the grandson of Sir Ferdinando Gorges, was one of the Barbadian planters petitioning the House of Commons in 1667 against a trade monopoly on the African trade and urging a return to a free trade in African slaves:

> that formerly theyr hath alwaies been a freedom of trade for all His Majesty's Subjects for negroes on the whole Coast of Giney, by reason whereof the said Plantation have been plentifully supplied with negroes of the best sort . . . to the great increase of the said Plantations. (BL, Tracts, 1029.e20.2)

42 Larry Gragg, '"To Procure Negroes": The English Slave Trade to Barbados, 1627–1660', *SA*, vol. 16, no. 1 (1995), pp. 68–9, 76–7. See note 51.

43 Letter from Jamaica, 15 February 1679, in the Correspondence Book of the Royal Company of Adventurers [actually now the Royal African Company], T/70/1; Christopher Jeaffreson, who said such practices in Nevis were 'rife', was told by a well-informed source that the interlopers were worth a good deal of money. John Cordy Jeaffreson (ed.), *A Young Squire of the Seventeenth Century: From the Papers (A.D. 1676–1686) of Christopher Jeaffreson of Dillingham House, Cambridgeshire*, 2 vols (London: Hurst & Blackett, 1878), vol. 2, p. 379.

44 PRO, will of James Teager? (probably Teague) of Bristol, died Jamaica, 15 March 1695 (1964), PROB 4/1790. Roger Hayden, 'Broadmead, Bristol in the Seventeenth Century', *Baptist Quarterly*, vol. 23 (1969–70), p. 349, notes that a John Teague was connected in the 1660s with the Baptist sugar merchants in Bristol.

45 P. F. Campbell, 'Merchants and Traders of Barbados', *JBMHS*, vol. 34 (May 1972), pp. 94ff; Harlow, *A History of Barbados*, pp. 320–2.

46 Robert H. Schomburgk, *The History of Barbados: Comprising a Geographical and Statistical Description of the Island . . .* (New York, 1971 reprint), p. 237. The town may have been named after William Speight, a Bristol-born planter resident there.

47 BL, Blathwayt's Barbados Papers, 1664–1706, Add. MSS 38714ff., 18–19.

48 PRO, T70/121, 16–18, cited in David Eltis, Stephen D. Behrendt, David Richardson and Herbert S. Klein (eds), *The Trans-Atlantic Slave Trade, 1527–1867: A Datatset on CD-Rom* (Cambridge, 2000).

49 C. S. S. Higham, *The Development of the Leeward Islands under the Restoration, 1660–1680* (Cambridge, 1921), pp. 162–4; Donnan, *Documents*, vol. 1, pp. 250, 260n, 261n; and for a lively popular account of the island's early history, see Vincent K. Hubbard, *Sword, Ships and Sugar: A History of Nevis to 1900* (Placenta, CA, 1993).

50 Unusually, the ship, under the command of a Captain John Bridges, appears to have come straight from Guinea to Bristol in May 1689, and the Earl of Nottingham directed the customs office at Bristol to allow the Royal African Company agents to unload and seize the ship; William John Harding (ed.), *CalSPDom, 1689–1690* (London: HMSO, 1895), pp. 122, 132.

51 McGrath cites the *Society* of Bristol, which was seized, 'laden with negroes and elephant's teeth', from the Guinea coast in Virginia in 1688, and the *Bettey* of Bristol. In McGrath, *Merchants and Merchandise*, p. xxii.

52 Richardson, *Bristol, Africa and the Eighteenth-Century Slave Trade*, vol. 1, p. xiii.

53 McGrath, *Merchants and Merchandise*, pp. 267, 268.

54 See, for example, Saintsbury (ed.), *CalSPCol, 1661–1668*, pp. 222, 321.

55 It is unclear whether he sent them as indentured servants or as slaves; see Table 1 and *The Deposition Book of Bristol, 1650–1654* (Bristol: Bristol Record Society), cited in D. P. Lindegaard, *Black Bristolians of the Eighteenth and Nineteenth Centuries* (Bristol: privately printed, n.d.), pp. 45–6.

56 Gragg, '"To Procure Negroes"', p. 73; R. Pares, *Merchants and Planters* (Cambridge: printed for the *Economic History Review*, 1960), pp. 38–9, 47–8, 53; Olivier (ed.), *Caribbeana*, vol. 3, p. 308. It required almost $4000 in the late seventeenth century to launch a working sugar plantation in the Caribbean, according to Nuala Zahedieh, 'Trade, Plunder and Economic Development in Early English Jamaica, 1655–1689', *Economic History Review*, second series, vol. 39 (1986), p. 208. The William Hilliard Pares refers to may, given the vagaries of early modern spelling, be identical to or a relative of William Helyar of Jamaica, who is discussed later in this chapter.

57 Farmer was characterized by his royalist enemies as a 'Magna Carta man', i.e. against the powers of the Crown; see Saintsbury (ed.), *CalSPCol, 1661–1668*, pp. 1, 308, 317–18, 325, 364–6; Olivier (ed.), *Caribbeana*, vol. 3, pp. 307–8; and Harlow, *A History of Barbados*, pp. 145, 157, 159. I am grateful to Ronald Hughes of Barbados for the additional information about Farmer's birthdate and time of death, and his ownership of a plantation in St Thomas. Farmer himself probably died in debt, perhaps owing to his political difficulties resulting in imprisonment.

58 PRO, *Spiar* v. *Hare*, C/105/27, contains the will of George Standfast and other documents relating to the legacy, including an account of the will of Thomas Spiar, who died in 1682. Spiar's widow, Mary, later married one of the largest planters in Barbados, Col. Thomas Walrond. For John Standfast's Barbados property in 1679, see John Camden Hotten (ed.), *The Original Lists of Persons of Quality . . . who went from Great Britain to the American Plantations, 1600–1700* (London: Chatto & Windus, 1874), p. 505; Olivier (ed.), *Caribbeana*, vol. 4, p. 113; and McGrath, *Merchants and Merchandise*, pp. 258–9, which shows Standfast's continuing relationship with Bristol via his uncle John Webb, who was a Merchant Venturer.

59 Robert Yeamans (probably the brother of John) is listed as owning land in Barbados in 1638 along with others such as Edward Southwell and Thomas Pocock whose names were subsequently associated with Bristol, in BL, *Memoirs of the First Settlement of the Island of Barbados and other Carribee islands, with the Succession of the Governors and commanders in chief of Barbados to the Year 1742 Extracted from Ancient Records papers and Accounts Taken from Mr. William Arnold, Mr. Samuel Balkly and Mr. John Summer, some of the First Settlers the Last of whom Was alive in 1688 Aged 82 . . .* (London: E. Owen, 1743), pp. 53ff.

60 For Yeamans, see James C. Brandow (ed.), *Genealogies of Barbados Families* (Baltimore: Genealogical Publishing Co., 1983), pp. 639–41, for his will and a family tree linking him to Bristol. A John Yeoman (probably Yeamans) was appointed an official to a newly formed 'prize office' in Barbados in 1654; BL, Historical Manuscripts Commission, *Portland Manuscripts*, vol. 2, p. 90. See *CalSPCol, 1661–1668*, pp. 1, 46, 154, 169, 267, 403–4, for entries on Yeamans's various activities, including his membership of the Barbados Council as early as 1661, and pp. 593–4 regarding murder allegations against him. See also BL, *Abstracts of Jamaican Wills, 1625–1792*, Add. MSS 34181, 222, for mention of his South Carolina dealings. Two Bristol mariners swore to city officials in 1674 that they had seen Sir John Yeamans, 'governor of the province of Caroline alive and in good health', the previous year, thus indicating the city's pride in this once-reviled son; BRO, Deposition Book of Bristol for 1674. See also Harlow, *A History of Barbados*, pp. 145, 157, 159. Beckles, in *White Servitude and Black Slavery*, p. 165, states that Yeamans was Lord Ashley's (later Earl of Shaftesbury) agent in Barbados. Shaftesbury regarded him as a particularly ruthless and grasping individual, and it was widely assumed at the time that he had murdered a business colleague, Col. Benjamin Berringer, in order to secure both his plantation and his wife, Margaret, for himself. Beckles states that the arrival of Yeamans and other Barbadians in South Carolina helped to ensure the colony's rapid development of 'the largest slave population in North America during the seventeenth century'. Richard Dunn concurs in this assessment in his *Sugar and Slaves: The Rise of the Planter Class in the English West Indies, 1624–1713* (London, 1973), pp. 58, 81n, 112–15. See also Karl Watson, '"The Barbados Endeavours to Rule All": A Socio-Political Commentary on the Barbardos/Carolina Relationship in the Seventeenth Century', *JBMHS*, vol. 43 (1996/7), pp. 86–7, and Harlow, *A History of Barbados*, pp. 153n, 160. See Warren Alleyne and Henry Fraser, *The Barbados–Carolina Connection* (London, 1988), pp. 7–9, 11, 13, 17, 19, 38–9, for Yeamans's skulduggery and for photos of the plantation mansion he 'inherited' from his allegedly murdered colleague. For a general overview of the links between Barbados and South Carolina, see Richard S. Dunn, 'The English Sugar Islands and the Founding of South Carolina', *South Carolina Historical Magazine* (April 1971), pp. 81–93.

61 Watson, '"The Barbados Endeavours to Rule All"', pp. 86–7.

62 Dunn, *Sugar and Slaves*, pp. 112–15. Yeamans was part of an elite which included a few other individuals with long-standing Bristol connections, such as Robert Daniel and members of the Cumberbatch family.

63 Joseph James, Henry Hunt, Robert Kirke as well as Anthony Swymmer are mentioned as Bristol merchants in Jamaica in the late seventeenth century in BM, Abstracts of Jamaican Wills, Add. MSS 34181. For Anthony Swymmer in Port Royal, see Michael Pawson and David Buisseret, *Port Royal, Jamaica* (Oxford, 1975), pp. 32, 64, 167, 169, 186, 193. For the will of Anthony Swymmer, proved in 1688, see 'Extracts from Wills Relating to the West Indies Recorded in England', *JBMHS*, vol. 12, no. 4 (August 1945), p. 179. His son, Capt. Anthony Swymmer, seems to have lived for a time after 1688 since he is listed as owning a 'factory' (i.e. plantation) in

1694, in an account by Richard Lloyd of Jamaican factory owners in 1694, 23 May 1699 to Council of Trade and Plantations, extracted from Cecil Headlam (ed.), *CalSPCol, 1699* (London: HMSO, 1908, reprinted Vaduz, 1964), p. 244, cited in www.genealogy-quest.com/collections/jamfact.html, 2000; see also Olivier (ed.), *Caribbeana*, vol. 5, p. 130. However, it is also possible that his nephew Anthony (d. 1719) owned the plantation by that date, though the reference to a *Captain* Swymmer makes it unlikely. The identities of Anthony Swymmer I (*c.* 1612–88) and Anthony II (b. 1675) are partly outlined by I. V. Hall in his notes on the Swymmer family, BRO 36722, Box 10. Hall cites Apprenticeship and Burgess records to show that Anthony I had been apprenticed to William Hayman, spent time in the Caribbean and ended his days in Bristol where he served as common councillor from 1684 to 1688. As the Swymmers named their male offspring William and Anthony throughout the seventeenth and eighteenth centuries, it is not always easy to distinguish between the various generations of Swymmers, and Hall's assertion that Anthony II was born 35 years after his brother William does seem unlikely.

64 The various Bristol activities of Alderman William Swymmer (*c.* 1640–1714), who served in Bristol as council member, alderman, sheriff, mayor and governor of the Incorporation of the Poor, as well as becoming Master of the Society of Merchant Venturers in 1690, have been derived from the Hall notes and from Latimer, *Annals of Bristol in the Seventeenth Century*, pp. 480, 482, and Patrick McGrath, *Records Relating to the Society of Merchant Venturers of the City of Bristol in the Seventeenth Century* (Bristol: Bristol Record Society, 1952), pp. 231–3. See also SMV, the anonymously compiled but generally reliable compendium of 'Merchant Venturers' Curricula Vitae' (unpublished typescript in alphabetical files, n.d., but *c.* 1970).

65 As described above in this chapter. William Hayman seems to have been involved in the abortive 1684 transaction only; DD/WHh 1089, item 111. If he was a contemporary of Anthony Swymmer I he would have been an old man by the 1680s and may have been the same William Hayman as is listed in Table 1 as a slave-owner in Bristol.

66 J. Napper reported to William Helyar from Jamaica in 1683 that 'I can't gett menn negroes here without women I . . . now sent to nevis for to buy 10 negroes.' He then purchased six men from one Capt. Henry Nurse there, who may or may not have been an agent of the Royal African Company; SRO, Helyar Papers, DD/WHh 1089, bundle 7, item 14 and bundle 2, item 22. According to Nuala Zahedieh, 'The Merchants of Port Royal, Jamaica and the Contraband Trade, 1655–1692', *WMQ*, third series, vol. 43 (1986), pp. 590–1, the illegal trade with the Spaniards was flourishing, with Spaniards purchasing slaves in Jamaica which the Royal African Company had brought to the island. Certainly the Helyars and the Swymmers discussed getting involved in a scheme selling slaves to Spaniards.

67 William's son Anthony, who lived in Bristol, had over a thousand acres of land in Orange Bay, Jamaica, and was reportedly said to have been worth £40,000 on his death on 18 June 1719. Although not listed by Richardson as a slave-ship owner or Africa merchant, the anonymous compiler of the 'Merchant Venturers' Curricula Vitae', which also recounts the report of his wealth and his political office, listed his principal occupation as West Africa trader, a discrepancy which may be accounted for by the fact that he may have had unreported shares in a number of ships. He was a member of the Bristol Council from 1684 to 1688 and from 1700 to 1719. Anthony's brother William Swymmer Jr is listed as a part-owner of only one slave ship in the period before 1729. See BL, will of (Hon.) Anthony Swymmer of Bristol Esq., 29 March 1717, Add. MSS 34181, and SMV, Anon., 'Merchant Venturers' Curricula Vitae'; Richardson, *Bristol, Africa and the Eighteenth-Century Slave Trade*, vol. 1, p. 171.

68 J. Harry Bennett, 'Cary Helyar, Merchant and Planter of Seventeenth-Century Jamaica', *WMQ*, third series, vol. 21 (1964), p. 53.

69 See Dunn, *Sugar and Slaves*, pp. 212–23, for a helpful chronology of the fate of the Bybrook Plantation; see also Michael Craton and James Walvin, *A Jamaican Plantation: The History of Worthy Park, 1670–1970* (London and New York, 1970), pp. 30–1.

70 SRO, Helyar Papers, DD/WHh 1089, bundle 2, item 111. A bill of exchange from 1676 referring to an earlier purchase of slaves by the Helyars specifically mentions the Royal African Company as a supplier, but in the 1684 transaction no mention is made of the company in the associated correspondence.

71 *Ibid*. It also seems unlikely that the factor would buy a consignment of largely sick slaves.

72 *Ibid*.

73 SRO, Helyar MSS, DD/WHh 1089, bundle 3, item 55.

74 '[It] being all one to him [Captain Swymmer] to pay me [John Helyar] as to pay the company for sd. 20 negroes'; SRO, Helyar Papers, DD/WHh 1089, bundle 3, item 4. See also DD/WHh 1089, bundle 2, item 87, and bundle 3, items 4, 6, for John Helyar's enthusiasm for a scheme of buying slaves direct on the grounds that the Royal African Company compels buyers to purchase slave 'in lotts', thereby taking the ill with the healthy.

75 Thomas Day, a wealthy merchant who later became mayor of the city, petitioned sometime around the 1670s to be Governor of Bermuda; BCRL, Petition of Mr Thomas Day to Lord Justice of England (n.d. but *c.* 1673), Southwell Papers, vol. 1.

76 MacInnes, *Bristol: A Gateway of Empire*, pp. 164–5; 'Extracts from Wills Recorded in England', *JBMHS*, vol. 12, no. 1 (1944), p. 23; Olivier (ed.), *Caribbeana*, pp. 272–3 and accompanying plate of the Bristol memorial tablet.

77 The will of Thomas Woodward also left to William and George Broadbent 'to each a Negro to be purchased by them at the first opportunity that presents and that meat, drink and apparrell and education until they shall attaine to the age of 15 years'; PRO, PROB 11/358/135.

78 Pares, *A West India Fortune*.

79 *CSPCol, 1677–1680*, p. 263.

80 Hall, 'Bristol's Second Sugar House', *TGBAS*, vol. 68 (1949), p. 152. For his Royal African Company investments, see PRO, Royal African Company Records for July 1677, T70/185.

81 Hall, 'Bristol's Second Sugar House', pp. 127–35. Sir John Knight (of Temple) was mayor in 1663–4, during which time he zealously persecuted the Quakers; *CalSPCol, 1661–1668*, p. 265, recounts that sailors of the *Mary Fortune* refused to transport three Quakers to Barbados against their will. See also Latimer, *Annals of Bristol in the Seventeenth Century*, pp. 324–6. A John Knight, 'marchant' of Bristol (who was probably our Sir John Knight of Temple), was named as a friend in a 1647 will by Daniell Smyth, a merchant in Nevis, according to John Titford, 'Settlers of the Old Empire, The West Indies: Nevis: Some Selected Examples of Transcripts of Records', *Family Tree Magazine* (November 1999), p. 59.

82 Hall, 'Bristol's Second Sugar House', pp. 133–9. Cary lived in Barbados *c.* 1653–6 according to a contemporary document cited in Olivier (ed.), *Caribbeana*, vol. 3, p. 299 and p. 299n. Thanks to Mike Hutson of El Paso, Texas, who, citing the *Biographical Dictionary of the South Carolina House of Representatives*, vols 2 and 3, told me that the Bristol Carys had a number of relatives who left Bristol to settle in Virginia in the seventeenth century.

83 J. W. Fortiscue (ed.), *CalSPDom, 1681–1685* (London, 1898), pp. 587, 653; Hall, 'Bristol's Second Sugar House', pp. 110–63. Hall states that it was Sir John Knight, the one-time partner of John Knight, who applied for the governorship of the Leeward Islands, which fell vacant in 1685, but Hall's own family tree of the Knight family indicates that that particular Sir John Knight (of Temple) died in 1683. I suspect the hopeful

candidate was the younger Sir John Knight (of the Hill), since he was resident in the Caribbean at the time. See his furious petition to the King's Most Excellent Majesty and the Lords of His Majesty's Most Honble Privy-Council, in BRL, Southwell Papers, vol. 2 and Jeaffreson, *A Young Squire*, vol. 2, pp. 88, 91, 98, 107; Henning, *The House of Commons*, vol. 2, pp. 692–5.

84 For details of these groups, see Hall, 'Bristol's Second Sugar House', pp. 139–40.

85 Pares, *A West India Fortune*, p. 25.

86 Cary attested in 1696 that William Miner, late of Nevis, owed Cary over £2805; PRO, 'Deposition of John Cary 28 August 1696 concerning William Miner late of Nevis', PROB 5/1170. A John Carey is listed as owning land in Antigua with Clement Tudway in 1679 and a few acres in Barbados in 1688 with Nathaniel Haggett; Olivier (ed.), *Caribbeana*, vol. 1, p. 166.

87 Sacks, *The Widening Gate*, pp. 339–43. Sacks does not mention Cary's attitude towards the enslavement of Africans and in fact devotes less than two pages to the subject of the slave trade in his book.

88 McGrath, *Records Relating to the Society of Merchant Venturers*, p. 231.

89 After 1688 some licences were sold to private traders as a way to bring in cash to the 'ailing' Royal African Company, and whilst most of the ships so licensed sailed from London, proposals for a ship setting out from Bristol were approved in 1690 according to K. G. Davies, *The Royal African Trade* (London, 1957), pp. 125–6. By 1696 there were six or seven Bristol ships allowed into the African trade; Rawley, *The Transatlantic Slave Trade*, p. 178 and p. 178n.

90 See H. J. Lane, 'The Life and Writings of John Cary' (MA dissertation, University of Bristol, 1932).

91 J. Cary, *An Essay on the State of England, in relation to its Trade, its Poor and its Taxes, for carrying on the present war against France*, pp. 74–5, cited in MacInnes, 'Bristol and the Slave Trade', pp. 164–5.

92 Huntington Library, John Cary, *A Discourse of the Advantage of the African Trade to this Nation, Extracted out of an Essay of Trade, Written by Mr. John Cary, Merchant* (London[?], 1712), accession number 297691. This extract is quite similar to Cary's original work *An Essay on the State of England*.

93 *Ibid.*

94 I am most grateful to Andrew Hanham, who has kindly supplied me with this information from a manuscript on Robert Yate which he is preparing as part of the History of Parliament Trust series on the *History of the House of Commons*.

95 They lost this battle, even after the ending of the Royal African Company's monopoly in 1698. African traders from the outports had to pay a 10 per cent duty to help the company continue its upkeep of its forts and factories in Africa.

96 W. E. Minchinton, 'The Voyage of the Snow *Africa*', *The Mariner's Mirror*, vol. 37 (1951), pp. 187–96; his 'Bristol – Metropolis of the West in the Eighteenth Century', *Transactions of the Royal Historical Society*, series four, vol. 5 (1954), pp. 69–89; 'The Slave Trade of Bristol with the British Mainland Colonies in North America, 1699–1770', in Roger Anstey and P. E. H. Hair (eds) *Liverpool, the African Slave Trade, and Abolition* (Historic Society of Lancashire and Cheshire, Occasional Series, 2, 1976), pp. 39–59; 'The Merchants of Bristol in the Eighteenth Century', Fédération Historique du Sud-Ouest, Actes du Colloque Franco-Britannique tenu à Bordeaux du 27 au 30 Septembre 1976), pp. 185–200 (*Sociétés et Groupes Sociaux en Aquitaine et en Angleterre*); and his edited collections, especially W. E. Minchinton (ed.), *The Trade of Bristol in the Eighteenth Century* (Bristol: Bristol Record Society, 1957).

97 Kenneth Morgan, *Bristol and the Atlantic Economy in the Eighteenth Century* (Cambridge, 1993), and his 'Bristol and the Atlantic Trade in the Eighteenth Century', *English Historical Review*, vol. 107 (July 1992), pp. 626–50. Morgan's 'Bristol West India

Merchants in the Eighteenth Century', *Transactions of the Royal Historical Society*, sixth series, no. 3 (1993), pp. 185–208, is also useful, as is his 'The Bright Family Papers', *Archives*, vol. 22, no. 97 (October 1997), pp. 119–29.

98 This has since been updated and included in a collaborative project in the form of a database of over 27,000 transatlantic slave-ship voyages made between 1595 and 1866. See Eltis *et al.* (eds), *The Trans-Atlantic Slave Trade*. Thanks to David Richardson for bringing this source to my attention and for kindly helping me with its interrogation.

99 Richardson, *Bristol, Africa and the Eighteenth-Century Slave Trade*, vol. 1, p. xv.

100 *Ibid.*

101 This estimate is based on the figure of 2114 voyages quoted from David Richardson, 'The Eighteenth-Century British Slave Trade: Estimates of Its Volume and Coastal Distribution in Africa', *Research in Economic History*, vol. 12 (1989), p. 169, quoted in Morgan, *Bristol and the Atlantic Economy*, p. 131. Richardson's estimates have been more recently revised downwards to 1658 as he continues with his ongoing statistical research. See the following note.

102 Calculated Eltis *et al.*, *The Trans-Atlantic Slave Trade*. These figures may be an underestimate of the numbers of slaves delivered, since (a) a small number of voyages did not record the number of slaves transported, and (b) voyages in which ships returned to Africa from America, rather than back to their original British port, are excluded. Figures employing other variables with regard to dates, ports of embarkation, etc. will differ. During the same period employed for evaluating Bristol and Liverpool voyages, London delivered some 468,078 slaves, but this statistic obscures the fact of London's predominance in the trade before 1720.

103 Richardson, *Bristol, Africa and the Eighteenth-Century Slave Trade*, vol. 1, p. xv.

104 Notably the Colonial Naval Office Shipping Lists (PRO, CO series) and the Wharfage books held at the archives of the Society of Merchant Venturers of Bristol. The Port Books are more properly called the Port.R. Exchequer Books (PRO E 190 series). For Richardson's discussion of sources and methodology, see Richardson, *Bristol, Africa and the Eighteenth-Century Slave Trade*, vol. 1, pp. viii–xiv.

105 I found the list in BL, Additional MSS 38373 f. 68. Its status is unclear, but it is part of the Liverpool Papers, which indicates some degree of some official status. I cross-referenced the ships named in the list with those listed in Richardson's *Bristol, Africa and the Eighteenth-Century Slave Trade*, vols 1 and 2. I then discounted any ships listed for voyages around the period 1727–31. According to this list, which lists in much detail the type and value of the cargo carried on each ship, along with the number of crew and slaves, roughly just over 3300 more slaves were carried aboard Bristol ships in the period around 1728 than Richardson had accounted for. As the number of slaves was given for each ship listed in January 1729, I assumed they had recently completed a slaving voyage which would have begun, allowing for between 12 and 24 months for such a voyage, around 1727. See also Morgan, *Bristol and the Atlantic Trade in the Eighteenth Century*, p. 133.

106 Richardson, *The Bristol Slave Traders*.

107 Minchinton, *The Trade of Bristol*, pp. 76–7.

108 Harris ensured a supply of trade goods through his East Indian stores and profited from imports bought on the proceeds of the sale of slaves by owning a sugar house. See PRO, will of Philip Harris December 1726, PROB 11/612/233.

109 See Chapter 3.

110 PRO, will of Joseph Swayne, 1735, PROB 11/674/237; Richardson, *Bristol, Africa and the Eighteenth-Century Slave Trade*, vol. 1, pp. 137, 149, 157, 162, 169.

111 See Donnan, *Documents*, vol. 3, pp. 498, 461, 481, 502. Other investors listed include Richard Farr, Henry Lloyd, and masters John Teague and Organ Furnell, who also invested in specific voyages.

112 Between 1698 and 1729 there were 322 masters employed aboard the Bristol slave ships, 16 of whom (less than 5 per cent) had invested in a slaving venture; figures derived from Richardson, *Bristol, Africa and the Eighteenth-Century Slave Trade*, vols 1 and 2. See also Stephen Behrendt, 'The Captains in the British Slave Trade from 1785 to 1807', *Transactions of the Historical Society of Lancashire and Cheshire*, vol. 140 (1990), pp. 107–10, regarding the wealth that captains, surgeons and other mariners could accrue from a voyage; see also pp. 91, 96, 104–5.

113 Bristol University Library Special Collections, Moravian Collection, Minister's Diary for 28 April 1757.

114 J. Latimer, *Annals of Bristol in the Eighteenth Century* (Bristol: privately printed, 1893), pp. 90, 127; John Carswell, *The South Sea Bubble* (London, 1960), pp. 46–7, 65–7; McGrath, *The Merchant Venturers of Bristol*, pp. 147–8. For Mary Baker's South Sea shares, see PRO, PROB 11/699.

115 Anon., *Shipshape and Bristol Fashion* (Liverpool, n.d. but *c.* 1951), p. 1.

116 As in the case of the *Eleanora*, which failed to sell all its Indian textiles when it went to Calabar in 1729 en route to St Kitts; Richardson, *Bristol, Africa and the Eighteenth-Century Slave Trade*, vol. 1, p. 180.

117 Eltis *et al.*, booklet accompanying *The Trans-Atlantic Slave Trade*, p. 22. The recent excavation of manillas in Bristol's King Street area attests to the importance of trading links between Bristol and the Bight of Benin, especially Old Calabar in what is now Nigeria.

118 PRO, *Hobbs* v. *Coster*, C/11/2246/14. Other Bristol merchants owning shares in the Bristol Brass Battery owned by Thomas and Mary Coster include John Andrews, Nehemiah Champion, Edward Harford, Nathaniel Hill, Thomas Daniel, Francis Devonsheir, Walter Hawksworth, Truman Harford, Charles Scandrett, Harford Lloyd, Corsely Rogers and Joseph Percival, almost all of whom had other African or slave-related business interests.

119 BM, Liverpool Papers, 38373 f. 68. By the 1790s, the well-known Quaker firm owned by Samuel Galton was an important provider of firearms; PRO, letter from Samuel Galton to James Rogers regarding the provisioning of the *Sarah*, 1790, James Rogers Papers, C/107/9.

120 *Journal of the Commissioners for Trade and Plantations* (London: HMSO, 1931, reprinted Nedeln, Liechtenstein, 1971), vol. 9 (1749–50), p. 20.

121 Bristol Central Reference Library, letters to Edward Southwell, the Merchant's Hall, 3 January 1740, and from Michael Becher, 31 October 1740, in the Southwell Papers regarding 'daggering', i.e. the financial abuses regarding the insuring of African ships, described by the earlier letter as 'an Evil having crept into the City for tradesmen and others not being any ways interested or Concerned in Ships to put in policys of Assurances commonly called Daggering for assrg. the bottoms of ships and vessels at an advanced premium to the great detriment of the partys concerned in the Ships and vessels'. For lists of individuals, see PRO, James Rogers Papers, list of insurers for the *Fame*, 7 January 1792, C107/6, and 9 October 1788, 107/3 for reference to a special policy taken out against 'Negro Insurrection' on the Africa-bound *Fly*.

122 Outset Notes for the *Jason* galley bound for Angola, 14 August 1743, belonging to the private collection of Edward Beaumont, who kindly supplied them to me.

123 This list of trade goods compiled from 'Invoice of sundry Goods shipd on board the *Jason* Gally . . . for Africa', August 1743 (private papers kindly supplied by Edward Beaumont); BRO, the Day family accounts, 40044 (2); PRO, James Rogers Papers, C107/1–15; Bristol Reference Library, 'Estimate for a cargo . . . for Purchase [of] 250 Negroes at Benny' to Isaac Hobhouse (n.d. but *c.* 1725), Jefferies Collection, vol. 13; BCRL, 'Abstract of a Cargo for a ship of 150 tons for Bonny on the coast of Africa', Southwell Papers, vol. 9. For reference to the beans used to feed the slaves, see BCRL,

Richard Lougher to Edward Southwell, 27 December 1740, Southwell Papers, vol. 6, and Minchinton, 'The Voyage of the Snow *Africa*', pp. 190–1; Specimen cargo to Africa, 14 April 1790, in the *Pilgrim*, in Minchinton (ed.), *The Trade of Bristol in the Eighteenth Century*, p. 60, and cargo shipped by Noblet Ruddock in the *Raymond* Galley to Africa in 1720, listed in 'The bills of lading of Noblet Ruddock and Co., 1720', in Minchinton, *The Trade of Bristol in the Eighteenth Century*, pp. 76–7.

124 J. F. Nicholls and John Taylor, *Bristol Past and Present*, 3 vols (Bristol and London: Arrowsmith, 1882), vol. 3, p. 165.

125 Charles Bell started in 1761 at a salary of £60 p.a. as a 'writer' for the Royal African Company. He soon became a factor and then a secretary at Cape Coast Castle. By 1765 he was chief of Commenda Fort at a salary of £250 and by 1769 Governor of Annamaboe at a salary of £500. He augmented his income by trading privately in slaves and was a friend and associate of the slave-trader Richard Miles. See PRO, T70/1454 p. 29; CO388/47; BRO, Letters of Charles Bell, 30189. Richardson, in *Bristol, Africa and the Eighteenth-Century Slave Trade*, vol. 3, p. 34, lists a Charles Bell as the master of the slaver *Swallow* in 1749, a date which would fit in with the subsequent career outlined above.

126 After the final demise of the Royal African Company in 1752, both Bell and Hippisley were employed by the Company of Merchants Trading to Africa. I should like to thank Professor Prothero for his helpful correspondence regarding Hippisley. John Hippisley was the Chief of Tantumquerry in 1759, and *JCTP*, vol. 11, p. 51, refers to his imminent dismissal from that post for undisclosed reasons; see also R. Mansell Prothero, 'John Hippisley on the Populousness of Africa: A Comment', *Population and Development Review*, vol. 24, no. 3 (September 1998), pp. 609–12, who reminds us that he was governor of Cape Coast Castle for some months before his death. Hippisley's attitudes towards Africans will be discussed in Chapter 2.

127 For Raymond's Bristol origins, see PRO, PROB 5/1149. For lists of slaving agents, see Richardson, *Bristol, Africa and the Eighteenth-Century Slave Trade*, esp. vol. 1, p. 203, and vol. 2, p. 156. Slaving factors Noblet Ruddock and Othniel Haggart also have Bristol connections.

128 Herbert S. Klein, *The Atlantic Slave Trade* (Cambridge, 1999), p. 103.

129 Paul Lovejoy and David Richardson, 'Trust, Pawnship, and Atlantic History: The Institutional Foundations of the Old Calabar Slave Trade', *American Historical Review*, vol. 104, no. 2 (April 1999), pp. 333–55. For the case of the son of the King of Popo, see *FFBJ*, 12 May 1759, and Charles Bell's complaint in the *JCTP*, vol. 66 (1759), pp. 17–18; see also p. 33 for a similar case of pawning gone wrong.

130 See William Snelgrave, *A New Account of some Parts of Guinea, and the Slave Trade* (London, 1734), in Donnan, *Documents*, vol. 2, p. 344, regarding the King of Dahmoney, and *JCTP*, vol. 66 (1759), p. 100. For the Hobhouse comment, see PRO, letter to Thomas Coster from Isaac Hobhouse, 23 April 1737, SP36/40 pt 2; see also University of Melbourne, Bright Family Papers, Francis Bright to Henry Bright, 25 October 1747, BFP/F6/28.

131 Latimer, *Annals of Bristol in the Eighteenth Century*, pp. 145–6, for reference to slaves languishing on board the snow *Bristoll Merchant* in poor health.

132 *JCTP*, vol. 9 (1749–50), p. 21, which refers to the meeting of the commissioners on 12 January 1749/50.

133 Philip M. Hamer (ed.), *The Papers of Henry Laurens* (Columbia, SC, 1968), vol. 2, p. 204.

134 BCRL, Japhet Bird to Isaac Hobhouse of Bristol, 27 February 1722/3, Jefferies Collection, vol. 13. See Behrendt, 'The Captains in the British Slave Trade', pp. 95–6, regarding the link between the experience of the captain and the rate of slave mortality.

Slave mortality figures derived from an interrogation of Eltis *et al.* (eds), *The Trans-Atlantic Slave Trade*.

135 University of Melbourne, Bright Family Papers, Francis to Henry Bright, 30 January 1747/8, BFP7/F7/1. See Morgan, *Bristol and the Atlantic Economy*, pp. 128–83, for a masterly account of the economic aspects of Bristol's slave trade.

136 Hamer (ed.), *The Papers of Henry Laurens*, vol. 1, p. 210.

137 I should like to thank Richard Burley of the Bristol Record Office for this information.

138 My thanks to Tom Duckenfield of Maryland for information on John and Robert Duckinfield. See also Richardson, *Bristol, Africa and the Eighteenth-Century Slave Trade*, vol. 1. for numerous references to Duckinfield.

139 *Ibid.*, p. 53.

140 *Ibid.*, p. 84; Donnan, *Documents*, vol. 2, p. 243n.

141 PRO, letter by John Normanton, master of the *Little Bristol*, to its owners in *Da Costa v. Scandrett*, C/1/77/20. David Richardson lists the ship as leaving Bristol in December 1717 but has listed Warren Cary as its sole owner and Alexander Barkley as its master. Normanton is listed as a slave-ship captain for a number of other African vessels before 1717; see Richardson, *Bristol, Africa and the Eighteenth-Century Slave Trade*, vol. 1, p. 63, for the ship and pp. 5, 6, 9, 28, 55 re Normanton. The fate of Normanton and his crew is not known, but a Moroccan envoy came to Bristol in 1739, and soon after, some sort of treaty protecting British ships from the raids of 'Salee rovers' was concluded; Latimer, *Annals of Bristol in the Eighteenth Century*, pp. 225–6.

142 PRO, Statement of Orators Isaac Da Costa, Andrew Broughton *et al.* in *Da Costa v. Scandrett*, C/1/77/20. The London merchants making the charge had gone to one John Gregory 'who keeps an office in the Royal Exchange for Insuring of Ships by the order and Direction of Matthias [Matthew?] Jones, London Freeman [and] made out a policy in the name of the said Matthias Jones for Insuring the ship called the *Little Bristol* whereof John Normanton was Master and her Cargo for a voyage from Bristol to any ports or places in Africa and . . . from there to . . . the West Indies and the said Matthew Jones and John Gregory reaffirming . . . that the said ship was strong and well built . . . Thinking she was safe having newly gone out about six weeks after they subscribed the money, Matthew Jones said the money had to be paid as the ship was lost and taken by Sally Rovers. But Orators' suspicions were roused as Jones could give no detail of the loss.' Later, before they had paid the insurance, they found the ship had set sail in December 1717 and was captured in January.

143 Richardson, in *Bristol, Africa and the Eighteenth-Century Slave Trade*, vol. 1, pp. xxiv, 75, 90, 91, reports only one other shipowner (Abraham Hooke) who dispatched a ship to Madagascar, though Latimer records that there were many more; Latimer, *Annals of Bristol in the Eighteenth Century*, pp. 127–8. See Virginia Bever Platt, 'The East India Company and the Madagascar Slave Trade', *WMQ*, third series, vol. 26 (1969), pp. 548–71.

144 The testimony of John Duckinfield to the East India Company cited in Platt, 'The East India Company', p. 559n and pp. 558–9. Given Duckinfield's Madagascar connections and his previous involvement in the *Tunbridge* Galley in 1711, it seems likely that he was also a part-owner of that same ship during her unlicensed voyage to Madagascar and Jamaica in 1721, though Richardson does not list him as such.

145 Richardson, *Bristol, Africa and the Eighteenth-Century Slave Trade*, vol. 1, p. 90; Platt, 'The East India Company', p. 559n and pp. 558–9; Latimer, *Annals of Bristol in the Eighteenth Century*, pp. 127–8.

146 Minchinton (ed.), *The Trade of Bristol in the Eighteenth Century*, p. 144n.

147 PRO, will of John Duckinfield, PROB 11/711/225; London Metropolitan Archives, 'Copy of Account of Mr. Robert Dukinfield's [*sic*] Estate in Jamaica . . . 21 July 1745', in Estate

Records of Duckinfield [*sic*] Hall, Jamaica, 771/802; list of landholders in Jamaica in 1750 in Olivier (ed.), *Caribbeana*, vol. 4, p. 95.

148 Richardson, *Bristol, Africa and the Eighteenth-Century Slave Trade*, vol. 3, p. 52. They were also sugar-traders; BRO, 'Account of the Swymmer family', in the notes of I. V. Hall, Box 10, 36772.

149 Donnan, *Documents*, vol. 3, pp. xli–xliii, esp. xliii n, who says this new regime led to even more abuses than those committed under the Royal African Company. For a list of the Company of Bristol Merchants trading to Africa, 1759, see Don Jones, *A History of Clifton* (Chichester, 1992), p. 88; an earlier list for 1755 appears in BCRL, Jefferies Collection, vol. 13, from which the total numbers cited are taken.

150 *JCTP*, vol. 9 (1749–50), p. 22.

151 Richardson, *The Bristol Slave Traders*, pp. 24–5; Richardson, *Bristol, Africa and the Eighteenth-Century Slave Trade*, vol. 4, p. xxiii.

152 *JCTP*, vol. 9 (1749–50), p. 7.

153 *Felix Farley's Bristol Journal*, 25 August 1753.

2

CULTURAL
EXCHANGES

THE REPRESENTATION OF BLACK PEOPLE AND
THE BLACK PRESENCE IN BRISTOL, c. 1700–75

Newspapers were . . . central instruments in the social production of information: both representing and verifying local experience, they refracted world events into socially meaningful categories and hierarchies of importance, bestowing order on the disordered and co-ordinating the imagination of social time and space.[1] (Kathleen Wilson, *The Sense of the People* (Cambridge, 1995))

The complexity of social relationships, reconstructible by the anthropologist through fieldwork, contrasts sharply with the one-sidedness of the archival sources that must serve as field material to the historian. (Carlo Ginzburg and Carlo Poni, 'The Name and the Game: Unequal Exchange and the Historographic Marketplace', in Edward Muir and Guido Ruggiero (eds), *Microhistory and the Lost Peoples of Europe* (Baltimore and London, 1991))

The representation of black people in English culture has been the subject of a number of important studies, but as yet none has addressed the way black people were portrayed or perceived in Bristol, despite the city's national importance.[2] Our task here is to attempt to fathom the way white Bristolians regarded black Africans and West Indians in the eighteenth century. But how are we to do this? Racial attitudes are notoriously difficult to elicit even when the subjects of one's study are alive. They become even more elusive when centuries intervene between the investigator and those investigated. One cannot even presume that 'race' was regarded as a useful conceptual tool in the past or that it shaped the way Africans were perceived more than did ideas about rank or religion. The views of some Bristolians, those of the propertied and educated male, are more easily discernible than those of the labouring poor, but even these can never be thoroughly salvaged.

The banter exchanged between mariners at the tavern or merchants at the coffee house, the whispered remarks between husband and wife, or among business partners, are forever cut off from our hearing. So too are the ephemeral cruelties and kindnesses shown to strangers, servants and slaves. Reduced to a dependence on documentary evidence, we know too that the newspaper editorial or parliamentary petition more often survives in the archive than do personal letters and ribald broadsides where franker, if less consistent, attitudes about black people might have been expressed.

Despite such difficulties, we shall first consider in this chapter the way those of property and education viewed Africans through the testimony of their newspapers, their wills, their personal correspondence and their art. We shall then turn to a small but rich cache of hitherto neglected writings by Bristol seamen to see what they can tell us about attitudes to race and to slavery. Our discussion will then progress to a consideration of the way black people resident in Bristol were discussed and treated. We shall conclude with a reflection upon the experience of two African princes whose arrival in Bristol in 1774 preceded the moment when notions about race and nation evolved into fully fledged ideologies of difference.

Representation and race

At first glance, Nicholas Pocock's handsome pen-and-ink sketch of the *Southwell* privateer (Figure 5), drawn in 1760 during the Seven Years War with France, seems a straightforward celebration of a Bristol ship. Bristling with guns, the beflagged vessel is an emblem of English patriotism. Like many Bristol privateers, however, the *Southwell* also served as a slaver in peacetime, and this explains the picture's lower panels with their African motif (Figure 6).[3] Here is the transatlantic slave trade literally and metaphorically marginalized.

These lower panels repay closer study, since they illustrate two moments in the slave-trading process. Their author, the son of a Bristol mariner and merchant, who spent much of his early career as a West India sea captain, was likely to have also had direct experience of the African trade. The drawing of the *Southwell* is one of three Bristol vessels he drew which featured African motifs. So, what exactly do they portray and what, if anything, do they reveal about racial attitudes and attitudes towards the slave trade in eighteenth-century Bristol?

The lower right-hand panel shows the *Southwell* moored off the African coast and a boat being rowed by British sailors towards the coast; two of the rowers appear to be black. Another boat portrayed has already landed, laden with trade goods, which are being unloaded with the help of Africans on shore. These Africans are armed and one is carrying what looks to be a box of guns with a Bristol label. Two other Africans are carrying a well-dressed Englishman aloft on a hammock, but they are not slaves, since one of them carries a sword at his side. On the far left of the picture we see an African scaling a palm tree and a jug of the indigenous liquor, palm wine, below.

This panel, then, accords closely with contemporary accounts of the slave-trading process in Calabar and other ports on the 'Guinea coast'. It conveys a picture not of conquest but of amicable trade. No slaves are shown, because, as explained in Chapter 1, the slaves would in such circumstances be purchased with the goods just delivered.

The left-hand panel, however, does picture slaves, manacled and naked, being forced by an armed African to board a canoe where British sailors receive them. The *Southwell* hovers expectantly at the side of the picture, another canoe crowded with slaves nearby. A close look reveals that its deck is already tightly packed with its human cargo. The slaves are portrayed matter-of-factly and the viewer is not explicitly invited to sympathize with their plight. Who, looking at this scene, would guess that on the *Southwell*'s last known slaving voyage in 1749, 284 Africans, over half the number estimated to be on board, died before reaching Virginia?

Most intriguing in this picture are the three figures placed slightly above the slaves. There is an African in a loincloth holding a great parasol over the second African, who is similarly attired except that he also wears what looks to be a three-cornered hat. Next to him is a more elaborately dressed Englishman in jacket and breeches and wearing a similar hat, who is probably meant to be the *Southwell*'s captain. What makes this such a significant grouping is the relationship of these three figures to one another. The man shaded by the parasol is a cabouceer (a trader imbued with the authority of the local ruler) or possibly even a headman or petty king. He is clasping the hand of the Englishman with one hand and has placed his other hand on the Englishman's shoulder in a gesture which denotes an equitable and friendly relationship between the two. This idealized image of African and Englishman as equal trading partners was not a common one in the period, but it was not unique. What this picture admirably demonstrates is that pro-slavery views could coexist alongside relatively favourable characterizations of African trading allies. This is not to say that Africans were commonly viewed as equals, but to underline the fact that British attitudes towards Africans were not monolithic, nor were they determined solely along a racial divide. Although one of the transatlantic slave trade's most insidious legacies has been the way it identified Africans in general with the status of slaves, Pocock's picture shows us that, by the mid-eighteenth century at least, this process was not quite as complete as some might have assumed.

Let us turn to a consideration of what the educated man of property in mid-eighteenth-century Bristol might have known about Africans. He might have derived some of his views about them from the wide range of books about African life and government then circulating in England. These, we are told, varied in the quality of their scholarship and analysis. Some showed empathetic insight into aspects of African government and life, but most conveyed a decided disdain for African religious beliefs and often contemptuous views of African political institutions.[4] Most of his knowledge, though, would have been gleaned from the press and from personal contacts, or from direct experience derived from a stay in the West Indies or North America. Although the local press was flourishing in this period, some merchants were said regularly to receive issues of the Caribbean newspapers. His assumption that Bristol's prosperity was dependent on the African slave trade and on the American and Caribbean colonies would have had a direct impact on the way he perceived Africans. Given the city's particularly close links with Jamaica, it is likely that the extreme forms of anti-black sentiment or

Figure 5 Nicholas Pocock, *The Southwell Frigate, c.* 1760. Drawing. Bristol City Museum and Art Gallery

'Negrophobia' so characteristic of the planter class there would have had a greater influence in Bristol than in most other English provincial cities.[5]

In the letters and newspapers that our eighteenth-century Bristol man of property might read, the African was almost invariably portrayed as a slave. The slave, in turn, was defined as a tradable commodity. The legal status of a slave in the British colonies was that of chattel or real estate. Yet the African was palpably a human being, and it was this contradiction inherent in the very concept of slavery which helped to make relations between black slaves and their white owners so pregnant with tension.[6]

The themes which emerge most commonly when we survey the representation of slaves in both private correspondence and public papers are those of fear and betrayal. The dehumanized representation of Africans employed so often by those involved in the provision of slaves to the Caribbean plantations is based on the assumption of the slave as thing. The language of the planters, merchants and factors involved in the provision of slaves to Caribbean plantations is in turns vividly engaged, when the prospect of profits is discussed, and emotionally distanced, when slave mortality is mentioned.[7] This coldly calculating approach first and foremost reminds us that, as wretched as plantation life could be for propertyless whites, it was blacks who were discussed in the same terms as were used to describe cattle. Indeed, slaves were regularly bequeathed as chattels in the Caribbean by Bristol merchants and planters. A Bristol surgeon who died in

Figure 6 Nicholas Pocock, *The Southwell Frigate* (details), *c.* 1760. Drawing. Bristol City Museum and Art Gallery

Jamaica in 1722 requested that his Negro boy, Quashee, be sent by his executor in England to his executor in Jamaica; in Bristol, a lady was said to have bequeathed a pious black youth to a wild young officer.[8] In 1718 John Opie described in a letter to his sister in Bristol how he had fought in the Virginia court to guarantee his ownership of the black slaves who had belonged to his recently deceased wife.[9] John Pinney, as a newcomer to Nevis in 1764, was soon able to reconcile his traditional Christian faith, steeped as it was with the idea of a divinely sanctioned social hierarchy, with his economic interest. Writing to a friend in England about his first attendance at a slave sale, he reported:

> I was shock'd at the first appearance of human flesh exposed to sale. But surely God ordained 'em for the use and benefit of us: otherwise his Divine Will would have been made manifest by some particular sign or token.[10]

Yet we can also find hints of the unease and ambivalence that some whites felt about treating people as things. Take, for example, the owner of the Bybrook Plantation in Jamaica in the late seventeenth century, the Somersetshire squire William Helyar, who was a valued patron of a number of Bristol merchants. In the rich collection of letters which still survive concerning the plantation is one from Helyar advising his first overseer to treat his slaves humanely, for what would the 'poor creature[s] . . . not do for a master that will but treat them a little kindly and with discretion?'.[11] Though the high turnover of overseers at Bybrook, as at other plantations, ensured that cruel or drunken individuals were sometimes in charge, at least one of Helyar's other overseers professed, with some passion, to pride himself in treating black and white alike. Even when the master, mistress or overseer felt affection and respect for certain individual slaves, as Helyar's sons undoubtedly did, the very fact of enslavement threw up a wall of distrust and resentment between them. In 1676, Quashee Eidoo, who had waited on Squire Helyar's son Cary when he was a young man, and who was one of the plantation's most skilled and trusted men, was implicated in a slave plot. Eidoo turned informer in order to avoid the most savage punishments meted out to the other slaves involved, who were left to starve to death after their arms and legs had been burned. In the event, Eidoo himself was transported and the owners of Bybrook sustained a substantial financial loss. What comes across in this and other Caribbean sources is the sense that the planters felt themselves sorely betrayed by the slaves they had personally trusted, and as a result racial boundaries were ever more firmly drawn.[12] Thus, twelve years later, John Helyar, another of the squire's sons dispatched to oversee the estate, informed his father in hardened tones of a violent uprising in 1686, adding, 'please do not forget to send me a couple of good blood hounds being very necessary creatures here to finde out runaways for such rogues are of the greatest eavle soare this island affords'.[13]

The provincial press in Bristol is a rich if underused source for excavating contemporary views of the African-as-slave. The various papers of the early and mid-eighteenth century all served as conduits for the views of merchants and planters. The progress of African and other merchant ships from Bristol was routinely followed from port to port. The world presented in their fiercely patriotic pages was a violent and uncertain one where Barbary pilots attacked English ships and Turks routinely bought and sold Christian slaves.[14] Freebooting buccaneer capitalism and a bellicose foreign policy characterized Britain between the Restoration and the American Revolution. Ships which in peacetime acted as slavers took to privateering or legalized piracy during wartime, often capturing 'Plunder, slaves and cattle etc.' from enemy vessels. Bristolians were said to have had a 'mania for speculating in these privateers', and the local papers enthused about their exploits, especially when local ships were involved or the prizes came to be sold in Bristol.[15] The lure of riches was made more urgent by aggressive notions of a masculine and Protestant national identity. Even in peacetime, anxieties were being constantly expressed lest the Dutch or French edge the British out of the lucrative African and West Indian trades. The world was divided, as one historian has quipped, into 'the good, the bad, and the impotent'.[16] In such an atmosphere, ethical anxieties about slavery were, it seemed, for sissies.

The image of the African, when it was evoked at all, was, with very few exceptions, that of the slave. Slaves in Bristol were rarely mentioned save in advertisements calling for the return of runaways in terms closely similar to those calling for the return of runaway apprentices. Most slaves covered by the press were those in Africa or, more frequently, those in labouring in the colonial plantations. The overwhelming image of the slave abroad was of a violent, treacherous and dangerous being.

The 1720s and 1730s were a time of widespread unrest amongst slaves in the British Caribbean. Refusals to work, arson, sabotage, suicide, rebellion and absconding all reached such a pitch that the Jamaican Governor, Council and Assembly sent an address to the King in 1734 'to implore your most gracious assistance in our present dangerous and distressed condition'.[17] Tellingly, the earliest reference to an African found thus far in the surviving Bristol papers was in the context of a slave revolt in Nevis in 1725.[18] The *Gloucester Journal* of 1729 forwarded a report from Bristol of a slave mutiny off the coast of Africa in which all but the cabin boy were killed. The Stono slave rebellion in South Carolina in 1739 must have been of particular interest to Bristol merchants, given their trading links there, and we know that news of mutinies and revolts were communicated through the reports of ships' captains and planters' letters to employers and friends in Bristol. In 1744 *Felix Farley's Bristol Advertiser* reported a slave plot in Jamaica whose discovery meant that a hundred slaves 'were condemn'd to be hang'd, burnt etc.'.[19]

A survey of the surviving local papers for the year 1750 affords us a glimpse into some of the anxieties which underlay the apparent confidence of those Bristolians with African and West Indian investments. In the spring of that year, an extract from a letter purporting to be from a resident in Charleston, South Carolina, to a merchant in Bristol was published by the paper 'For the good of People trading to Guiney and the West Indies'. Its alleged purpose was to publish, in the *Bristol Weekly Intelligencer*, a recipe for an antidote which had saved the life of a Carolina gentleman who had been poisoned by two of his slaves only six months earlier.[20] The gentleman, readers were told, lay in a melancholy condition, imagining he had the Flux; and so thought the most ablest Physicians. After some time, by meer accident, it was discovered the Cook had given him something in his Gruel; and upon being taken up, owned the whole affair; for which she, and the Poisoner have both suffer'd Death.[21]

The slave-owner, however, continued to languish, despite the efforts of the doctors, until a 'Negro who said [he] . . . had not the least Doubt but that he could cure him' was sent for and administered the antidote in question. The antidote, evidently an African herbal remedy, was published in full, with the assurance that several other people in Carolina had 'since received the same benefit from the said Negro'.[22]

In giving such prominence to this story, the *Intelligencer* played on the point that Africans had mysterious specialist knowledge unknown to Western medical men. The underlying point was that seemingly loyal slaves had used such knowledge to try to kill their master. True, the fact that there was a slave willing and skilled enough to help a white master was reassuring. So too was the news that he was duly rewarded for his loyalty with both his freedom and an annual pension. This last point enabled readers to feel that justice was done and thereby avoid having to ask why the other slaves wished to poison their master in the first place. But there was also a disturbing subtext. The unstated question which arises from the story is, what would have happened if the good slave had not come forward? What if he too had proved hostile? Did not this story implicitly remind readers that resentful black slaves might someday invoke their collective power in a way which could prove fatal to slave regimes in general?[23]

That same year, readers were told about the grisly murder of a white woman in New York by her 'Negro slaves'; a burning down of a 'great part of the town of Port Royal of Jamaica' by 'Negroes'; and a slave revolt aboard the Bristol ship the *King David*, where it was reported that the

> Negroes rose and killed all the Crew except four they kept alive to navigate the ship back again to their own Country, but being near the Island of St. Vincent they got her in there and with assistance of the French carried into [Guadelupe].[24]

Despite this rare example of Anglo-French cooperation, much anxiety was expressed that year about French competition in both the African and colonial trades. Bristol, along with other outports, was fighting for free entry into the African trade in 1750. The *Bristol Weekly Intelligencer* led on the story that spring, stressing the importance of a 'free trade to Africa' for the survival of the sugar colonies, and later featured a letter from Barbados expressing the hope that the matter be quickly settled lest the French, 'who are very numerous on the coast', gain an advantage over the British.[25]

But beneath such fevered rivalry, there seems to have been, as the case of the *King David* mutiny indicates, an implicit solidarity between the French and English which surfaced whenever black slaves challenged white rule. Such solidarity was again in evidence when plantation revolts threatened to undermine the Caribbean plantocracy during the revolt in Martinique of 1752 when 700 houses were burned and 'a great number of people' killed. The *Bristol Weekly Intelligencer* presented a fearsome image of black antipathy when it reported to its readers that

> This great fire was chiefly owing to the resentment of a Negro woman who resolved to be revenged on her Master by setting fire to his House. She was apprehended and atoned for her Crime by horrible Tortures, which she endured to the last Gasp with out the least shriek or Groan, telling the Spectators that the torments she suffered were not equal of the Pleasure she felt at having ruined her master, doing him more Harm than he could have done her.[26]

This image of vengeful courage is iconic in its intensity, but what drove this unnamed woman to such desperate acts was not thought worthy of mention.

As these examples illustrate, Bristolians reading the local press in the mid-eighteenth century would have been left in no doubt that with few exceptions, Africans were a violent and alien lot with a decided potential for harm.[27] The Seven Years War with the French was by then under way, affording some slaves a chance to earn their freedom by serving with the British forces, but those who did so were routinely categorized as 'negroes' rather than as 'men' when casualties were reported.[28] Violence was part and parcel of privateering, but black violence seems to have been singled out for especial notice.[29]

In 1760 this impression intensified, with news of what we have now come to call 'Tacky's Rebellion'. *Felix Farley's Bristol Journal* in the summer of 1760 reported a revolt that had flared up in Jamaica. According to the journal's correspondent, a ship's captain from Jamaica, no fewer than three different insurrections had recently occurred in St Mary's in the north of the island, in which fifteen overseers had been killed and four plantations had been 'burnt and destroyed'.

> The insurrection of the Negroes at Jamaica was occasioned by one of their Masters refusing them a holiday on Easter Monday, a Custom on that Island for many years. Three of the ring leaders were taken and executed which put a stop to the affair.[30]

Despite such summary action, the revolt continued, and the following week, readers learned of a disturbing ritual dimension to this black violence:

> A young man was shot as he passed by some Negro huts in Kingston Savannah, which informing the guard of, a file full of men immediately marched thither when several of the Negroes jumped over the Fence and made their escape. One however was seized, and on searching his hut was found a sword of an extraordinary size and weight, the hilt covered with black velvet and studded with brass nails and under the velvet a Parrot's red feather, which it seems, is with the Coromanteees the Banner of War. This Sword we are assured has been seen at Spring Path, the three Sundays last past; and it has been observed, that the Coromantee negroes about Kingston have been very audacious since the account . . . of the Insurrection in St. Mary's.[31]

The existence of a sword with fetishistic significance recalls the observations reported over a century before by the overseer of the Bybrook Plantation about the use of magical ritual in a slave plot. In that incident, water was used in a divination ritual preparatory to revolt. In both conspiracies, 'Coromantee' or Gold Coast Africans from the Ashanti, Akan and Fanti peoples were implicated. Long admired and feared for their martial bearing – Christopher Codrington had famously characterized them as 'everyone a hero' – Gold Coast inhabitants had traditionally fetched the highest prices in Jamaica despite their reputation for rebelliousness. As the poet James Grainger warned his readers in his 1764 ode 'The Sugar-Cane':

> if thine own, thy children's life, be dear,
> Buy not a Cormantee, tho' healthy, young.
> Of breed too generous for the servile field;
> They born to freedom in their native land,
> Chuse death before dishonourable bonds.
> Or fir'd with vengeance, at the midnight hour, sudden they Seiz[e] thine
>   unsuspecting watch,
> And thine own poinard bury in thy breast.[32]

Coupled with such a fearsome reputation, the magical ceremonies and fetishes they employed made them seem positively diabolical in the eyes of British planters and merchants.[33]

The 1760 revolt continued to rumble on, and 30 conspirators were tried in St Thomas-in-the-East, of whom 12 were hanged. One, reported *Felix Farley's Bristol Journal*, 'named Davy having said he would kill 10 white men had his arms broken before Execution. Five were burnt alive.'[34] The burning alive of rebels echoes the punishment of witches a century before. There is a ceremonial aspect too, both to the tortures inflicted on rebellious slaves and in the reportage. At times the press treatments of these incidents have a ritual tone to them, as if the very reeling off of tortures and punishments might serve as an incantation against the spirit of future rebellion.

Take, for example, the way that *Felix Farley's Bristol Journal* so tersely and, one senses, so grudgingly reported the Mansfield judgment of 1772. The paper's dry account of the substance of this historic judgment, which was popularly, if wrongly, assumed to guarantee slaves free status in England, stands in striking contrast to the treatment of the story placed directly below it. This concerned the execution of a slave convicted of the 'barbarous assassination' of a plantation overseer in Jamaica. The punishments of all those convicted of this crime were reported in detail. Three accomplices, it was related, had their noses cut off, two were transported and one flogged. The cruelty of the punishment to the chief plotter was implicitly justified in the description of the way he met his death:

> Sam a mulatto man was staked to iron bars and burnt. The Fire being set at a small distance and continued til it came to his feet. He bore it with such savage sullenness and brutal ferocity, as if he was deprived of inward and outward feelings.[35]

Did not this story, and the very way it was positioned on the page, attempt to undermine the confidence that readers might otherwise have felt in the wisdom of the Mansfield judgment? Was this not a way of warning its readers that the Mansfield judgment might open the way to the freeing of such brutal beings as Sam the mulatto?

Mark Steele has contended that the particular vulnerability of the slave regime in Jamaica to slave resistance led to the development of a particularly virulent brand of racial antipathy there. I would add that Bristol, with its especially close and long-standing links with Jamaica, was uniquely well placed to imbibe such antipathy and fear, and that Bristol's press was instrumental in this process.

So far it has been argued that the stereotypical image of the African presented in the city's newspapers has been that of the violent or treacherous slave, and that very occasionally that image was counterbalanced by a reassuring story of a slave whose devotion to his or her master superseded all other loyalties. This contention, however, is not completely true. Very rarely, Africans were presented in the press not as slaves, but as chiefs, kings or princes whose trade was important to Britain and whose loyalty had to be secured despite the flattering attentions of rival powers. Take this example from the foreign news column of the *Bristol Weekly Intelligencer*:

> The son of the King of Annamabo came to take a View of the Castle and Grounds of Versailles. As the Reception of a Negro Youth Shews the French Court have views upon this Place [Annamabo], which belonged to the Royal African Company of England, whose Fort there lies in ruin, Orders no Doubt are already given to rebuild and put it in a state of Defence.[36]

Bristolian readers of the *Gentleman's Magazine* might have connected this news item with the reported fate of another prince of 'Annamaboe' and his friend, who, after being dispatched to England for an education, were apparently sold into slavery in Barbados instead. They were eventually rescued but only after the prince's father, John Currantee, protested and suspended all trade with the British in favour of the French. The young men were fêted on their arrival in England and their betrayal publicly condemned.[37] Their story was also the subject of a popular novel published in 1749, *The Royal African: or Memoirs of the Young Prince of Annamaboe*. Other sons of African cabouceers and kings, including the younger brothers of this particular prince, were soon sent to Britain and lavishly treated for similar 'diplomatic' reasons, though not all English officials liked the idea.[38]

A decade later, *Felix Farley's Bristol Journal* indignantly condemned the kidnapping of an African prince, this time the only child of the King of Popo (the actual name of the ruler, Ashampoo, is not deemed to be of sufficient interest to be cited):

> The father of the Prince being lately dead, and the Captain being then upon the Coast, was sent for to inform him that they wanted the young Prince brought home; but the Captain not giving them a satisfactory Account . . . was seized, imprisoned and ironed, and then confessed the Truth: upon which an Order was sent to a Merchant in that trade here to procure the Prince's Enlargement

[freedom] which was done by purchasing him of the gentleman who bought him; and he now appears suitable to his Rank, and is to return to his native Country in a very little time, and then the Captain, no doubt will receive his just Deserts.[39]

This account seems to flatter the role which Bristol African merchants (acting as members in the Company of Merchants, now in charge of African trade) played in the affair. The truth, it transpires, was that the man who sold the prince, along with a companion, was a former officer of the company, and did so when the company had refused to underwrite the expense incurred by their journey to England. After interviews with the Commissioners of Trade in London, with company representatives and the ex-officer involved, it was resolved that the young men would be returned to their families along with compensatory gifts.[40] The whole tenor of this episode bespeaks a cynically pragmatic attitude to the Africans who were cultivated as slave-trading partners in a competitive market.

No press mention seems to have been made of the visit that same year to Bristol of an 'African prince'. Yet the city's Moravian minister, Brother Nyberg, reported receiving a guest who sounded very much like one of the Anamaboe sons of John Currantee. In his diary for 4 April 1759, Nyberg recounts:

> An African Prince, GongGlass [sic] sent by the Government to take shipping at Bristol – came to see our chapel – I played him a few tones on the organ and told him of our labours among his countrymen. He has been three years at Paris, speaks good French and said he would be very glad to see me in Africa.[41]

Nyberg's polite and cordial encounter with the prince was informed by his hopes for the evangelization of Africans. Though Nyberg was evidently impressed by the young man's linguistic accomplishment and rank, he did not question the nature of the government's 'shipping' business. Moravianism at that time, a self-professed 'religion of the heart' founded on universal love, was far more interested in converting Africans than in understanding them on their own terms, or in freeing them from temporal enslavement. Nyberg's Bristol congregation of 200 followed reports of the progress of their Jamaican mission amongst their 'negro brethren' with warm enthusiasm. Although they were still Eurocentric, and disdainful of 'heathen' mores, the willingness of the Moravians to accept as equals those Africans who would adhere to their creed nevertheless stands in striking contrast to the attitudes exhibited in Bristol's merchant press.

Crewmen's tales

One neglected source for the study of slavery and racial attitudes in Bristol has been the small cache of writing by men employed on the slave ships. Three first-hand accounts survive, two of which were published as pamphlets in the eighteenth century and one of which, a manuscript diary, has only recently been put in the public domain. (There is also a second-hand summary of an account of a captain of a slaving ship, which purports to describe events dating from the 1790s. We shall not discuss it here, save to say that the original on which it was based was destroyed sometime around the 1960s by a descendant who reportedly thought it 'too lurid' to be kept.)[42]

Some key characteristics of the accounts are summarized in Table 4. Although these accounts are a welcome alternative to those by propertied men, we should remember that their authors were not from the lowest sections of the labouring poor. These were literate and, with the possible exception of Told, skilled men who were moved to record their experiences. Their accounts respectively span most of the century, and aside from providing incidental information about life aboard a slave ship, they reveal an illuminatingly messy range of attitudes towards black Africans and slavery.

The sensationalist tone of Barker's and Told's accounts has perhaps made historians wary of using them.[43] Yet external evidence suggests their authors did indeed serve aboard Bristol slave ships. To take Told's account first, although his exploits pre-date the keeping of crew lists, the Guinea captains he names did exist and with one exception they sailed on the ships and at the times he mentions.[44] More research is needed to analyse the accuracy and veracity of Told's descriptions of Guinea and Calabar – his garbled versions of African expressions and his mention of people speaking in 'moorish' and 'negroish' hardly inspire confidence. Yet the specificity of some of his other observations seems more convincing. After his return to Britain, Told converted to Methodism and became a well-known preacher in London. We do not know when he wrote his account, only that it was published after his death and was used as part of the Wesleyan campaign against the slave trade. The heavy hand of an Evangelical editor can certainly be discerned in the 1786 text and may account for its curiously hybrid style – a mixture of the picaresque and the pious. Given its provenance, this is in no way an innocent narrative. The question is, what if anything can be learned from it?

If the purported aim of his story is to expose the cruelties of the slave trade, most of the narrative energy goes into detailing the cruelty of a particular slave captain, Timothy Tucker of the *Loyal George*, to the crew in his employ, and most especially towards Told himself. One of the first facts evinced to show Tucker's depravity is that he transported a 'European' woman aboard his ship to sell to 'the black Prince of Bonny'. It is hard to discern whether it is the cruel treatment of this woman (she later dies aboard ship in 'circumstances too shocking to mention') or the fact that she was to be 'sold' to a black man which most exercises its author.[45] Certainly Told did not seem to object to the prostitution and sale of African women, since he notes without comment that one of the heroes of his narrative, the 'good' slave captain James Roach, 'esteemed among Africans for his courteous behaviour', 'purchased a fine black girl for his own use' when anchored off the Calabar coast.[46]

As a genre, seamen's tales of Africa are notoriously contemptuous of African customs, tending to feature the most gruesome or sexually explicit customs for the titillation of their Western audiences. At first sight, Told is no exception; when he goes on the coast of Bonny he relates the evidence of human sacrifice in the form of 40 or 50 human heads hanging from the door of the palaver house, and

Table 4   Bristol seamen's accounts of their experiences on board slave ships in the eighteenth century

Author	Title	Type of work
Robert Barker	*The Unfortunate Shipwright or Cruel Captain: Being a Faithful Narrative of the Unparallel'd Sufferings of Robert Barker, Late Carpenter Aboard the* Thetis, *Snow of Bristol, in a Voyage to the Coast of Guinea and Antigua*	Published pamphlet
Silas Told	*An Account of the Life, and Dealings of God with Silas Told* ii) *Authentic History of a British Seaman Who Was Eleven Years in the Slave Trade, With Some Account of the Cruelties Practised on Those Poor Unfortunate Creatures*	Published pamphlet in two versions. Version one is longer; version two omits much of Told's account of his religious conversion. There were at least eight editions of the longer
Joseph Banfield	'Joseph Banfield's Autobiography' – seems to have been written retrospectively towards the end of the eighteenth century	Manuscript in diary form
J. D. Spinney	'Misadventures of a Slaver', based on Baker's memoirs, was published in *Blackwood's Magazine,* 1629 (July 1951), pp. 26–37	Secondary account of the memoirs of Charles Baker, commander of the *Princess*

witnesses the sacrifice of a dog. He ascribes no fewer than 600 concubines to the King of Bonny, though he concedes that only 30 or 40 actually lived in his compound. Yet some of his descriptions demonstrate the common humanity of the Africans he describes: the clever ruse devised by one of the Queen of Bonny's entourage to remedy Told's headache; the astonished laughter of some Calabar headmen after Told confessed he had frightened off a fearsomely disguised fetish figure, 'Egbo', with his pistol.[47] He mentions the ritual sprinkling of palm wine as part of a ceremony common in West Africa.

Date	Date of events covered which are relevant to slave-trading	Background and Bristol connection
1760	1751–5?	Born Wigan, Lancs., 1722, apprenticed in Liverpool, worked in Shrewsbury and arrived in Bristol *c.* 1750 and served aboard two Bristol slavers. Left Bristol, probably for London, *c.* 1755.
(i) 1786 (ii) not known	1726–*c.* 1733	Born in Lime Kilns, Hotwells, Bristol, 1713, son of a physician who was ruined in a speculation. Raised in Kingswood and then attended Colston's School before being apprenticed on the *Prince of Wales* at 12 years of age. Served on Bristol slavers; ended his days as a Methodist preacher at Newgate in London.
Not known – seems to have been written retrospectively, probably around the 1780s	1767–78	Born in Falmouth, Cornwall, *c.* 1742, son of a cordwainer, went to sea on a whaler at 12 years of age; arrived in Bristol 1765, where he served on the *Sydenham* to Gibraltar before going on to serve on Bristol guineamen. Served on board a Bristol whaler owned by Sydenham Teast in 1786. Went on to sail on London ships in Latin America before becoming master of his own West India ship
	1790–1	Born in Devon. Father a sea captain, apprenticed at a young age to serve at sea. Was master of the *Princess*, a slave ship, but went on only one voyage.

What is striking about Told's narrative is the close physical contact and often warm personal relationships he professed to have with some of his West African trading partners. After having being horsewhipped by Tucker and reduced to a feverish illness, Told describes going offshore to stay with his African hosts in 'Bonny':

One day I accompanied the king Arigo on shore for the benefit of my health (as the savage [Tucker] had almost put an end to my life) and continued there for a space of six weeks, and slept with the king's son, prince Arigo during the same.[48]

This degree of casual intimacy with Africans, which had been customary between English traders and their African partners in the early part of the century, would have been unthinkable for their social counterparts in South Carolina or the Caribbean. It is worth noting too how Told implicitly characterizes Tucker and not the Africans as the 'savage'. And though he expresses shock, as a piously brought up Christian, at some of the Africans' 'diabolical' customs, he also professes his respect for the 'benevolent' Dick Ebrew and another African associate: 'these two men I have often admired for their meek and loving spirit, exceedingly far beyond tens of thousands who call themselves Christians'.[49] The fact that these two men were slave-traders did not seem to alter Told's opinion and they are favourably contrasted with their countryman Tom Ancora, another New Calabar trader. Yet even Ancora, whom Told accuses of murdering Captain Roach after a row over Roach's African 'girl', is vividly described as an accomplished linguist and duplicitous charmer who outwits Roach in order to poison him.[50]

Told seems at pains to judge men as individuals. In one incident, a Portuguese who returned some money stolen from him on the African coast is praised for being more 'actuated by principles of honour (especially in this instance to a foreigner), than many thousands of my countrymen' would have been to their own kind. A Virginian skipper of mixed race who taught Told how to catch fish and turtle is celebrated by Told for his kindness and skill.[51] Told's encounters with people in foreign parts seem to have made him more reflective about the behaviour of his own countrymen. However, only those Africans whose rank Told judges as equal or superior to his own merit this treatment. Told's attitude towards the slaves appears to be much less nuanced. He portrayed them with either pity or fear, depending on their submissiveness. Told seems genuinely aghast at the flogging and shooting to death of a slave condemned as being too 'sulky' to eat his food – describing the man's quiet resignation in some detail. Yet he portrays with seeming approval the execution of slaves who mutinied. One gets the sense from this source that it was individual cruelty rather than the institution of slavery itself which was the primary object of Told's disquiet.

The second source under consideration is Robert Barker's account *The Unfortunate Shipwright or Cruel Captain*. First published in 1760, it appeared well before the abolitionist movement became established in Britain, and was written in the hopes that it would vindicate its author against the charges made by the 'cruel captain' of the title. Barker's work is much better corroborated by other sources than is Told's. We know that Barker sailed on board the slaver *Thetis* as a carpenter in 1754. As he described, the *Thetis* had indeed been taken over by the chief mate, Robert Wapshutt, after the death in Africa of its original master, Captain Fitzharding. We know too that Barker, along with three other men, was charged with piracy whilst on board. Other records also confirm that Barker went blind as a result of 'a distemper raging amongst the Slaves' on board the *Thetis*, and was initially allowed a pension of 3s 6d per week by the Merchant Seamen's Hospital in Bristol.[52]

In his pamphlet, Barker charged that Wapshutt and the ship's surgeon had conspired to poison Captain Fitzherbert whilst off the coast of Andonny in West Africa. Blaming the death on West African traders, Wapshutt took over command,

and the picture of shipboard life aboard the *Thetis* thereafter is one of despotic victimization and cruelty, closely echoing Told's description of Tucker's regime aboard the *Loyal George*. Nakedness and exposure to the elements is a theme which runs through Barker's narrative. He is sent out to gather firewood on the coast without shelter; he is sent out in a longboat up a creek where he and his colleagues soon find themselves surrounded by 'upwards of an hundred negros, and with pistols and cutlasses, who stripped us all stark-naked . . . and robbed us of everything we had, which they took into canoes and carried the same clean off'.[53]

The focus of the narrative is on the cruel treatment meted out to Barker and other crew members, and it is this aspect of his writing that has excited the little attention it has received from historians.[54] The pamphlet, however, also affords us glimpses of a reign of sexual terror meted out to the African woman aboard the ship. At one point Barker describes a row which erupted between Wapshutt and John Roberts, the surgeon, over

> a negroe girl purchased with the [embezzled] goods of Mr. Pope our late second mate deceased, which arose to such a pitch they were determined to cut her in two, Wapshutt to take one half of her, and the doctor the other though she was no property of either.[55]

The woman was not killed, but such wrangling indicates a sadistic disregard for life. Barker, who by this time had been accused of piracy, was kept naked in all weathers on deck:

> In this naked condition I remained till the ship arrived at Antigua, and during al that time was obliged to go on the Quarter Deck to drink water there, when Wabshutt and the doctor for their beastly diversion, would frequently order the negroe women and girls to haul me backwards and forwards by the privities.[56]

Though the reader's attention is directed to Barker's humiliation, the fact that young girls and women were forced to carry out a sadistic act for the 'entertainment' of their male captors suggests that they too were subject to other abuse.

Barker's own relations with West Africans appear to have been much more remote than do Told's. The fact that he asserted that the 'girl' sold to his masters was 'no property of either' implies, however, a democrat's aversion to enslavement. The very fact that he attempted to pursue his case against a social superior might also indicate a degree of political radicalism on his part.[57]

Whatever his motives, Barker's publication was seen by Bristol's mercantile establishment as an insolent affront. Despite the fact that he had gathered sworn statements from crewmen attesting to the truth of his pamphlet, it was the pamphlet which proved to be his undoing. The Society of Merchant Venturers, which administered Barker's pension, was outraged by its publication:

> Robert Barker, late carpenter of the snow *Thetis* has imposed on the Publick by publishing a Pamphlet entitled the Unfortunate shipwright and Cruel Captain wherein he has inserted several falsehoods calculated to blacken the character

of persons who appear to be innocent and to raise the compassion of the Publick on his behalf and get money as an unfortunate seaman. It is ordered that the Pensin [*sic*] of the said Robert Barker be from henceforth stopped.[58]

The autocratic and peremptory treatment of a man judged 'insolent' for publishing his version of events reminds us of the plight of those whites without property or powerful friends in Georgian society. The fact that the merchants refused to countenance, much less investigate, the charges against Wapshutt, despite the corroborating evidence submitted, speaks volumes.

Joseph Banfield's unpublished and manuscript account, by contrast, had a very different provenance and was written to serve no practical purpose. Covering his long and varied career as a sailor aboard whalers, merchantmen and privateers, this rare document is neither polemical nor didactic in tone. So far as we know, Banfield, who by 1783 had risen to become master of his own ship on the New York–Montego Bay run, was neither an Evangelical nor a political radical. Indeed, Banfield's 'autobiography', as it is called, has not been shaped into a continuous narrative but is organized more along the lines of a diary, with events of his various voyages being given greater prominence than his private life.[59]

Married to a Bristol woman, Catherine McMullin, in 1765, Banfield served aboard Bristol slavers for a decade from 1767.[60] Banfield was no convert to the anti-slavery cause. He seems to have found favour enough with Bristol Guinea captains in so far as two of them rehired him for successive voyages.[61] Yet his account of his misadventures whilst on the *Gambia* under Captain Willis in the early 1770s shows that his attitudes towards black people were more complex than his career on board slavers might initially suggest. When his ship arrived on the River Gambia in 1770, Banfield recalls setting out on a longboat with two companions – 'one White man and one Black man' – to make contact with African traders. Their boat, however, was soon 'overset by a Tornado'. His white companion was lost, but Banfield reports managing to pull the other man back onto the boat. He relates their adventures after they swam ashore, referring throughout to his 'Black companion' as they wandered naked and afraid in unknown territory, met other Africans and found themselves taken hostage by the headman of a small trading village. In all this, Banfield shows no trace of racial antipathy or contempt.

Consider the passages where Banfield describes the 'dismal condition' that he and his 'Black companion' found themselves in immediately after their shipwreck:

After wee had moved some miles toward the wood whence we knew not; Lamenting our circumstance, Providence guided us so well that have [?] uss In the way of two Black Men armed with Bows and Arrows.

When ass soon ass the[y] saw uss advancing toward them, the[y] stood their ground, and putt them selves in a posture of Defense to Defend them Selves Supposing me to be some wild-creature that the[y] might have never saw. But that Idea soon forsook them for I sent my black Companion to Speake to them while I stood at a distance, he then acquainted them of our Sad Accident, the[y] then Instantly disarmed themselves and realy Participated in our sorrows and directed uss whitch way to go and we should come to a Town.[62]

Figure 7   (Attributed to) Philip Vandyke, *Broad Quay, Bristol* (detail), *c.* 1785. Painting. Bristol City Museum and Art Gallery

Though Banfield was clearly in a position to order his companion forward to meet the strangers, we do not know whether he did so because his associate was from the region himself or simply because he was black. But Banfield shows empathy with the indigenous people he encountered in that he realized that he must have seemed an unknown and alarming creature, given his whiteness. His description of the men 'participating in our sorrows' affirms their common humanity.

Banfield then relates that he and his companion (who, significantly, is never named) reached the town mentioned and were received by 'our host, the Master of the Town', who separated the two men and gave Banfield food, drink and clothing: 'The Old man my Host, observing my condition, ordered me a cloth for to cover my nakedness with whitch I readily accepted off'.[63] Banfield, though treated well, was detained there for a fortnight until news was received that a trading vessel had arrived at the trading post nearby. On board, it seems, was the wife of the governor of the 'Foort James', who on hearing of Banfield's plight

> instantly came to release me and to Demand me off the Old man, whitch he Denyed without one Slave in my Room [i.e. place], she then told him if he wold not lett me go without a slave in my room she would return . . . to the foort and bring up a company of soldyars and Destroy his town for them. Soon then [illegible] to the fury of the woman he consented to lett me go away with her, for whitch I must be forever Beholden to this good woman for I must so caul her.
>
> So wee got our Release, me and my black Companion and in about twenty days I got safe to . . . my Vestle again . . . [and] we soon sailed after I got back for

Barbados . . . [where we] sold our Negros to some Gentlemen to cary them over to the Dutch main.

So here we have Banfield, referring respectfully enough to his captor as an 'Old man', and his 'host', solicitous enough about the fate of his nameless companion to ensure that he too is released, yet scrupling not at all to ship other black people to Barbados as slaves.[64]

All three narratives serve to illustrate how white attitudes towards black Africans were complicated by notions of rank, gender and individual circumstance.

Africans in Bristol: subaltern voices on the black presence

The lives of black people in Britain and the attitudes they encountered from the host population are only briefly glimpsed in the fragments of evidence available to us. Very few pictures of the period attest to the presence of black people in Bristol. Two, a 1734 engraving, *The South East Prospect of the City of Bristol* by Nathaniel and Samuel Buck (Figure 11, p. 102) and the painting of Broad Quay attributed to Philip Vandyke (*c.* 1785) (Figure 7), show liveried male servants. In the Buck engraving a crudely drawn young man is attending a lady and her baby. In the Vandyke painting of the Broad Quay in Bristol, a bewigged young man can just be discerned by a row of barrels in the lower middle of the picture pointing the way to an Englishman.

The local press occasionally printed advertisements placed by masters anxious to locate runaway slaves and, in one case, to sell a 14-year-old boy. Table 5, largely constructed from the findings of local researcher Doreen Lindegaard, shows our dependence on parish records and newspapers for any knowledge we might have of the city's black residents. Whilst the 50 or so names listed here for the first half of the century grossly under-represent the actual number, there does not seem to be any evidence to suggest a large community of Africans in Bristol akin to that which existed in London. The number of black servants after 1750 certainly increases, as West Indian planters retired to Bristol and nearby Clifton with their entourage of servants. Smollett, in his novel *Humphry Clinker*, postulates the existence of some boisterously defiant black musicians who were the liveried servants of a Clifton visitor.

Press representation, then, of black people resident in mid-eighteenth-century Bristol was generally rare. The one exception to this observation so far found was an enigmatic spoof ad placed in the spring of 1751 in the *Bristol Weekly Intelligencer*. Addressed 'to the Ladies' by a 'gentleman . . . who proposes himself for a husband', this description follows:

He is of the Age of 32 . . . He is a black Man, generally reputed comely; His Nose inclines to the Roman; His Teeth are White and even; His forehead is high; His Eyes are full of fire and the hopes of Sweetness; And his Beard as Sir Richard Steele says, when fresh shaved, looks blue upon his chin.[65]

Readers were informed that the gentleman in question was 'to be at Mrs. Benchley's near Dowry Square' for the next fortnight, and that 'entire secrecy may be depended upon'.

What are we to make of this curious anomaly? It seems to allude to some secret liaison between a Bristol lady and an African, and the ironic use of flowery description suggests that the black man in question was possibly an actor or visiting African notable who had been favourably received in polite society. The figure so delineated certainly reminds one of the noble African prince Oroonoko, the character of Aphra Behn's novel which had been dramatized by Thomas Southerne and performed in Bristol as early as 1726 and into the 1740s.[66] The Dowry Square address and the fact that the supposed suitor threatened to 'set out for Bath' if he did 'not receive an answer within a fortnight' suggests that he was a fortune-hunter thought to have had a dalliance with the lady named. True or not, the advertisement's knowing tone ridicules any genteel white woman who might have entertained the idea of an interracial romance.

Yet Bristol men, especially when they were safely abroad in the Caribbean or an African fort or aboard a slave ship, were not averse to interracial liaisons. In the case of Robert Duckinfield, the son of the merchant John Duckinfield, such romance was publicly affirmed. In 1755 he left much of his sizeable estate to his siblings in Bristol. However, a substantial portion of his Jamaican property – a house, 101 acres of land and coterie of slaves, and property in Kingston, Jamaica – was left to his consort, the free black woman Jane Enugson. Enugson was to have use of his 'principal house' in Kingston as well, until his brother Samuel came to claim it, at which point she was to have £300 to build her own home there. Duckinfield bequeathed 1200 acres purchased from another Bristol merchant in Jamaica, Zachary Bailey, to his 'mulatto children' by Jane Enugson: William, Escourt and Elizabeth Duckinfield. All the children were allotted slaves; Escourt's slaves had previously belonged to his late uncle after whom he had been named. Escourt was also given money in order to finance his own apprenticeship as a bricklayer 'or such other trade as he shall choose' and a cash settlement so that he could exploit the land he inherited. Elizabeth, who received only female slaves along with her land, was promised £1000 on the condition that she married a white man.

> But in case my said Daughter should Intermarry with any but a White Man then I hereby declare the said Bequest of . . . One thousands Pounds and all and every the Lands and Slaves to her hereby Devised, Null and Void. And in that case, tis my Will and Desire that my said Daughter shall only be Maintained out of the Annual Interest of the said sum of One thousand Pounds for and during her Natural Life. And that after her Decease . . . the said Principal sum of one thousand pounds as all the Lands and Negroe or other Slaves herein before Devised to her be equally Divided between my said two sons . . . and their Heirs lawfully begotten.[67]

Duckinfield's sons were under no such strictures to 'marry white', though only their legitimate offspring would be eligible to inherit. Duckinfield's will eloquently

Table 5   Africans resident in Bristol, *c.* 1700–50

1702	Mary Columbus and Joseph Thompson	'A negro' and 'a negress [both] of Jamaica and Bristol, two Jamaica Black servants to Merchant Heathcote, a sojourner in the parish of St. Stephen's, Bristol', married
1702	Edward Peter Scipio	Servant to Edward Jones, Warden of the Society of Merchant Venturers, 1721–2
1704	Ann Jones	Adult 'blackmore of riper years', baptized Temple church
1712	Jacob Fony	Buried St James's Church
1713	Scipio	Runaway slave belonging to Capt. Foye
1715	Hannah	'Nigro servant of Mr. Richard Lathrop, about 8 years old'
1715	Unnamed man	'Negro' described as aged about 20 having three or four marks on each cheek, belonging to Captain Stephen Courtney of the *Duchess*
1720	Scipio Africanus	'Negro servant' to Rt Hon. Charles William, Earl of Suffolk and Bradon, buried Henbury Church, Bristol*
1718	'Tallow'	'Negro boy' belonging to Becher Fleming, bequeathed to Mary Becher*
1720	William	'Negro, adult', baptized All Saints' Church
1721	Commodore and Venus	Married St Michael's Church. (Commodore described as a gingerbread maker)*
1721	Thomason Lawsen	'Black boy' baptized Temple Church
1723	Thomas James	Baptized St Philip and St Jacob's Church
1723	Francis Bristol	'A negro boy, was baptised in case of extreme danger of death, 28th March 1723'. Godfather and probable master was Francis Creswick
1723	Lencey	'Young black girl belonging to Mr. Gibbs', baptized St James's Church
1725	Christina Black	Maidservant to Mr Thomas Whitchurch, baptized Temple Church
1726	Thomas Quaqua	'A negroe man aged about 20 years', baptized St Michael's Church
1728	Mary Tiroo	'A black woman' baptized at Temple Church – probably wife of Thomas Quaco
1728	William Rice and Rebecca Neale	'Blacks' married at St Augustine the Less*
1727	William Owen, formerly known as 'Chance'	'A blackmore', baptized Doynton, Glos.
1728	Unknown man	About 20 years old, from the Gold Coast; 'of a docile disposition', fit to be trained as a gentleman's servant or instructed in a handicraft. Ran away from Captain Gwythen
1729	Noah	'Black boy' 5 years of age, servant to Mr Richard Eagles, buried Temple Church
1731	Black Jonis	'A little boy' buried St Andrew, Clifton
1732	Judith	A negro woman aged about 50 years, baptized St Mary Redcliffe
1733	Mary Reece	Baptized St Augustine's the Less*

Table 5 – *continued*

1734	Sabina	'A negro, maid of Mrs. Round's, buried St Philip and Jacob's
1737	Richard Cornwall	Black man falsely accused in paternity suit by white Englishwoman
1738	John (and Benjamin) Cambridge	Son of Benjamin Cambridge, a black, buried St Augustine's
1739	Faith Danby	'Adult negro girl', baptized Bristol Cathedral
1739	Four unnamed servants	Servants to Bristol-bound American travellers on board the *Baltick**
1740	John	Buried St Stephen's
1743	John Quaqua and Penelope Webb	Married St Michael's Church
1744	Mary Milward	'A mulatta', baptized St Stephen's
1744	John Ancoo	Servant to Capt. Jos. Smith, baptized St Andrew's Church*
1744	Elizabeth (John and Ann Cambridge)	'A negro child', daughter of John and Ann Cambridge, baptized St Augustine's. A John Cambridge is listed as a seaman aboard a number of African voyages.
1745	Clare Smith	A black, baptized St Augustine's Church
1746	John Gloucester	'A negro' married a white woman, Mary Ven, at St Leonard's
1746	Mingo	Runaway, 'of a good black complexion, smooth face, wears a black wig, had two short blue waistcoats and black breeches, his upper teeth scagg'd and broken, has a cut on his right wrist which stands up in a bunch. He speaks pretty good English; has been in and out of this City about 8 years.'*
1747	Sarah Lewis	'A negro', baptized St. Augustine's
1747	John Coffee	'Adult negroe', baptized Bristol Cathedral
1747	'Free Essex'	'A negroe' who survived a voyage on the *Duke of Queensbury* to Africa and Jamaica and returned to Bristol in 1749*
1748	Unnamed boy	'Negro boy' eloped from Mr Josiah Rose of Redcliffe St
1748		A 'Negro servant belonging to Col. Two-Good' was arrested for a knife attack in Stapleton on Mr Pontin, the 'Master of the Fire-Engine, and an overseer of the Coleworks in Kingswood'.
1750	Halifax	Seaman aboard the *Peggy*; usual place of abode was Bristol
1750	Lewis Fortune	Baptized St Michael's Church

Sources: Derived from D. P. Lindegaard, *Black Bristolians of the Eighteenth and Nineteenth Centuries* (Bristol: privately printed, n.d.) except those entries marked by an asterisk, which are taken from Pip Jones and Rita Youseph's *The Black Population of Bristol in the Eighteenth Century* (Bristol: Bristol Historical Association, 1994). For details about Mingo, see *Felix Farley's Bristol Journal*, 15 November 1746; a Lewis Mingo of Bristol is listed as a seaman aboard the *Tyall Trugold*, which returned to Bristol from a voyage to Africa and Virginia in 1749 according to SMV, Muster Rolls for 1748–51, no. 109; for 'Free Essex', see SMV, Muster Rolls 1748–51, no. 166. For John Cambridge, see SMV, Seamen's Hospital Orders 1747–69, no. 126; for Col. Two-Good's servant, see *Bristol Journal*, 22 October 1748.

demonstrates how personal affection coexisted alongside racialist sentiments within the slave system.

Not all were so generous to their mixed-race offspring as was Duckinfield. The Bristol merchant Samuel Delpratt, who moved to Kingston before his death in 1783, is a case in point. Though his four lawfully begotten children, Samuel, Edward, Mary Ann and Elizabeth, each inherited £5000, his 'reputed natural daughters', all 'free quadroon women', Sarah and Elizabeth Delpratt and Mary Foord, received only £200 each.[68] Jacob Rickett of Westmorland, a probable scion of the Bristol Ricketts, awarded, in his will of 1754, 'my Negroe Amelia, now big with child' her freedom and insultingly promised that if her child was a mulatto, he would be freed at 21 and inherit £100 or three 'Negroes'.[69]

Of course, we know nothing of all the Bristol planters and merchants who had children by slaves whom they refused to acknowledge as their own and left in a state of enslavement. It is impossible to know if the pregnant Amelia consented to sex with her master, was raped by him, or attempted to use his sexual interest for her own ends. Love might conquer all, but lust is another matter, especially within an oppressive system.

Though the sources are coy about it, some of the mixed-race offspring of Bristol merchants and planters undoubtedly came to England. Nathaniel Milward, a Bristol merchant who became a wealthy and well-respected planter in Jamaica, bequeathed £2000 to his friend George Bush of Bristol to be executor for his three 'natural' quadroon children, Edward, Judith and Benjamin Milward. The two boys appear to have been put under the care of a Yorkshire vicar until they were 14 with the hope that they would then be apprenticed to 'the foundery on the back of Bristol' or 'to a carpenter of some repute'. The daughter was to go to England under the care of a midwife of Milward's acquaintance or, failing that, to stay with Milward's cousin in Bath until she was old enough to be apprenticed as a midwife or mantua-maker. In the event, Edward died some years later whilst a mariner on the coast of Africa, and his surviving siblings received the rest of the legacy. We know no more of their fate, but here too is a case where paternal regard crossed the racial divide.[70]

The poet Robert Southey reports that there were 'a good many Creoles', some of mixed race, at his school in the 1770s, as there were 'at all the Bristol schools'. Southey maintained that the Creole boys he knew

> were neither better nor worse than so many other boys in any respect. Indeed though they had a stronger national cast of countenance, they were, I think, less marked by any national features of mind or disposition than the Welsh, certainly much less than the Irish.[71]

But this assurance does not accord with Southey's recollections of individual mixed-race boys who seem in various ways to have had a tragic time in Bristol. One of them, 'the most fiendish boy I had ever known', is likened by Southey to a pagan demon with 'black eyes' that glowed with 'devilish malignity' and a 'countenance [that] would darken with his black passion'. Also describing him as being of partial 'French extraction', Southey felt strongly that his evil nature was a result of 'bad blood' because the boy's nephew, who later lived in Clifton whilst training as a surgeon, had a similar character, and after a profligate life, committed suicide in prison. Readers today might not dispute the severe abnormality of the boy's and his nephew's behaviour, but wonder if the terms which Southey used to describe them implicitly conflated race-mixing with pathology. It is true, however, that the second boy Southey mentions knowing in Bristol was of a different character. The natural son of a 'coloured' (mixed-race) woman and a wealthy planter, he is portrayed as a paragon of virtue: inoffensive, gentlemanly and quiet. Yet he too committed suicide after falling into debt because his father failed to provide for his illegitimate son in his will.[72]

But it is his description of a third schoolmate which is the most poignant, for it reveals the casual cruelty that could be suffered by a child of mixed race. Southey's favourite teacher, we are told, did not suffer fools willingly and was 'greatly provoked' by 'stupidity', but Southey's very description of the lad suggests another reason for the teacher's dislike:

> There was a hulking fellow (a Creole with Negro features and a shade of African colour in him), who possessed this stupidity in the highest degree; and Williams [the schoolmaster], after flogging him one day, made him pay a halfpenny for the use of the rod, because he required it so much oftener than any other boy in the school. Whether G—— was most sensible of the mulct or the mockery, I know not, but he felt it as the severest part of the punishment. This was certainly a tyrannical act; but it was the only one of which I ever saw William guilty.[73]

Creole children of wealthy planters aside, most black West Indians who were not servants worked as seamen in eighteenth-century Bristol. Again, visual evidence of their presence is very rare. However, a Pocock sketch of Sydenham Teast's shipyard at Wapping on the Bristol Docks *c.* 1760 (Figure 8) shows divers craftsmen and labourers at work. A very close look at the figures on the second and the third ships from the left reveals that two of the workers there are of African origin and appear to be dressed differently from the others.

These visual survivals accord with the documentary evidence, which indicates that many of the 50 or so black residents thus far revealed to be have been living in Bristol by 1750 came as servants by way of the Caribbean. A few came directly from Africa, like the two black sailors, probably grommettoes (free black Africans in the employ of the Royal African Company), who arrived in Bristol in 1710 on board the *Michael* of Glasgow[74] or the young man, born on the Gold Coast, who ran away from Captain Gwythen in 1728 (see Table 5). Whilst the seamen on board the *Michael* were soon called to London, others stayed. At least one black seaman, Thomas Quaco, had a family in Bristol and served aboard Bristol slavers in the 1750s, and the muster rolls for Bristol list a few others. William Richardson, a seaman who came to Bristol from Jamaica in 1768, stayed for some months with the Moravian congregation in the city in their communal house for single men. Both Richardson and Quaqua were acknowledged as free men,[75] but generally speaking, the legal status of black residents in Bristol before 1772 was uncertain.[76]

Figure 8   Nicholas Pocock, *Wapping, Bristol* (detail below), *c.* 1760. Drawing. Bristol City Museum and Art Gallery

But if the free status of black people was disputed in law, the free status of white people was undermined in practice, a point that may have had a direct bearing on relations between the two races. As has often been pointed out, propertyless whites in Britain shared many, though certainly not all, of the disabilities suffered by enslaved blacks, especially in the period before 1760. Apprenticeship and indenture, after all, were not forms of free waged labour, and could in some ways seem to echo the conditions of chattel slavery. Paupers, though variously treated, were still vulnerable to abuse. Nevertheless, the English labouring poor perceived themselves as protected against arbitrary and absolute power by the political settlement of 1688. They were jealous of their 'freeborn' status which 'belongs to All, and is everyman's Birthright', a status which distinguished them from mere 'slaves'. They were increasingly resentful, as the century wore on, of any measures that seemed to undermine this status, especially that of impressment – the practice of seizing or impressing able-bodied men to serve aboard British naval ships.[77] The Bristol press had first welcomed impressment in 1744, assuming that it was a good way of ridding the city of its most troublesome elements:

No Tradesman or working artificer shall be compelled to service, but it shall extend to Vagrants, and all idle Persons; the fewest of which are to be found in this City, perhaps above all the cities in England, owing to the natural industry and assiduity of its Inhabitants, whose ardour for Trade and Navigation cannot admit of any such useless creatures to dwell among them.[78]

Not surprisingly, poor Bristolians viewed things differently, fearing impressment to such an extent that when one press gang went to work in the city in 1759, during the Seven Years War, its captain reported to the Admiralty that 'three hundred Seamen gathered in a riotous manner, almost killed a person whom they thought belonged to us, wounded the drummer . . . threatening Death and destruction of the officers'.[79] Within a short time, after further affrays with seamen and Kingswood colliers, every member of his gang had been wounded and one had been murdered.[80]

Of course, impressment might have had the effect of making the 'vagrants' and 'useless creatures' more determined than ever to distinguish themselves from slaves, especially those who were unbaptized 'heathens'. Alternatively, it is equally conceivable that a common experience of poverty and subjection to arbitrary power might foster, in some, a sense of solidarity. Many merchant seamen were used to working with people from different nations.

The reception of black Africans and Creoles in the city may also have been affected by considerations of gender. Most of the Africans resident seem to have been men and there are instances, as in the case of John Quaqua, of marriage between Africans and Englishwomen. Sexual liaisons were not always sanctified by the law, and confusions over the notion of racial difference are indicated by two anecdotal pieces of evidence connected with unlawful relations. The first is that when Sarah Elliott accused Richard Cornwall, 'a Christian Negro, servant to Captain Day in College Green', of fathering her child, a baby was produced in evidence, and according to a press report of the case, 'the woman artfully to deceive the fellow procured a borrow'd child with its skin smutted over but he calling for a wet Napkin and rubbing the child's face found it a fair complexion quite different from his specie'.[81] Cornwall's accuser was committed to prison. This documented case lends credence to another instance, immortalized in a contemporary ballad, where a Bristol wife, delivered of a black baby whilst her husband is at sea, tries to assure him that the baby's colour is due to the charcoal she purported to crave whilst pregnant.[82]

These disparate pieces of evidence suggest that notions of racial difference were not yet consistently developed in Bristol in this period. African people are variously referred to as 'blackamore', 'negro' and 'black', but 'black' was applied to others besides Africans. When, for example, Captain Anthony Fox, master of the snow *Peggy*, recorded the names, birthplaces, sailing histories and 'complexions' of his crew who served on an African voyage in 1748, he labelled 28 of his men as 'browne', including those from England, Sweden, Holland and Ireland, and the rest as 'Blacke', including John Goodboy of Guinea, but also sailors born in Scotland, Ireland, Wales and Genoa.[83] It is difficult to know how precisely to interpret the significance of this curious document except to say that parochial notions of difference loomed large in people's minds up to very recently and that particular distinctions between race and nation were not as developed in this period as they were later to become. Southey's remark about the Irish and the Welsh cited earlier seems to confirm this. As late as the early nineteenth century, a local tobacco firm commonly conflated Amerindian figures with those of Africans in its advertising.

Bristolians would have had decidedly negative perceptions of African religious practices. Yet Christianized Africans were noted approvingly for their piety as early as the mid-seventeenth century. Edward Terrill, who chronicled the progress of the Baptist Church of Christ meeting in Broadmead in Bristol, remembered the

> blackymore maide named Frances a servant to one of that lived upon the Back of Bristol which thing is somewhat rare in our dayes . . . to have an Ethyopian or blacmore, to be truly convinced of sin . . . and to be truly converted to the Lord.[84]

According to Terrill, her advice on her deathbed inspired great respect, 'it being the dyeing words of a Blackmore fit for a white Heart to Store'. These words reveal that though her coffin was carried by the 'Elders and the chiefest of note of the brethren in the congregation', her status was not quite equal to that of whites. A similar blend of affection and ethnocentric condescension can be found on the tombstone dedicated to one Scipio Africanus, a young servant to the Earl of Suffolk, who died at the age of 18 years in 1720:

> *I who was born a PAGAN and a SLAVE*
> *Now sweetly sleep a CHRISTIAN in my GRAVE*
> *WHAT tho' my hue was dark, my SAVIOUR'S sight*
> *Shall change this darkness into radiant Light.*[85]

Black servants were both a badge of social status and, if they were slaves, a source of cheap labour. In 1757 Caleb Dickinson, who combined his life on a Wiltshire estate with the ownership of a Jamaican sugar plantation and Bristol sugar-trading, remembered with annoyance his promise to a Jamaican associate to look after a young slave in Britain. He gave instructions that the child, recently shipped to London, should be put on a coach to Bristol and allowed an inside seat as the weather in December was severe.[86] Dickinson planned, as he confessed to his brother Ezekiel, to offload the child and the expense of his upkeep onto a fellow Quaker, the merchant Thomas Goldney III. He writes in a good-humoured but contemptuous tone, 'I expect Brother Goldney who loves amusement will take him – I'll keep one of his birds instead.'[87] Such views would not have been expressed had the child been of a paler complexion and higher rank. In practice, however, either generosity or economic self-interest motivated him to provide some education for the child, as his letter to an acquaintance in Jamaica indicates: 'I give my compliments to Mr. M[uchutchion] – whom I shall write to sh[o]rtly . . . his boy Champayne is here and goes to School.'[88]

There are a number of other examples of black domestic servants being treated with some affection if not with respect, and of living lives comparable or even superior in material comforts to those enjoyed by their white counterparts. Pero, the personal servant of the Nevis planter John Pinney, lived in relative comfort in Bristol, and amassed enough money pulling people's teeth and performing other services that he was able to lend money on a small scale to his fellow servants. If Pero ever fretted about his sister in the Caribbean, whom Pinney had sold to a notoriously sadistic master, we have no evidence of it.[89]

Many impoverished white migrants to eighteenth-century Bristol suffered illness, loneliness, abuse and the disruption of family ties. Many of the poorest, particularly those from the west of Ireland, had also to contend with learning a new language. The situation of African migrants, however, was of a different register. A young African newly placed in the home of some Liverpool merchants around this time was reported to have joyfully mistaken his own reflection in a mirror for the presence of another African child and to have been inconsolable at his inability to embrace the figure he saw.[90] Consider, too, what must have been the mental state of the 10-year-old boy who had survived smallpox only to be sold in a Bristol coffee house.[91] Brother Parminter, of Bristol's Moravian congregation, recalls in his diary his visit to a dying young black man who had earlier attended his chapel's services with enthusiasm. Now, slumped in front of his employer's kitchen fire on a cold November day, the evidently lonely youth seemed too frightened to talk to him or his companion, Brother Walters:

> I went to see the poor sick Negro but he was got down by the Kitchen Fire and there being a Heap of Servants about he told Br[other] Walters the less said about our Saviour there the better . . . therefore we soon walked home again. Yet I really liked the young Man.[92]

These incidents should make us reconsider the cultural dislocation and social isolation which affected even such seemingly pampered children like Champayne or Scipio Africanus.

The case of the Old Calabar princes

The two young Africans who in 1774 found themselves in Bristol merit our especial attention. For they arrived at the port at a time when abolitionist sentiment was beginning to gain ground. Their subsequent experience and treatment reveal some intriguingly complex attitudes held by their hosts towards Africans just at a time when abolitionist sentiment was beginning to gain ground.

These two 'brothers', as they were often called, were probably not brothers at all, but cousins. They were the kinsmen, possibly the son and the nephew, of Ephraim Robin John, the most important man in Old Calabar, in what is today the Biafran part of Nigeria. Their names, Little Ephraim Robin John and Ancona Robin Robin John, are Anglicized versions of their real names, and unlike slave names were chosen by themselves, probably for the purpose of more easily trading with foreigners.

Bristol and Old Calabar, on the Niger Delta, had been trading together since at least the late seventeenth century. Old Calabar's elite had grown wealthy on the slave trade, and by the mid-eighteenth century a rival trading community called New Calabar challenged their hegemony.

In 1767 three young kinsmen of the Old Calabar ruler had headed a party of some 300 men who set out in a convoy of canoes to confer with their rivals and perhaps compete for trade with the English slavers then anchored offshore. The idea seems to have been that the presence of English slavers would afford some sort of neutral ground in which to sort out their trade dispute. However, the English captains (including two from Bristol), angry at the high prices for slaves demanded at Old Calabar, had colluded with their New Calabar rivals in a plan to massacre them. The young men were forcibly taken on board one of the English slavers. The eldest was soon delivered to his rivals, who quickly beheaded him. Most of the rest of the Old Calabar party, still in their canoes, were killed as they fled towards the shore. The two young kinsmen of Old Calabar's ruler, Ancona Robin Robin John and Little Ephraim Robin John, were still on board.[93]

In the event, they were not killed, but carried off and sold into slavery in the Americas. After various ordeals they found themselves in Virginia with a master who routinely whipped them. In 1773 they were reportedly recognized by some of their compatriots who were crewing aboard a Bristol-bound ship, the *Greyhound*. As Ruth Paley relates, the Africans testified that the *Greyhound*'s captain agreed to take them aboard with a view to their getting back to Calabar via Bristol. The captain, however, claimed that they stowed away.

Once they arrived in Bristol, the captain delivered the two men to a slave trader who was 'the agent acting for their supposed Virginia owner'. They found themselves imprisoned and in chains aboard the *Brickdale* in Kingroad, awaiting a favourable wind which would enable their return to Virginia. That would have been the end of the story, but somehow the two Africans had managed to get a letter or message smuggled out to an old trading associate of their father, the Bristol slave-trader Thomas Jones. After two weeks, Thomas Jones found them and issued warrants for the arrest of their jailers.[94]

Now Ancona Robin Robin John had met the Bristol slave-trader Thomas Jones at Old Town years before. The records indicate that Jones had visited the town several times, probably as a slave-ship captain, when he was establishing a stable trading relationship with the Efik traders there. Jones was not implicated in the 1767 massacre, so it was understandable that the two young men should contact him for help. By their lights, they (unlike the Africans they had undoubtedly helped to sell in the past) had been free men, wrongfully kidnapped and enslaved. Possibly they saw their own original enslavement as exceptional because of its particular circumstances: they had not been kidnapped outright but lured aboard a ship in bad faith.

As Ruth Paley has ably pointed out, their situation raised important questions about the implications of the Mansfield judgment of 1772 for the status for slaves who came to England. Here were two men claiming they had been unlawfully enslaved, and their adversaries ultimately thought it safer to argue that they should be imprisoned for debt (as they had not paid their fare to Bristol) than that they were to be imprisoned as slaves. Paley observes that if these two Africans were judged to have been wrongfully enslaved, then British traders would in future have needed to enquire into the particular circumstances of every slave they hoped to sell, lest they sell one who was wrongfully enslaved![95] Jones obtained an interview for Little Ephraim Robin John and Ancona Robin Robin John with Lord Mansfield, who, Paley tells us, was reluctant to reach a judgment which might grant free status (and the possibility of suing for back wages) to the 15,000 or so displaced Africans then currently in London. In the event, the case went to the King's Bench, and a compromise, which effected their release but which still left the status of slaves unclear, was reached.[96]

During their time in Bristol, the two Africans' closest relationship seems, initially at least, to have been with Thomas Jones. It was Jones who rescued them and started legal proceedings. It was Jones who 'took us to his house' and Jones who 'sends us to school to read', and probably Jones who enlisted a Mrs Forrest to take them to Charles Wesley 'to learn about God'.[97]

Why would a dyed-in-the-wool slave-trader go to all this trouble? The obvious answer is that he saw a golden opportunity to ingratiate himself with Ephraim Robin John, who by 1767 was the acknowledged grandee or king of Old Calabar. Certainly he seems to have succeeded in doing just that. The trust informing the personal relationships which undoubtedly did exist between English and Biafran traders must have been seriously undermined by the 1767 massacre. Jones was in correspondence with Old Calabar traders after 1767 and had a bell cast for 'Grandy' Ephraim Robin John at John's request: 'Pls send me one larg Bell to make chop [?] for my war canow [canoe]'.[98] This fine bronze bell, which is now in Bristol, is inscribed 'from Thomas Jones of Bristol to Grandy Robin John of Old Town'.[99] Grandy Robin John also appears to have asked Jones about the whereabouts of his two 'sons' well before their arrival in Bristol.[100] Jones was under no illusion about the probity of the Calabar slave-traders and was at first suspicious of the identity of the two African youths, writing to a participant of the 1767 massacre for confirmation of their identity. This correspondent, Ambrose Lace, speaks favourably of young Ephraim, whom he appears to have 'schooled' briefly in Liverpool before the 1767 massacre. But he informs Jones that the history of Ephraim Robin John 'would exceed any of our Pirates, the whole sett at Old Town you know as well as me'.[101] Though Lace was hardly one to make a moral judgement, it is the case that the Old Calabar rulers killed many and enslaved even more for their own personal gain.[102]

During their stay in Bristol, 'the brothers' were introduced to Elizabeth Johnson, a local Methodist known for her piety and philanthropy. They also developed a close relationship with Charles Wesley, who baptized them in January 1774. Wesley sent them books and letters on their departure back to Calabar. The two youths wrote in February to thank him whilst they were on board the *Maria*.[103] In the summer of that year, Elizabeth Johnson was astonished to find them back in Bristol, distressed and in rags after their rescue from the shipwrecked *Maria*.[104] Johnson informed Charles Wesley, who was in London, that 'the poor souls ran to your house and from thence to ours' on their return. It is clear from her letter that she was anxious for their welfare:

> they were near starved [and] our pain for them is not to be described. They appear greatley distressed but yet confident[.] [W]e have our fears that . . . Jones will not any more attend to them . . . we was engaged to leave Bristol on the Tuesday morning but recommend them to the care of Mrs. Parnell for the time of our absence when we return we shall be ready to give our poor assistance, but what shall be done if the Lord doth not help us I dare not give place to thought at presence [*sic*].[105]

In the event, the two unlucky youths seem to have stayed with Johnson for some eight or nine weeks until they were successfully reinstated back home to Old Calabar. Five weeks before their final departure, they wrote to Charles to report that 'Your brother [John Wesley] has been so kind as to talk to us [and] has given us the sacrament twice.'[106] They wrote to him again during their voyage home and also corresponded with Charles Wesley Jr, with whom they were on first-name terms. 'Bristol friends', they wrote, 'are kind.'[107]

Johnson's fears about Thomas Jones appear to have been unfounded, to the extent that he fitted out a ship for the youths' return home. Thomas Jones had done more than simply return two pawns; he had rescued two important kinsmen without any prior credit agreement and gone to considerable trouble and expense to do so. He had obtained for them an audience with the Lord Chief Justice. Moreover, he had provided them with an English education – something much prized by West African traders. According to the Bristol Moravian minister who met them in 1774, both could 'talk English as to be under stood and read tolerably well, which they learned here', though another source suggests that Little Ephraim may already have had schooling in Liverpool before he was kidnapped.[108]

Why, though, was Jones willing to risk Mansfield adjudicating on a case which could have, had there been no compromise, had such adverse effects on slave-trading? Why did Jones send the Africans to the Wesleys, who not only converted them but also tried to turn them from slave-trading?

The motives the Evangelicals had for befriending the young Africans were more transparent. Johnson, Wesley and the Moravian minister who met these 'two pretty young men of a family of note' in July 1774 wanted very much to establish a mission in Old Calabar. The plan was that on their return to Africa the converted princes would not only leave off their slave-trading but would also receive a Methodist missionary and thus enable the spread of the gospel there. However, once back in Africa, they swiftly returned to slave-trading. Nevertheless, as a direct result of their relationship with Elizabeth Johnson and the Wesleys, two Methodist missionaries were sent out to Calabar either with the princes or shortly thereafter, in 1776 or 1777.[109]

This whole episode marks a transitional phase in the Evangelical attitude, both to the slave trade and to the Africans they encountered. The Wesley brothers wanted to end the trade and naively felt that their charges would give up the trade despite the political and economic pressures on them to do otherwise. On the other hand, the Wesleyans were prepared to send a mission to work under the patronage of slave-traders, both Bristolian (Thomas Jones) and Biafran (Grandy Robin John). Thomas Jones's motives must have been primarily commercial. Though he had showed great kindness to the John brothers, his contact with them did not alter his willingness to trade for slaves in a most ruthless and murderous manner. Around this time, perhaps in order to consolidate further his relationship with the Old Calabar traders, his ship the *Wasp* would participate in the shelling of New Calabar, in which many Africans were killed.

Conclusion

The contacts between Bristol and Calabar traders demonstrate that not all black–white relations could be simply categorized as relations between master and slave. The rough cameraderie of the mixed-race crews aboard some Bristol ships, the instances of shared religious worship, the documented instances of interracial marriages and liaisons and their mixed-race offspring further complicate the picture.

Nevertheless, economic interest set the parameters for racial attitudes in this slaving port. Within these parameters, attitudes might vary, depending on whether individual Africans could claim a superior rank or were baptized Christians. A sense of national and religious superiority, even among the more tender-hearted, also informed the way most white Bristolians viewed black people. The fear of black violence, amplified by the reports in the Bristol, London and colonial press, seems particularly to have informed the anxieties of many whites, especially those with Caribbean connections. In the midst of all this, however, individuals existed in all classes who were repulsed by the cruelty of the slave trade. But until the last quarter of the eighteenth century, few in the city questioned the propriety of the slave trade itself.

Notes

1 Kathleen Wilson, *The Sense of the People: Politics, Culture and Imperialism in England, 1715–1785* (Cambridge, 1995), p. 40.

2 Peter Fryer, *Staying Power: The History of Black People in Britain* (London, 1984); F. O. Shyllon, *Black Slaves in Britain* (London, New York and Ibadan, 1974); Ron Ramdin, *The Making of the Black Working Class in Britain* (Aldershot, 1987); James Walvin, *Black and White: The Negro and English Society, 1555–1945* (London, 1973) and his *Black Presence: A Documentary History of the Negro in England, 1555–1860* (London, 1971); Gretchen Gerzina, *Black England: Life before Emancipation* (London, 1995); Norma Myers, *Reconstructing the Black Past in Britain, 1780–1830* (London, 1996).

3 Francis Greenacre, *Marine Artists of Bristol: Nicholas Pocock 1740–1821, Joseph Walter, 1783–1856* (Bristol: City of Bristol Museum and Art Gallery, 1982), pp. 6–8, 18–21; David Richardson, *Bristol, Africa and the Eighteenth-Century Slave Trade to America*, 4 vols (Bristol: Bristol Record Society, 1986, 1987, 1991 and 1996), vol. 3, pp. 22, xvii.

4 There is a full discussion of these works and their varying approaches in *The African Link: British Attitudes to the Negro in the Era of the Atlantic Slave Trade, 1550–1807* (London, 1978), pp. 17–25; see also Philip Curtin, *Image of Africa: British Ideas and Action, 1780–1850*, 2 vols (University of Wisconsin Press, 1964), vol. 1, pp. 12–23.

5 M. J. Steel, 'A Philosophy of Fear: The World View of the Jamaican Plantocracy in a Comparative Perspective', *Journal of Caribbean History*, vol. 27 (1993), pp. 1–20.

6 See, for example, the observation of David Brion Davis in *The Problem of Slavery in the Age of Revolution, 1770–1823*, extracted in Thomas Bender (ed.), *The Antislavery Debate: Capitalism and Abolitionism as a Problem in Historical Interpretation* (Berkeley, Los Angeles and Oxford, 1992), pp. 17–18.

7 The Hobhouse Letters, BCRL, Jefferies Collection, vol. 13, are a case in point. The Helyar Manuscripts discussed in Chapter 1 also confirm this contention and are valuable since they contain evidence concerning a Caribbean slave plantation before the 1760s. Much more material about plantation regimes survives from the late eighteenth century, when the prospect of abolition seemed imminent and when there was a more self-conscious attempt to prove the humane nature of plantation life.

8 See BL, will of Anthony Bigg, 7 August 1722, Add. MSS 24181, no. 213. In 1766 a Moravian worker in the Bristol congregation reported the death of a devout young man who had been one of two young black men regularly attending Moravian services in the city. The report states that the deceased had 'had a real Love for our Saviour [and] . . . I believe indeed our Saviour took him and that very opportunely for his Mistress dying had bequeathed him to a wild young officer'; BULSC, 25 December 1766, Bristol Choir-House diary (single men's choir house), Moravian Collection, DM451; see also Table 5 in this chapter.

9 BRO, letter from John Opie to Francis Creswick (?), Frogmore St, Bristol, 5 November 1712, Creswick Papers, 206(16)r. Thanks to Margaret McGregor of the BRO for assistance in the deciphering of this document.

10 Cited in Richard Pares, *A West Indian Fortune* (London, 1950), p. 121.

11 SRO, 26 August 1678, Jamaica Letter Book, Helyar MSS, DD/WHh 1089. 'Poor creatures' is a recurring description of slaves right up to the twentieth century (MacInnes), and whilst admittedly it was sometimes applied to pets and mistreated animals, it was also used in conjunction with particularly wretched paupers as well.

12 SRO, Helyar MSS, DD/WHh 1089, bundle 3, item 47; see also the innovative work by Richard Price, *Alabi's World* (Baltimore and London, 1990), which opens with a Surinam planter's sense of hurt and astonishment that a slave to whom he had given a scarf on the occasion of his child's birth would run away.

13 SRO, Helyar MSS, DD/WHh 1089, bundle 3, item 2.

14 See, for example, *Samuel Farley's Bristol Postman*, 19 December 1715. The survival of local newspapers before 1750 is patchy; Bristol Public Libraries, *Early Bristol Newspapers: A Detailed Catalogue of Bristol Newspapers Published up to and Including the Year 1800 in the Bristol Reference Library* (Bristol: Corporation of Bristol, 1956).

15 See, for example, *FFBJ*, 23 June 1759. During the Seven Years War, English privateers operating in the Caribbean were said to 'daily bring up Plunder, Slaves, Cattle etc.'. See also *FFBJ*, 11 February 1758. For local sales of seized cargo, see *FFBJ*, 21 January 1758 and 12 July 1760; see also BCRL, 'The Old Bristol Privateers', *The Bristol Times* (n.d. but c. 1860) in the Jefferies Collection, vol. 12.

16 Kathleen Wilson, 'The Good, the Bad and the Impotent: Imperialism and the Politics of Identity in Georgian England', in Ann Bermingham and John Brewer (eds), *The Consumption of Culture, 1600–1800: Image, Object Text* (London, 1995), pp. 237–62. See also Jack P. Greene, 'Empire and Identity from the Glorious Revolution to the American Revolution', in P. J. Marshall (ed.), *The Eighteenth Century*, vol. 2 of *The Oxford History of the British Empire* (Oxford and New York, 1998), ed. William Roger Louis, 4 vols, pp. 208–31.

17 Cited in Richard B. Sheridan, 'The Formation of Caribbean Plantation Society, 1689–1748', in Marshall (ed.), *The Eighteenth Century*, p. 406.

18 In which it was reported that 'the Negroe slaves in that island rose against their Masters'; *Farley's Bristol Newspaper*, 20 November 1725.

19 *Farley's Bristol Advertiser*, 30 March 1744.

20 *Bristol Weekly Intelligencer*, 3 March 1750.

21 *Ibid*.

22 *Ibid*.

23 See the remarks about poisoning by slaves in the Caribbean in Barbara Bush, *Slave Women in Caribbean Society, 1650–1838* (Kingston, Bloomington and London, 1990), pp. 73–7, and the discussion in Chapter 5 about obeah.

24 *BWI*, 25 August 1750, re the New York murder; *BWI*, 21 July 1750, re the Jamaican uprising; and *BWI*, 14 July 1750, for the mutiny on board the *King David*. The voyage but not the mutiny is reported in the account of the voyage in Richardson, *Bristol, Africa and the Eighteenth-Century Slave Trade*, vol. 3, p. 31, though Richardson observes that only eight (not four, as the papers attest) of the original crew survived to the West Indies.

25 *BWI*, 3 March 1750 and 11 August 1750. Before 1750, out ports had to pay a tax to enter the trade.

26 *BWI*, 7, 14 and 21 October 1752; see also 18 January 1752 for a report of the violent destruction of a sugar plantation by slaves in Surinam in 1751.

27 The sole exception to this is an article by Voltaire published in 1760 in *Felix Farley's Bristol Journal*, which will be discussed in Chapter 4.

28 *FFBJ*, 23 June 1759. Note how it is only the whites who are called 'men', whilst the blacks are referred to as 'Negroes', a convention also employed when reporting war casualties in the Caribbean.

29 See, for example, the reporting of a deposition of a sailor of a Bristol ship which had been seized by a French privateer: 'some of them, particularly a Negro, shot the said Captain Calihall and . . . his second mate'; *FFBJ*, 28 June 1760. The only instance I could find of sympathy for the suffering of slaves in the Bristol press was during a storm aboard a slave ship when the crew, terrified of a mutiny, pushed the slaves down into the flooded hold of the listing ship. When another ship came by them to rescue them, only the white people were saved; *FFBJ*, 8 January 1763.

30 *FFBJ*, 28 June 1760. It is interesting to note that the slaves were revolting not against the fact of their enslavement but against a deterioration in their working conditions.

31 *FFBJ*, 5 July 1760.

32 James Grainger, *The Sugar Cane: A Poem in Four Books* (London: R. and J. Dodsley, 1764), pp. 128–9.

33 There are many references to the 'Coromantee' in both the primary and the secondary literature. The Kingston-based slave factors Tyndall and Ashetton told Isaac Hobhouse in a letter dated 13 March 1729 that Gold Coast slaves were favoured, especially by the South Sea factors. See the testimony of witnesses called to speak to the Commissioners for Trade and Plantations on the Gold Coast Africans being 'best esteemed', and whilst one witness asserted that they were of a 'good temper, if well used', another said that though 'fitter for labour' than other Africans, they were 'of a dangerous rebellious disposition, and promote disturbances', and thus needed to be mixed with those from other nations. *JCTP*, vol. 9, pp. 8–9, 13. Their participation in slave rebellions may well have to do with the martial nature of Ashanti culture, which, if the following story, first related by the planter historian Bryan Edwards, is to be believed, contrasted sharply with that of the Ibos:

> A gentleman of my acquaintance, who had purchased at the same time ten Koromantyn and the like numbers of Ibos (the eldest of the whole apparently not more than thirteen years of age) caused them all to be collected and brought before him in my presence to be marked on the breast. This operation is performed by heating a small silver brand, composed of one or two letters, in the flame of spirits of wine, and applying it to the skin. . . . The application is instantaneous and the pain momentary. Nevertheless, it may easily be supposed that the apparatus must have a frightful appearance to a child. Accordingly, when the first boy, who happened to be one of the Ibos, and the stoutest of the whole, was led forward to receive the mark, he screamed dreadfully, while his companions of the same nation manifested strong symptoms of sympathetic terror. The gentleman stopped his hand; but the Koromantyn boys, laughing aloud, and immediately coming forward of their own accord, offered their bosoms undauntedly to the brand, and receiving its impression without flinching in the least, snapped their fingers in exultation over the poor Ibos. (Bryan Edwards, *History of the West Indies*, cited in A. B. Ellis, *A History of the Gold Coast of West Africa* (London: Chapman & Hall, 1893), pp. 95–6)

Bristol slave-traders complained that 'Eboes' were 'prone to suicide'. It is tempting to dismiss such stereotyping out of hand, but it may be a garbled misinterpretation of actual cultural differences shaped by specific historical and geographical circumstances. If the Ibos were thought to be less spartan, they were noted for their linguistic skill and their business acumen. In all events, this preference for the Coromantyn (whom Christophere Codrington characterized as 'every one a hero') recalls the preference of British administrators in India for the 'martial virtues' of the Sikhs to the inhabitants of Bengal or south India, whose bearing was commonly condemned as 'effete' or 'servile'. Such preferences probably tell us mostly about the martial and masculine nature of British culture at this time. One could imagine a student at a pre-Arnoldian public school being encouraged to bear physical pain in a manner very similar to that of the young 'Koromantyns' mentioned by Edwards.

34 *FFBJ*, 4 October 1760.

35 *FFBJ*, 27 June 1772.

36 *BWI*, 27 June 1752; see also *BWI*, 23 September 1752; *FFBJ*, 12 May 1759.

37 Wylie Sypher, 'The African Prince in London', *Journal of the History of Ideas*, vol. 2, no. 2 (1941), pp. 239–43; Anthony J. Barker, *The African Link: British Attitudes to the Negro in the Era of the Atlantic Slave Trade, 1550–1807* (London, 1978), pp. 27–8. Margaret Priestley's wonderful book *West African Trade and Coast Society: A Family Study* (London, Ibadan and Nairobi, 1969) has a picture of William Ansah, the 'Annamabo Prince', and places John Currantee and others in context (pp. 20–4, 39–41). John

Corrantee was indeed the King of Annamaboe; see PRO, 21 January 1751/2 entry in *JCTP*, vol. 9, p. 259, and PRO, 13 November *c.* 1754, CO388/46/63.

38 'Two of the young Negros [*sic*] who went to England are already rated in your Books much beyond their Deserts, and the addition of two more will only rouse the greediness of our labourerrs, who will be tearing us to send home their young slaves, who after they have been cared for as Princes in England will come back to Africa to be made quills to suck through, according to the Negro phrase, for whatever we allow to maintain them goes half to their Masters'; PRO, Charles Bell to the committee of the Company of Merchants Trading to Africa, 20 March 1756, CO388/47.

39 *FFJB*, 12 May 1759.

40 John Roberts had been the officer upon the coast at the time and was held responsible by the Commissioners for Trade for the incident. It is not clear if he was the 'Captain' reportedly held by the Africans or whether such imprisonment was a fabrication, since Roberts reported in person to testify to the commissioners about this incident in 1759. It appears that the two young men had been kidnapped as early as 1756. The Company of Merchants Trading to Africa explained that its decision not to fund Roberts was due to its own financial problems. Representatives of the company and Charles Bell of Cape Coast Castle had brought the matter to the attention of the commissioners because of their concern about the 'disturbances and obstructions to our trade at Popo' which this incident occasioned. See *JCTP*, vol. 10 (1757), p. 336, and vol. 11 (1759), pp. 14, 17–18, and PRO, copy of the deposition of Edward Gregory, 12 April 1757, CO388/47.

41 BULSC, Bristol Minister's diary, 4 April 1759, Moravian Collection. The Moravians (Church of the United Brethren) had set up a short-lived mission in Guinea in 1737, which is what Nyberg was probably alluding to.

42 My thanks to Susan Brittain of Bristol, a direct descendant of Charles 'The Brave' Baker, as he was called by his family, for kindly affording me access to her family's papers on Baker. Baker lived from 1770 to 1832 and was the captain of the slave ship the *Princess*, which sailed from Bristol in 1791. Just off the coast of Africa the ship was badly damaged, and Baker and his crew decided to build a raft and try for the shore. They made it but were captured by local people and ultimately enslaved for some weeks. Most of his crew died from illness and mistreatment, but he and two others survived. The ship was later found, still floating. This was his first and last involvement in the African trade, and there is a family tradition that he subsequently supported abolition. See Richardson, *Bristol, Africa and the Eighteenth-Century Slave Trade*, vol. 4, p. 193.

43 Ken Morgan does mention Barker, but only en passant. Jonathan Press, in his *The Merchant Seamen of Bristol, 1745–1789* (Bristol: Bristol branch of the Historical Association, 1976), does discuss Barker's account, but not with reference to the racial attitudes expressed therein.

44 See Richardson, *Bristol, Africa and the Eighteenth-Century Slave Trade*, vol. 1, p. 157. Although there is no record of Captain Roach and his chief mate, James Seabon (or Seabourn), on board the *Scipio*, the names of both men are listed for other slaving voyages around this period in Richardson, *ibid.*, vol. 1, pp. 159, 171, and vol. 2, pp. 15, 45. A Timothy Tucker (not Thomas Tucker, as Told has it) was indeed commander of the *Royal George* on the dates Told mentions.

45 Silas Told, *An Account* (London, 1786), pp. 19, 22. The woman died in St Thomas, an island off the coast of Calabar, so it is not clear whether she was purchased by an African before her death. According to the shorter (and I believe earlier) edition of Told's account, the woman had been trepanned by the captain.

46 Though it must be admitted that Roach's involvement with her led to his death; *ibid.*, pp. 19, 26–7.

47 Told's racy description of a fearsomely disguised figure called 'Egbo' chasing local women from hut to hut and whipping their bare bottoms may seen preposterously far-fetched. However, in Old Calabar a secret religious society under a priest had long been established there to impose financial discipline on the community and regulate slave-trading activities. By the 1790s it was reported that its methods had evolved into a form of extortion and terror. Disguise or masquerade was employed, and to 'run ekpe' was to go from ward to ward of Old Calabar imposing summary justice on offenders through whipping them or taking their goods. According to Lovejoy and Richardson, 'Egbo' seems to refer to 'Ekpe', though an early eighteenth-century account by William Snelgrave (which Told may have read) refers to the god Egbo in its discussion of Old Calabar. See Paul E. Lovejoy and David Richardson, 'Trust, Pawnship, and Atlantic History: The Institutional Foundations of the Old Calabar Slave Trade', *American History Review*, vol. 104, no. 2 (1999), pp. 347–8.

48 Told, *An Account*, p. 20.

49 *Ibid.*, p. 28. Dick Ebrew cannot be a reference to Richard Brew of Cape Coast since Told's voyages pre-date the appearance of the African Brews, who in any case did not reside near Old Calabar. See Priestley, *West African Trade*, pp. 108, 121–3.

50 Told, *An Account*, pp. 27–8.

51 *Ibid.*, pp. 32, 43.

52 Richardson, *Bristol, Africa and the Eighteenth-Century Slave Trade*, vol. 3, p. 88 for details of the *Thetis* and p. 66 for information on the *Ann*, which Barker says was at Andony (in the Bight of Biafra) along with the *Thetis*, and which, as he attests, was captained by Alexander Robe. See also p. 42 for details of the *Tryal*, on which Barker earlier sailed, as his pamphlet attests. Disabled Bristol seamen had to apply to the trustees of the Seamen's Hospital, who were members of the Society of Merchant Venturers, for relief, which was administered through the Seamen's Hospital. For the records concerning Barker, see SMV, 5 October 1756, Seamen's Hospital Orders 1747–69, no. 50.

53 Robert Barker, *The Unfortunate Shipwright or Cruel Captain: Being a Faithful Narrative of the Unparallel'd sufferings of* Robert Barker, *late Carpenter on Board the* Thetis *now of Bristol, in a Voyage to the Coast of Guinea and Antigua* (London: 'printed for and sold by the sufferer for his own benefit; and by no one else, 1760), pp. 11–12.

54 J. W. Damer Powell, *Bristol Privateers and Ships of War* (Bristol, 1930), p. 188; Press, *The Merchant Seamen of Bristol*. See Stephen Behrendt, 'The Captains in the British Slave Trade from 1785 to 1807', *Transactions of the Historical Society of Lancashire and Cheshire*, vol. 140 (1990), pp. 107–10, regarding the wealth captains, surgeons and other mariners could accrue from a voyage; see also pp. 91, 96, 104–5.

55 Barker, *The Unfortunate Shipwright*, p. 24.

56 *Ibid.*, p. 27.

57 According to one source, Wapshutt was arrested in 1757 and the case settled in 1758, with Barker getting £26 in compensation instead of the £150 asked for. Barker published the pamphlet after the judgment, presumably in order to get more money; see Damer Powell, *Bristol Privateers*, p. 188.

58 SMV, 2 December 1760, Seamen's Hospital Orders 1747–69, no. 50; see also 15 November 1763 and 9 November 1767 for the refusals of Barker's appeals against the withdrawal of the pension. The trustees at that time included Henry Swymmer, Joseph Daltera, Henry Casamajor, Thomas Farr and William Reeve. Barker, who by this time lived in London with his wife and young child, sent the affidavits and letters to the Merchant Venturers up to 1772, but his pension apparently was never reinstated. For the affidavits of Barker's shipmates attesting to the truth of Barker's charges against Wapshutt, including their accusation that Wapshutt forged one of their signatures on a document vilifying Barker, see SMV, 17 August 1760, Seamen's Affidavits, 5 January

1761 to 10 October 1765, bundle IV, and letter to Messrs. Kington & Vaughan from H. Bostock, 2 November 1772. The Merchant Venturers also withdrew the pension of one William Cozzins, another seaman blinded on the Africa run, who wrote what was seen as an 'anti-merchant pamphlet'. Astonishingly, Barker (or friends on his behalf) reprinted an extended version of the pamphlet when he was 80 years of age, no doubt taking advantage of a sea change in public opinion towards the slave trade; see *The Genuine Life of Robert Barker, dictated By Himself while in a State of Total Darkness* (London: printed by Galbin & Marchant for the author, 1809).

59 Huntington Library, San Marino, California, the 'Autobiography of Joseph Banfield', HM57345. I am grateful to Mary Robertson of the Huntington Library for bringing this document to my attention.

60 Although after preliminary investigations I could find no record of his marriage, Banfield's name does occur in the muster rolls of the slaver *Gambia* for the two voyages he mentions in his memoirs, and there is also confirmation that he had served aboard another slaver, the *Andrews*, at the time he said he did. See SMV, Ships' Muster Rolls for 1770–1, no. 68, and 1771–2, no. 127 . I have not researched the muster rolls for his later voyages, but a perusal of Richardson, *Bristol, Africa and the Eighteenth-Century Slave Trade*, vol. 3, pp. 216, 228, and vol. 4, pp. 17, 72, 74, shows that Banfield named both the captains and the ships and their particulars in accordance with Richardson's findings.

61 Banfield served on one slaver, the *Gambia*, on two successive voyages under Captain Willis and made three voyages aboard another, the *Colston*, rising to the rank of chief mate under Captain Jackson.

62 'Autobiography of Joseph Banfield'.

63 *Ibid.*

64 *Ibid.* The attitude of the governor's wife is interesting too. Her surprisingly vigorous assertion of military authority does not fit into the usual stereotype of Georgian femininity and shows that the informal conditions of the African coast may have provided a broader scope for women's activities. She seems ready to negotiate with her African counterpart, but only up to a point. She may well have been of mixed Portuguese and African origin since she is referred to as Signora Linda 'Debatt' – possibly Delpratt – and since Englishmen stationed in Africa often had 'country wives' there. This incident suggests that the role of women in the slaving forts merits further investigation. For another instance of shipwrecked sailors being taken prisoner and ransomed by Africans, see *FFBJ*, 26 May 1764.

65 *BWI*, 4 May 1751.

66 The 1726 performance was in Bristol's earliest theatre on St Augustine's Back, near the city docks; *Farley's Bristol Newspaper*, 3 September 1726. For performances in 1747, see BCRL, 'Account Book of Jacob's Well Theatre, 1741–1748', and an article by Sybil Rosenfeld, 'Actors in Bristol, 1741–1748', held at the BRO, 8981 (4). She refers to the account book listing a small payment to a black boy to play in *Oroonoko* in 1747, but I could not find this reference when I checked the source myself.

67 London Metropolitan Archives, copy of account of Robert Duckinfield's estate in Jamaica taken by himself, 29 July 1745, Acc. 775802, and will of Robert Duckinfield, 17 November 1755, Acc. 775803. Duckinfield's sisters Rebecca Hale and Martha Richards both lived in Bristol. I am indebted to Tom Duckenfield of Maryland, who is currrently researching his descent from Jane Enugson and Robert Duckinfield, for drawing my attention to this will and other relevant information.

68 BL, will of Samuel Delpratt, 17 June 1783, Add. MSS 34181, no. 143.

69 BL, will of Jacob Ricketts, 8 April 1754, Add. MSS 34181, no. 198. Bush, in *Slave Women*, esp. pp. 110–18, reminds us that enslaved women often used their sexual favours as a way of securing goods and freedom for their offspring.

70 These documents are inexplicably categorized as 'Pedigrees of the Lloyd and Harford families, 25 Jan. 1791' but refer to a will made in 1773 along with a later settlement on the death of Nathaniel Milward's eldest natural son. They can be found in BCRL, Jefferies Collection, vol. 11, pp. 93, 94.

71 See Richard Charles Cuthbert Southey, *The Life and Correspondence of Robert Southey* (London: Longman, Brown, Green & Longman, 1849, 9th edition), vol. 1, p. 95.

72 *Ibid.*, p. 97.

73 *Ibid.*, p. 95.

74 Nigel Tattersfield, *The Forgotten Trade: Comprising the Log of the* Daniel and Henry *of 1700 and Accounts of the Slave Trade from the Minor Ports of England 1698–1725* (London, 1991), p. 399n.

75 John Quaqua was described in 1765 as having been a free man 'above one and twenty years and never out of employ'. He was granted a pension by the Seamen's Hospital in Bristol which was briefly suspended when it was discovered that he had continued to work after the pension was granted. The pension was reinstated in 1765. See SMV, Seamen's Hospital Orders 1747–69, no. 123, and SMV, Seaman's Hospital Certificates for Financial Help 1751–1806, bundle 4. See D. P. Lindegaard, *Black Bristolians of the Eighteenth and Nineteenth Centuries* (Bristol: privately printed, n.d.), pp. 34–6, for a reference to one John Quaco (1711–80), the husband of Penelope Webb. It seems likely that Quaqua and Quaco are the same person. The 'Negroe' William Richardson had claimed to be baptized at the age of 12 by a Bristol Moravian missionary in Jamaica, Br. Caries. He stayed with the Moravians for some months, claiming he could not get a passage back from Jamaica, but left the congregation after some disagreements the following year; see BULSC, Moravian minister's diary, 27 July 1768, 25 October 1768, 20 December 1768, 14 June 1769 and Elders' Committee minutes, 24 February 1769, 22 April 1769 and 16 June 1769, Moravian Collection. The muster rolls also list 'Black Jack' of Bristol aboard the *Little Pearl*, an African ship (Muster Roll, 13 July 1786, no. 138) and Sam Joe, who boarded the *Brother in Africa* (Muster Roll, 22 July 1785, no. 146). For other listings of black seamen after 1750, see Lindegaard, *Black Bristolians*.

76 Judith Alleyne, a Barbadian heiress who was buried in Bristol Cathedral in 1763, freed her servant John Hylas in 1758 so that he could marry Mary, who belonged to a Mr and Mrs Newton. After eight years of marriage, Mary was kidnapped on behalf of her former owners and sent to the plantations. A court case ensued, but although it was ordered that Mary Hylas should be returned to England since her husband was a free man, the status of slaves in England had not been clarified. Even after the *Somerset* judgment, residence in Britain did not, as we shall later see, automatically guarantee free status; Shyllon, *Black Slaves in Britain*, pp. 40–3, and York Minster Library, 'A Short Report of a Trial before Lord Chief Justice Wilmot in the Court of Common Pleas . . . 3 December 1768 . . . Thomas John Hylas vs. John Newton', letter book of Granville Sharp, pp. 11–22. I have not been able to ascertain whether or not Hylas or the Newtons resided in Bristol or when Judith Alleyne moved to Bristol, although, intriguingly, the letter book appears to have been purchased in 1896 from a dealer in Bristol.

77 'The happy Island of Great-Britain is not only the Head, but the Last Quarter of True Liberty. That Liberty which is founded in law and which cannot be invaded but by subverting the constitution. This Liberty is not restrained, as in Poland, to the Nobility; or as in Genoa, to certain rich families . . . but belongs to ALL, and is everyman's BIRTHRIGHT.' This statement opened an editorial which warned against the overzealous use of the press gang in *FFBJ*, 28 June 1755, in marked contrast to the enthusiasm the editor had evinced for impressment a decade earlier.

78 *FFBJ*, 28 April 1744.

79 Captain Gordon's report to the Admiralty, cited by Nicholas Rogers, 'Vagrancy, Impressment and the Regulation of Labour in Eighteenth-Century Britain', in Paul E. Lovejoy and Nicholas Rogers (eds), *Unfree Labour in the Development of the Atlantic World* (London, 1994), pp. 108–9.

80 *Ibid.*

81 *Gloucester Journal*, 22 February 1737, cited in Lindegaard, *Black Bristolians*, p. 17.

82 'A full . . . account of A Lady who Longed for Charcoal and was safely delivered this morning of a Fine Black Boy . . .', cited in Pip Jones and Rita Youseph, *The Black Population of Bristol in the Eighteenth Century* (Bristol: Bristol Historical Association, 1994), pp. 17–18.

83 SMV, Muster Rolls for 1748–51, no. 77. The term 'blackamore' is used less often by the mid-eighteenth century.

84 Edward Terrill, *The Records of a Church of Christ Meeting in Broadmead, Bristol, AD 1640–AD 1688* (London: J. Heaton & Son, 1865), p. 30.

85 The tombstone is in Henbury Churchyard in Bristol.

86 'Sir/I had really forgotten the request Mr. Machutchion——— . . . made to me to take care of the little Negro boy he bot. On the Bay of the Black River in Jamaica untill I rec'd a letter from my brot[her] dated 19 Nvr where he said you have him with orders to deliver him to me! – If you'l please to send him Down, by the machine, and place him under the care of one or other of the passengers, I will receive him on the acct. of Mr. M. . . . please to write me when you intend to send him, that I may send the Inn here to meet him, the weather being severe, he had need be an inside passenger – and as he is a negro child, his passage may be paid here on his arrival' (BCRL, 11 December 1757, Caleb Dickinson to Capt. Barwell at the Jamaica Coffee House, London, Caleb Dickinson's letter book).

87 BCRL, 15 December 1757, Caleb to Ezekiel Dickinson, Caleb Dickinson's letter book.

88 BCRL, 4 February 1758, Caleb Dickinson to Mr Brearey, Caleb Dickinson's letter book.

89 Christine Eickelmann and David Small, 'Who was Pero?' (unpublished manuscript, Bristol, 1999).

90 Reported in Christiana C. Hankin (ed.), *Life of Mary Anne Schimmelpenninck* (London: Longman, Brown, Green, Longmans & Roberts, 1858), pp. 243–4. The story was told to Mary Anne Schimmelpenninck when she was a girl by the mistress of the boy in question.

91 *FFBJ*, 26 July 1760.

92 Cited in M. Dresser (ed.), 'The Moravians in Bristol', in J. Barry and K. Morgan (eds), *Reformation and Revival in Eighteenth-Century Bristol* (Stroud: Bristol Record Society, 1994), p. 138. This young man almost certainly was the same person who was reported to have died in December 1766 just before his owner was going to pass him on to a 'wild young officer'; see BULSC, 25 December 1766, Bristol Choir-House diary (single men's choir house), Moravian Collection, DM451.

93 Gomer Williams, *History of the Liverpool Privateers* (London: William Heinemann and Liverpool: Edward Howell, 1897), p. 533; for other versions of this event, see Ancona Robin Robin John's vivid account of the Calabar massacre in the John Rylands Library (Ancona Robin Robin John to Charles Wesley, 17 August 1774, DDCW 2/4) and the depositions of Thomas Jones, William Floyd and James Bivins in PRO, '*King* v. *Lippincot and others*', KB/1/19/3. I should like to thank Marika Sherwood for her detailed information about the collection of Charles Wesley's correspondence at the John Rylands Library (DDCW) and its relevance to Calabar, and I should like to thank Ruth Paley and Stephen Behrendt for referring me to the letters and affidavits in the King's Bench Papers (KB/1/19/3) mentioned above.

94 Ruth Paley, 'After *Somerset*: Mansfield, Slavery and the Law in England, 1772–1830', in Norma Landau and Donna Andrews (eds), *Crime, Law and Society* (Cambridge,

forthcoming), p. 3. My thanks to Ruth Paley for allowing me to see her article before its publication and for her helpful suggestions regarding sources.

95 The Virginia merchant Henry Lippincott, whose premises were in Corn Street, Bristol, and the William Jones listed as a merchant in King Square, Bristol, co-owned the *Brickdale*. See Paley, *ibid.*, p. 3, and Bryan Little (ed.), *Sketchley's Bristol Directory for 1775* (reprinted Bath, 1971).

96 Paley, 'After *Somerset*', pp. 4–7.

97 JRL, Little Ephraim Robin John to Charles Wesley, 17 August 1774, DDCW 2/5.

98 PRO, 16 June 1769, Ephraim Robin John [aka King George] to 'Jones Marchant', KB/19/3.

99 My thanks to Stephen Behrendt for his information about this bell, which is now in the collection of the Society of Merchant Venturers in Bristol. Whether or not the bell was ever sent to Calabar is open to question, since it has long been in the possession of the Society of Merchant Venturers of the City of Bristol, of which Jones had been a member. But according to Behrendt, it is possible that the bell was sent out to Calabar and returned on the death of its owner. A photograph of the bell will be found in M. Dresser and S. Giles (eds), *'Bristol and the Atlantic Slave Trade' Exhibition* (Bristol: Bristol City Council, forthcoming). It appears that the Thomas Jones who was last a slaving master aboard a ship to Old Calabar in 1763 was the same as the slave merchant Thomas Jones who is reported to have financed slaving ventures as early as 1767. The latter did not begin to trade with Old Calabar until 1770, the year the bell was produced. Records are incomplete, but it seems Jones's slavers sailed again to this port at least four more times, including the year (1774) when the two princes were returned. His last ship to Old Calabar seems to have been in 1782, after which he primarily traded with New Calabar until his death in 1795. See Richardson, *Bristol, Africa and the Eighteenth-Century Slave Trade*, vol. 2, pp. 157, 214, and vol. 3, pp. 13, 25, 50, 53, 59, 72, 83.

100 See PRO, 16 June 1769, Ephraim Robin John [aka King George] to 'Jones Marchant', KB/19/3 – though the King's handwriting and use of pidgin English and the similarity of the Anglicized names of the various Efik traders makes this difficult to confirm with certainty. Jones wrote to Ambrose Lace, one of the captains involved in the 1767 massacre in 1773, asking him to corroborate the princes' story, and received the reply that he knew Litttle Ephraim well: 'I brought young Ephraim home and had him at School, then sent him out, he cost me above sixty pounds and when his Fathers [Grandy Ephraim] gone I hope his son will be a good man.'

101 It is not clear when precisely Little Ephraim was in Liverpool; presumably before his abduction in 1767. See letter to Thomas Jones from Ambrose Lace, captain of the Liverpool slaver the *Edgar*, 11 November 1773, in Williams, *History of the Liverpool Privateers*, pp. 541–2. See also Paul Lovejoy and David Richardson, 'Trust, Pawnship, and Atlantic History: The Institutional Foundation of the Old Calabar Slave Trade', *American Historical Review*, vol. 104, no. 2 (1999), pp. 339–47, for a penetrating assessment of the nature of the economic and social relations between English slave-traders and their Old Calabar counterparts, and Behrendt, 'The Captains in the British Slave Trade from 1785 to 1807', p. 82, for more on Ambrose Lace.

102 Most of the primary sources on Calabar society (as opposed to travellers' accounts) begin in the 1780s or later. But it is clear from the diary of Antera Duke, which begins in 1785, as well as from the testimony of various English traders that bloodshed and enslavement were endemic, and though to some extent regulated by indigenous custom and restraint, were exploited for the personal advantage of the ruling elite in this period. This goes counter to Basil Davidson's glowing account of Efik institutions, especially that of Ekpe, though even he concedes that personal wealth motivated its leaders more than the common good as the slave trade developed. See Basil Davidson, *Discovering*

Africa's Past (London, 1978), p. 140. See G. I. Jones, *Efik Traders of Old Calabar: Containing the Diary of Antera Duke, an Efik Slave-Trading Chief of the Eighteenth Century Together with an Ethnographic Sketch and Notes by D. Simons and an Essay on the Political Organisation of Old Calabar* (Oxford, 1956), pp. 27–75; for a general survey of Old Calabar and Efik society, see A. J. H. Lathan, *Old Calabar, 1600–1891: The Impact of the International Economy upon a Traditional Society* (Oxford, 1973), esp. pp. 3–35. See also Ekei Essien Oku, *The Kings and Chiefs of Old Calabar (1785–1925)* (Calabar: Association for the Promotion of Efik Language, Literature and Culture, 1989), pp. 4–18; see also David Northrup, 'Igbo: Culture and Ethnicity in the Atlantic World, 1600–1850', *Slavery and Abolition*, vol. 71, no. 3 (December 2000), pp. 2, 8–10, on the Old and New Calabar peoples.

103 JRL, Little Ephraim Robin John and Ancona Robin Robin John to Charles Wesley, 22 February 1774, DD CW 2/7; see also Little Ephraim to Charles Wesley Jr, 26 December 1774, DDCW 2/10.

104 JRL, Elizabeth Johnson to Charles Wesley, 6 July 1774, DDCW 2/8.

105 *Ibid.*

106 JRL, Ephraim Robin John and Ancona Robin Robin John to Charles Wesley, 17 August 1774, DDCW 2/5; see also Charles Wesley to the Revd William Perronet, 23 January 1774, DDCW 6/93a. The Johns' relationship with John Wesley, so far as can be gleaned from the evidence, was a rather formal one, but it is clear that John Wesley, who had been informed of their shipwreck by a friend, had been following their progress with interest. Thanks to Marika Sherwood for drawing my attention to this material.

107 These friendly letters to 'Dear Charles', i.e. to Charles Wesley's son, from both brothers are in JRL, 10 October 1774, DDCW 2/11. See also Little Ephraim to Charles Wesley Jr, 26 September 1774, DDCW 2/10.

108 BULSC, Bristol minister's diary, 14 July 1774, Moravian Collection; Williams, *History of the Liverpool Privateers*, pp. 541–2.

109 Their fate was reported to the Elders' Committee of the Bristol Moravian congregation in June 1777:

> By letters from Old Calabar which Miss Johnson communicated to [the Moravian] Br[other] Steinhauer, we learned that Mr. Syndman and his Brother, who went from here to Guinea [*sic*] to see whether Missionaries might be settled here got safe to Calabar but died both of a sickness within 4 weeks.
>
> . . . the King of Calabar in his Letter to Mr. Jones the Merchant and owner of the Ship [in which presumably the missionaries were sent] mentions their Death and writes, that he is sorry for it. Miss Johnson wishes that a mission unto those Parts might be still [tried]'; BULSC, Bristol Elders' Committee minutes, 13 June 1777, Moravian Collection.

3

GENTILITY AND SLAVERY

BRISTOL'S URBAN RENAISSANCE RECONSIDERED, c. 1673–c. 1820[1]

The World's A Citty full of Crooked Streets
And Death the Market Place Where All Men Meets.
If Life was Merchandize that men could buy
The Rich would always live, the Poor alone would Die.

(*Bristol Weekly Intelligencer*, 23 December 1752)

There is not a brick in the city but what is cemented with the blood of a slave.
(Anonymous comment on Bristol cited in J. F. Nicholls and John Taylor, *Bristol Past and Present* (3 vols) (Bristol and London, 1881–2), vol. 3, p. 165)

Can it be truly said that Bristol was 'built on the slave trade'?[2] Were the 'grand stone mansions' on the slopes between Bristol and Clifton which began to spring up by the mid-eighteenth century really financed by merchants grown rich on slave-grown sugar?[3] This chapter examines to what extent Bristol's urban development in the eighteenth century was based on the profits derived from the slave trade and the trade in slave-produced commodities. The establishment of links between slavery and urban development has significant implications for the more general debate about the economic importance of the slave trade for Western commercial and industrial development.[4] It relates also to new work done on the 'rise of gentility' and the importance of consumption in this period as a generator of economic growth and cultural transformation.[5]

Local historians of Bristol have, when they have considered the question at all, generally failed to investigate it in any substantive way.[6] Historians dealing with the larger national picture of Britain's urban development have demonstrated little interest in ascertaining the relationship between the slave trade and the development of what was, for much of the eighteenth century, Britain's second city.[7] Even Peter Borsay's important and influential work *The English Urban Renaissance*, though it includes Bristol, virtually ignores the impact of the slave trade.[8]

According to Borsay, the post-Restoration period saw the 'resurgence of urban fortunes' in Bristol and elsewhere in England. English cities were, he says, characterized by increasing physical and demographic growth, prosperity and refinement. He documents the increase in population, the burgeoning of town squares, the proliferation of paved streets, assembly rooms and theatres, and he attributes this urban development to 'the three springs . . . of commerce, industry and services'.[9] He even mentions in his discussion of commerce the importance of 'overseas markets', including the West Indies and North America. Such trade at least trebled in value between 1650 and 1750 and, he reminds us, led not only to an increase in shipbuilding but also to an expansion in the demand for manufactured goods. When discussing industry, Borsay duly lists Bristol's glassmaking, sugar refining, soap boiling, brass and copper smelting, earthenware production, brewing and distilling.[10] When discussing the concomitant expansion in service industries he cites the growth of such spas as Hotwells and the increasingly genteel tastes of its inhabitants, which had cultural as well as economic implications.[11]

The period Borsay singles out as the period of urban renaissance is precisely the period in which Britain's involvement in the slave trade and the trade in slave-produced goods took off. Indeed, as we have seen, it is in the period between 1730 and 1745 that Bristol briefly surfaced as the nation's foremost slaving port.[12] Yet the slave trade is peripheral to Borsay's interests; he is content to emphasize the importance of the link between economic development and urban regeneration. Yet by his failure to articulate the particular role the wealth from slavery played in the English urban renaissance, the process is sanitized. When slavery is obscured, the relationship between exploitation and gentility is inadvertently airbrushed out of the historical picture.

It will be argued here that as processor of slave-produced commodities, as supplier of goods to West African slave-traders, as the purveyor of both slaves and goods to the plantations, and as planters and planters' agents, Bristol's merchant community derived wealth from the slave colonies. Some of this wealth was recycled into the city's infrastructure in the form of new housing, infrastructure and public buildings.

Certainly contemporaries were in no doubt as to the centrality of the African and West Indian trade to the city's prosperity. They did not make the tendentious distinction which some subsequent scholars have made between the African slave trade and the West Indian and American plantation trades.[13] Though it is true that Bristol merchants were shifting their energies away from the African trade to the West Indian and American plantation trade by mid-century, Bristol was still an important slave port in European terms. More to the point, as *Felix Farley* had said, 'Commerce is a Circle'; without the demand for slave labour from the plantations, the 'African trade' could not flourish.

This interdependency between the colonial trades and the trade in slaves is reflected in the wide-ranging business interests of leading African merchants. Whilst it is true that many had interests in seemingly unrelated trades, such as the Baltic or Levant trade, others diversified as a way of consolidating their interests through backward integration. Thus, a merchant with Swedish interests might thereby obtain the ore needed for his iron manufactory, which produced trade goods for the Guinea coast. Links with Venice or the East Indies could ensure supplies of trade goods such as glass bugle beads or calicoes.[14] We need also to go beyond the counting house, the plantation and the dockyard to consider the role of Bristol slave merchants as property developers, patrons and cultural consumers. This chapter will attempt to demonstrate some of the links between trade and consumption, between brutality and innovation, between go-getting avarice and gentrified social improvement. In particular, we shall explore how housebuilding constituted a recognized method for becoming 'rich and respectable'.[15]

The particular approach adopted is to consider specific areas of Bristol between the 1670s and the early nineteenth century and investigate the business interests of those developing and/or utilizing the sites. We shall go on to consider the ownership of some of the grand houses erected or renovated in the wider Bristol area to see how pervasive were the links between gentrification and slave-based wealth. Throughout the chapter we will take note of the way such development, both in the city and in its suburban and rural hinterlands, was accompanied by a growing refinement of manners. Such an approach combines original prosopographical[16] and topographical research. Building upon the impressive work of economic historians and archaeologists researching the city,[17] I have been able to determine, in some cases at least, which owners or tenants of specific buildings were involved in 'the African trade' or its colonial derivatives. Poor Rate books, local directories, newspaper advertisements, invoices, wills and chancery court case documents (used in conjunction with Richardson's work in particular) have further enabled me to identify the business interests and kinship connections of individual inhabitants of a particular area.[18]

The city, 1676–1713

It is evident that post-Restoration Bristol did indeed experience a 'renaissance'. In particular, the period in between the publication of two of the city's earliest maps – Millerd's map of Bristol in 1673 (Figure 9) and Rocque's 1742 map of the city (Figure 10)[19] – is also, especially after 1713, the very period in which the African trade was most dynamic and important to Bristol. It is also the time when the trade to the Caribbean and the slave-holding colonies of Maryland, Virginia and the Carolinas and Rhode Island became so significant. By the 1780s, Bristol's role as a slaving port, whilst still significant, had long been eclipsed by Liverpool. This increasingly gentrified era saw too a new self-consciousness about the propriety of the slave trade. Merchants such as Thomas Harford or Henry Bright increasingly preferred to identify themselves with

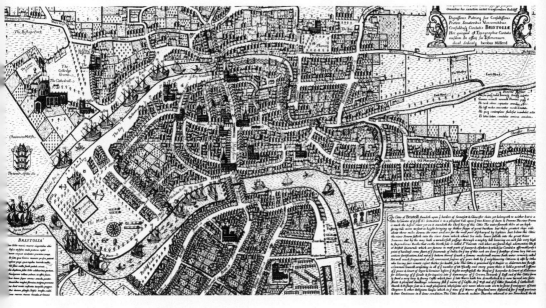

Figure 9 (above) James Millerd, *An Exact Delineation of the Famous Citty of Bristoll and Suburbs*, 1673. Bristol City Museum and Art Gallery

Figure 10 (below) John Rocque, *A Geometrical Plan of the City and Suburbs of Bristol*, 1742. Bristol City Museum and Art Gallery

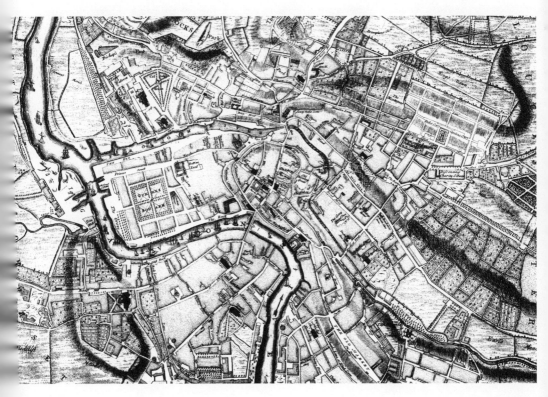

their West Indian or American interests and distance themselves from 'the Guinea trade'.

The Millerd map of 1673 shows the centre of Bristol still discernibly in the shape of a cross. The city walls remained largely intact, and there were few suburbs. Generally speaking, the urban infrastructure is shown to be in a relatively primitive state. Merchants still worked under a covered 'Tolzey' or pergola. The main 'Bristol bridge' was a medieval structure, picturesque but unable to sustain the growing traffic from the rural hinterlands. Small Street, where many merchants lived,[20] was cramped and old-fashioned, though conveniently close to the quay. The quay fronted onto the River Frome – which, along with the River Avon, is shown at the centre of the map. Bristol's notoriously tidal harbour was a thirteenth-century creation, and 'The Marsh', bordering the harbour, was relatively undeveloped save for the roperies shown by Millerd on either side.

Although late seventeenth-century Bristol showed little evidence of any urban renaissance, the trading networks which were being consolidated at that time laid the groundwork for both the financial prosperity and the physical transformation which was to characterize much of the early Georgian period. Some of the most important of these trading networks involved the plantations of Virginia and the Caribbean, which were increasingly dependent on African slave labour. As we have seen in Chapter 1, a number of prominent Bristolians had extensive interests in the plantations of the Caribbean and Virginia in the late seventeenth century.[21] As early as 1679, Bristol was already the centre of an internationally based sugar-refining industry. In that same decade, a coffee house, that symbol of the brave new regime of colonial consumption, opened its doors in the city's High Street.[22] By this time too, tobacco had become an increasingly important trade commodity and Bristol's mercantile elite had already acted to ensure that tobacco produced on colonial plantations supplanted home-grown varieties.[23] Formally barred from participating in the slave trade until the 1690s, some Bristol traders, as we have seen, supplied plantations with slaves from at least the 1680s.[24] After 1698, and the repeal of the Royal African Company monopoly, the 'African trade' in Bristol began in earnest, though war impeded its growth until 1713. In addition to slaves, the slave plantations of the Caribbean, Virginia and Maryland also needed commodities and manufactured goods which Bristol was happy to supply.

The surviving evidence does not permit us to make a definitive causal link between slaving interests and urban development in Bristol much before 1713, although the stirrings of an urban rebirth can perhaps be first discerned as early as the 1680s. In 1681 William Swymmer built two warehouses on the docks whose purpose, according to one source, was to accommodate sugar imports from Barbados and Jamaica, and probably Antigua, where William Swymmer's son-in-law Sir William had investments. Given Swymmer's activities during the 1860s as a purveyor of slaves to the Caribbean (discussed in Chapter 1), it is notable that in 1692 he advanced the Society of Merchant Venturers £600 towards the building of a new quay and cranes on the Bristol docks, for which he was soon reimbursed. There were also other buildings and public works in evidence by the 1690s: in 1696 an almshouse was erected and in 1699 the city's medieval High Cross restored. In 1704 a new city council house was erected.[25]

The urban renaissance in Bristol

Industry as well as trade was beginning to make its mark on Bristol by the early eighteenth century. A fine series of 'Prospects of the City of Bristol' by Samuel and Nathaniel Buck made in the 1730s is a visually vivid source for the city's development (Figure 11).[26] Their *South Eastern Prospect of Bristol* directs the viewer's eye towards the Temple and Redcliffe areas of the city, full of smoking glass houses. In the foreground a black slave in livery attending a white mother and child indicates the genteel lifestyle that trade and industry could bring.

The 1742 Rocque map (Figure 10), too, shows unmistakable indications of the 'urban renaissance' described by Borsay. The expansion of industry is evidenced by the proliferation of glass cones and a new crane featured in the map's borders, not reproduced here. At least ten glass cones are recorded in detail in the Redcliffe and Temple areas in the subsequent (1743) edition of Rocque's map.[27]

Poor Rate books for the parish confirm that the entire area had been full of glass houses,[28] which Daniel Defoe asserted produced 'a very great Number of Glass Bottles, which they send fill'd with Beer, Cyder and Wine, to the *West-Indies*, much more than goes from London'. Bottles of brandy were also sent to West Africa.[29] Distilling, glass-making, sugar-refining and slave-trading, then, enjoyed a symbiotic relationship. Philip and William Freke, slaving merchants, were part-owners of a sugar house in Temple Street. Philip Freke, a Tory with parliamentary ambitions (he stood unsuccessfully for a Bristol seat in 1715), had interests in a brandy distillery by 1731 and co-owned a sugar house in the nearby Old Market.[30] The slave-trader Isaac Hobhouse was also reported to have had shares in a sugar refinery in Redcliffe in the first part of the eighteenth century. Similarly, John Berrow, an African merchant, co-owned a glass house in Redcliffe Back.[31] In 1713 John Vigor, a maltster in the Redcliffe parish, was, along with a sugar house owner, one of the higher Poor Rate payers in the area and a Joseph Vigor was by then a partner in a new brass battery company, and by 1723 Vigor & Co. co-owned a slave ship with Philip Freke's brother Thomas, who was himself one of Bristol's most active slaving agents.[32]

All this industrial activity stimulated the development of new streets too, including one pointedly named 'Guinea Street' in Redcliffe Parish. The original owner of one of the earliest houses on Guinea Street was one Edmund Saunders, a churchwarden at nearby St Mary Redcliffe Church. David Richardson has established that Saunders had been a slave-ship captain and then one of the city's leading slaving agents in that period.[33] Saunders rose to membership of Bristol's commercial elite when he became a member of the Society of the Merchant Venturers before his fall into bankruptcy in 1740. The inventory taken of Saunders's house on his bankruptcy affords a vivid glimpse into the possessions of this once affluent agent. In addition to the china, glassware and mahogany

Figure 11 Samuel and Nathaniel Buck, *The South East Prospect of the City of Bristol* (detail), 1734. Bristol City Museum and Art Gallery

furniture were 'a parcel of Negro caps', pipes of Madeira and bales of textiles specifically destined for trade with West African slavers. There was an impressive array of jewellery as well, gold rings and exotica such as gold-tipped antelopes' horns and the chillingly triumphalist addition of 'a blackamore's head in gold'.[34] Saunders appears also to have dabbled in property speculation, as early in 1727 he advertised '4 large new houses with gardens and both sorts of water' for let in Guinea Street. By 1743 some eleven houses on the same street, described as 'lately built', were sold as part of his estate.[35]

Development was also taking place across the docks, close to the quayside. Rocque's map shows a new street called Princess Street (also variously known as Princc's or Prince Street) on the site of what had previously been known as 'the Marsh'.[36] T. L. S. Rowbotham's atmospheric painting of Prince's Street was

Figure 12   T. L. S. Rowbotham, *Prince's Street*, watercolour, 1826. Bristol City Museum and Art Gallery

completed in 1826, over a century after its initial development during the period 1700–27 (Figure 12). A great crane and slipway had been put in at the bottom of the street, which faces onto the docks, by 1733.[37] At the top of the street, not visible in the painting, a new Merchant Venturers Hall, built on the site of an older one in 1711, ensured the street's commercial tone.[38] But Prince's Street was a mixture of warehouses, residential dwellings and public buildings, most of which seem to have been linked either directly or indirectly to the slave trade.

One fine terrace, partially visible behind the ship's rigging on the left of the picture, was built early in the century by three Bristol merchants. Two of these men, Henry Combe and John Becher (1677–1743), served as Bristol's mayor, and also invested in slaving vessels.[39] Both men were linked by friendship and family networks to other slaving interests. In 1718 Becher's wife, Mary, was bequeathed 'my negro boy named Tallow' by a Jamaican friend of the family recently retired to Bristol. Combe also had a slave plantation in Nevis. When he ran unsuccessfully for Parliament against Edward Southwell in 1739, it was said that he had 'amassed wealth eno' to buy 1/2 a nation'.[40] John Becher's son Michael soon took over his father's slaving firm, whilst another son (by his second marriage), Edward, was resident as a merchant in Jamaica by 1737.[41] One of Becher & Co.'s slave ships, the *Jason*, would in 1760 be the subject of a sketch by Nicholas Pocock, who lived with his family on Prince's Street from 1756. As discussed in the previous chapter, Pocock's celebratory pen-and-ink drawing of the ship is bordered by vivid scenes of slaving off the African coast.[42]

Perhaps one of Prince's Street most prominent early residents was Thomas Coster (Figure 4). Born in 1684, he was Tory MP for Bristol from 1734 until his death in 1739. That year, the *Gentleman's Magazine* published an epitaph in his honour proclaiming him:

> *From commerce rich, yet rich without a stain,*
> *Tho' wealthy humble and tho' wise not vain.*[43]

Just how stainless Coster's wealth was, however, is open to debate. He had inherited from his father property in Bristol and a complex of copper works in Bristol, the Forest of Dean and Neath, in whose affairs he took an active part. Indeed, he was instrumental in adding a brass battery to his holdings.[44] Much of Bristol's brassware and copper wire was designed for the export trade to Africa. Copper nails and sheathing were needed for protecting the hulks of Bristol slave ships against the ravages of the West African teredo worm. It is not surprising to find, then, that between 1730 and 1739 he co-owned six slaving vessels, including the *Amoretta*, which in 1738 sold 206 Africans (including 37 children) in South Carolina. Coster, a business associate of Isaac Hobhouse, would in 1739 leave his daughter an estate worth £40,000.[45]

Some of Coster's new neighbours on Prince's Street were even more heavily involved in the slave trade. Henry Tonge and Noblett Ruddock were also leading slaving agents. Tonge, a stuff maker, managed some 42 slaving voyages between 1730 and 1753 and left shares in brass and copper concerns and in the Bristol Crown fire office – a firm which grew rich on the needs of the city's fire-prone sugar-refining industry. Tonge managed to leave £50,000 and extensive properties to his children, who soon joined the gentry.[46] Like Tonge, Christopher Willoughby, another Prince's Street resident, was by 1750 a member of the Bristol contingent of the Company of Merchants Trading to Africa, the government-approved group that replaced the Royal African Company.

Bisecting the street today is Farr Lane, named after Richard and Thomas Farr, of the Farr rope-making firm, who also managed many of the city's slaving voyages. Thomas was an eminent solicitor and principal clerk to the custom house.[47] Richard's son Richard Farr Jr was a member of the Society of Merchant Venturers, rising to become a master of the society in 1762 before ascending to the post of Bristol's lord mayor the following year.

Further down the street and slightly lower down the social scale lived Hollis Saunders, a merchant with some slaving investments. For a time, Saunders lived comfortably enough in Prince's Street. His furniture included a mahogany bedstead, chairs, tables and a bookcase full of good modern books. But Saunders, who financed a slaving expedition on the *Alexander* in 1758, found his part-share in a subsequent voyage in 1759 to be a disaster, and this may account for why he had to sell his house and goods the following year.[48] His house was advertised as being 'extremely convenient for a merchant or substantial tradesman whose business may occasion a frequent attendance at the Custom-House or Key'.[49]

In addition to houses and warehouses, Prince's Street had its share of buildings devoted to entertainment. The African House was a tavern or coffee house whose name reveals the preoccupation of the traders who frequented it. In 1757 a master advertised for the return of his slave 'Starling', 'A Negro lad about 18 years of Age [who] blows the French Horn very well', to another tavern on the street, the Rising Sun.[50] Further down, towards the Merchants' Hall, the Assembly Rooms (visible halfway down on the left of Figure 12) were constructed in 1755, financed by a tontine of merchants contributing £30 each. This token of increasing refinement came into being because, as Defoe acutely observed, in this context 'luxury must always follow riches'.[51]

By 1769, though Bristol's role in the slave trade had already begun to decline, the West India trade showed no signs of flagging. The Farrs and Willoughbys and the African merchant Thomas Deane (who is possibly the scion of an early Bristol sugar merchant of the previous century) are all Esquires by this date. They are joined on the street by the West India merchant Samuel Span and the sugar-refiner Edward Brice. Across the docks, Redcliffe Terrace, a residential development for this increasingly gentrified breed, was nearing completion. It was developed by the shipbuilder Sydenham Teast, whose shipyard is pictured in Figure 8.[52]

Just around the corner from Prince's Street, another development, Queen Square, had already grandly embodied the relationship between slavery, urban development and the rise of gentility. In a detail from the Bucks' *North West Prospect of the City of Bristol* of 1730 (reproduced in Figure 13), we see Queen Square – also visible in Rocque's map (Figure 10) – 'against a background of smoking glasshouses and girded in ship's masts, the classically elegant symbolic epicentre of shipping and manufacture'. Although the square was designed in imitation of London squares rather than as a commercial development, one of its earliest and most prominent buildings was a new custom house, which was completed by 1710.[53]

In any case, the genteel aspirations of the square's residents and developers must be understood in context. The lamps and railings around the square, which, as Borsay tells us, were prototypical of early provincial urban developments elsewhere, helped to transform the area from a marsh 'open to all social classes'[54] to a socially exclusive residential enclave. By the time it was completed in 1729, Queen Square was, as Borsay notes, the first of a number of elegant squares built in the city in the eighteenth century, and remains the largest of its type in England.[55] What Borsay does not mention is that the square was developed at precisely the same time that Bristol became Britain's premier slaving port, displacing even London, whose slaving fortunes had been badly upset by the bursting of the South Sea Bubble.

As Figure 13 attempts to illustrate, most of Queen Square's most prominent residents were connected in a dense web of business and kinship interests either to the African slave trade or, increasingly as the century wore on, to the trade in slave-produced commodities. At least 10 out of the 24 substantial ratepayers on the square were engaged in the African trade in 1730. Aside from Woodes Rogers (Figure 13),[56] another early resident was John Day, a leading merchant whose *Dover Galley* made four successful slaving voyages between 1707 and 1713, and who served as the city's spokesman at Westminster during the hearings concerning the Africa trade between 1711 and 1713.[57] Other residents and probable relatives were

Some Eighteenth-Century Residents of Queen Square
and their connections to the Atlantic slave trade

Abraham Elton II

Abraham Elton II (1679-1742) inherited the largest house on the Square from his father Abraham I, the founder of an impressive mercantile empire in the city. His son, who invested in at least three slaving voyages, had investments in the slave colonies of Maryland and Virginia and replaced his father as MP for Bristol in 1727. He also supplied copper sheathing for African ships, copper rods for trading on the African coast and copper vats used for processing gunpowder. His brothers Jacob and Isaac were also involved in slave-trading.

John Anderson

He owned a number of slavers and directly managed some 66 voyages between 1764 and 1797 including the *King George*, which in 1764 shipped 280 Africans from the Windward and Cape coasts to Kingston, Jamaica.

Isaac Hobhouse

A leading slave-trader in the city, he managed 44 slaving voyages before 1747 and partnered James Laroche in several slaving ventures. Hobhouse sold plantation produce in Bristol and oversaw the education of the children of his West Indian clients sent to England. By 1760 he lived on the Square and also had property in Clifton, then a fashionable village near Bristol.

Joseph Jefferis

From a prominent merchant family, both he and his brother William, the city's leading Carolina merchant in the first half of the century, were slave-traders. Joseph Jefferis was mayor of Bristol in 1724 as well as organizing 14 slaving ventures by 1729. His ship the *Pearle*, which he co-owned with his brother, William Swymmer Jr and others, delivered 355 slaves to Barbados and South Carolina in 1728.

James Laroche

Bristol's most important slaving agent in this period, who managed some 132 slaving voyages between 1728 and 1769. The 360 slaves who were carried aboard his ship the *Loango* from Angola and delivered to South Carolina in 1737 included 40 children.

Woodes Rogers

A famous privateer, he was amongst the first to let a plot in the Square and to build 'a substantial mansion house' there. He invested in slaving ships and ended his days as Governor of the Bahamas, which had a slave regime. One of his Bristol-born sons was an official of the Royal African Company.

Thomas Freke

From an established merchant family, he managed 14 slaving voyages before his death in 1730 including the *John and Betty*, which embarked from Guinea in 1729 with 250 slaves and delivered 158 to Kingston, 11 of whom died on arrival. Two other members of the Freke family were also slave-traders in Bristol, as was his brother-in-law John Brickdale.

Henry Bright

He served as a factor in Jamaica and returned to Bristol in 1746 to marry Sarah Meyler, the daughter of his former employer (Richard Meyler, an African and West Indian merchant). Bright's shipping interests included a substantial interest in the African and Carolina trades. He also traded directly in slaves.

Other residents

John Becher	John Gresley
John Day	Abel Grant
Nathaniel Day	Thomas Harris
Nathaniel Foy	

Figure 13   The background is from a detail of Samuel and Nathaniel Buck, *The North West Prospect of the City of Bristol*, 1734. Bristol City Museum and Art Gallery. The information is taken in part from David Richardson, *Bristol, Africa and the Slave Trade to the Americas*, vols 1 and 2.

Nathaniel Day, part-owner along with Edward Colston of St Peter's Sugar House,[58] and Peter Day, a sugar merchant who joined Richard Farr on at least four slaving ventures and married the daughter of Abraham Elton I, owner of the largest house on the square.[59] They were joined by the merchant Joseph Earle (later to become MP for Bristol) whose *Earle Gally* in 1702 was pressed into royal service after it sold its slaves in Jamaica.[60] As early as 1711 other prominent slaving merchants owning warehouses, cellars and homes on the square included John Becher, Lewis Casamajor, Abel Grant and Isaac Elton, who also owned a Jamaican plantation.[61]

Isaac's father, the immensely wealthy Abraham Elton I, a partner in Thomas Coster's father's copper firm,[62] died two years before the square was completed and passed his house on to his son Abraham Elton II (Figure 13). Abraham Jr joined Thomas Coster in 1733 to promote the erection of the handsome bronze Rysbrack statue of William III which graced the square's centre. (Their critics attributed their action more to their interests in the copper and brass industry than their aesthetic sensibilities.[63]) Both Isaac and Abraham were listed in 1750 as members of the Company of Merchants Trading to Africa.[64]

Thomas Freke owned a house in Queen Square. He left it in 1730 to his young son Thomas. The Freke estate, which included a prodigious number of urban and rural properties in and around Bristol, was administered by Freke Sr's son-in-law, John Freke Brickdale, another African merchant. Brickdale appears to have let the house in 1742 to the enormously wealthy grocer and African merchant Michael Miller.[65]

Nearby was Bristol's most important slaving agent in this period, James Laroche, whose activities are summarized in Figure 13.[66] Laroche dominated Bristol's trade with Old Calabar in what is now Nigeria and liaised with a number of other merchants in slaving ventures, including Edmund Saunders of Guinea Street, Thomas Coster of Prince's Street as well as four of his neighbours in Queen Square: Noblett Ruddock, Joseph Jefferis (Figure 13), the slaving captain Thomas Quirk[67] and Isaac Hobhouse (Figure 13). Hobhouse, who does not appear to have moved into the square until around 1760, partnered virtually every Bristol merchant on the square. Aside from Laroche, his slaving associates living elsewhere in the city included Edmund Saunders, Captain William Swymmer (probably the grandson of Alderman Swymmer) and Thomas Coster.[68]

Interestingly, rate books for the 1730s show that although the square was mainly residential, lofts, cellars and warehouses were also still let for what must have been, in some cases at least, commercial purposes, and by 1761 there was the Marine Coffee House and Tavern on the square, which no doubt further facilitated business dealings.[69]

By 1775 Bristol's first trade directory[70] listed other residents with slaving connections. These included Nathaniel Foy, Thomas Harris and John Anderson (Figure 13). Their neighbour John Gresley owned, amongst other slaving ships, the *Minerva*, which shipped some 300 enslaved Africans from Cape Coast to Kingston, Jamaica, that same year;[71] Henry Bright (Figure 13) served in Jamaica as an ensign during the Maroon War as well as being a slaving agent, before returning to Bristol in 1746 to live on the square.[72] Bright's extensive shipping interests included a substantial interest in the African and Carolina trades, and he too traded directly in slaves. The published letters between South Carolina planter and slave-trader Henry Laurens and such Queen Square residents as Bright, Isaac Hobhouse and William Reeve demonstrate the close interest which traders in slave-produced commodities such as indigo, rice and sugar took in the supply of slaves.[73]

Those American merchants who lived on the square also had slaving connections. Bristol had been a major supplier of slaves to South Carolina before 1750, and by the 1760s merchants like Thomas Deane of Prince's Street continued the trade, whilst Edward Neufville, a Carolina merchant, lived at 12 Queen Square by 1775.[74] Elias Vanderhorst, a Carolina planter and slave-owner who came to Bristol in the 1770s, was in 1792 made the American Republic's first consul in Britain. It seems particularly appropriate that the consulate was also in the square.[75]

As the century wore on, residents increasingly preferred to distance themselves from the slave trade itself. It was a dirty trade and, as we shall see in the next chapter, increasingly at odds with the image of a refined gentleman of sensibility. Thomas Harford the ironmaster, for example, was careful to conceal the fact that much of his exportware consisted of 'Guinea pots' and 'Guinea kettles' used in the barter for slaves.[76]

As we have seen, a number of Queen Square's residents were in the Bristol Corporation, and some held high office in the city. These same men dominated the list of those who helped to found the city's more genteel cultural institutions. The Assembly Rooms and the nearby Theatre Royal, which opened in 1766, are two cases in point.[77] By the time the Farr family tried to sell their 40-year lease on their Queen Square house in 1768, their advertised bid in a local paper included not only the house but a second house in King Street 'opposite the Library', a share in the Bristol theatre, a share in the new Assembly Room and a share in the circular stables in St James.[78]

The 'chief enlargement' of Bristol had, as one contemporary noted, been made since the building of the 'elegant and spacious' Queen Square. Since its erection, he continued, there has been in the city '[the] addition of so many fair Streets and stately Edifices on every side that at present it is near one third Part bigger than it was forty years ago'.[79] However, by this time Queen Square was just beginning to lose some of its social cachet. It was a time when the city's African trade had been decisively outstripped by that of Liverpool. The city's social structure was also changing, with the increasing importance of the professional classes becoming evident.[80]

Borsay cites the growth of genteel suburbs and the marked proliferation of country houses for 'the gentry and pseudo-gentry' in this period. Clifton was Bristol's most fashionable suburb in this period. Much Clifton property was owned by the Society of Merchant Venturers, and the eighteenth century saw its progressive development in both bespoke and speculative housing. Donn's map of 1769 (Figure 14) lists nine names of note in the Clifton area, five of whom – Farr, Hobhouse, Brickdale, Freeman and Jefferies – were prominent African traders, and one of whom – Codrington – had extensive West Indian holdings. This short list of names is, however, misleadingly brief, for Clifton was awash with slave-based wealth. Donald Jones's careful study of Clifton shows that a few Africa and West India merchants played a major role in the development of the fine houses which began to make Clifton such a fashionable place. The linen draper Paul Fisher built the distinguished Clifton Hill House by 1747. Fisher, the son of an important African merchant and himself a member of the Company of Merchants Trading to Africa, also had a financial interest in a Grenada plantation and the West India and Carolina trades.[81]

By 1755 Abraham Isaac Elton had bought Fremantle House and in 1764 Henry Hobhouse (Isaac's son) built Cornwallis House.[82] Thomas Pedler, a wealthy merchant of 'Pimlico and Bristol', who built Beaufort House (now demolished) in 1767, almost certainly owed some of that wealth to the West Indian plantations. (A Robert Pedler is mentioned in a 1650 will of a man with Bristol connections as a tobacco merchant of Nevis.) Robert Pedler's grandson, who was Thomas's direct heir, seems to have inherited a Jamaican plantation from him and on his own death in 1823 bequeathed money to his 'reputed natural daughter Jane Pedler, a slave on Catherinemount estate' in order to free her, and also willed 'my Horse ferryman and my mule Dick and all my household furnityre and my Canoe . . . [and] the following Slaves, namely Ellen and her children, Sarah and Sucker, Beck, Nancy, Adam, John, Fortune, Big William and Little William' to his apparently black consort, Jane Boswell, stipulating that on her death they should go to their three children and Jane Pedler.[83]

Near the picturesque Avon Gorge in Clifton, a fashionable Georgian dwelling, still popularly known as 'St Vincent's Rocks', belonged to Josias Jackson, who owned a similarly named property in the Caribbean island of St Vincent. Clifton's famous Royal York Crescent, with its colourful wrought-iron balconies, raised walkway and distinctively 'colonial' style, was conceived in 1782 as a tontine financed by six merchants, most of whom had African or West Indian links.[84] By the 1790s James Lockier and James Macalay, developers who were responsible for much of Georgian Bristol, including Berkeley and Portland Squares, took over the troubled development. Both men had interests in the Africa trade and investments in the Honduras, probably in mahogany plantations.[85] Booms and busts in the speculative housing market affected Clifton's growth. But by the end of the eighteenth century, Clifton had the most important concentration of retired West Indian families outside London. As Olivier observed in 1910, 'Bath and Bristol hav[e] . . . been very favourite residential places for West Indians, no doubt on account of the hot springs and climate, as well as their gaiety and fashion.'[86]

Most of the 50 or so memorials to white West Indian families in Clifton recorded by Olivier and local researcher Mary Campbell date from the late eighteenth to the mid-nineteenth centuries. These émigrés included some politically prominent Caribbean families, including the Alleyne family of Barbados, the Mills family of St Kitts and the Baylys of Jamaica. It was families such as these who helped to finance some of Bristol's urban and industrial development.[87] Even those who came simply to die created a demand for accommodation. John James Vidal had been a member of the Jamaican Assembly and a Supreme Court judge of that island before he came to Richmond Terrace, Clifton, where he died in 1823.[88] The Cumberbatch family, who appear to have had long-standing Bristol links, lived since at least the early eighteenth century as planters in Barbados before Edward

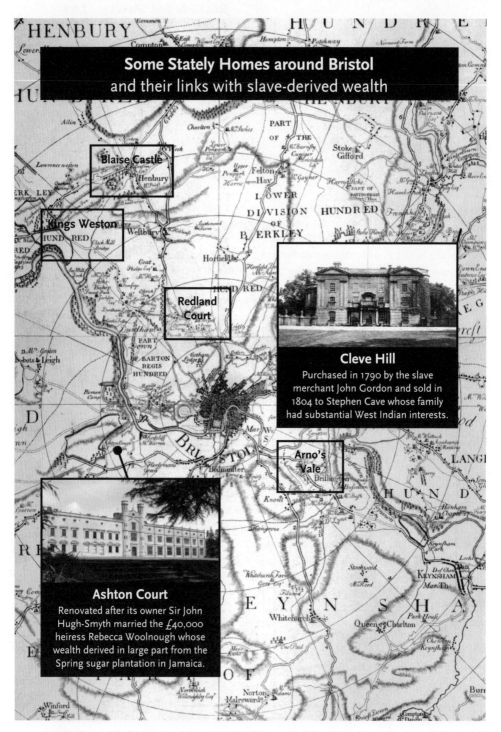

Some Stately Homes around Bristol
and their links with slave-derived wealth

Blaise Castle

Kings Weston

Redland Court

Cleve Hill
Purchased in 1790 by the slave merchant John Gordon and sold in 1804 to Stephen Cave whose family had substantial West Indian interests.

Arno's Vale

Ashton Court
Renovated after its owner Sir John Hugh-Smyth married the £40,000 heiress Rebecca Woolnough whose wealth derived in large part from the Spring sugar plantation in Jamaica.

Figure 14   The map is Benjamin Donn's 'This map of the country 11 miles around the city of Bristol', 1769. Bristol Museum and Art Gallery

Carleton Cumberbatch moved to Clifton sometime before 1821.[89] The solicitor James Tobin (1737–1817), son of a Nevis planter, worked in Bristol as a West India merchant and pro-slavery pamphleteer before retiring to Clifton.[90]

Green mansions: stately homes and slave wealth

An increasing number of merchants grown rich on the African and/or West Indian trades moved out to country houses as the eighteenth century wore on. As well as these 'pseudo-gentry' were those more established aristocrats who were able to enlarge or renovate their manor houses thanks to an infusion of West Indian wealth.[91] Some moved quite a distance from Bristol; Henry Hobhouse, for example, acquired land at Castle Cary, and the Harfords bought property in Cardiganshire in Wales.[92]

Though establishing the relations between slavery and the building of country houses is fraught with methodological snares, it is an essential task if we are to document the progress of a significant number of Bristol merchants from rough-edged slave-traders to refined country gentlemen. Quite a bit of painstaking detective work is involved and much more remains to be done. For a start, there is no register of country houses or substantial landowners for the Bristol region in this period, though Gloucestershire country houses are well documented by Nicholas Kingsley's modern study. The rest of the surrounding region is dependent on more partial accounts, including Robert Cooke's less scholarly but very useful *West Country Houses* and eighteenth-century accounts.[93] Wills, court records and various indentures and deeds need to be examined in relation to each individual property. Once the various owners are established, cross-referencing them with David Richardson's register of African merchants or with various Caribbean and American genealogical studies can establish direct connections with the slave trade, or with colonial slave plantations.

Donn's 1769 map of the Bristol region claims to include all the 'seats' and 'noted' houses in the area and is the best starting point for our survey. Dedicated to Bristol's civic and mercantile elite and financed by subscription, this is hardly an enterprise steeped in scientific detachment, nor does it distinguish between an ancient manor and a newly constructed house. However, it would have been in Donn's interests to have included as many properties as possible in his map, and in any case it is the most definitive local survey for that period.[94] Figure 14 highlights a few of the houses mentioned on the map whilst Table 6 details all those for whom I could establish some links with either the slave trade or slave plantations. Admittedly, this 'snapshot' approach does not take into account the way particular estates developed and changed hands over our period, but I have tried to detail the evolution of a few of these estates in the discussion that follows.

Some estates classified in Table 6 were built in the seventeenth century and had differing types of associations with colonial wealth. Others were erected or taken over at a later date by those with African or West Indian investments. It is outside the scope of this study to research the definitive history of each of the estates Donn lists, but enough research already exists to indicate that the connections between country house development in the Bristol region and slave-generated wealth are much more widespread than has previously been suggested.

Table 6 Houses listed on Donn's 1769 map of the country around Bristol with West Indian or African associations

Distance from Bristol	Name of house and/or area	Name of owner/ occupier
Within 1 mile	The Royal Fort	Thomas Tyndall
Within 2 miles	Redland Court	[John] Innys
	Between Redland and Westbury	The Misses Day
	—	The Farrs
	—	Mr Jones
	—	Mr Cornish
	Ashley	Mrs Elton
	—	Mr Bailey
	Arnos Court	Mr [William] Reeve
	Knowle	Mr Brickdale
	Clifton	Mr Brickdale
	Clifton	Mr Codrington
	Clifton	Mr Hobhouse
	Clifton	Mr Elton
	Clifton	Mr Freeman
Within 3 miles	Cote House, Westbury	Mr Phelps Esq.
	Stoke Bishop	Mrs Lloyd
	—	Whitchurch Esq.
	—	Mr Deane
	Stapleton	Mrs Perceval
	—	Mr Parsons
	—	Mr Arding
	Ashton Court	Smith Esq.
	Long Ashton	Mr Bayly
Within 4 miles	Blaise Castle, Henbury	Robert Farr
	Upper Penpark	Mr Harris
	Highridge	Baker Esq.
	Leigh Court	Mrs Gordon
	Cleeve Hill, Downend	Charles Bragge/John Gordon/Stephen Cave
Within 5 miles		Mr Brickdale
	Frenchay	Mr Harford
	Frenchay	Mr Champion
	Frenchay	Mr Draper
	Keynsham	The Duke of Chandos
	Northwick	Willoughby Esq.
	Kingsweston	Edward Southwell
6–10 miles (partial list)	—	Morgan Esq.
	Aust	Jefferies
	Tockingham	Casamajor
	Nr. Tockingham	Tonge
	Codrington [Doddington] Ct	Codrington
	Clevedon Court	Elton Esq.
	Dirham [Dyrham Court]	William Blathwayt

Donn lists over 100 houses within an eleven-mile radius of the city. This chapter pays particular attention to the 65 houses and/or their owners situated within a five-mile radius (Figure 14). At least 30 of these 65 can be confidently linked to wealth derived from the African and West Indian trades or to the ownership of slave plantations. Most of the houses within this five-mile radius are the houses of merchants. Table 6 lists all those houses associated with slave-generated wealth which stood within a five-mile radius of the city. It also includes a partial list of those houses within a six- to eleven-mile radius of the city that also had slaving associations.

Nearest to the centre of Bristol was the Royal Fort, built by Thomas Tyndall *c.* 1767. Tyndall, a banker, was the scion of a family which had had extensive interests in the African and West Indian trades since the late seventeenth century (Tyndall & Assheton, for example, were slaving agents in Jamaica for a number of Bristol merchants). This house (now part of the University of Bristol) was built in 1739 on the site of an older mansion which had previously been the residence of another Bristol merchant, philanthropist and slave plantation owner, John Elbridge.[95] The exquisite plasterwork and beautifully wrought staircase of Tyndall's new house attested to the growing gentility and refinement of Bristol's merchant class by the 1760s.

Just to the north-west of the Royal Fort was Redland Court, an estate historians traditionally associated with the 'wealthy London grocer' John Cossins, who acquired it in the 1730s and built a new mansion (on the site of an Elizabethan one) shortly thereafter. Its long-standing West Indian connections have been largely ignored. The house survives today (as a school), and so too does Redland Church, originally built by Cossins as the estate chapel.[96] Two stylized African heads on the back of the chapel are still visible, and have been assumed to have had no historical significance. In fact, the estate's history is shot through with Caribbean connections. It is worth devoting a few lines to it in order to illustrate this point.

The estate itself was held by the Bristolian Sir Robert Yeamans in the 1680s. His brother Sir John was, as we have seen, one of the early settlers of Barbados and a founder and Governor of South Carolina. Sir Robert bequeathed the Redland estate to his wife and on her death the estate was to revert to his nephew Colonel Robert Yeamans of Barbados, the son of Sir John. The Barbadian Yeamans sold the estate in the early eighteenth century to another Barbadian planter, Thomas Maycock, who in 1731 bequeathed the lifetime use of the estate to his mistress, Ann Ely (who also owned a slave plantation), with the proviso that it then went to his legitimate son Thomas Maycock. In 1735 the Redland estate was purchased from a Thomas Maycock by a City of London merchant and it changed hands twice more before it was purchased by John Cossins in 1738. The renovation of Redland Court (now Redland Girls' School) by Cossins appears to have coincided with his marriage to Martha Innys, a wealthy West Indian heiress. On his death in 1756, his wife inherited Redland Court and she in turn left it to her brothers Jeremy and John Innes.[97]

Still within a two-mile radius of the city centre, en route to Bath, stood Arnos Court and its flamboyantly gothic Black Castle. 'Ordered into existence' (*c.* 1756–8) by the Quaker copper-smelter, brass-founder and slave merchant William Reeve, the castle itself (which still stands) was made out of the slag from his brass foundries.[98] Reeve, who had extensive property holdings in Clifton and the Bristol region, went bankrupt in 1775. Robert Vigor and Thomas Cave were appointed, with another man, as commissioners for his estate, which appears to have been sold to a member of the Tonge family, whose fortunes were also founded in large measure by the slave trade.[99]

On the extensive downs which grace Bristol's north-west borders stood Cote House. Originally built by John Elbridge, it was occupied by 1769 by one William Phelps Esq.[100] Very possibly this was the heir of James Phelps who, Richardson records, captained a slaver for James Laroche in 1743 before launching his own ship later that same year.[101] The neighbouring Cotes estate seems to have been occupied in 1769 by Mrs Hort, whose name is connected with the Elbridge family and the sugar industry,[102] but sometime before 1814 George Daubeny IV, the heir of the Daubeny sugar-refining, glass and banking fortune, retired there.[103] Nearby Stoke Bishop (now Trinity Theological College) is probably of medieval origin but was enlarged to more stately proportions around 1666 by Sir Robert Cann. Cann, related to the Yeamans on his mother's side, owned properties in Jamaica at a time when the 'sugar revolution' caused planters to supplement their supply of indentured white labour with African slave labour. We have discussed his connection with the 'spiriting' of white labour to the plantations earlier in the book. A century later, the house appears to have been occupied by Mrs Lloyd, possibly a member of the Quaker Lloyds of Bristol, whose involvement in the Carolina trade and ownership of some Carolina plantations was supplemented by investments as African merchants.[104] Nearby Sneed (now Sneyd) Park was originally owned by the seventeenth-century merchant Joseph Jackson. I have been unable to trace any African or West Indian connection but have found that in 1823 the West Indian magnate and slave-owner Thomas Daniel Jr resided there.[105]

Not much is known about Henbury Manor or about Sir Samuel Astry, its owner in the late seventeenth century. We do know that an African slave, Scipio Africanus (d. 1719), lived in the Great House as a servant of Sir Samuel's son-in-law, the seventh Earl of Suffolk. The Earl lived at the Great House in Henbury until his own death in 1720. Scipio's tombstone can still be seen in the Henbury parish churchyard, though the fact of his actual burial there is not documented. The estate was split and passed on to members of the Smyth family, and eventually fell into the hands of the solicitor Jarrit Smith, who married a Smyth heiress. In 1764 Jarrit sold the Great House to his friend the grocer and African trader Michael Miller (formerly of Queen Square). Two years before, this canny lawyer had sold part of the estate, called Blaise estate, to Thomas Farr, and it is Farr's name which appears on Donn's map. Thomas Farr, who as we have seen had extensive interests in the slave trade, proceeded to build a £3000 folly called Blaise Castle, the better, it was reputedly said, to view his ships sailing back up to Bristol. The Farrs' family role as active slave-traders was cut short by the American War of Independence, which caused Farr financial ruin. The estate was later sold to John Scandret Harford, a banker and partner in a wholesale ironmongers which traded to Africa. Harford demolished the old manor house at Henbury and built the fine Blaise Castle House in 1792.[106]

Other Bristol slave-traders also moved out to country residences which their wealth enabled them to 'improve'. Tockingham Court, which was purchased by merchant and slave-ship investor Lewis Casamajor (d. 1743)[107] in 1753, was substantially enlarged, and sold in the 1780s to Samuel Peach, a Bristol banker and slave-ship owner. Peach was the father-in-law of Henry Cruger MP, who himself had plantations in Jamaica and St Croix.[108] Clevedon Court estate was purchased by Sir Abraham Elton I after 1717, but his grandson, another Sir Abraham and the fourth baronet, substantially renovated it over the period 1761–88.[109]

Thomas Player rebuilt Cleve Hill House, an old manor, in the early eighteenth century, and in 1736 Charles Bragge inherited it. Bragge married into the Bathurst family, whose members had long been involved in both African and West Indian affairs (Benjamin Bathurst was Deputy Governor of the Leeward Islands in the late seventeenth century and a heavy investor in the Royal African Company). His son, who took the name Bathurst (and served as a Tory MP for Bristol from 1796 to 1807 before becoming Treasurer of the Navy), kept the rights to the manor but sold the house to the slave merchant John Gordon in 1790. In 1804 both the house and the manor were purchased by Stephen Cave Esq. The Cave family had investments in banking, the glass industry and Caribbean plantations, and Stephen's second son married into the Cumberbatch family of Barbados.[110]

At times, slave-produced wealth could enable country gentry to renovate their properties – a case in point being Ashton Court. Sir John Hugh-Smyth, the son of Jarrit Smith and Florence Smyth, married the £40,000 heiress Rebecca Woolnough, whose wealth derived in large measure from the Spring plantation in Jamaica, and began to improve his property and dress his servants in fancy livery thereafter.[111]

Plantation wealth could ease the erection of grand houses by the grander gentry in less direct ways. Take Dyrham, a house built by William Blathwayt in the mid-eighteenth century. Blathwayt is perhaps best remembered as Secretary of State for both James II and William III and as MP for Bath until 1710. Blathwayt took an active interest in the African trade, concurring with his acquaintance John Cary about its importance. Blathwayt also took a personal interest in the Caribbean, growing wealthy in no small measure because of the emoluments connected with his posts as Clerk in the Plantation Office, Secretary to the Lords of Trade, and Surveyor and Auditor General of the Royal Revenue in Virginia, Jamaica, Barbados, the Leeward Islands and other colonies. Christopher Jeaffreson, a young squire sojourning in the Caribbean, observed in the early 1680s that Blathwayt expected 'gifts' whenever he was asked to assist the interests of planters and officials in St Christopher (St Kitts).[112] Blathwayt inherited Dyrham Park on his marriage in 1686 to Mary Wynter, whose family wealth also owed much to colonial exploits in the Caribbean, and began to renovate it in 1691.[113]

Blathwayt was a close friend of Robert Southwell, government envoy and MP, who in 1679 bought the Kingsweston estate from Sir Humphrey Hooks, a man with 'important family and political ties in Bristol, Gloucestershire and Barbados'.[114] Robert refurbished his house in 1680. His son, Edward, asked Vanbrugh to design a new house around 1710. A government minister for Ireland, Edward seems (like his father) to have been actively involved in West Indian administration as well. In any case, as MP for Bristol, and as member of the 'Gentlemen Natives of Gloucestershire', he was intimately connected with advancing the interests and concerns of Bristol's slaving merchants.[115] In the 1780s the Kingsweston estate was purchased by the sugar merchant and Jamaican planter Caleb Dickinson, whose son refurbished the house.

Codrington Court (as it appears on the Donn map) was purchased by Christopher Codrington II (1668–1710), Fellow of All Souls College and Governor of the Leeward Islands. His large fortune (he left £10,000 to All Souls College, Oxford) derived in good measure from his grandfather's acquisition of extensive West Indian plantations, including properties in Barbados, Antigua and Barbuda.[116] His heir, Christopher Bethel Codrington, built Doddington House at the end of the eighteenth century, whilst his family's involvement in Antigua continued well into the next century.

The relation of other properties to the slave trade awaits further research. Wraxall Court, originally built by Samuel Gorges, and rebuilt in 1720 by John Codrington, is probably riven through with slave-trading connections since the Gorges family were associated with holdings in Barbados and John Codrington is possibly the younger son of Christopher Codrington I. On a more modest scale, Oldbury Court House, which belonged to the Winstone family in the eighteenth century, was purchased by the 'West Indian sugar baron' Thomas Graeme, who called in Humphrey Repton to remodel the gardens in 1800.[117] Naish House of Portishead (not on the Donn map) was built in 1785 by James Gordon, a Scot who had made a fortune from his West Indian plantation.[118]

Gentility

The merchants of Georgian Bristol had a reputation for boorishness and greed, and for being 'as rough mannered as their sailors'.[119] One mid-Georgian contemporary sneeringly observed that they even preferred the street to the more refined surroundings of their newly built Corn Exchange.[120]

It is certainly true that at the end of the seventeenth century Bristol was not conducive to living a 'life of the mind'. Alderman Swymmer, resplendent though he might have appeared in his aldermanic robes, attended by his black slave, was revealed by his letters to be a crude and grasping fellow, and his son Anthony, who served as the city's mayor, reportedly combined immense wealth with a boorish parsimony.[121] It is symbolic, too, that the first work to be printed by Bristol's first printer, William Bonney, was John Cary's *Essay on . . . Trade* (1695),[122] and in 1704 the mercantile bent of the city's cultural life can be discerned in the range of books Bonney, who also edited the city's earliest newspaper, had himself taken to selling:

Bibles, Common Prayer Books . . . Primers, Shop-books, pockets books, Paper to hand Rooms, writing Paper, vocal and instrumental music books and blank ale licences; also blank Commissions for privateer men of war . . . [and] a new map of . . . England and Wales containing all the cities and market-towns with roads from Town to Town, the days on which their several markets are kept . . . and what towns are navigable.[123]

As Thomas Cox observed of the city in 1727, 'It is very populous; but the People give up themselves to Trade so entirely that nothing of the Politeness and Gaiety of Bath is to be seen here.'[124]

But as prosperity increased, so did the range of books and cultural events available in the city. Even as Cox wrote, the climate was visibly changing. In the autumn of 1726, Bristolians were invited to attend either the London Coffee House or the Tolzey to hear lectures on the philosophy of John Locke, to see an orrery at the Castle Green Tavern and to attend a performance of *Oroonoko* at the theatre in St Augustine's Back.[125] By the early 1730s booksellers were advertising – along with the Bibles and the Psalters, the pocket books and the navigation manuals – novels, history books and books on architecture.[126]

This is not to say that merchants were transformed immediately. The wealthy grocer Michael Miller bridled at having his written style corrected by his young clerk (later the philosopher) David Hume and retorted that he had made £20,000 by his English and would not have it improved.[127]

But, whatever their polish, early eighteenth-century merchants like Joseph Vigor, Henry Tonge and Thomas Freke were socially ambitious and canny enough to amass considerable properties in and around Bristol which enabled their descendants' more formal ascent into gentility.[128] Bristol shops were selling luxury items like chocolate and coffee as early as 1750, and silks and brocades, as well as 'cloths for the African trade', were advertised increasingly in the local press.[129] A number of African merchants established one of the country's earliest provincial banks in 1750 and other West Indian and African merchants established more soon after. These banks (which were later to be absorbed into the National Westminster Bank) had originally functioned in part to help finance the West Indian trade. These banks also provided their founders with a new and refined commercial persona.[130]

By 1760, luxury had challenged parochialism and there was talk of 'the London itch' – that is, a desire to ape the manners of the metropolis. As the economy expanded, the dividing lines between merchant and manufacturer, professional and squire, were further blurred by prosperity, partnerships and marriage.[131] 'Mr Thomas Farr of the Custom House', who died in 1760, had a collection of 300 fine prints, whilst his nephew Thomas Farr, of Blaise Castle, was eulogized in a poem[132] as 'The *connoisseur*, the merchant and the friend'.[133] The Eltons, whose founding father Abraham I had started life as the son of a lowly road scavenger, were grand enough by the third generation not only to improve the fabric of Clevedon Court but to cultivate a newer, more self-consciously cultured identity.[134] When Philip John Miles built Leigh Court in 1814 on the grounds of an older house, he filled it with a Continental art collection as a badge of his discernment.[135] As Hancock points out, the acquisition of country houses was not only about social transformation but also about the transformation of self.[136]

As luxury followed riches, then, refinement followed luxury. The wealth injected into the economy by both the African trade and the slave plantations of the Americas helped to make this process possible. The historiography of consumption in the Georgian era dealing as it does with the way such consumption fulfilled the aspirations and shaped the communal identities of social groups, needs to reconsider consumption's economic and political roots. To blandly ascribe the increase of wealth to the increase of 'colonial trade' is to fail to consider the importance of slavery in the production of that wealth. Surely that is a point worth exploring.

This peculiar configuration of gentility and brutality became increasingly difficult, as the nineteenth century wore on, for the descendants of Bristol's Africa and West Indian merchants to acknowledge. Nevertheless, the evidence shows that Bristol's urban renaissance was exceptionally reliant on the exploitation and dislocation of African labour.

Notes

1 A shorter version of this chapter has appeared as 'Squares of Distinction, Webs of Interest: Gentility, Urban Development and the SlaveTrade in Bristol . . .', in *Slavery and Abolition*, vol. 21, no, 3 (2000), pp. 21–47. I wish to thank Gad Heuman and the editorial board for their helpful comments about a draft version of this article and for their cooperation in allowing me to use this material here in this book.

2 Andor Gomme, Michael Jenner and Bryan Little, *Bristol: An Architectural History* (London, 1979).

3 Anton Bantock, *The Later Smyths of Ashton Court from Their Letters, 1741–1802* (Bristol, 1984), p. 155.

4 For an up-to-date perspective on this debate, see Seymour Drescher, 'Capitalism and Slavery after Fifty Years', *Slavery and Abolition*, vol. 18, no. 3 (1997), pp. 212–27.

5 Jonathan Barry, 'Provincial Town Culture, 1640–1780: Urbane or Civic?', in Joan Pittock and Andrew Wear (eds), *Interpretation and Cultural History* (Basingstoke, 1990), pp. 198–234; Neil McKendrick, John Brewer and J. H. Plumb (eds), *The Birth of a Consumer Society: The Commercialization of Eighteenth-Century England* (London, 1982); John Brewer and Ann Bermingham (eds), *The Consumption of Culture, 1600–1800: Image, Object, Text* (London, 1995); John Brewer, *The Pleasures of the Imagination: English Culture in the Eighteenth Century* (London, 1997). Only two essays (Felicity Nussbaum's 'Polygamy, *Pamela* and the Preoccupation of Empire', pp. 217–32, and Kathleen Wilson's 'The Good, the Bad and the Impotent: Imperialism and the Politics of Identity in Georgian England', pp. 237–63) out of the 26 in *The Consumption of Culture* explicitly address the transatlantic slave trade in their consideration of consumption and cultural activity. Amanda Vickery's *The Gentleman's Daughter: Women's Lives in Georgian England* (New Haven and London, 1998) is similarly silent on the subject.

6 Only J. R. Ward's article 'Speculative Housing in Bristol and Clifton, 1783–1793', *Business History*, vol. 20, no. 1 (1978), pp. 3–19, specifically addresses the link between West Indian wealth and urban development in the latter part of the eighteenth century and then only for the decade after 1783. A partial exception to this general tendency is Donald Jones's book on Bristol's most genteel suburb, which begins to substantiate such links, documenting as it does that the original owners of at least three substantial

Georgian residences, Clifton Hill House, Clifton Court (now Chesterfield Hospital) and Clifton Wood House, were all involved in the African slave trade; Donald Jones, *A History of Clifton* (Chichester and Guildford, 1992), pp. 32, 39–46, 82–3, 98. Alan F. Williams, 'Bristol Port Plans and Improvement Schemes of the Eighteenth Century', *Transactions of the Bristol and Gloucestershire Archaeological Society*, vol. 80–1 (1962–3), pp. 138–40, does mention briefly the importance of the slave trade to the city's urban development.

7 Jonathan Barry's 1991 essay 'Provincial Town Culture, 1680–1780', whilst explicitly admitting the shift in Bristol's economy towards the colonial trade from 1650 onwards, does not develop this in any detail. Ken Morgan's 1993 book on Bristol and the Atlantic trade is too focused on entrepreneurship and relative economic decline in the late eighteenth century to concentrate much attention on urban development; see Kenneth Morgan, *Bristol and the Atlantic Trade in the Eighteenth Century* (Cambridge, 1993); so too is his richly documented and important prosopographical study of Bristol West India merchants, 'Bristol West India Merchants in the Eighteenth Century', *Transactions of the Royal Historical Society*, sixth series, no. 3, pp. 185–206.

8 Peter Borsay, *The English Urban Renaissance: Culture and Society in the Provincial Town, 1660–1770* (Oxford, 1989).

9 *Ibid.*, pp. 16–28.

10 *Ibid.*, p. 28.

11 *Ibid.*, pp. 32–8.

12 Morgan, *Bristol and the Atlantic Trade*, pp. 132–3.

13 Patrick McGrath, *The Merchant Venturers of Bristol: A History of the Society of Merchant Venturers of the City of Bristol from Its Origin to the Present Day* (Bristol: Society of Merchant Venturers, 1975), pp. x–xi.

14 See David Hancock's pioneering *Citizens of the World: London Merchants and the Integration of the British Atlantic Community, 1735–1785* (Cambridge, 1995), pp. 37–8, 172ff., which examines London merchants who were involved in slave-trading along with a range of other business activities.

15 Hancock, *Citizens of the World*, pp. 320–47.

16 By 'prosopographical' I mean research that investigates the biographical data of a group of historical actors to uncover the connections amongst them as well as information about them as individuals.

17 Hancock, *Citizens of the World*; David Richardson, *Bristol, Africa and the Eighteenth-Century Slave Trade to America*, 4 vols (Bristol: Bristol Record Society, 1986, 1987, 1991 and 1996); David Richardson, *The Bristol Slave Traders: A Collective Portrait* (Bristol: Bristol Historical Association, 1985); Morgan, *Bristol and the Atlantic Trade*; Roger Leech, *The Topography of Medieval and Early Modern Bristol: Part I* (Bristol: Bristol Record Society, 1987) and his *The Precinct of the University of Bristol: Medieval and Early Modern Topography* (Bristol: Bristol Record Society, 2000). I have also availed myself of the researches of urban archaeologists working in Bristol.

18 I should like to thank Guy Grannum of the Public Record Office, Kew, for drawing my attention to the Chancery Masters' Exhibits in this regard.

19 Both are held at the Bristol City Museum and Art Gallery, which kindly gave me permission to reproduce them here.

20 Leech, *Topography of Medieval and Early Modern Bristol*, pp. 152–9.

21 Bristolians such as Aldworth Elbridge, John and Sir Robert Yeamans, John Combe, Azariah Pinney, Thomas Cann, John Knight Jr and his son all had interests in sugar plantations in the Caribbean. For Aldworth Elbridge, see Donald Jones, 'The Elbridge, Woolnough and Smith Families of Bristol in the Eighteenth Century with Special Reference to the Spring Plantation, Jamaica', M.Litt. dissertation, University of Bristol, 1972, A712, p. 40; for John Combe, see V. Olivier (ed.), *Caribbeana: Being Miscellaneous*

Papers Relating to the History, Genealogy, Topography and Antiquities of the British West Indies, 6 vols (London, 1910), vol. 5, p. 279; R. S. Mortimer, 'Quakerism in Seventeenth Century Bristol, 1654–1700', MA thesis, University of Bristol, 1946, A170, p. 326. The others mentioned are fully documented in Chapter 1.

22 Borsay, *English Urban Renaissance*, p. 145, cites the existence of four coffee houses from perhaps as early as 1666, but the earliest record I could find of a coffee house in the city was 1679 in BCRL, extract from a deed dated 18 April 1677, High Street bundle, 'Inns and Taverns', p. 6, Braikenridge Collection. For references to Bristol's other coffee houses, see *Felix Farley's Bristol Journal*, 28 February 1758 (Exchange Coffee House), 7 February 1761 (Maritime Coffee House and Tavern), 27 March 1763 (Foster's Coffee House) and *Bristol Journal*, 2 May 1772 (American Coffee House and the West-India Coffee House).

23 McGrath, *The Merchant Venturers of Bristol*, p. 68.

24 John Latimer, *The History of the Society of the Merchant Venturers of the City of Bristol* (Bristol 1903), p. 178; John Latimer, *The Annals of Bristol in the Seventeenth Century* (Bristol, 1900), p. 368; C. M. MacInnes, *England and Slavery* (Bristol, 1934), pp. 27–8. Patrick McGrath, *Merchants and Merchandise in Seventeenth-Century Bristol* (Bristol: Bristol Record Society, 1955), p. xxii, plays down the number of Africa-bound illegal traders by referring to the fact that few were ever seized by the authorities, but it seems likely that the early eighteenth-century practice of Africa-bound ships sailing under the fiction that they were bound for Madeira or Cape Verde may have some relevance for the period before 1698. Certainly the cargo on some of the ships listed by McGrath as Madeira-bound seems to have been destined for a West African market; see Richardson, *Bristol, Africa and the Eighteenth-Century Slave Trade*, vol. 1, p. xiii.

25 See BRO, I. V. Hall's notes on the Swymmer family, 36722 Box 10, regarding warehouses and sugar trading which Hall derived from the minutes of Bristol's Common Council and from the port books. For Swymmer's loan, see Patrick McGrath (ed.), *Records Relating to the Society of Merchant Venturers of the City of Bristol in the Seventeenth Century* (Bristol: Bristol Record Society, 1952), p. 153. New research by Roger Leech corroborates my argument that slave-based wealth stimulated urban development in the late seventeenth century. See his *The St. Michael Precinct of the University of Bristol: Medieval and Early Modern Topography* (Bristol: Bristol Record Society, 2000).

26 The Bucks' 'Prospects of Bristol' are in the possession of the Bristol City Museum and Art Gallery.

27 Glass cones are proudly pictured on the bottommost left-hand picture on the map's margins, not shown in the portion of the map reproduced here. See also BRO, Temple Parish, 1720–9, 2A27; BRO, Poor Rates for St Mary Redcliffe Parish, December 1721, and *Farley's Bristol Newspaper*, 21 November 1730, for the sale of a glass house in the adjoining St Philip and St Jacob's parish, and 28 November 1731, for a reference to Humphrey Perrot's glass houses in Temple Street.

28 BRO, 2A27 Temple Parish 1720–9; BRO, Poor Rates for St Mary Redcliffe Parish, December 1721. See also Joe Bettey (ed.), 'A Bristol Glassworks *c.* 1730', in Patrick McGrath (ed.), *A Bristol Miscellany* (Gloucester: Bristol Record Society, 1985), pp. 15–20.

29 Daniel Defoe, *A Tour thro' Great Britain*, ed. Samuel Richardson (New York and London, 1974), vol. 2, p. 271. BRO, Poor Rate Book, June–December 1721, for St Mary Redcliffe; BCRL, see for example the order for 40 'whicker bottles of brandy' in the Isaac Hobhouse papers, specifically the 'Estimate for a cargo for purchase of 250 negroes at Bonny' (n.d.), Jefferies Collection, vol. 13, p. 9; PRO, invoice from Lucas, Pater & Coathupe, 4 May 1792, James Rogers Papers, CO107/3; Invoice from Wadham, Ricketts & Co., 21 December 1790, James Rogers Papers, CO107/6; Invoice from

Stevens, Cave & Co., 3 May 1792, James Rogers Papers, CO107/3 all show trade goods destined for African slaving ships owned by James Rogers.

30 Thomas (d. 1730), Philip and William appear to be brothers; PRO, will of William Freke, May 1731, PROB 11/644. See also BRO, Freke Papers, BRO, 133325 (40) and (60), and will of Thomas Freke, 4 August 1730, AC/JS/40. BRO, V. Hall notes on indenture dated 10 December 1704 of Old Market Sugar Refinery, 36722 Box 13; and PRO, will of Thomas Freke, PCC, 6 March 1706, which refers to his nephews Philip and Thomas Freke; both state that Freke's partners in the sugar house included the slaving merchants Francis Rogers and Christopher Shuter. For Philip Freke's parliamentary candidacy, see W. R. Williams, *Parliamentary History of the County of Gloucestershire* (Hereford: privately printed, 1898), p. 124.

31 *FFBJ*, 7 June 1760. The article refers to the sale of Berrow's goods and the letting of an already established glass firm, Crosse & Berrow's. Berrow is listed as a member of the Company of Merchants Trading to Africa in 1755; BCRL, Jefferies Collection, vol. 13, pp. 159–161.

32 Joseph Vigor was a partner in John Coster's brass battery in 1709; PRO, *Hobbs* v. *Coster*, C11/2246/14. In 1742 Thomas Goldney III records that John's son William Vigor (listed elsewhere as a gentleman) married a Mrs Rondeau. He died in 1761. By 1760, John's grandson Robert Vigor and the African merchant Isaac Hobhouse's son Henry Hobhouse are both part of a corporation-appointed commission to supervise the building of a new Bristol bridge joining Redcliffe and Temple to the rest of the city. By 1784 Robert would become the co-owner of a glass house on premises leased from another prominent African merchant, Joseph Harford; *FFBJ*, 19 February 1760; BRO, Harford to Vigor and Stevens, 4 November 1783, 151784; P. K. Stembridge, *The Goldney Family, a Bristol Merchant Dynasty* (Bristol: Bristol Record Society, 1998), pp. 154, 159.

33 Richardson, *Bristol, Africa and the Eighteenth Century Slave Trade*, vol. 1, pp. xxii, 14, 16, 109, 117, 126–7, 131, 141, 143, 151, 172, 175–6, and Richardson, *The Bristol Slave Traders*, p. 30.

34 Bankruptcy statement of Edmund Saunders, 10 August 1740; BRO, AC/JS 62 (20); see also notice of auction of Saunders's house in *FFBJ*, 31 March 1743.

35 *Farley's Bristol Newspaper*, 25 February 1726/1727 (these dates refer to the old calendar), and Walter Ison, *The Georgian Buildings of Bristol* (London, 1952), p. 156. The Captain Bartlett also of Guinea Street who died in April 1760 was likely to have been the slave-ship master of the same name who co-owned a number of slave ships and invested in some eight slaving voyages from Bristol between 1730 and 1745; *FFBJ*, 12 April 1760, and Richardson, *Bristol, Africa and the Eighteenth Century Slave Trade*, vol. 2, pp. 6, 19, 40, 49, 53, 72, 92, 134. Saunders's original residence still survives.

36 Celia Fiennes described the Marsh on her visit to Bristol in 1698 as by 'a long rope yard which is encompas'd by trees on either side . . . which compasses round a large space of ground which is called the Marsh' where the 'Company of the Town' would engage in 'the diversion of walking in the evening'; Christopher Morris (ed.), *The Journeys of Celia Fiennes* (London, 1949), p. 238.

37 See Ison, *Georgian Buildings*, and William Barret, *The Antiquities of the City of Bristol* (Bristol, 1789), p. 690. A look at Richardson, *Bristol, Africa and the Eighteenth-Century Slave Trade*, vol. 2, pp. 175, 206, shows that Teast's involvement in the slave trade was more indirect. He seems to have invested in only one slave ship, but benefited from the trade in the repair and refitting of slave ships at his dock.

38 C. F. W. Denning, *The Eighteenth-Century Architecture of Bristol* (Bristol: Arrowsmith, 1923), pp. 71, 103.

39 W. Barrett, *The History . . . of the City of Bristol*, pp. 697, 699. Combe served as sheriff of Bristol in 1726 and mayor in 1740.

40 W. R. Williams, *Parliamentary History of the County of Gloucestershire* (Hereford: privately printed, 1898), p. 125; see *BWI*, 2 May 1752, regarding the funeral of Henry Combe Esq. and his 'immense fortune'.

41 BRO, will of Becher Fleming, 1718. I am grateful to Edward Beaumont, a descendant of the Becher family, for the information about the relationship between John and his sons.

42 See Francis Greenacre, *Marine Artists of Bristol: Nicholas Pocock (1740–1821), Joseph Walter (1783–1856)* (Bristol, 1982) and David Cordingly, *Nicholas Pocock (1740–1821)* (London, 1986). The sketches of the *Jason* and the *Southwell*, both slavers turned privateers, are part of the collection of the Bristol City Museum and Art Gallery.

43 *Gentleman's Magazine*, 30 September 1739, cited in W. R. Williams, *Parliamentary History*, p. 125. Coster also had a dwelling house in College Green adjoining Bristol Cathedral; *Farley's Bristol Newspaper*, 26 August 1738; PRO, will of Thomas Coster, 21 November 1739, PROB 11.699 sig. 230.

44 For property in College Green, Bristol, see BRO, Bristol Bargain Book, 7 August 1700, p. 93, 04335(8); PRO, *Coster* v. *Ball*, C/11/2246/14, for joint stock company set up for a brass battery works near Bristol united with the Eshare brass wire society; for John Coster, see John Latimer, *The Annals of Bristol in the Eighteenth Century* (Bristol, 1893), pp. 66–7, and Joan Day, *Bristol Brass: A History of the Industry* (London, 1973).

45 Richardson, *Bristol, Africa and the Eighteenth-Century Slave Trade*, vol. 2, pp. 88, 15, 64, 68, 7, 15, 64, 68, 88, 100; PRO, will of Thomas Coster, 21 November 1739, PROB 11.699 sig.230.

46 PRO, will of Henry Tonge Esq., proved February 1762, PROB 11/873; WRO, Tonge Family Bible, 226/2.

47 Thomas Farr died in 1760; see *FFBJ*, 2 February 1760. Richard Farr was his son or brother. According to Philip M. Hamer (ed.), *The Papers of Henry Laurens* (Columbia, SC, 1968, 1969), p. 210n, Richard Farr Jr was a member of the Society of Merchant Venturers in 1737, Warden in 1748 and 1759 and Master in 1762 as well as a member of the Bristol Corporation 1746–82, sheriff 1746, mayor 1763 and alderman 1767–82. He died on 15 May 1782. Richard's four sons, Thomas, John, William and Paul, were also prominent merchants.

48 *FFBJ*, 23 February 1760 and 21 November 1761. The *Kingston*, the final ship in which he invested, was taken by the French after delivering slaves to Charleston, South Carolina; see Richardson, *Bristol, Africa and the Eighteenth-Century Slave Trade*, vol. 2, pp. 108, 112, 123.

49 *FFBJ*, 17 May 1760.

50 BRO, Poor Rate Book, Parish of St Stephen, September–March 1732, PR/ST5/25–33; Richardson, *Bristol, Africa and the Eighteenth-Century Slave Trade*, vol. 1, pp. 188, xxi–xxii, 26, 32, 38, 44, 55–7. There is a reference to the African House in Prince's Street in *FFBJ*, 21 January 1758.

51 Defoe, *A Tour*, p. 271.

52 Ison, *Georgian Buildings*, p. 209. According to Richardson, *Bristol, Africa and the Eighteenth-Century Slave Trade*, vol. 3, pp. 175, 206, Teast was a part-owner of one slaving vessel and benefited from the rebuilding and refitting of at least one other.

53 Denning, *Eighteenth-Century Architecture*, p. 37. See also Pat Hughes, Jane Root and Christopher Heath, *The History and Development of Queen Square: Appendix to the Application to the Heritage Lottery Fund by Bristol City Council for the Restoration and Enhancement of Queen Square* (Bristol: Bristol City Council, 1996), p. 16. My thanks go to Stephen Price, Director of Bristol City Museum and Art Gallery, for this last reference.

54 Steven Poole, '"Till Our Liberties Be Secure": Popular Sovereignty and Public Space in Bristol, 1780–1850', *Urban History*, vol. 26, no. 1 (1996), pp. 40–54; Borsay, *English Urban Renaissance*, pp. 73–5.

55 Borsay, *English Urban Renaissance*, p. 75. Other squares included St James's, Orchard and Dowry Squares by the mid-1720s and by the 1770s Berkeley, King and Brunswick Squares; Hughes *et al.*, *The History and Development of Queen Square*, p. 69.

56 BRO, Bristol Bargain Book, 8 December 1720, p. 160, 04335(8). Damer Powell, in *Bristol Privateers and Ships of War* (Bristol: Arrowsmiths, 1930), states that William Whetstone Rogers was a member of the council of the Bahamas and one of the three chief merchants of the Royal African Company. He was born in Bristol *c.* 1706 and died in Whydah, Dahomey (now Benin), in 1735.

57 John Day, Master of the Society of Merchant Venturers in 1716 and Mayor of Bristol the following year, led the local campaign to stop the Royal African Company from attempting to reimpose its monopoly. He was an elder member of the Day family, who were heavily involved in the slave trade. John Day also invested in three other slaving voyages before 1738; Richardson, *Bristol, Africa and the Eighteenth-Century Slave Trade*, vol. 1, pp. 8, 15, 20, 24, 32, 53; W. E. Minchinton (ed.), *The Trade of Bristol in the Eighteenth Century* (Bristol: Bristol Record Society, 1957).

58 Latimer, *The Annals of Bristol in the Seventeenth Century*, p. 478. Nathaniel Day, who was listed as a soap boiler, served as mayor in 1705; Latimer, *The Annals of Bristol in the Eighteenth Century*, p. 534. St Peter's Sugar-House appears to have refined slave-produced sugar from the Azores or Madeira.

59 BRO, Marriage Settlement of Peter Day and Miss Elton, 20 October 1711, 59181 (46).

60 Romney Sedgwick, *The History of Parliament: The House of Commons, 1715–54* (London: HMSO, 1970), vol. 1, p. 2. The *Earle Gally* was pressed into service at Jamaica by the British government, presumably because of the outbreak of the War of the Spanish Succession in 1702, but its cargo of Caribbean goods was brought back to Bristol by another ship. For details of the voyage, see Richardson, *Bristol, Africa and the Eighteenth-Century Slave Trade*, vol. 1, p. 3. See Chapter 1, Table 2 regarding his career as an MP.

61 BRO, Poor Rates for St Stephen's Parish 1711, PR/St S/9. For Isaac Elton's plantation, see Margaret Elton, *Annals of the Elton Family: Bristol Merchants and Somerset Landowners* (Stroud, 1994), p. 39.

62 He died leaving £100,000; Elton, *Annals of the Elton Family*, pp. 16, 53.

63 Elton, *Annals of the Elton Family*, pp. 38–48. Elton and Coster chose the very sculptor who carved the stone monument of Edward Colston, Bristol benefactor and director of the Royal African Company, in All Saints Church.

64 *Ibid.*, pp. 17–20.

65 PRO, *Freke* v. *Freke*, C/108/4. Thomas also seems to have had a half-share of a property in King St; BRO, Bristol Bargain Book, 30 November 1700, p. 105, 04335(8).

66 See Richardson, *Bristol, Africa and the Eighteenth-Century Slave Trade*, vol. 2 for Laroche's activities.

67 Derived from Richardson, *Bristol, Africa and the Eighteenth-Century Slave Trade*, vols 1 and 2.

68 PRO, Isaac Hobhouse to Thomas Coster MP, 23 April 1737, SP36/40, vol. 249. Neither is listed by Richardson, *Bristol, Africa and the Eighteenth-Century Slave Trade*, vol. 2, p. 86 as an investor in this particular venture, which, as Hobhouse's letter confirms, was managed by Edmund Saunders. It seems clear, however, that Hobhouse was an investor and likely that Coster was. In any event, Hobhouse seems to have had no reservations about the propriety of lobbying Coster in his official capacity to look after his (Hobhouse's) commercial interests. For some of Hobhouse's other liaisons with Coster, see Richardson, *Bristol, Africa and the Eighteenth-Century Slave Trade*, vol. 2, pp. 15, 66, 77, 100.

69 *FFBJ*, 7 February 1761.

70 *Sketchley's Bristol Directory for 1775*, ed. B. Little (Bath, 1971).

71 Richardson, *Bristol, Africa and the Eighteenth-Century Slave Trade*, vol. 3, pp. 162, 180. See also Richardson, *The Bristol Slave Traders*.

72 This information was taken from an unpublished study by P. Bright, a descendant of the Bright family, a copy of which was made available by the Bristol City Museum and Art Gallery.

73 Hamer (ed.), *The Papers of Henry Laurens*, vol. 1, pp. 209, 210, 214, 252; vol. 3, p. 33n; vol. 4, p. 110.

74 D. Richardson, 'The Bristol Slave Trade to Colonial South Carolina', *Slavery and Abolition*, vol. 12, no. 3 (December 1991), pp. 138, 144, 146; Hamer (ed.), *The Papers of Henry Laurens*, vol. 2, p. 212.

75 BRO, Schedule for the Vanderhorst and Duncombe Papers, and 8032 (5) and (49).

76 See Day, *Bristol Brass*, p. 169, on the reluctance of the Harfords to reveal the links between their brassware and the slave trade.

77 BRO, Theatre Royal Register Book, 8978 (1a) includes the names of Bright, Harford, Laroche, Miller and Farr amongst the subscribers. Many of the other subscribers are also involved in either the slave or the sugar trade.

78 BCRL, Jefferies Collection, vol. 8.

79 *Sketchley's Bristol Directory for 1775*, p. 117.

80 E. Baigent, 'Economy and Society in Eighteenth Century English Towns: Bristol in the 1770s', in Dietrich Denicke and Gareth Shaw (eds), *Urban Historical Geography: Recent Progress in Britain and Germany* (Cambridge, 1988), p. 123.

81 Jones, *A History of Clifton*, pp. 39–40, BCRL, Jefferies Collection, vol. 13, p. 159; Olivier (ed.), *Caribbeana*, vol. 1, pp. 153–4.

82 Jones, *A History of Clifton*, pp. 86–7.

83 BRO, Pedler and Wheeler Family Papers, 21500 (1a) and the will of Thomas Pedler Jr, 17 January 1823, 21500(M). Pedler refers to his 'reputed' natural daughter Jane Pedler, who was a slave on Catherinemount Estate in Jamaica and to whom he bequeathed £10 per annum, as he did to his three children by Jane Boswell, but he also gives money to Jane to effect her freedom. Thomas Pedler Jr's relationship to his namesake who built Beaufort House is in a note in BRO, 21500 (2)(R).Other Clifton residents who built houses there include Samuel Worrall, a Bristol solicitor and the clerk to the Society of Merchant Venturers, who represented Bristol's interests in the African slave trade to the Commissioners for Trade and Plantations in 1757. In 1776 he purchased the prestigious Church House in Clifton and the year after built Shortgrove House there; see BRO, Worrall Family Papers, 12149 (5). The Nevis reference is from a will of 1650 cited in John Titford, 'Settlers of the Old Empire: The West Indies: Nevis: Some Selected Examples of Transcripts of Records', *Family Tree Magazine* (November 1999), p. 59.

84 The merchants involved were John Cave, Joseph Harford, George Daubeny, Richard Vaughan and William Fry; see BCRL, Jefferies Collection, vol. 12, p. 195.

85 Both men were part-owners of at least one African ship in 1797; Richardson, *Bristol, Africa and the Eighteenth-Century Slave Trade*, vol. 4 (1996), p. 7; for their Honduran holdings, see Ward, 'Speculative Housing in Bristol', p. 16n., and for other speculative activities see Penelope Mellor, *A Kingsdown Community* (Bristol, 1985).

86 Olivier (ed.), *Caribbeana*, vol. 1, p. 24.

87 Ward, 'Speculative Housing in Bristol', p. 11. They were both members of an anti-abolitionist consortium organized by the Bristol Merchant Venturers; Society of Merchant Venturers Hall, West India Trade Minutes, 15 April 1789.

88 Olivier (ed.), *Caribbeana*, vol. 1, p. 219.

89 See 'Monumental Inscriptions in England Relating to West Indians: Clifton Church Bristol', in Olivier (ed.), *Caribbeana*, vol. 2, pp. 309, 371, 377, 379; see also pp. 82–5 in the same volume. My thanks to Mary Campbell, who kindly lent me her list of Clifton church memorials. For Cumberbatch, see *Journal of the Barbados Museum Historical Society*, vol. 9, no. 1 (1941), pp. 42, 47–9.

90 Thanks to David Small, who showed me his manuscript on James Tobin which is to be submitted for publication. William Miles, who owned more than Jamaican plantations, married into the Berrow family of Clifton according to Bill Evans, 'Leigh Court' (unpublished manuscript, 1998). Thanks to Bill Evans for the loan of this manuscript. Another notable was Thomas Oliver Cave, the eldest son of the Bristol merchant and banker John Cave and the grandson of Lt. Gov. Thomas Oliver of Bristol, Boston, Massachusetts, and Antigua. The widow of Lewis Cuthbert, the owner of Clifton Plantation in Jamaica, died in Clifton, Bristol, in 1830. See Olivier (ed.), *Caribbeana*, vol. 2, p. 141. Thanks also to James Brennan for information on Lewis Cuthbert.

91 See Alistair Hennessy, 'Penrhyn Castle', *History Today* (January 1995), pp. 40–6. My thanks to Professor Hennessy for bringing this work to my attention. He is currently researching a longer piece on the links between British estates and Caribbean slavery.

92 W. E. Minchinton, 'The Merchants of Bristol in the Eighteenth Century', *Fédération Historique du Sud-Ouest, Actes du Colloque Franco-Britannique tenu à Bordeaux du 27 au 30 Septembre 1976*, pp. 185–200. Sociétés et Groupes Sociaux en Aquitaine et en Angleterre.

93 Nicholas Kingsley, *The Country Houses of Gloucestershire* (Cheltenham, 1989); Robert Cooke, *West Country Houses: An Illustrated Account of Some Country Houses and Their Owners in the Counties of Bristol, Gloucester, Somerset and Wiltshire . . . (Clifton, Bristol, 1957)*. Contemporary accounts consulted included Sir R. Atkyns, *The Ancient and Present State of Gloucestershire* (London: 1712); S. Rudder, *A New History of Gloucestershire* (Cirencester, 1779); F. Weinard and Revd E. Bates (eds), *Collinson's History of Somerset* (Taunton, 1898); John Rudder, *Delineations of the North Western Division of the County of Somerset and of Its Antediluvian Bone Caverns* (London, 1829).

94 Bristol City Museum and Art Gallery, B. Donn, *The Map of the Country in Miles Round the City of Bristol*, 6 November 1769.

95 An original house was built on the site of the Royal Fort by John Elbridge in 1739. When Elbridge left the fort to build an even grander house a mile or two further out of the city (Cote House), the site was sold to Thomas Tyndall. Both men derived much of their wealth from slavery. For the Elbridge family, see Donald Jones, 'The Elbridge, Woolnough and Smyth Families of Bristol in the Eighteenth Century with Special Reference to the Spring Plantation of Jamaica', M.Litt. thesis, University of Bristol, 1972. Elbridge was one of the founders of Bristol's Royal Infirmary and of other charitable projects. For the Tyndall family, see Joseph Betley, *The Royal Fort and Tyndall's Park: The Development of a Bristol Landscape* (Bristol: Bristol Historical Association, 1997), pp. 8–9, and Leech, *The St. Michael Precinct of the University of Bristol*.

96 Latimer, *Annals of Bristol in the Eighteenth Century*, p. 173.

97 See University of the West of England, Lease and Release of Redland Estate, Samuel Perry to John Cossins, 23/24 February 1738, Redland Hill House Deeds; BRO, abstract of Giles Hungerford's will, 3 October 1638, Slade Baker Collection 8015 (2); copy of Sir Robert Yeamans's will, 26 January 1686, 8015 (83d); articles of agreement between Col. Robert Yeamans Esq. of . . . Barbados and his son and heir Robert Yeamans the younger . . . and the Hon. Thomas Maycock of . . . Barbados, 21 September 1725, 8015 (81a); extract from the Registry of the PCC, Barbados 23 June 1731, 8015 (81a); will of John Cossins Esq., 23 December 1756, 8015 (10); copy of will of Martha Cossins, 1761,

8015 (12); conveyance of Samuel Perry Esq. *et al.* of London to John Cossins, late of Redland Court, 4 February 1778, 8015 (79); Ison, *Georgian Buildings*, p. 164.

98 Timothy Mowl, *To Build the Second City: Architects and Craftsman of Georgian Bristol* (Bristol: Redcliffe Press, 1991), pp. 64–5; Richardson, *Bristol, Africa and the Eighteenth-Century Slave Trade*, vol. 3, pp. 13, 80, 113, 123, 171, 210.

99 BRO, 25 July 1775, copy of a conveyance dated 1 March 1775 from R. Scudamore and Henry Hobhouse Esq., 1775; memorial to William Nores Tonge Esq. of Arnos Court at Olveston Parish Church near Bristol.

100 The history of the Cote estate is particularly complex since no fewer than three estates, Cote, Northcote and Cote House, were virtually adjacent to each other in the eighteenth century. According to Kingsley, *Country Houses of Gloucestershire*, pp. 107–10, the earliest owners of Cote House cannot be ascertained, though he is satisfied that it passed in 1745 to William Phelps and thence from his widow to John Thomas 'after 1760'. According to the Donn map, the estate belonged to 'Phelps Esq.' as late as 1769. Kingsley states that the property went in 1775 to Capt. John Webb, MP for the city of Gloucester, and was owned by John Wedgwood between 1797 and 1806. It passed to the Ames family in 1825 and was demolished in 1925 to make way for St Monica. According to an archaeological survey done by the Bristol City Museum, Northcote was part of the estate originally built upon by John Elbridge and was acquired by John Webb in 1777, briefly acquired by the Wedgwoods by 1804 and thereafter owned by the Protheroes; Bristol City Museum, Excavation and Survey of Badminton School, Westbury on Trym (1993). In either case, both the Ames family (through African trading) and the Protheroes (through their West Indian plantations) made money from slavery. My thanks to John Bryant of the Bristol City Museum and Art Gallery for helping me to disentangle the three estates, though I take full responsibility for any remaining inaccuracies.

101 Richardson, *Bristol, Africa and the Eighteenth-Century Slave Trade*, vol. 2, pp. 135, 137.

102 See PRO, 'Indenture between James Day, Bristol Merchant and Mary His Wife (Which Said Mary is Aunt and Heiress at Law of Anne Elbridge late widow and relict of Thomas Elbridge late of Coate within the parish of Westbury)', 15 April 1745, C107/171; BRO, I. V. Hall notes, box 6, 36772.

103 I. V. Hall, 'The Daubenys: One of the Most Energetic Sugar Baker Families in Eighteenth Century Bristol at the Temple St. and Halliers Lane References'. Part I under GEORGE DAUBENY I, *Transactions of the Bristol and Gloucestershire Archaeological Society*, vol. 84 (1965), p. 115.

104 Hamer (ed.), *The Papers of Henry Laurens*, vol. 3, p. 33n. 'John Lloyd, Charleston Merchant was born in Bristol England in 1735 and died in Charleston in 1807. In 1769 he purchased "Springfield" plantation on the Ashley River.'

105 BRO, bond, James Vaughan Philip Vaughan to Thomas Daniel the younger of Sneed Park, 12171 (8).

106 The iron wholesalers' firm was Daniel, Harford, Weare & Payne, who were financed in part by a bond from the Alleyne family and who supplied various iron pots for one of James Rogers's slavers, the *Fanny*, in 1792. Daniel and Weare had slave-trading interests as well. See PRO, James Rogers Collection, c107/3 and c107/4; BRPO, Articles of Partnership in 1788 (Daniel, Weare, Harford, etc.), Harford Family Papers, 28948/p23; and bond for £4000 to Fanny, Ann and Mary Alleyne, 29 December 1789, Harford Family Papers, 28048/p25/5; Kingsley, *Country Houses of Gloucestershire*, vol. 2, pp. 79–81. Harford was later a friend of Wilberforce.

107 Casamajor came from a Huguenot family who settled in Bristol in the late seventeenth century.

108 Thanks to Richard Tovey of Tockington School, who informed me that a beam inscribed with the date 1753 had been uncovered during a recent renovation of the Georgian

portion of the house. Samuel Peach Esq. of Tockington died in 1785 and was father-in-law to Henry Cruger, MP for Bristol. Peach, linen-draper and banker, co-owned two slave ships. Thanks to John Gunnery for his advice on local families and for showing me Peach's memorial in Olveston Parish Church near Bristol. See Olivier (ed.), *Caribbeana*, vol. 2, p. 79, for information on Cruger.

109 Cooke, *West Country Houses*, p. 22; Elton, *The Elton Family*, pp. 32–6, 126–9.

110 For Charles Bragge Bathurst, see J. F. Nicholls and John Taylor, *Bristol Past and Present* (Bristol: Arrowsmith, 1882), vol. 3, p. 232, and Revd Arthur E. Jones, *Our Parish Mangotsfield Including Dowend in a Brief Account of Its Origins and History* (Bristol: W. F. Mack & Co., n.d. but *c.* 1899), pp. 123–5; see also pp. 118–23. John Gordon Sr is listed as a member of the African Committee of the Society of Merchant Venturers and was part of the anti-abolitionist alliance organized by the society in 1789. Messrs Cave were listed as 'manufacturers' involved in the same alliance. Society of Merchant Venturers, West India Trade Minutes, 15 April 1789; Olivier (ed.), *Caribbeana*, vol. 2, p. 85. I should like to thank Belinda Waddington for the loan of a schedule for Cleve Hill House which she inherited from her family.

111 See Anton Bantock, *The Later Smyths of Ashton Court: From Their Letters, 1741–1802* (Bristol, 1984) at BRO Schedule for the Woolnough Papers, Ashton Court Collection.

112 John Cordy Jeaffreson (ed.), *A Young Squire of the Seventeenth Century: From the Papers (A.D. 1676–1686) of Christopher Jeaffreson of Dillingham House Cambridgeshire*, 2 vols (London: Hurst & Blackett, 1876), vol. 2, pp. 15, 101, 112–14.

113 For Blathwayt's views on the slave and plantation trades, see PRO, *CalSPCol*, 1677–80, vol. 46, p. 1631. For his office-holding and finances, see G. M. Jacobsen, *William Blathwayt: A Late Seventeenth Century English Administrator* (New Haven, London and Oxford, 1932), pp. 100–3, 434–68. See *Dictionary of National Biography*, ed. L. Stephen (London, 1885), vol. 5, p. 206.

114 David Harris Sacks, *The Widening Gate: Bristol and the Atlantic Economy, 1450–1700* (Berkeley, CA, 1991), p. 298.

115 See BCRL, Southwell Papers, for Southwell's correspondence with James Laroche and his concern over the illegal insurance practices which dogged slaving vessels. See *BWI*, 22 August 1752, for his attendance at the Gentlemen Natives of Gloucestershire, one of several similar associations of (mainly) Bristol residents from the adjacent counties.

116 Olivier (ed.), *Caribbeana*, vol. 4, p. 314; see advertisement for Doddington in *Farley's Bristol Newspaper*, 8 January 1725–6 (old calendar), GRO, Schedule for the Codrington Papers D1610 p. iv.

117 Kingsley, *Country Houses of Gloucestershire*, vol. 2, p. 296.

118 Bristol City Museum and Art Gallery, *Archaeological Evaluation of Land at 115 High Street, Portishead for Cowlin Design and Bristol* (Bristol and Regional Archaeological Series, 1997), BA/F3T2, p. 4.

119 BULSC, Special Collections, Anon., *Observations Made during a Tour through Parts of England, Scotland and Wales in a Series of Letters* (London: T. Becket, 1780), p. 91.

120 Anon., *Observations Made during a Tour*, p. 91.

121 Nicholls and Taylor, *Bristol Past and Present*, vol. 3, p. 162. Anthony was said to be worth £40,000 on his death.

122 The full title is *An Essay on the state of England, in relation to its Trade, its Poor, and its Taxes, For Carrying on the Present War against France*; see Latimer, *Annals of Bristol in the Seventeenth Century*, p. 474.

123 *The Bristol Post Boy*, 7–10 September 1709. For an erudite analysis of the development of a reading culture in Bristol, see Jonathan Barry, 'The Press and the Politics of Culture in Bristol, 1660–1775', in Jeremy Black and Jeremy Gregory (eds), *Culture, Politics and Society in Britain, 1660–1800* (Manchester, 1991), pp. 49–81.

124 Thomas Cox, *Magna Britannia*, 1727, IV. Cited in Peter T. Marcy, 'Eighteenth Century Views of Bristol and Bristolians', in Patrick McGrath (ed.), *Bristol in the Eighteenth Century* (Newton Abbot, 1972), p. 30.

125 The Tolzey was a sort of open-air pergola under which merchants plied their wares and conducted business until 1744, when the Corn Exchange was built on the site; *Felix Farley's Bristol Advertiser*, 30 March 1744. For the events advertised, see *Farley's Bristol Newspaper*, 3 September, 17 September and 19 November 1726.

126 *Farley's Bristol Newspaper*, 27 January 1732–3 (old calendar).

127 Ernest C. Mossner, *The Life of David Hume*, cited in Minchinton, 'The Merchants of Bristol', p. 190.

128 See Vickery, *The Gentleman's Daughter*, pp. 27–36, on the similarly porous nature of social divisions in eighteenth-century Lancashire.

129 *BWI*, 3 March 1750, for one of a number of chocolate advertisements, and 25 April 1752 for William Stephen's advertisement for cloths for the African trade.

130 The first bank was called Bristol Bank and later Old Bank. It opened in 1750 by the partnership of Onesiphorus Tyndall, Harford Lloyd, Isaac Elton, William Miller, Thomas Knox and Matthew Hale, all of whom were members of the Company of Merchants Trading to Africa. West Indians and African merchants were also important to the partnerships of the New Bank and Miles Bank, founded in 1752, the Harford Bank and the Exchange Bank, whose partners included Michael Miller, John Cave, Henry Bright, [Wm?] Swymmer and James Read. See Charles Henry Cave, *A History of Banking in Bristol from 1750 to 1899* (Bristol: privately printed, 1899), pp. 9–16, 52. Additional material was obtained from the NatWest archives, Bristol Old Bank Papers and Accounts, 4633, 4634, 4636, 8233, 4194, 5194, 3373; Miles Bank Papers, 4635, 3375. My thanks to Susan Snell and Fiona McCall, formerly of the NatWest archives, for their assistance.

131 Bantock, *The Later Smyths of Ashton Court*, p. 70.

132 'Clifton – a poem', quoted in Blaise Castle, in Nicholls and Taylor, *Bristol Past and Present*, vol. 3, p. 197; emphasis added.

133 Elton, *Annals of the Elton Family*, pp. 8, 12, 52–4.

134 *Ibid.*

135 Bill Evans, 'Leigh Court'. My thanks to Bill Evans for allowing me to see his unpublished manuscript.

136 Hancock, *Citizens of the World*, p. 320.

== 4 ==

THINKING ABOUT
THE SLAVE TRADE

ABOLITION AND ITS OPPONENTS, 1760–91

When you see the flowing eyes, the heaving breast or the bleeding sides and tortured limbs of your fellow-creatures, was you a stone or a brute? Did you look upon them with eyes of a tiger? When you squeezed the agonizing creatures down in the ship, or when you threw their poor mangled remains in the sea, had you no relenting? Did not one tear drop from your eye, one sigh escape from your breast? Do you feel no relenting now? (John Wesley, 'Thoughts upon Slavery', *The Works of the Rev. John Wesley* (London: John Mason, 1800), vol. II, p. 74)

The Negroes at Cherry Garden I find complain and make the most of their suffering . . . 'tis fortunate for them they are under the eyes of a humane man who knows their Proprietor is both able and willing to relieve their real wants, which I flatter myself I have complied with. (Caleb Dickinson to Messrs. East & Dickinson, 23 November 1784)[1]

A long-standing and lively debate still continues over the abolition of slavery in the British colonies. Should the laurels for the moral victory rest exclusively on the heads of British 'saints' and humanitarians? Or had slavery, as the Trinidadian historian and prime minister Eric Williams argued, by then outlived its economic usefulness to the West? What credit should go to the resistance waged by the enslaved Africans themselves? Was it God, Mammon or the threat of bloody rebellion which effected the end of formal slavery in the British Empire?[2]

The next three chapters sidestep these larger questions to consider who supported and who opposed the anti-slavery campaigns in Bristol and in what terms they did so. The present chapter will deal with the early years of the abolitionist movement before 1792. We shall then consider the abolition campaign after that date, when political circumstances seemed much less propitious for its political success. Chapter 6 will then investigate the emancipation campaign from the unpromising days of 1808 up to its parliamentary success of 1833.

The campaign for the abolition of the slave trade began in the 1780s, led in Parliament by William Wilberforce and supported at grass-roots level by a combination of Quakers, Evangelicals and those imbued with the principles of rationalism and the rights of man. At first, progress was limited to the regulation of conditions aboard British slave ships in 1788 under the Dolben Act. But the inspired doggedness of anti-slavery campaigners both inside and outside Parliament helped to ensure that abolition, of the *British* slave trade at least, was finally achieved in 1807–8. By this time, given the wars with post-revolutionary France, the political climate was hostile to further reform. The emancipation of those already enslaved in British colonies would have to wait three more decades, to be finally achieved in 1838.

As we are already well served by scholarly examinations of Bristol's abolition and emancipation campaigns in terms of their parliamentary progress and the activities of their elite players,[3] there may seem little left of interest to say about the subject. Yet as we examine the identities, social networks and mindsets of those involved on all sides of the slavery question, a richer and more nuanced picture emerges, a picture which involves white women and black Africans, English artisans as well as merchants and MPs. Along with a trawl of political and business records, private papers, religious records and court proceedings have also been consulted. The focus in these three chapters will also be on those sources which previous scholars have dismissed as scurrilous, sketchy or peripheral. We shall examine with particular interest the ways in which election literature and ritual, playbills, poetry and popular pamphlets dealt with slavery and slaves. I shall argue that it is precisely those sources which can offer us an entrée into once widely shared values regarding race, propriety and civic identity.

I must stress here that anti-slavery campaigners in Bristol did not operate in a social vacuum but had a variety of links with those involved in the slave economy. In the following discussion I shall attempt to demonstrate how the growth of an anti-slavery culture in the city, infused as it was by Enlightenment and Romantic ideals, could also be compromised to accommodate vested economic interests, social aspirations and notions of African inferiority. The role that popular literature, much of it written by women, played in the early abolitionist campaign will next engage our attention. Finally, we shall consider the social backgrounds, motives and tactics of those opposing abolition.

The culture of abolition

Quakers, rational thinkers and Evangelicals: anti-slavery sentiment before 1787

Historians of British abolition identify three main streams feeding into the growth of anti-slavery sentiment: Quakerism, 'Rational Dissent'[4] and Evangelicalism. Research reveals that in Bristol there was a good deal of personal and ideological mixing among these three groups. Baptists corresponded with Evangelicals, Evangelicals considered the new French philosophy, Methodists read Quaker tracts. Specific individuals amongst them also had personal contact with Africans, and though it is impossible to quantify the impact of such contact, the evidence does suggest that such encounters with Africans could in some instances significantly shift these individuals' own attitudes towards slavery. At the same time, although these groups were crucial in articulating new attitudes towards slavery and race, they themselves were bound up in terms of kinship and class, business interests and racial attitudes to the more traditional world of the slave-owner.

For example, the widely celebrated role of the Society of Friends in the abolitionist movement obscures (at a local level at least) the significant involvement of Quakers in the slave trade and wider slave economy. Eight of the 20 largest contributors to Bristol's new Quaker Meeting House, built in Quakers Friars in 1747, were by 1755 also members of the newly formed Society of Merchants Trading to Africa.[5] Devonshire, Lloyd & Reeve was a Bristol Quaker firm involved in the export of slaves to South Carolina, and another Quaker, Corsely Rogers, was similarly involved.[6] Certainly a ban on 'the Negro trade' does not seem to have prevented Quakers from trading in slave-produced commodities or in goods which were sold to West Africans from the decks of Bristol slavers. Thus William Champion, who had been part-owner of a slaving vessel in 1758, continued as a partner in Warmely Brass Company, whose battery work was reportedly designed for the 'Guinea Trade'.[7] William's cousin Joseph Champion was in 1758 one of the three Bristolians heading the nine-strong management committee of the Company of Merchants Trading to Africa.[8] William Reeve, who traded in slaves throughout his career, was expelled from the Friends in 1775, but this seems to have been on account of his bankruptcy rather than on account of his slaving.

However, there had always been a tension, as David Brion Davis and Roger Anstey have shown, between slave trading and Quaker notions of spiritual equality and pacifism. A minority of Friends had long felt distinctly uneasy about slavery.[9] Some Quakers had repudiated slavery in the seventeenth century, and in 1696 the Philadelphia Friends meeting first mooted the notion that their members should be advised against participating in the slave trade. By 1719 those members of the Philadelphia meeting who persisted in the trade were disciplined. However, vested interests being what they were, it was not until nearly half a century later, in 1761, that similar disciplines were adopted by Friends in England. That year, the Bristol men's meeting minutes record that a deputation of four men were instructed 'to enquire if any Friend is concerned in the Negro Trade'. By 1762 the deputation reported that

> it appears only one Friend is actually concerned in the African Trade who soon proposes to sell out and to have no connections with it and another who has been applied to says that he has lately parted with his Interests in that Branch of the Business.[10]

Of course, by then Bristol's participation in the African trade was in decline, with many merchants transferring their interests to trading with the West Indian and American slave colonies. The ties of economy, kinship and politesse meant that the social gap between slave-traders and Quakers in Bristol was not, in the 1760s and 1770s, as absolute as modern readers might assume. Slave-holding and trading cut right across political lines. Joseph Champion's son, the porcelain manufacturer and prominent Bristol Whig Richard Champion, was a close political ally of the slave-trader Thomas Farr, and in 1776 Sarah Champion reports that she and her brother dined with Edmund Burke at Farr's. Richard Champion, who appears to have left the Quakers in 1778, owned a number of West Indian ships, and the collapse of his porcelain business eventually led him to retire to Carolina as a planter, where we may reasonably assume he owned slaves.[11] As late as 28 November 1785, the Bristol men's monthly meeting recorded that it had again launched an inquiry into which of its members were involved in the African trade and yet again concluded that although Bristol Friends were 'generally clear',

> not one person being engaged therein, or holding anyone in slavery, but . . . some few in the course of business furnish goods to merchants in that trade and . . . one family . . . have not yet been able to withdraw their [West Indian] property, and [so] hold a mortgage on an estate whereon slaves are employed.

Yet the records of the slaver James Rogers show that Joseph Harford's firm was still exporting brassware aboard Guinea ships as late as the 1790s, by which time he had converted to Anglicanism.[12]

Similar inconsistencies can be discerned in the activities of some Bristol Evangelicals in the 1770s. Evangelical Christianity, though less inclined to political radicalism than Quakerism, has often been cited as another important wellspring for anti-slavery sentiment. Yet, as Drescher reminds us, Evangelicalism in this decade did not necessarily demand a rejection of slavery per se.

For example, the Countess of Huntingdon, who had Evangelical chapels in Bristol and Bath, also owned an Evangelical college in Georgia which derived income from the rice yields of its adjoining slave plantation. Her chaplain, the preacher George Whitefield, had partnered John Wesley in evangelizing Bristol during the Great Awakening of 1739. Whitefield later visited Georgia (which had originally prohibited slavery) and wrote in defence of slavery, though urging the conversion of the slaves. Whitefield's position seems particularly anonmalous given his close friendship with a Quaker leader in the abolitionist campaign, Anthony Benezet, who hosted him when he visited Philadelphia.[13] It has been argued that Quakers inspired John Wesley's widely read tract against the slave trade, which was published in 1774. Certainly Wesley had read Benezet's pamphlet two years before and probably obtained a copy from local Quakers with whom he was in contact. (William Fry and some fellow Friends had since 1769 been buying up multiple copies of Benezet's *Caution to Great Britain and her Colonies* in London and bringing them back to Bristol to distribute.)

However, it could also be argued that it was John Wesley's own personal encounter with Africans in Bristol which precipitated his public conversion to the abolitionist cause. We have earlier seen how the wrongfully kidnapped African 'princes', Little Ephraim Robin John and Ancona Robin Robin John, came to the city in 1773 and 1774, how close they had been to Charles Wesley and how John Wesley had spoken to them and thrice given them the sacrament. It was John Wesley too who in 1774 passed on to Benezet the particulars regarding the brutal massacre at Old Calabar which had occurred seven years earlier and which came to light during the court case fought to secure the release of the two Africans.[14]

By 1783 *The Arminian Magazine*, the journal of the Wesleyans, published extracts of the testimony of the Bristol mariner William Floyd about the Calabar massacre of 1767, along with the corroborating account by the 'John Brothers', as they were called. The young Africans detailed their subsequent fate, and a later issue carried a flattering description of their Bristol experiences.[15]

That same year, 1783, also saw Bristol Friends launch a series of extracts from anti-slavery literature in the local press. Two years later, they resolved to distribute 300 copies of Benezet's anti-slavery works.

The second edition of Benezet's anti-slavery tract *A Caution to Great Britain* was published in 1784. In 1788 he published *Some Historical Account of Guinea . . . with an Inquiry into the Rise and Progress of the Slave Trade*, which included a substantial account by a Bristolian, Harry Gandy (1722–99). Sarah Champion, who first met Gandy in 1777, was clearly intrigued by this 'very agreeable and sensible' middle-aged Bristol lawyer who had returned to his native city after a long time in the West Indies. Sarah and her brother Richard would soon discover that Gandy had had first-hand experience as a slave-trader, first as a novice seaman who found himself helping to quell a slave revolt at sea, and later as a slave-ship captain in 1752 and 1767. Gandy's early encounters had clearly been traumatic, and the guilt he felt at witnessing the atrocities endemic to the trade both at sea and during his twenty years in the Caribbean turned him towards Quakerism and into an ardent anti-slavery campaigner.[16]

The Wesleyans converted another traumatized Bristol veteran of the slave trade and enlisted him in the abolitionist cause, albeit posthumously. Silas Told's (1711–79) graphic account of his mistreatment by a Bristol slave-ship captain and of the cruelties and corruptions of the trade, discussed in Chapter 2, was first published in 1786 and an abridged version appeared the following year in *The Arminian Magazine*.[17]

'A young negro' was baptized by Wesley in Bristol that same year, and Wesley noted that the 'whole congregation' was as 'deeply serious' and as 'much affected' by the event as was the youth himself.[18] Given that baptism was popularly associated with free status and that baptized members of the congregation had equal status with one another, it seems reasonable to suppose that this event, along with Wesley's publications and sermons, disposed Bristol Wesleyans towards abolition. Since many of the Bristol Wesleyan congregations were from the labouring classes, it also can be inferred that abolitionist sentiments were held by people from very modest backgrounds.[19]

Sense and sensibility: Enlightenment and Romantic influences

Quakers and Wesleyans aside, there were other influences at work which were beginning to raise questions about the propriety of slave-trading. Increased wealth, as we have seen, brought gentility with it. Reading became more widely diffused, and though the overwhelming majority of books published in Bristol in the 1770s were religious, mainly Wesleyan, publications, secular writing from France was beginning to find a wider audience amongst educated Bristolians, who also enjoyed domestic novels, travel writing, poems and plays. The Bristol poet Robert Southey recollects that 'Bull's Circulating Library' acted as the 'Bodleian Library' for his linen-draper father. The establishment of a grand subscription library in King Street, largely by local Whigs (including Champion and the banker and slave-ship owner John Peach, and the African trader Joseph Smith), further diffused Enlightenment ideas. Although its merchant patrons preferred history and travel books, new works by French and Scottish writers also had their place, and one of the most-borrowed books between 1774 and 1784 was the English translation of Abbé Raynal's *A Philosophical and Political History of the Settlements and Trade of the Europeans in the East and West Indies*, a work which, though it denigrated Africans, was noted for its scathing attack on the institution of slavery.[20]

As early as 1760, Enlightenment ideas were being disseminated in the press. *Felix Farley's Bristol Journal*, never known as a repository of liberal values, published without comment an essay purportedly by Voltaire entitled 'A Remarkable Account of a White Moor Brought from Africa to Paris'. In it, its author purports to have seen a 'white Moor' in Paris (possibly an albino African). Reflecting on this 'Moor's' singular appearance, Voltaire goes on to survey the different characteristics of the human species as evidence of the richness of nature and explains such variations as adaptations to different climates rather than as evidence of a divinely inspired hierarchy. With characteristic irony, Voltaire goes on to state that he'd been told that white Moors believed themselves to be 'peculiarly favor'd by Heaven', and that 'they have a Holy Horror of all men' who do not have white woolly hair like themselves. The white Moors, Voltaire relates, thought that the universe was created for them alone and that they were destined to be the 'masters of the Negroes and other whites, men eternally rejected by Heaven'. Perhaps, Voltaire concludes, 'they may be deceived, but if we think ourselves much better than them, we deceive ourselves with equal stupidity'.[21] Voltaire's particular brand of satire did not address the notion of slavery directly, but its implications were clear enough. Although the essay does not seem to have stimulated any debate in the local press on either race or slavery, the fact that it was printed at all suggests there was interest in the subject.

The ambivalence people of 'sensibility' (a term which was coming into vogue in this era) felt about enslaving Africans is plainly articulated in a 1766 essay by John Hippisley. Hippisley, the son of Bristol's early theatre impressario of the same name, spent some years in the slave forts as an officer of the Company of Merchants Trading to Africa. The essay, which received national attention, implicitly accepts that the slave trade is attended by an unacceptable level of cruelty.

But his premise is that the slave trade is far too important to be abandoned, and though people should not be treated as things, Africans are a breed apart:

> To declaim upon the horrors of this trade would have been beside the question, and as far as I can see, could have answered no good purpose: for the impossibility of doing without slaves in the West-Indies will always prevent this traffick being dropped. The necessity, the absolute necessity, then, of carrying it on, must, since there is not other, be its excuse. We would not, however, be quite silent upon this occasion. A hint will be forgiven by those who *do not* need it, inconsideration of those who *(Perhaps) do.* We hope then, it will be every remembered *that the traffick is in human creatures;* that sensibility and deep reflection upon their sad state do not operate very powerfully among the negroes; yet they are not *totally* devoid of them; that certain ties there are, which, when broken, affect even brutes; and that feeling, bodily feeling at least, is the portion of everything that has life. Shall we then forget that many of these poor creatures, to say nothing of their common misfortune, in leaving their native country for ever, have been torn from the woman, the child, or the parent that they loved? Circumstances of so piteous a nature, as, instead of inspiring wanton cruelty, or cold neglect, should teach the white possessors to soften the misery of their condition by every safe and reasonable indulgence that their humanity can suggest, and that the nature of the case will admit.[22]

Such sentiments were being diffused in Bristol at a number of levels. *Oroonoko*, Southerne's reworking of Behn's play about the cruelties of slavery, had been staged by Hippisley's father at least five times in Bristol between 1761 and 1763 at his theatre in Jacob's Well Road.[23] The Southerne play, as we have seen, decried the cruelties inflicted on an African of noble lineage and a decidedly Europeanized visage, but did not attack the trade itself. In a somewhat more militant but still romantic vein, the young poet Thomas Chatterton's *African Eclogues*, written around 1770, portray an array of handsome, well-born black hunters and their beautiful sweethearts amid a lushly verdant African idyll. In floridly resounding tones, Chatterton too celebrates black nobility and condemns the white venality of those 'pale children of the feeble sun' who 'in search of gold thro'' every climate run':

> *The children of the wave, whose pallid race*
> *Views the faint sun display a languid face . . .*
> *Fear, with a sicken'd silver, tinged their hue;*
> *The guilty fear when vengeance is their due.*[24]

Here again the message is mixed, as Alan Richardson points out, for though Chatterton may attack the slave trade and subvert the conventional European symbolism around blackness and whiteness, he still represents 'African culture only in starkly primitivist terms'.[25] Africa for Chatterton is still full of savages, however noble they may be, and Chatterton's political writing shows him to be unquestioning about the propriety of English colonization in the Caribbean.

Nonetheless, the *Eclogues* had a particular resonance, composed as they were in a slaving port.

It is, however, a short essay published in Bristol in 1775 by a minor writer, William Combe, which perhaps reveals most about the local diffusion of Enlightenment ideas and their impact on attitudes towards the slave trade. Combe was a hack writer who produced three short pieces for the genteel end of the Bristol market in the 1770s. In his *The Philosopher in Bristol Part the Second*, he extols the virtues of the 'respectable merchant' and the 'fair retail dealer' and tells his audience that he knows many such men in Bristol:

> [I] happened about a fortnight ago to be in company, where the Guinea Trade was the topic of conversation: – and I could not forbear from expressing my concern and indignation at the inhuman traffic. – I had spoken some time upon the subject, – and enlarge[d] [up]on the excellent observation of Montesquieu, – *'that if Negroes are men, they who traded in them could not be christians.'*[26]

Combe tells his reader that at this point he was interrupted by two slave-traders. The first, a 'genteel' man of 'a very pleasing appearance', agreed that the trade was 'not to be justified upon any principles of humanity and religion' but said that he continued in it because he could see no practicable alternative:

> 'If any substitutes [to the trade] could be found, that would exempt a part of the rational creation from slavery I should rejoice, and would willingly forego a commerce which is so dishonourable to the human species. – But while it continues there cannot be any good reason why I may not receive those profits, which if I were to relinquish them, would be eagerly pursued and gladly obtained by another.'[27]

The genteel slave-trader assures Combe that he makes certain that his slaves are treated with 'the utmost humanity' and expresses the hope that '"while the trade itself is deservedly stigmatised, – they, who follow it upon the most liberal and humane principles of which it is capable, may not be involved in the general censure"'. Combe is so impressed by this man that he says he could 'with real pleasure have taken him to my bosom'. The prospect of such an embrace was at this point, Combe tells his readers, rudely interrupted by another slave-trader, who stormed noisily out of the room and then returned to revile Combe's new acquaintance:

> 'you may say what you please of the Guinea-Trade – that it is contrary to religion and humanity and all that' – 'but this I know,' added he, holding forth his hat, 'that I have got this full of money by it:' – and then he shut the door again with his former violence and departed. – This is the sordid character whom I have marked for disgust . . . [and] have endeavoured to hold forth to public censure.

The implication is clear. The first merchant is in the mode of that prince of Bristol merchants, 'the excellent, the pious and benevolent MR. COLSTON'. He is a man of sensibility and virtue and is a credit to his city. The second merchant, by contrast, is a boor. It is his lack of gentility and manners which most offends Combe. By distinguishing between these two ideal types, Combe gives Bristol's African merchants a means by which they could pay lip-service both to Anglican benevolence and to fashionable French philosophy without jeopardizing their profits. They could still trade in slaves, but sensitively!

Combe knew his market well, for there were such individuals in Bristol at the time. One abolitionist recalled asking a Whig friend how he could reconcile himself to be a slave merchant and was told, 'I own I do not like it but my interest leads me to it.'[28] Thus was participation in the slave trade *rationalized*, in every sense of the word.

The idea that one could be a humane slave-trader had its attractions. Gandy had tried to treat his slaves well when he went on (despite his early traumatic experience as a young seaman on board a slaver) to captain two slave voyages, but found to his horror that brutality was built into the system as sickness and suicide undermined his best efforts.

The African merchant Thomas Jones knew all about the brutalities involved in the trade, having served as a slave captain in his early career. Yet he too was no unthinking brute, for although he continued to trade in slaves up until his death in 1795, his will makes clear that he did not want his son to do the same, but to go to university instead.[29]

The American Revolution helped in a number of ways to promote abolition. For a start, the war it occasioned badly disrupted Bristol's Atlantic trade, with the African trade in particular becoming 'virtually suspended'. As a result, a number of African traders, including Farr, went bankrupt.[30] At the same time, the American Revolution had helped to disseminate further the idea of the 'natural rights of man'. Supporters of the American rebels were not necessarily abolitionists, as the example of Cruger demonstrates, but many were. Linda Colley suggests that abolition gained in popularity also because it reasserted Britain's symbolic role as a beacon of liberty despite the government's opposition to American independence.[31]

By 1777 even the Bishop of Bristol, Thomas Newton, used Enlightenment rhetoric when he privately praised the anti-slavery campaigner Granville Sharp for being 'a real lover of liberty and a friend to mankind', though he does not seem to have made his sentiments public.[32] Edmund Burke, MP for Bristol until 1780, indicated his distaste for the slave trade as early as 1778, a point that could not have endeared him to his constituency, though he certainly opposed the immediate ending of the trade.[33]

In July 1787 Gandy hosted Thomas Clarkson, a young Evangelical who was dispatched by the newly formed (and largely Quaker) Abolition Committee in London to Bristol on a fact-finding mission. Clarkson was to gather evidence on the abuses of the slave trade, including the high mortality rates of the crews aboard the slaving vessels. As is well known, the small group who supported Clarkson were mainly Quakers, but included the reformist Anglican cleric Josiah Tucker, formerly the rector of St Stephen's Church in Bristol and later Dean of Gloucester. John Wesley's name did not appear in this committee, but he did write an encouraging letter to Granville Sharp in October of that year affirming his 'perfect detestation of the horrid slave trade'.[34]

Figure 15
British School,
*Portrait of
Hannah More.*
Miniature
(watercolour on
ivory). Bristol City
Museum and Art
Gallery

In charting the rise of the abolitionist movement in Bristol, it is all too easy
to convey a picture of a cleanly heroic progress from Old Corruption to Reform.
But the evidence indicates a messier picture, blurred by patronage, kinship and
the persistence of older attitudes. Tucker was a friend of such abolitionists as the
Reverend James Newton and Hannah More (Figure 15); he provided Clarkson
with useful contacts in the West Country. He condemned Locke and Rousseau
for pretending 'to justify – the making of slaves of others whilst they are pleading
so warmly for Liberty for themselves'. He attacked Jamaican planters who pressed
for the limitation of the power of the Crown over their own affairs so that they
could be 'at full Liberty themselves to whip and scourge and torture their poor
Negroes, according to their own brutal will and Pleasure'. He rounded on George
Washington and other founders of the new American republic for having 'no
objection against slavery, provided they shall be free themselves'.[35] Yet Tucker
also enjoyed a 'considerable legacy', as well as the Queen Square residence of
Miss Peloquin, the sister and sole heir of David Peloquin, a sugar magnate whose
immense wealth had to be in large part slave-derived. Hannah More, for her

part, regarded the abolitionists the Reverend James Newton and Olney as mentors, but she also respected her friend Samuel Peach, then a Bristol linen-draper with investments in slave ships.[36] John Wesley, who remained a Tory to his dying day, supported Matthew Brickdale in 1784 despite his associations with slave-trading, though it must be said that his Whig opponent, Cruger, also had slaving connections. Nor, as we shall see, did abolitionist sympathies by any means rule out racialist attitudes towards Africans.

Bristol's local abolitionist group was set up in 1788 to petition Parliament and help support at grass-roots level the campaign which Wilberforce was to launch within Parliament. As Table 7 shows, it was made up of a number of Quakers, but was supported also by three Anglican clerics and by Dissenting ministers. It was a well-connected group with a number of Esquires and professionals.[37] A public meeting was called in January 1788 at the Guildhall in Broad Street, Bristol, on the slavery question and was reportedly well attended. A small coterie of women were reportedly amongst the original subscribers.[38]

The Quaker and amateur scientist Charles Dyer (an employee of an African merchant who was also a gunpowder manufacturer) recalls in his diary that he 'signed a Petition at Guildhall to Parliament for abolishing the Slave Trade [and

Table 7 Members of Bristol's Abolition Committee, January 1788

Dr John Hallam	Dean of Bristol
Josiah Tucker	Dean of Gloucester
Revd Dr Camplin	Prebendary, Bristol Cathedral
Revd J. P. Estlin	Presbyterian/Unitarian minister of Lewin's Mead
Revd Thomas Wright	Dissenting minister
Revd Caleb Evans	Broadmead Baptist Church
Harry Gandy	Solicitor/member of Society of Friends
John Harris	City alderman/Dean of Broadmead Baptists
Dr [Edward Long?] Fox	Medical doctor
Mr W. Lunnell	Merchant, Brunswick Square, Castle Green (Congregationalist) Meeting House
John Collard Esq.	Merchant, Orchard Street
Joseph Harford Esq.	Iron manufacturer, originally a Friend, later an Anglican
Thomas Rutter	Quaker; brush and bellows manufacturer?
Matthew Wright	Merchant, Society of Friends
Mr Coates	Possibly Joseph Coates, wine merchant
Mr Edward Griffiths	Member of Bristol Corporation, Brunswick Sq.
Rowland Williams Esq.	Sugar baker?
Dr John Wright	Bristol Royal Infirmary
Joseph Beck Esq.	Gentleman, Society of Friends
George Daubeny Esq.	City alderman/sugar refiner

that] . . . it was signed by a great number'.[39] The young assistant pastor at Broadmead Baptist Church, Robert Hall, wrote to his father a few weeks after the meeting to report that over 800 people signed the petition, a great number 'considering that *no application has been made to any*' and that 'much opposition is made by the merchants and the dependants who are many, perhaps most of them engaged in it'.[40]

Hall was an enthusiastic abolitionist, but though religious Dissenters have generally been cited as bastions of anti-slavery support, those in Bristol had a more complicated relationship with the abolitionist movement. On the one hand, their emphasis on rational thought, literacy and a distrust of state religion, and their formal exclusion (as non-Anglicans) from political life, inclined them to favour political reform. On the other hand, a significant number of dissenters were merchants or industrialists with African or West Indian interests. The wealthy Lewins Mead congregation, identified as Presbyterian until the late 1770s, had long been the spiritual home of a number of wealthy African traders such as the Eltons, the Tyndalls and the Farrs. In 1788, during the launch of the local abolitionist campaign, their largest subscribers included prominent slave-ship owners such as Thomas Deane, John Anderson and William Gordon, West Indian slave-holders such as Richard Bright and sugar-traders such as Samuel Munckley. Although officially barred from politics as Dissenters, in practice these wealthy men often circumvented the law and held civic office and became Merchant Venturers.[41] However, their minister since 1770 had been one John Prior Estlin, who steered them steadily towards Unitarianism, a religiously radical brand of Christianity which rejected the idea of the Holy Trinity.[42] This religious radicalism had political implications and led John Prior Estlin himself to join the abolitionists. One might think that his congregation would not have tolerated a minister with such views, but he remained in post until 1817. The record does not reveal what disquiet his stand on slavery may have caused them.

The picture for Bristol's main Baptist congregation at Broadmead is also contradictory, though in a different way. The congregation was not as wealthy as that of Lewins Mead. Their minister was Caleb Evans, an erudite man. He had succeeded his father, Hugh, in the post, and at first sight appears to have been straightforwardly in favour of abolition. In 1788 the Western Association of Baptists, in which Evans played a leading role, signed a letter proclaiming support for the abolition of the slave trade and subscribed money to the London Abolition Committee. Evans was also listed as a member of the committee set up to distribute anti-slavery petitions in 1788.[43] But Evans was no Wesley on this matter. As with the Lewins Mead congregation, early Bristol Baptists included sugar merchants such as the Terrills, whose Barbadian plantation, Cabbage Hall, later went to the Popes. The Pope family continued to give financial support to the Bristol Baptists even after they had ceased their membership at Broadmead. In a preliminary study, Dr Roger Hayden notes that Caleb Evans had long-standing and intimate connections with other members of both London's and Bristol's mercantile elite, which were to make an abolitionist stand increasingly awkward.[44] It is perhaps significant that his 1788 sermon *British Freedom Realized*, preached and published on the centenary of the Glorious Revolution, made no reference to African slavery.[45] By contrast, his young assistant pastor, Robert Hall, was passionately eloquent on the subject, and his letters to the local press, under the pen name of '*Britannicus*', made no secret of his distaste for the trade.[46] Hall, however, was at this stage of his life a rationalist and a radical, who was coming under increasing scrutiny for suspected 'Socinian' tendencies.[47]

Charles Dyer's Quakerism and John Wesley's Arminianism represented a more mystical strain in abolitionist thought. Both these men, though intensely interested in scientific discoveries (especially those concerning electricity), had been influenced by the writings of the mystic Jacob Boehme, which conceived of the universe in the most impenetrably symbolic terms reminiscent of earlier occult writers. Wesley's own view of the cosmos was not Newtonian, but suffused with providential meaning. For Wesley all things were connected by God. No wonder his Bristol sermon against slave-trading, delivered on 6 March 1788, was appropriately interrupted by a supernatural occurrence:

> A vehement noise arose, and shot like lightning through the whole congregation. The terror and confusion were inexpressible. The benches were broken in pieces, and nine-tenths of the congregation appeared to be struck with the same panic. In about six minutes the storm ceased. None can account for it without supposing some preternatural influence. Satan fought lest his kingdom be delivered up.[48]

If intense religiosity was at the heart of the abolitionist movement, the most rational means and men were employed to advance it. 'Benevolus', an abolitionist writer, larded his letter to the local press with quotations from Montesquieu and expressed his 'astonishment' that those 'who have had all the advantages of a liberal education' still persisted in the 'trade in rational beings'.[49] 'Benevolus' was joined by 'Britannicus' (Robert Hall) and others in a letter-writing campaign to the Bristol press which was replicated elsewhere and accompanied by a flurry of petitions presented to Parliament from around the country. The rational way the campaign was organized was at least as important as the rational arguments it employed.

As a result of this public pressure throughout the country, a Select Committee was established to inquire into the African slave trade and its impact upon Britain and her colonies. The Select Committee interviewed over 60 abolition witnesses, most of whom had been obtained by Clarkson's heroic struggle to find people willing to testify. Bristol witnesses included the slave-ship captain Thomas Deane (not to be confused with Thomas Deane Esq. of the Lewins Mead congregation), and seamen who had served aboard slavers off the West African coast (William James, Knight and Brucc). Perhaps most important of all was the surgeon James Arnold, whose damning testimony of conditions aboard slave ships did much to counter the anodyne picture provided by John Anderson, the slave merchant representing the interests of Bristol's Society of Merchant Venturers. Clarkson's real triumph was to show, using a sample of 20,000 names derived from ships' muster rolls, that far from being a 'nursery for British seamen', as anti-abolitionists had argued, 'more persons would be found dead in these slave vessels from Bristol, in a given time, than in all the other vessels put together, numerous as they were, belonging to the same port'.[50]

However, the findings of the Select Committee would not, thanks to the delaying tactics of the anti-abolitionists, be completed until 1790. Throughout 1788, abolitionists in Bristol continued their campaign, writing to the press, raising money, though the amount of money raised by the local committee in 1788 was small: £146 compared to over three times that amount raised in Manchester.[51] During this time Clarkson continued his labours and came to Bristol on several more occasions. By then, the MP for Oxford University, Sir William Dolben, had managed to introduce his bill for regulating the conditions for slaves aboard slave ships, which, despite hearty opposition from Bristol's MPs, received Pitt's support and became law in the summer of 1788.[52]

Literature, gender and abolition

Despite their doggedly rational and hard-headed campaigning, abolitionists were not slow to recognize the importance of appeals to the heart. Poetry as well as sermonizing became an important tool in the mobilization of public opinion. Hannah More, who had personal links with Wilberforce, Walpole and Johnson, published a highly influential poem, 'The Black Slave Trade', early in 1788 precisely to help Wilberforce's parliamentary campaign. Before its publication it is said that More showed her poem to her old Latin tutor, the Reverend James Newton of the Bristol Baptist Academy, and his young student Joseph Cottle. Her act indicates the existence of an informal local network of abolitionists. Bristol's Baptist Academy would, as we shall see, infuse a whole generation of missionaries with anti-slavery principles, and Joseph Cottle would later go on to join Robert Southey and his friend Samuel Taylor Coleridge in writing against the slave trade.[53]

More's poem itself contains romantic elements, and owes as much to Southerne's *Oroonoko* and Chatterton's *African Eclogues* as to Montesquieu, but it is transmuted by its sheer vivacity and its Evangelical fervour. Addressing an educated audience, More stresses the humanity of the enslaved African and strongly hints at the moral corruption that the slave trade brought to both black and white:

> *Whene'er to Afric's shores I turn my eyes,*
> *Horrors of deepest, deadliest guilt arise.*
> *I see, by more than Fancy's mirror shewn,*
> *The burning village, and the blazing town:*
> *See the dire victim torn from social life,*
> *See the scar'd infant, hear the shrieking wife!*
> *She, wretch forlorn! is dragged by hostile hands,*
> *To distant tyrants sold in distant lands!*

More speaks directly to the merchants themselves and, invoking traditional patriotic pride in the rights of the freeborn Englishman, asks them to empathize with the Africans they enslave:

If warm your heart, to British feelings true,
As dear his land to him as yours to you;
And Liberty, in you a hallow'd flame,
Burns unextinguish'd, in his breast the same . . .
Revere affections mingled with our frame,
In every nature, every clime the same;
In all, the love of HOME and FREEDOM reign.

More is sufficiently influenced by the Enlightenment to argue that Africans 'are still men, and men shou'd still be free'. But her Evangelicalism inclines her to classify them as 'dark and savage, ignorant and blind', because they are not yet Christianized. Towards the poem's end, she declares that 'Faith and Freedom spring from Britain's hands', and thereby conflates the Christian's mission to evangelize with a Briton's mission to colonize. This is More at her most radical, for her writings on black people in the years succeeding the French Revolution would stress the need for their obedience and civilization.

More's protégé Ann Yearsley, the so-called 'Lactilla' or milkmaid poet, also published an anti-slavery poem early in 1788. Yearsley, impoverished through enclosure, was in fact of yeoman stock and possessed a sturdy independence of character which would later lead to her break with More and may even have been behind her timing the poem's publication to coincide with that of her former patron.[54]

Yearsley's 'Poem on the Inhumanity of the Slave Trade' was, as Mary Waldron contends, altogether more politically radical than that of her patron.[55] In it, Yearsley bitterly contrasts the savage property laws which condemned petty thieves in England to the scaffold with the impunity enjoyed by the slave-traders whose business involved murder, robbery and rape. England's

laws, with prudence, hang the meagre thief
That from his neighbour steals a slender sum,
Tho famine drives him on. O'er him the priest,
Beneath the fatal tree, laments the crime,
Approves the law, and bids him calmly die.
Say, doth this law, that dooms the thief, protect
The wretch who makes another's life his prey,
By hellish force to take it at his will?

Is this an English law, whose guidance fails
When crimes are swell'd to magnitude so vast
That Justice an eternal distance keeps
From England's great tribunal, when the slave
Calls loud on Justice only?[56]

However sensitive Yearsley proves herself to be to the injustices of rank and class, in this poem at least, she is (as Richardson insightfully shows) parochial about race. But the poem's 'dingy' hero-victim Luco, who in many ways, says Ferguson, is 'a

Figure 16
Trade card for
Stansfield & Co.,
tobacconists, of
Castle Street,
Bristol, late
eighteenth century.
Bristol City
Museum and Art
Gallery

declassed and feminised version' of Oroonoko, is ascribed a confused mixture of
African and Indian characteristics.[57] This tendency to conflate non-white groups
together into an undifferentiated savage 'other' was not unusual at the time, as a
contemporary Bristol tobacco advertisement (Figure 16) demonstrates.

In March 1788 'Della Crusca' (possibly Mary Robinson) sent in to the *Bristol
Gazette* an elegy against slavery which foreshadowed the later campaign against
the consumption of slave-produced sugar:

> *Are drops of blood the Horrible Mauve*
> *That Fills with luscious juice the teem[ing] cane?*
> *And must our fellow creatures thus endure*
> *For traffic vile the indignity of pain [?]*[58]

That same month saw another woman's poetical work employed for the abolitionist
cause. The *Bristol Gazette* published extracts of three poems sent in by a reader,

under the headline, 'Specimens of the Practical Genius of an African Girl'. The apolitical and self-consciously genteel verses call to mind those of the African-American poet Phillis Wheatley, a volume of whose poems was published in Britain in 1788. The very fact that 'an African Girl' was capable of such polished work was supposed to counter arguments for the inherent intellectual inferiority of black people.

Propriety as well as intellectual inferiority was invoked as a reason for excluding white women from the slavery debate. 'Amelia' of College Green, Bristol (possibly Mary Robinson, who originally hailed from College Green), wrote to *Bonner and Middleton's Bristol Journal* arguing against such exclusion:

> If it be deemed improper for our sex to take an active part on the present popular subject of the Slave Trade; yet we are allowed to possess at least in equal degree with the men, every tender impression, every endearing affection of the soul; we have our sentiments and our feeling respecting every virtuous sensibility of the heart – and what more interesting to the susceptible mind than the cause of sweet humanity.

Having couched her argument in the most 'feminine' terms, Amelia goes on to debunk the 'sophistries' contained in a pamphlet justifying the slave trade on biblical grounds. Disavowing any knowledge of the 'science of logic', Amelia confidently appeals instead to the 'common sense and plain good understanding' of her readers.[59] Her approach recalls Clare Midgely's observation that '"masculine" reason and "feminine" sensibility were enlisted as complementary qualities in the fight against the slave trade'.[60]

Sarah Champion (1742–1811) never wrote or publicly campaigned for abolition. Her private diary, however, affords us the opportunity not only to see how anti-slavery sentiments grew in a private individual but also to glimpse some of abolition's leading figures in their more private moments. Sarah Champion's experience exemplifies that mixture of sensibility and reason of which Midgely writes. Her questioning about slavery, begun perhaps when the Bristol Friends first condemned slave-trading in 1761, was certainly intensified in 1777 when she began to care for a 12-year-old African boy who may have been the servant of her brother-in-law John Lloyd or brought by one of the West India captains in her brother Richard's employ. 'Poor Black Ned', as she calls him, became ill in the Bristol climate and was 'boarded out', probably to a local family. Sarah took it upon herself to call on him. In March 1777 she reports regularly visiting this 'little innocent negro boy', and as the child's condition deteriorated, her emotional attachment grew. Aware of the boy's 'lonely, orphaned state', she seemed much saddened when he died, alone, in January 1778: 'I visited him at short intervals but no one was with him at the time he expired, which gave me some concern.'[61] She comforted herself with the thought that the boy seemed to have died peacefully, and recalled in her diary that 'He had much desired to be released before the following week', when he was to have been put on board ship to try the effect of the voyage and the change of climate on his health.

But although he contemplated death without terror, yet from an early impression he had received, he connected his body with his soul in a future happy state; and therefore he feared if he died on board ship the crabs would eat him, which would prevent his going to Heaven where he said he should go to God and see his mother again.

Sarah Champion was clearly perplexed by what was a widely held West African belief that one's body must be intact in order to be able to rejoin one's ancestors after death. But the poignancy of Ned's situation did not escape her, and she was clearly moved by his death. Although it is evident that she did not see him as a social or intellectual equal, she does imply that he was her spiritual equal, and it is this which makes her think more deeply about the human impact of the slave system: 'the amiable simplicity of the boy, *whom I really loved* led me to reflect on the abuse of the advantages we enjoy in his favourite isle, for surely *untaught* he adored his great benefactor'[62] (emphasis added). Sarah Champion's meeting with Harry Gandy in 1778 and her encounter a decade later with Thomas Clarkson further deepened her interest in the plight of African slaves, but it was clearly her encounter with 'Ned' which affected her most emotionally and made slavery more than an abstract political issue.

In November 1788 Sarah Champion records receiving Thomas Clarkson at her home. It is not clear with whom she was now living, her brother having departed for South Carolina in 1784 and her father only an occasional visitor. But it is clear from the diary that she moved in largely Quaker and Evangelical circles:

we had a visit from Clarkson. From his character and present engagement, expectation ran high, but it did not as was often the case, lead to disappointment. His person was agreeable, his address modest and manly, neither eager to talk nor affectedly silent. Yet I thought he seemed oppressed with the weight of the good work which now brought him to Bristol. At the entrance of a person whom he believed to be no friend to the abolition, he was almost wholly silent. Falconbridge (once a surgeon on board a slave ship, but now engaged on the right side) was with him, also Harry Gandy, Sampson Lloyd of Birmingham [the banker and relative by marriage of Richard Champion], John Helson, John S[candrett] Harford, . . . [Thomas] Rutter and Dr. Fox [a doctor who pioneered the more humane treatment of the mentally ill]. But to me the subject of the slave-traders is attended with effects which make great inroads on my peace, and even on my rest. Yet I trust the time is not far distant when the same glorious Power, who has been pleased so to employ so many instruments in their service, will enable them so to accomplish the glorious work of their deliverance.[63]

This vivid record of a meeting of Clarkson and his local allies indicates the importance of informal networks in the campaign and reveals Clarkson's feelings of vulnerability and isolation. It also represents abolitionist organization as an almost exclusively male affair, with Sarah Champion now a firm convert to the cause, content to trust in Providence and root from the sidelines.

Yet we have seen the role women played as writers against the slave trade, and both in London and in Bristol they played the crucial role of providing the venues for abolitionists to meet with like-minded people. That same November, for example, Sarah Champion reports visiting the Park Street residence of Hannah More, where Miss More and her sisters hosted the same informal clique of anti-slavery activists. Clarkson, we are told, was again relatively silent on this occasion, '*his* aim being evidently to get Harry Gandy talking about the interior of Africa, [and] a beautiful description he gave us'.[64]

By January 1789 Sarah Champion was still socializing with some anti-abolitionists, but she had begun to find their views increasingly repugnant. She records a visit by Gandy and Clarkson when her father, Joseph Champion, a Swede named Wadstrap and another man called Shurmer were also present: 'Two of the company so much opposed Clarkson on the subject of the Abolition that the conversation became irksome . . . but on *two* withdrawing before supper, at which was added Truman Harford, we passed an agreeable evening.[65]

During the early years of the French Revolution, many middle-class Dissenters, along with numbers of artisans, were thrilled at the prospect of reform and saw abolition as one plank amongst many in their radical platform. Indeed, Drescher informs us that Clarkson 'freely expressed his belief in the identity of the aims of abolitionism and the French Revolution' when touring the provinces. Many opponents of immediate abolition were to assert their support (often, but not always, one suspects, disingenuously) for the gradual abolition of the trade.

How far such democratic ideals inspired abolitionists in Bristol is unclear. Wesley and More exercised an undoubtedly conservative influence on their respective circles, and the fact that many artisans in the city depended on the Atlantic trade for their livelihood must have depressed their reforming zeal. Nevertheless, this upsurge of radicalism was alarming, especially to those merchants and planters whose interest depended on the continued vitality of the British slave trade.

Anti-abolition

Who were the anti-abolitionists?

As early as 1783, the planter and West India merchant John Pinney had complained to his business partner in Nevis, James Tobin, that

> the people have seem[ed] devoted to our destruction, they entertain the most horrid degrees of our cruelties – it now pervades all ranks of people – they think slavery ought not to be permitted in any part of the British dominion: it is incompatible with the Spirit of Our constitution. I assure you: expect to see all our sugar colonies under the dominion of some wiser European power.[66]

Tobin himself, who had returned to Bristol in 1784, took on the abolitionists in the form of a pamphlet war against James Ramsay, who had written an attack on the treatment of slaves in the West Indies. Tobin's first effort was published anonymously in Bristol and London in 1785, with subsequent pieces appearing in

London. Tobin's keenness to play down the cruelties of the slave regime was matched only by his antipathy to mixed-race relationships, an antipathy due in part at least to the fact that his father had mixed-race children in addition to his legitimate heirs. A partner in Pinney's Bristol firm, Tobin soon became a Merchant Venturer and a member of the local West Indian Association, and played a significant role in the anti-abolitionist campaign nationally.[67]

In Bristol the Society of Merchant Venturers, which had organized a memorial against abolition in March 1788, went on in the following year to organize a group of African and West India merchants and manufacturers with related interests to rally around the anti-abolitionist cause. This was part of a nationally orchestrated campaign coordinated by the West India interest in London.[68] Table 8 shows that there were only ten African merchants listed but more than twice that number of men (21) listed as West India merchants and planters. Of the African merchants, it is striking that two Scotsmen (Gordon and McTaggart) and two Welshmen (Jones and Rogers) number within this group. Four of the West Indian merchants and/or planters had investments in either the cargo or the ships involved in slaving ventures.

Table 8   African and West Indian merchants listed at the anti-abolitionist meeting on 15 April 1789 convened by the Society of Merchant Venturers of the City of Bristol[69]

African Committee members	West India merchants, planters, etc.
Anderson, [John]	Claxton, R.
Biggs, [Isaac and/or Samuel]	Gibbs, G.
Deane, [Thomas] (Ald.)	Gordon, J.
Elton, W[illiam]	Laroche, James (Sir)
Fowler, John	Maxse, J.
Gordon, John (Sr)	Oliver, Thomas
Harford, Charles	Palmer, [probably Arthur]
Jones, Thomas	Prothero[e], Philip
McTaggart, James	Span, Samuel
Rogers, James	Miles, W.
	Bright, R[obert]
	Bright, L[owbridge]
	Pinney, John
	Bailie, E[van]
	Brice (Ald.)
	Daubeny, (Ald.)
	Daniel, T.
	Reid, John
	Reid, G.
	Tobin, J[ames]
	Weare, J. F.

Table 9   List of 'manufacturers' who joined the Anti-Abolitionist Committee established by the Society of Merchant Venturers of the City of Bristol, 15 April 1789[70]

Ames [Levi?]	Unitarian	Dry salter	Clifton Hill
Bach			
Baugh	Unitarian	Gunpowder manuf.	St James Sq.
Bence		Wood importer	Wine St
Blanning [William?]		Shipbuilder	
Bush			
Bush, H.			
Cave	Anglican	Banker	
Chubb		(Wm Chubb) deal merchant	
Cross, J.		(James Cross) Distiller	
Cross, T		(Thomas Cross) Grocer	
Delpratt [William?]		Merchant	
Farr, P. and/or W.	Unitarian	Family firm manufactured rope	
Fisher		Linen draper/shipowner	Clifton
Gardiner [and sons?]		Hat manufacturers	Wine Street/Broad St.
Gibbons			
Hales, Messrs.		Brass and pewter manuf.	
Hayward		Ship block maker/chandler	Queen Square
Hillhouse	Unitarian	Shipbuilder	
Huntley			
James			
Jones, W.		Possibly Maltster and Brewer	
Lewis			
Lockier		Timber merchant/speculative builder	
Lucas, R[obert?]		Glass manuf.	
Morgan, Messrs.	Unitarian ?		
Protheroe		Iron manufacture/hat manuf.?	
Randolph, W.		Merchant	Redcliff Parade
Shapland	Unitarian	Probably soap-boiler	
Shatton			
Tombs, Richard		Shipbuilder	
Vaughan, Richard		Banker	
Wilcocks			
Winwood, Thomas		Iron-master	

The most surprising feature of the anti-abolitionist meeting is the number of 'manufacturers' involved (Table 9). Although it has not proved possible to research this list completely in terms of occupation, residence and religious affiliation, it does appear that the Merchant Venturers 'padded out' these names to include some of their friends who were not necessarily manufacturers, such as Merchant Venturer Richard Vaughan, who was a banker. Three were shipbuilders, and a number seem to have been in the export trades such as iron and glass. Some, like Lockier and Bence, imported timber from the Caribbean to supply their activities as speculative builders.

Many opponents of immediate abolition were to assert their support (however disingenuous) for the gradual abolition of the trade.

Alderman Daubeny, a sugar refiner who had publicly supported the abolitionist cause the year before, was one of the signatories. So too was the West India trader and plantation owner Lowbridge Bright, though he was evidently unwilling to resume his slave-trading activities when the trade was being debated in the Commons.[71] Unitarians such as Deane Anderson Baugh and Bright also signed, and although there do not seem to be any signatories from the Broadmead Baptist congregation, one of their number, Alderman John Harris, who was briefly Mayor of Bristol in 1790, went over to the anti-abolitionist cause at about this time. Harris, a long-time associate of Broadmead's minister, Caleb Evans, supported Evans in a bitter public dispute with Evans's abolitionist protégé Robert Hall in 1790. Although the precise nature of the dispute has never been made clear, charges that Hall was a religious radical, a 'Socinian', suggest that his political radicalism and his abolitionism may have proved unacceptable to the leaders of the Broadmead congregation.[72] In any case, the widely popular Hall, whom Hannah More deemed an 'incomparable' abolitionist spokesman, left for Cambridge that same year and did not return to Bristol for over a decade.

The theatre of race

That same spring, the Theatre Royal, which as we have seen was largely founded by a consortium of Merchant Venturers, staged George Colman's version of *Inkle and Yarico*. The story of Inkle and Yarico had existed in various prose and poetic forms since the late seventeenth century. Colman's comic opera version was an ephemeral farce with little left of the anti-slavery sentiments which had characterized some of its predecessors.[73] Davis dismisses it for this reason, but it repays analysis precisely because it was staged at the height of the local abolition campaign. It proved so popular with 'its genteel and numerous' audience that it was staged again in the autumn. Colman knew Bristol and Bath since he stayed in lodgings on the Upper Bristol Road when his play was being staged in the two cities.[74] The plot revolves around the money-mad 'cannibal catcher' Inkle, who sails to Barbados from North America after a brush with death. He takes with him his Amerindian lover, Yarico, who had saved his life, only to attempt to sell her into slavery to a Barbadian planter and marry the Governor's daughter. The plot ends with Inkle apologizing to Yarico, who forgives him for his behaviour.[75]

The opera, intellectually inconsistent as it is, both satirizes and reinforces racial stereotypes and offers a critique of slavery which accommodates the existence of slave regimes. In the passage below, Inkle's honest servant, Trudge, who himself has a liaison with Yarico's kinswoman Wowski, confronts another servant's revulsion towards the idea of interracial liaison:

PATTY (a chambermaid): Oh! The monster! The filthy fellow! Love with a black-a-more!

TRUDGE: Why there! No great harm in it I hope.

PATTY: Faugh! I wouldn't let him kiss me for the world; he'd make my face all smutty.

TRUDGE: I'd have you know, Madam Patty, that Black a Moor ladies as you call 'em are some of the very few whose complexions never rub off![76]

The virtues of women of colour, then, are contrasted with the artifice of their English counterparts. Yet though Yarico's copper colour makes her 'quite dark but elegant, like a Wedgwood tea pot', darker African women are dismissed as unattractive: 'thick lip'd, flat nos'd, squabbly, dumpling dowdies!'.[77]

The cruelties of slavery, though implicitly condemned, are not directly confronted. The whole anti-slavery message is muted by the sheer beneficence of the character General Curry, the slave-owning Governor of Barbados. A colonial version of Combe's enlightened slave-trader, Curry apparently holds slaves for humanitarian reasons: 'I can't help thinking that the only excuse for buying our fellow creatures, is to rescue 'em from the hands of those who are unfeeling enough to bring them to market.'[78]

At the end of the play it is acknowledged that interracial liaisons are unacceptable in polite society, but the audience is invited by Patty the chambermaid to express its support at least for the sanitized fictional liaisons portrayed in the play:

Sure men are grown absurd
Thus taking black for white,
To hug and kiss a dingy Miss
Will hardly suit an age like this,
Unless here, some friends appear,
Who like their wedding night![79]

This invitation to the audience to applaud Yarico and Inkle's romance was a graceful way of asking them to applaud the performance itself. It was hardly intended to incline them towards abolition. 'Happily ever after' in this context did not envisage the end of slavery or even the trade itself. As Mary Pratt has said in a wonderfully titled essay 'Eros and Abolition', Colman's play is typical of a genre which underwrites rather than undermines the existing colonial regime.[80] This point is driven home when we consider the audience which came to view the play in Bristol. By the time of its second staging, in November, King George III was seriously ill and the play ended with a rendition of 'God Save the King' during which, it was reported, 'scarcely an eye appeared without the tears of loyalty gently steeling from it'.[81] Thus did urbanity and anti-abolition drape themselves in the cloak of patriotism.

Evasive manoeuvres: Bristol anti-abolitionists and the middle passage

Aside from theatricals, memorials and political lobbying, some Bristol merchants showed themselves willing to resort to less orthodox means to frustrate abolitionist aims. As Clarkson found to his cost, slave-ship captains and sailors were unwilling to testify about abuses aboard the slave ships, since to do so would have jeopardized their future employment prospects. The cache of business papers left by African merchant James Rogers reveals how at least one slave merchant and his associates responded to the challenge of the abolitionist campaign.

When the Dolben Act was passed in July 1788, limiting the number of slaves that could be 'packed' into slaving ships, James Rogers's Dominican associates advised him to evade the Act by sailing under French colours. This would have, they argued, the added advantage of allowing him to claim the generous bounties the French government was paying for every slave landed in Mustique and Guadeloupe.[82] Rogers seems to have been very open to operating the fraud, for in September 1788 Thomas Gillett & Co. of Bordeaux wrote to him from Bristol with formal proposals. A Bristol vessel equipped to carry 300 to 500 'negroes' could be fitted out with a full array of African trade goods ('except for brandies', which the French presumably planned to supply themselves). The ship would proceed to Bordeaux, at which point a 'sham sale' of the cargo would be held and '²/₃rds of the ships' crew would be exchanged for French sailors', although the English captain would remain in charge. French papers would be supplied, and then the ship was to proceed to the African coast 'to take on board as many Negroes as the ship will carry without paying any attention to the new Regulations made in England, and carry them to any Port in St. D[omin]g[ue]'.[83] Allies in St Domingue would sell the slaves and furnish the captain or supercargo with 'good Bills on Bordeaux for the Neat Proceeds' and Rogers's vessels would be entitled to the bounties.[84] It is likely that the outbreak of the Revolution scuppered these plans, but the correspondence does indicate the willingness of traders like James Rogers to circumvent ameliorative legislation.[85]

Nor did James Rogers stop the flagrant abuse of female slaves on board his own ships during this period. The case of the voyage of the *Juba* to Old Calabar provides a grim insight into racial and sexual attitudes on the eve of the abolition campaign. The ship's surgeon, Matthew Neely, professing that he had a reputation for being 'very tender of both of white and Black', complained to Rogers about the general conduct of the ship's captain, John Kennedy. The captain, wrote Neely, suspected him of 'having to do with his girl which I never had', and assaulted him brutally with a horsewhip. The pretext was Neely's own punishment of another female slave, the 'whore' of the captain's brother, with whom he had a 'little difference'.[86] Neely, whose reputation for honesty was later backed up by other members of the ship's crew, made another, more telling revelation, namely about

Kennedy's treatment of yet another enslaved woman, the 'sister of the girl he [the captain] did commonly sleep with':

> He beat her unmercifully on acct she would not submit to sleep with him tho a Savage, yet at last was forced to comply . . . even in the middle of the day and on deck his actions were more like a Beast than a man.[87]

Despite such conduct, it was the captain, rather than the surgeon, whom Rogers rehired.[88] Like Silas Told before him, Neely pointedly contrasts the civilized behaviour of the 'savage' with a slave captain's bestial conduct.

Another dissident aboard one of Rogers's slaving ships was a crewman named Harrison who claimed he had been imprisoned and enchained by Africans on account of his captain's conduct towards them on a previous voyage. (It seems that Captain Walker, the man accused, had kidnapped six hostages and later dispatched the unsuspecting Harrison to sell goods to the very people whose relatives had been seized.) The crewman, who claimed that he had never received his wages, complained to James Laroche, Rogers's associate. The captain denied everything, saying he had never engaged Harrison aboard his ship. It is not clear whether Harrison was black, but Laroche warned Rogers that he had to be handled carefully since he was 'connected . . . with Granville Sharp the chairman for abolishing the African Trade – and they [sic] support him'.[89]

Even the most ruthless slavers could sense the change in public opinion. In 1790 the prominent African trader Richard Miles wrote to Charles Bell (now resident in Bristol) anticipating the impact of abolition:

> from my Heart I believe they have already done all the Mischief they can . . .
> I mean the seed is sown and tho' it may not happen this year or next . . . I verily
> believe we shall soon lose all our West Indian Islands.[90]

Marshall has outlined the political tactics by which Bristol Merchant Venturers helped to delay a vote on Wilberforce's bill until 1791.[91]

The small number of anti-abolitionist letters published in the Bristol press between 1788 and 1792 belies the passion and political clout which the anti-abolitionist lobby could still muster. They were fired not only by the direct attacks on them in the press, but by the indirect effect the campaign was having on their business. It seems that the very prospect of abolition caused some of their suppliers to suspend trade with them.[92] On the other hand, the threat of abolition could work to the slave-traders' advantage, as one of Rogers's agents in Grenada informed him that same year:

> From the late accounts of the success of Mr. Wilberforce in the House of Commons (tho we have yet hopes the business will not pass the House of Lords) we are certain good slaves would command very high prices. If any of your ships gives us a call, you may depend upon our taking advantage of the times to make them high.[93]

Political activity: anti-abolition rhetoric in Bristol

Anti-abolitionists told the public in no uncertain terms of the economic ruin abolition would bring to the city and the nation. Whilst it was decidedly unfashionable, in the press at least, to advocate slavery as a moral *good*, it was still argued to be an economic and political *necessity*. If the British withdrew from the slave trade, warned one anonymous correspondent, it 'would be eagerly seized by other nations, deprive us of the benefit of fitting out annually 200 sail of ships, be a very considerable detriment to our manufactures, and materially injure our British settlements in the West Indies'. Only 'the French, our deadly rivals', would benefit.

Underlying these anxieties were deeper ones about the Africans themselves. It was said that abolitionists were more concerned about the plight of slaves than the plight of Irish or English workers, though one could equally argue that Bristol's pro-slavery elite were not noted for their generous treatment of the poor.[94]

A few anti-abolitionists did go further to imply that the slave trade performed a positive function by arguing that if there were no slave trade, Africans would be left to the depravity of their own tyrannical rulers in Africa or to insurrection in the Caribbean. For example, one letter in *Bonner and Middleton's Bristol Journal*, written shortly after the public meeting on abolition in 1788, feared that 'the present zeal [for abolition] may be productive of a great national injury', for once the slave trade ceased, Africans would be left to cannibalism at home. Another correspondent, signing himself or herself 'Impartial', argued that the trade was

> so interwoven into the Trading Constitution of the Kingdom that to abandon it to our rivals the French would be to stab the vitals of this nation, as a trading people and leave our posterity to be in time Slaves themselves.

Similarly, 'An Englishman and Fellow citizen' maintained that abolition would be 'rash and ruinous' and could end in the British making slaves of themselves because once freed, the 'negro population of the West Indies' 'would cause sad calamities of fire and sword . . . [and plunge the English into a] gulph of misery and desolation'.

The wilder rhetoric of some pro-slavery advocates in the Bristol press needs to be understood in both its iconographical and its historical contexts. Graphic images of the body politic dismembered, dishonoured or otherwise harmed were a familiar trope in the discourse of British political caricature at least since the Civil War. The image of Britannia enslaved and ensnared was tied in not only to the particular political crisis alluded to, but to deeper notions of masculine honour and national identity. Both Jews and blacks were invoked as figures of ridicule in popular political discourse, as a 1784 spoof playbill against the Tory candidate of the day illustrates. It was entitled 'All in the Wrong or the blue's Turned blacks', and its stock characters (thinly veiled references to real local people) included 'the artful jew candidate', 'the white negro', 'Shylock the Jew' and 'Gaby Short Cock'.[95] The particular images invoked by the anti-slavery lobby during the abolition controversy are oddly reminiscent of those employed during the opposition to the naturalization of Jews thirty years earlier. In that controversy, the rite of circumcision provided a handy trope which enabled opponents to forecast the dissolution of the Christian constitution should Jews be admitted to the political process. Circumcision was conflated with castration and even crucifixion; all three represented a loss of political and moral integrity and autonomy which naturalization was seen to imply. The spectre of African liberation which abolition implied engendered an analogous set of metaphorical threats to British national identity: cannibalism replaced crucifixion; enslavement, castration; and pagan witchcraft, 'Pharisaical' Judaism.

In 1790 two anti-abolitionists, Lord Sheffield and Henry Cruger, were returned as MPs. The following June, a benefit performance held at the Theatre Royal was entitled *Liberty or Two sides of the Water*, featuring such stock characters as John and Lady Bull, the Jew, the Irishman, the Scotsman, an English sea captain and the French Grand Confederation. Although slaves were not explicitly mentioned, the configuration of characters bespeaks an anxiety to affirm the integrity of British national identity in politically unsettling circumstances and could only have acted to affirm the 'otherness' of those who were not white 'freeborn Englishmen'.[96]

The political circumstances of the day lent added force to all the images of terror and destruction, and all the affirmations of British sovereignty in the face of foreign threats. This was a threatening time for British traditionalists, and indeed for property-holders of any significance. By 1791 the French Revolution was becoming more radical. The French King had been arrested, territories such as Avignon and Alsace unilaterally annexed. A slave rebellion in the French colony of St Domingue in August 1791 struck terror into the hearts of British West Indian slave-holders. 'Calamities of fire and sword' were all around.

Notes

1 WRO, Dickinson Papers, 282/2.
2 Eric Williams, *Capitalism and Slavery* (London, 1944).
3 See Peter Marshall, 'The Anti Slave-Trade Movement in Bristol', in Patrick McGrath (ed.), *Bristol in the Eighteenth Century* (Newton Abbot, 1972), and his *Bristol and the Abolition of Slavery: The Politics of Emancipation* (Bristol: Bristol Historical Association, reprinted 1998), as well as A. Mary Richards, 'The Connection of Bristol with the African Slave Trade, with Some Account of the Currents of Public Opinion in the City', MA thesis, University of Bristol, 1923. The other substantive major treatments of the English abolitionist movement do not focus on Bristol. They include Roger Anstey, *The Atlantic Slave Trade and British Abolition, 1760–1810* (London, 1975); Seymour Drescher, *Econocide: British Slavery in the Age of Abolition* (Pittsburgh, 1977), though his *Capitalism and Antislavery: British Mobilization in Comparative Perspective* (New York, 1977) does refer to the Bristol press. David Brion Davis's *The Problem of Slavery in Western Culture* (Ithaca, NY, and London, 1966), *The Problem of Slavery in the Age of Revolution, 1770–1823* (Ithaca, NY, and London, 1975) and *Slavery and Human Progress* (New York, 1984) are more concerned with the intellectual grounding of anti-slavery thought than with the political campaigns associated with it. J. R. Oldfield, in *Popular Politics and British Anti-Slavery: The Mobilisation of Public Opinion against the Slave Trade, 1787–1807* (Manchester, 1995, repr. London and Portland, OR, 1998), looks at both the London and the provincial abolition campaigns, but does not deal in any depth with Bristol, nor does Colin Turley's *The Culture of English Anti-Slavery,*

1780–1860 (London, 1991). All these works, however, have, in various ways, set both the standard and the agenda for local studies such as my own.

4 According to Colin Turley, 'Rational Dissent' refers to those non-Anglican Protestant groups (such as English Presbyterians and General Baptists) who stressed the importance of rational individual inquiry and by the beginning of the nineteenth century was epitomized by Unitarianism. Given Bristol's particular experience, I would argue that rationalism as derived from the French Enlightenment was an influence on the development of anti-slavery sentiments of both Dissenters and Anglicans before the 1780s.

5 These were Nehemiah Champion, John Bull, Caleb Dickinson, Richard Franks, Francis Freeman, Joseph Kill, Caleb and Edward Lloyd, Charles Scandrett, Samuel Smith, Joshua Willcox; see BRO, 'Account of Money Collected . . . between 1747 and . . . 1751 for the rebuilding the Fryars' in SF/A12/1 and Proceedings in building Meeting Houses, 1670, 1747 . . . ', 'Building Book' (Friars Records *c.* 1842, H. 7), cited in M. H. Simpson, 'Bristol Friends and the Friends Meeting House', *Journal of the Friends Historical Society*, vol. 47 (1955), p. 26n. The names derived from these sources were then checked against the names of Bristol African merchants listed in 'Members of the Company of Merchants Trading to Africa', 23 June 1755, in BCRL, Jefferies Collection, vol. 13, p. 159, and a similar list dated 1 June 1759 cited in Donald Jones, *A History of Clifton* (Chichester, 1992), p. 88. Four of these Friends were on the twelve-strong committee overseeing the erection of the meeting house. Some 200 Friends contributed to the fund between 1747 and 1751.

6 Philip M. Hamer (ed.), *The Collected Papers of Henry Laurens*, 6 vols (Columbia, SC, 1968), vol. 1, pp. 252, 258, 267, 276.

7 Jones, *A History of Clifton*, pp. 45–6.

8 Elizabeth Donnison, *Documents Illustrative of the History of the Slave Trade to America* (Washington, DC, 1931), vol. 2, p. 522n; Jones, *A History of Clifton*, p. 88.

9 Anstey, *The Atlantic Slave Trade*, p. 202.

10 BRO, Men's Monthly Meeting, 31 August 1761 and 4 January 1762, SF/AC/10a, and see also 1 July 1785 and 28 November 1785, SF/A1/15.

11 Hugh Owen, *Two Centuries of Ceramic Art in Bristol being a History of the Manufacture of 'the True Porcelain' of Richard Champion: with a Biography Compiled from Private Correspondence Journals and Family Papers . . .*, 2 vols (London: Bell & Daldy, 1873), vol. 2, p. 271.

12 PRO, James Rogers Papers, invoice from Harfords & Co. for the *African Queen*, 9 June 1792, C107/13. This firm supplied Guinea goods to Rogers in the 1780s as well.

13 The Penn Street Tabernacle was opened by Whitefield in 1753 and the Countess of Huntingdon was a patron; Ignatius Jones, *Congregationalism in Bristol* (Bristol, 1947), p. 24; see Aaron Crossley Hobart Seymour, *The Life and Times of Selina, Countess of Huntingdon*, 2 vols (London: Simkin Marshall & Co., 1839), vol. 2, pp. 264–5; Drescher, *Capitalism and Antislavery*, pp. 116–17.

14 JRL, letter to Charles Wesley from Ephraim Robin John, 17 August 1774, Methodist Collection, DDCW 2/5. Thanks to Marika Sherwood for this reference. See also PRO, deposition of William Floyd, in *R. v. Lippincott and others*, KB1/19/3 Mich 1773, Anstey, p. 240. Thanks to Ruth Paley for the reference to the King's Bench material.

15 John Wesley New Rooms Library, *The Arminian Magazine* (1783), pp. 98–9, 151–3, and (1785), pp. 211–12. My thanks to Jeffrey Spittal, librarian of the New Rooms, for his kind help.

16 Friends House Library, Antislavery Collection microfilm, A. Benezet, *A Caution to Great Britain and Her Colonies In a Short Representation of the Calamitous State of the Enslaved Negroes in the British Dominions*, 2nd edition (Philadelphia and London, 1784); Gandy's letter is in *Some Historical Account of Guinea . . . its Situation, Produce, and the*

General disposition of its Inhabitants with an Inquiry into the Rise and Progress of the Slave Trade, its Natures, and Lamentable Effects (London: J. Phillips, 1788), pp. 125–31. For Champion's views, see Woodbrook College, 'Extracts from the Diary of Sarah Fox (née Champion), 1745–1802, copied by . . . Theodore Naish', 1873, Bevan–Naish Collection.

17 Silas Told, *An Account of the Life, Dealings of God with Silas Told, Late Preacher of the Gospel* . . . (London, 1786); *The Arminian Magazine*, vol. 10 (1787), pp. 183–5, 628. See references to the Wesleys dining with Told in London in JRL, Catalogue of the Charles Wesley Papers, vol. 2 (1994), DDCW 7/27, and Thomas Jackson (ed.), *The Journal of the Rev. Charles Wesley*, 2 vols (London, 1849), p. 263. According to the Revd Mark Guy Pearse, in 'A Newgate Class Leader and Tyburn Chaplain', *The Wesleyan Methodist Magazine*, vol. 132 (1909), pp. 52–7, 135–9, Told was converted on his return to England at the Foundery in London and ended his days comforting condemned prisoners in Tyburn and is portrayed doing so by William Hogarth in his print *The Idle Prentice Executed at Tyburn* . . .

18 Nehemiah Curnock (ed.), *The Journal of the Rev. John Wesley*, 7 vols (London: Epworth Press, 1938), vol. 7, pp. 144, 333n.

19 For a fuller explication of Wesleyan membership in this period, see John Kent, 'Wesleyan Membership in Bristol, 1783', in D. Walker, A. Percival, W. J. Sheils and J. Kent (eds), *An Ecclesiastical Miscellany* (Gateshead: Bristol and Gloucestershire Archaeological Society Records Section, 1976), vol. IV, pp. 105–32.

20 For Raynal, see Anthony J. Barker, *The African Link: Attitudes to the Negro in the Era of the Atlantic Slave Trade, 1550–1807* (London, 1978), p. 21; for books consulted at Bristol's new library, see John Brewer, *The Pleasures of the Imagination: English Culture in the Eighteenth Century* (London, 1997), p. 181; John Latimer, *The Annals of Bristol in the Eighteenth Century* (Bristol: privately printed, 1893), pp. 403–4. The present building was erected in 1789.

21 *FFBJ*, 22 March 1760.

22 John Hippisley, '"On the Populousness of Africa": An Eighteenth Century Text', reprinted in *Population and Development Review*, vol. 24, no. 3 (September 1998), pp. 601–8. My thanks to Professor Mansell Protheroe for providing me with a copy of this essay.

23 BCRL, notices and playbills from 9 August 1761, 1 August 1762, 20 June 1763, 25 July 1763 and 15 August 1763, in the Richard Smith Theatre Collection, vol. 1, pp. 189, 196, 204.

24 'Narva and Mored: An African Eclogue' and 'Heccar and Gaira: An African Eclogue', *The Poetical Works of Thomas Chatterton*, ed. John Richmond (London: Walter Scott, 1885), pp. 37, 40.

25 Alan Richardson, 'Race and Representation in Bristol Abolitionist Poetry', in Tim Fulford and Peter J. Kitson (eds), *Romanticism and Colonialism: Writing and Empire, 1780–1830* (Cambridge, 1998), p. 137.

26 Anon. [William Combe], *The Philosopher in Bristol. Part the Second* (Bristol: G. Routh, 1775), pp. 50–2. Thanks to Michael Richardson of the University of Bristol Library, Special Collections for this reference. See also James Bandinel, *Some Account of the Trade in Slaves from Africa as Connected with Europe and America from the Introduction of the Trade into Modern Europe, down to the Present Time; Especially with Reference to the Efforts Made by the British Government for Its Extinction* (London, 1942, reprinted 1968), pp. 68–72, on Enlightenment and Evangelical influences which promoted abolitionist sentiment.

27 Anon., *The Philosopher in Bristol*, pp. 50–2.

28 See BL, *Proceedings of the Anti-Slavery Meeting held at the Guildhall, Bristol* (Bristol, 1826), 8156.a.14.

29 In his 1795 lecture on the slave trade, Coleridge distinguishes between sensibility and benevolence; see David Richardson, *Bristol, Africa and the Eighteenth-Century Slave Trade to America*, 4 vols (Bristol: Bristol Record Society, 1986, 1987, 1991 and 1996), vol. 4, p. xxxvii.

30 John Latimer, *The Annals of Bristol in the Eighteenth Century* (Bristol: privately printed, 1893), p. 416; Wesley R. Savadge, 'The West Country and the American Mainland Colonies, 1763–1783, with Special Reference to the Merchants of Bristol', B.Litt. thesis, University of Oxford, 1952, p. 120.

31 Linda Colley, *Britons: Forging the Nation, 1707–1837* (London, 1992), p. 354.

32 Gloucestershire Record Office, Granville Sharp Papers, correspondence of Bishop of Bristol with Granville Sharp, 29 May 1777, also 7 October and 16 May 1777, D3549, 13/1/B36.

33 Davis, *The Problem of Slavery in Western Culture*, p. 398.

34 Curnock, *The Journal of the Rev. John Wesley*, vol. 7, p. 333n.

35 Josiah Tucker, 'A Treatise Concerning Civil Government' (1781), reprinted in Robert Livingston Schuyler (ed.), *Josiah Tucker: A Selection from His Economic and Political Writing* (New York, 1931), p. 493.

36 Martin Crossley Evans, *Hannah More* (Bristol: Bristol Historical Association, 1999), p. 2.

37 *The Bristol Gazette* of 31 January 1788 lists names of the committee of 20 men who oversaw the petition campaign. Table 7 cross-references these names with those listed in *Sketchley's Directory of 1775* and *Matthew's Directory for 1789*.

38 Oldfield, *Popular Politics and British Anti-Slavery*, p. 138.

39 Dyer: 30 January, p. 244; extracts from William Dyer's diary.

40 Olinthus Gregory (ed.), *The Miscellaneous Works of Robert Hall with a Memoir by Olinthus Gregory* (London: Bell & Daldy, 1868), cited in Richards, 'The Connection of Bristol with the African Slave Trade', p. 33.

41 BRO, Olive M. Griffiths, 'Sidelights on the History of Presbyterian-Unitarianism from the Records of Lewins Mead Chapel, Bristol' (typed MS, n.d.), p. 8.A3; BRO, list of subscribers, Lewins Mead congregation, 1781–90, 39461/F/4a, and minutes and list of members, 1813, 39461/M/1(a); Savadge, 'The West Country and the American Mainland Colonies', pp. 93–4.

42 Griffiths, 'Sidelights on the History of Presbyterian-Unitarianism', pp. 1–12.A3; for the increasing tendency towards Unitarianism, see also Jones, *Congregationalism in Bristol*, p. 21.

43 *Bristol Gazette*, 31 January 1788.

44 Roger Hayden, 'Caleb Evans and the Anti-Slavery Movement in Bristol', paper delivered at the Baptist College, Bristol, 13 May 2000. I am indebted to Dr Hayden for allowing me to cite from his paper, which is based on original archival research.

45 Caleb Jones, *British Freedom Realized: a Sermon Preached at Broadmead Bristol 5 November 1788 being the Hundreth Anniversary of the Glorious Revolution . . .* (Bristol: William Pine n.d. but *c.* 1788).

46 Richards, 'The Connection of Bristol with the African Slave Trade', p. 57.

47 BCRL, obituary of Robert Hall, Jefferies Collection, vol. 12; 'Socinianism' was a Christian heresy which denied the divinity of Jesus and thus denied the validity of a trinitarian view of God. It was associated with Arianism and the two were associated by the 1760s with Unitarianism. For a fuller discussion of its complex theological and political implications, see J. C. D. Clark, *English Society, 1688–1832* (Cambridge, 1985), pp. xiii, 281–2.

48 Latimer, *Annals of Bristol in the Eighteenth Century*, p. 482.

49 *Bonner and Middleton's Bristol Journal*, 4 August 1787.

50 Anstey, *The Atlantic Slave Trade*, p. 265.

51 Richards, 'The Connection of Bristol with the African Slave Trade', p. 73.

52 Anstey, *The Atlantic Slave Trade*, pp. 268–72; Marshall, 'The Anti-Slave Trade Movement in Bristol', pp. 195–9; Richards, 'The Connection of Bristol with the African Slave Trade', pp. 33–5.

53 Clare Midgely, *Women against Slavery: The British Campaigns, 1780–1870* (London and New York, 1992), p. 32; for the links between Newton, More, Sarah Wesley (the daughter of Charles) and Cottle, see Basil Cottle, 'The Life (1770–1853), Writings and Literary Relationship of Joseph Cottle of Bristol', Ph.D. dissertation, University of Bristol, 1958, pp. 12–13.

54 Diary of Sarah Fox, 2 February 1777.

55 Mary Waldron, 'The Slave Trade and the Women of Bristol', paper delivered at the John Cabot Conference, University of the West of England, Bristol, 1 May 1997. My thanks to Mary Waldron for a copy of this paper and other related information.

56 Ann Yearsley, 'Poem on the Inhumanity of the Slave Trade', in Moira Ferguson, *Subject to Others: British Women Writers and Colonial Slavery, 1670–1834* (London and New York, 1992), pp. 170–2; for a full and engaging treatment of Yearsley's life and work, see Mary Waldron, *Lactilla: The Life and Writings of Ann Yearsley, Milkwoman of Clifton, 1753–1806* (Athens, GA, 1996).

57 A. Richardson, 'Race and Representation', pp. 140–1; Ferguson, *Subject to Others*, p. 170. It should be noted that one of Yearsley's correspondents and friends, Elizabeth Dawson, was an admirer of the writings of Ignatius Sancho, the first African to be published in Britain, as well as of Yearsley's 'Poem on the Inhumanity of the Slave Trade'. It seems, therefore, possible that Yearsley would also have been familiar with Sancho's writing, but there is no direct proof for this. See West Yorkshire Archive Service, correspondence of E. Dawson, 23 March 1788 and 14 April 1788, TA/18/9, and Mary Waldron, 'Ann Yearsley: The Bristol Manuscript Revisited', *Women's Writing*, vol. 3, no. 1 (1996), pp. 35–45. My thanks to Mary Waldron for bringing the existence of this collection of letters to my attention.

58 *Bristol Gazette*, 13 March 1788; Richards, 'The Connection of Bristol with the African Slave Trade', p. 64.

59 *BMBJ*, 5 July 1788.

60 Midgely, *Women against Slavery*, p. 35.

61 Woodbrook College, November 1788, 'Extracts from the Diary of Sarah Fox'.

62 *Ibid.*, March 1777 and 8 January 1778.

63 *Ibid.*, November 1788.

64 *Ibid.*

65 *Ibid.*, 3 January 1787. Shurmer was possibly one William Shurmor, whom *Sketchley's Bristol Directory for 1775* lists as a gentleman resident in Dighton Street. And Wadstrup was possibly C. B. Wedstrom, a Swede associated by 1790 with the Sierra Leone settlement discussed below; Anthony J. Barker, *The African Link: British Attitudes to the Negro in the Era of the Atlantic Slave Trade, 1550–1807* (London, 1978), p. 28.

66 John Pinney to James Tobin, 30 October 1783, in R. H. Pares, Microfilm Notes on his *West India Fortune* (Rhodes House Library), p. 252.

67 In his *Cursory Remarks upon the Reverend Mr. Ramsay's Essay on the Treatment and Conversion of the African Slaves in the Sugar Colonies, by a Friend to the West-India Colonies and Their Inhabitants* (Bristol and London, 1785), Friends House Library. See also David Small, 'James Tobin (1736–1817)', unpublished MS, 1999. My thanks to David Small for letting me read this paper.

68 Lilian Penson, 'The London West India Interest in the Eighteenth Century', *English Historical Review*, vol. 36 (1921), p. 385.

69 BSMV, West India Trade Minutes of meeting 15 April 1789. Additional biographical material on many of those listed can be found in Richardson, *Bristol, Africa and the*

Eighteenth-Century Slave Trade, vol. 4, p. xxii. Information about West India merchants/planters' investments in slaving voyages is also gleaned from vol. 4 of Richardson's book.

70 BSMV, West India Trade Minutes of meeting 15 April 1789. Additional material on religious affiliation, occupation, residence, etc. gleaned from W. Matthews, *Matthews Complete Bristol Directory* (Bristol, 1789), and *Sketchley's Directory of Bristol for 1775*, ed. B. Little (Bristol, 1775, reprinted Bath, 1971). I also checked the names listed against the subscription lists of various Dissenting chapels in Bristol, which are held in the BRO.

71 Kenneth Morgan, 'The Bright Family Papers', *Archives*, vol. 22, no. 97 (October 1997), p. 122.

72 Hayden, 'Caleb Evans and the Anti-Slavery Movement'.

73 The opera was written by George Colman the Younger; Davis, *The Problem of Slavery in Western Culture*, pp. 12–13.

74 According to Southey, the Bristol and Bath theatres shared the same company, and what was performed in Bristol on Monday was performed in Bath on Tuesday and Thursday. Cumberland, author of *The West Indian*, and Sheridan also stayed at the same lodgings when their plays were staged in the two cities; Southey, *Life and Correspondence of Robert Southey*, pp. 41, 73.

75 BRO, Macready's Prompt Book for *Inkle and Yarico* (n.p., n.d. but *c.* 1799?), 8979 (11).

76 *Ibid.*

77 *Ibid.*

78 *Ibid.*

79 *Ibid.* See Gretchen Gerzina, *Black England: Life before Emancipation* (London, 1995), pp. 8–9, which discusses the play, though not in its Bristol context.

80 The reference is to an (uncontextualized) version of the story which ends with Yarico enslaved and alone, but even in the sanitized theatrical version discussed in this chapter, 'the vision of "cultural harmony through romance" is not fulfilled'; Mary Louise Pratt, *Imperial Eyes: Travel Writing and Transculturation* (London, 1992), pp. 99–100.

81 *FFBJ*, 22 November 1788.

82 PRO, James Rogers Papers, William Webb to James Rogers, 6 July 1785, C/107/14. Webb, a Bristolian resident in Dominica, proposed an elaborate scheme for using French merchants and crew with the British captain masquerading as an American in order to qualify for the bounty; a letter from Francis (?) and Robert Smith, also in Dominica, to James Rogers, 21 July 1788, C/107/7 part 2, explicitly refers to the 'late restrictions on the African trade' as a further reason for 'turning some of our own ships under French colours'.

83 PRO, James Rogers Papers, Thomas Gillett & Co., 'Proposals for Sale of Negroes . . .', 30 September 1788, C107/7, part 2.

84 *Ibid.*

85 Abuse of the Dolben Act also appears to have been a factor in a case brought against another of Rogers's slave-ship captains, John Goodrich, by the ship's own surgeon around 1791; PRO, James Rogers Papers, invoice from the solicitors Hughes & Co., n.d. but *c.* 1791, C107/13.

86 Neely reports, 'Having a little difference with [the Captain's] Brother's whore she came to make her complaint and finding no just cause against me she was ordered down on which I give her a little twig on the elbow it would not have hurt the eye with a small line about as thick as a goose quill and in length about 18 inches'; PRO, Matthew Neely to James Rogers, 10 May 1789, James Rogers Papers, C/107/2.

87 PRO, Matthew Neely to James Rogers, 10 May 1789, James Rogers Papers, C/107/2.

88 Kennedy's re-employment seems even more inexplicable given the negligence and cowardice he displayed when the ship was wrecked off the Irish coast on its return to

Bristol; PRO, letters from Kennedy, O'Donnell and others during May 1789, James Rogers Papers, C107/2. See Richardson, *Bristol, Africa and the Eighteenth-Century Slave Trade*, vol. 4, pp. 126, 130 for the voyage of the *Juba* and pp. 200, 206, 228 for Kennedy's later employment by Rogers.

89 PRO, James Rogers Papers, James Laroche to James Rogers, 27/8/89, C/107/9. I could not find Harrison's name on any of the muster rolls held by the Merchant Venturers for that period, but it is not necessarily a complete list.

90 BRO, letter from R. Miles to C. Bell, Charles Bell Papers, 38109(2).

91 *Ibid.*, pp. 34–5; Marshall, 'The Anti Slave-Trade Movement in Bristol', pp. 195–9; Anstey, *The Atlantic Slave Trade*, pp. 268–72.

92 PRO, James Rogers Papers, Robinson and Heywood to Rogers & Co., 9 April 1792, C107/7, part 2.

93 PRO, James Rogers Papers, Munro McFarlane & Co. to James Rogers, 14 June 179? [2?].

94 A distinction might be made between Wilberforce and other abolitionists. Granville Sharp, that most indefatigable campaigner for poor blacks, also campaigned against the impressment of (white) British seamen, whose lot anti-abolitionists had compared to that of the slave. See GRO, Granville Sharp Papers, D3549, 13/3/36.

95 BCRL, B13035.

96 *Sarah Farley's Bristol Journal*, 25 June 1791; Kathleen Wilson, *The Sense of the People: Politics, Culture and Imperialism in England, 1715–1785* (Cambridge, 1995), p. 20, talks about the way the term 'the people' was 'used to delimit the political nation' and sanction government policy, and how it excluded as 'others', 'those who were considered at vairous times not to be fit for membership: the feminine and effeminate . . . Catholics, Scots, Irish, Africans and Jews'.

5

ABOLITION IN A COLD CLIMATE, 1792-1807

In war-time the most good-humoured men are apt to be irritated by the persistent agitation of a controversial question not directly concerned with the winning of the war. And such little connexion as there was between the Slave Trade and the war told against Abolition. (R. Coupland, *Wilberforce: A Narrative* (Oxford, 1923))

The bells of Bristol's grandest church, St Mary Redcliffe, were rung to celebrate the defeat of Wilberforce's Abolition Bill in 1791.[1] By the following year, Tom Paine was publicly burned in effigy in the city, and local abolitionists were tending to stress the moral corruption which the slave trade engendered rather than the rights of man. As the backlash against the French Revolution gained momentum, those fighting for the end of the slave trade in Parliament did all they could to disassociate their cause from the taint of radicalism.

Our agenda here is to trace the progress of this 'respectable anti-slavery'. We shall explore the role local women played in the abolitionist culture in Bristol and then discuss some of the anti-slavery rhetoric employed by some of the Romantic poets, notably Coleridge, Southey and those in their immediate Bristol circle. Moving somewhat further afield, we shall go on to consider, for the first time, Bristol's international links with the newly founded 'free' settlement of Sierra Leone on the grounds that it reveals a good deal about the different currents within English abolition as a whole. Turning homewards, we shall evaluate what evidence survives about the position of black people in Bristol during the 1790s, the way slavery was represented in Bristol's theatre and how Bristol's press dealt with the abolitionist victory of 1807.

Respectable anti-slavery

When Wilberforce delivered his speech in the Commons on abolition in April 1792, Bristol press coverage was intense. Wilberforce had accused a number of ships, including the Bristol slavers *Thomas*, *Recovery* and *Wasp*, of being involved in the August 1791 bombardment of New Calabar.[2] He also accused John Kimber, the captain of the *Recovery*, of assaulting and causing the death of a 15-year-old African girl who had refused to dance naked for him on deck during that same voyage. The extensive newspaper coverage given to both Wilberforce's speech and Kimber's case has been amply described by Marshall. Though no Bristol broadsides on the Kimber case have as yet come to light, the combination of local actors and prurient appeal makes it seem likely that the case was discussed in the city even by those who did not read a newspaper. Both Kimber and Walter Jacks, one of the *Recovery*'s owners, were local men, and it was Jack's testimony which was crucial in Kimber's acquittal.

But readers of Bristol's newspapers had few excuses for not knowing about the sexual and physical abuse endemic on slave ships. The Kimber case confirmed Alexander Falconbridge's account of his experiences as a slave-ship's surgeon which had earlier been serialized in *Felix Farley's Bristol Journal*:

> On board some ships, the common sailors are allowed to have intercourse with such of the black women whose consent they can procure . . . [and] the officers are permitted to indulge their passions among them at pleasure; and are sometimes guilty of such brutal excesses as disgrace human nature.[3]

Precisely how enslaved women aboard such ships were thought to have been able to withhold consent is not discussed. We have seen what was alleged to have happened to one woman aboard the *Juba* when she attempted to refuse the attentions of Captain Kennedy, and the girl aboard the *Recovery* was said to have fared even worse. Such revelations of sexual exploitation and degradation had particular resonance for white women in Britain. As Mary Wollstonecraft had pointed out, white Englishwomen and African slaves had much in common with regard to their lack of legal status and their economic dependence. Both groups were also sexually vulnerable, a point which was not lost on Wollstonecraft's friend, the Bristol-born actress and writer Mary Darby Robinson (aka 'Perdita'). A former pupil of Hannah More, Robinson wrote a number of anti-slavery poems, including 'The Negro Girl', 'The Negro Child' and 'The African'. The cast-off mistress of both the Prince Regent and the pro-slavery lobbyist Banastre Tarleton, Robinson had been reduced to poverty when her male protectors abandoned her, and as Moira Ferguson observes, her poems are full of parallels between the plight of impoverished and dependent Englishwomen and that of enslaved Africans. In 'The Negro Girl' Robinson condemns, as she does so often, those who 'nurs'd in splendour, deal Oppression's blow', and the sexual predation of slavers is a recurring theme.[4] In 'The African', Robinson describes the humiliation of the enslaved man when

The darling of his heart, his sable love
Selected from the trembling timid throng
By the wan TYRANT, whose licentious touch
Seals the dark fiat of the Slave's despair.[5]

Immensely popular in her day, Robinson began to suffer from her association with radicalism and her sexual 'improprieties' as the century drew to an increasingly puritanical close. Though admired by Coleridge, Robinson would, by Victorian times, be dismissed by one Bristol writer as 'the girl who strayed', her 'reputation [deemed] too bad for . . . [her poetry] to be seriously considered'.[6]

Respectable ladies might more safely manifest their abolitionist sympathies by flocking to sermons given by abolitionist vicars. No such sermons survive for Bristol in this period, though it is known that the fashionable Reverend John Stonhouse of Hotwells was passionately opposed to the trade. When Sarah Champion visited the More sisters in Bath in December 1791, she accompanied them to hear their 'favourite preacher' there, a 22-year-old son of a stonemason. She records in her diary that 'The chief subject of this afternoon was the abolition of the slave trade. A West India planter was of the company and a sister of Lord Sheffield.'[7] Champion notes these members of the audience precisely because they would have been discomfited by the sermon's content. Lord Sheffield, then the Whig MP for Bristol, was a vigorous opponent of the abolitionist cause on behalf of the city, and had published a pamphlet defending the slave trade the previous year.[8] The fact that such high-ranking people would attend such a sermon indicates that a cultural shift had occurred since the 1760s when the Quakers first began their lonely battle against the slave trade.

By this time, the 'acceptable face' of abolitionism came to be associated with moral purity rather than egalitarian ideals in a way that reminds one of the evolution of the late Victorian women's movement. If, as has been suggested, abolitionism was a way of rebranding England's symbolic role as a beacon of liberty after the American Revolution, the brand of liberty on offer was to be paternalistically *conferred*, rather than seized.[9]

Women were also involved in the successful abolitionist campaign to boycott slave-produced sugar which was launched in 1792. Ignored in Marshall's account of the anti-slave trade movement in Bristol, this consumer-led activity marked an important new development in political mobilization. Because of its domestic base, it involved women as active participants from the start. Hannah More was prominent in the boycott. She or her friend William Cowper probably wrote the poem extracted below, a rare example of abolitionist humour. Published anonymously in a Bristol paper, it chided genteel society for its moral inconsistency:

I own I am shocked at this purchase of slaves,
And fear those who buy them and sell them, are knaves:
What I hear of their hardships, their tortures and groans,
Is almost enough to draw pity from stones.
I pity them greatly, but I must be mum,
For how could we do without sugar and rum?
Especially sugar, so needful we see,
What, give up our desserts, our coffee and tea?[10]

The 'anti-saccharites', as they were called, were themselves satirized for their double standards, and their sanctimonious asceticism. Hannah More's poem aside, humour seemed to be a weapon more frequently exploited by the anti-abolitionists. One spoof letter reprinted in Bristol from the London press is worth citing here. Addressed to 'Lady L——', it is purportedly from a 6-year-old boy who asks to be released from his promise to abstain from sugar:

> I cannot think, dear Lady . . . how anybody who will not eat sugar because it is eating Negro flesh, can handle gold or silver or find themselves with silver spoons or forks; for if eating sugar is eating negroes' flesh, sure every time anybody puts a fork or spoon in their mouth, it is putting a dead negro's finger or toe there.[11]

This satire conveys anti-abolitionists' conviction that abolitionists were dangerously ill-informed and acting in an emotional 'frenzy' – a word used more than once in local sources. Its willingness to use the gruesomely cannibalistic images to make the joke also reveals a tough-minded indifference to the allegations of distress and suffering amongst the slaves.

Although 'the sugar interest from Bristol to Liverpool' did feel the impact of the boycott at the height of the accompanying petition campaign of 1792, its impact was short-lived.[12] The slave revolt in St Domingue (Haiti), which spread into the neighbouring Spanish colony of Santo Domingo, was to limit the supply of sugar to the advantage of British producers. The reports of the 'very serious insurrection at St. Domingo' came to one Bristol trader from some London associates:

> it is said 50,000 negros [*sic*] are in arms and that they have burnt several plantations and Houses, there is every reason to believe this . . . [will] make some alteration in West India produce, at present the sugar market is very dull *and unless the news gives it a lift* the prices will be lower.[13] [emphasis added]

As it happened, the interruption of supplies from St Domingue did boost Continental demand for British sugar, a fact which undermined the boycotters' objectives. But the public image of West Indian sugar had been changed for ever, and a whole new section of the British populace had been invited to think about the slave trade in terms of their own personal responsibility.

Romanticism and anti-slavery

Abolitionists in Cottle's circle in the days of mounting political reaction included the 'clever young Quaker' Robert Lovell (1770–96); that son of a Bristol linen-draper, Robert Southey; and Southey's brilliant friend Samuel Taylor Coleridge. In 1794, when they were little known, these men were dreaming of a 'Pantosocratic' utopia, a place where they could live and work in equality and according to the laws of nature. Their vision was in part inspired by Keane's South Pacific idyll.[14]

All four writers published works criticizing the slave trade in this period. Cottle, in his 'Malvern Hills', condemns

the SLAVE MERCHANTS, Britons Blush to Own!
Who consecrate their influence, all their power,
Not to improve, reform, and elevate
But to abase . . .

And alone of his poetic associates, he provides a vivid picture of the European and African slave trader, 'lured by the love of gold!', on the coast of Benin:

There they meet!
The white men and the black, pre-eminent,
Each in his way: both lured by love of Gold!
The merchant, who, so late, his footmarks left
On Niger's boasted margin, gathering still
His merchandize, indifferent how, now stands
Upon Benin's wide shore. He looks around,
Hope realized, with a majestic fort
On Wares of flesh and blood. The buyer, too,
No whit behind his peer, in consequence,
Emcompassed by select commodities
(Powder, or 'slaughter weapons', spirits, beads)
Offers, denies, rejects, each master-fiend
In trick and subterfuge . . .

Coleridge and Lovell both invoke the spectre of Chatterton when they lambast slave-trading and the materialism which underlies it. The satirist Lovell decries those Bristol merchants who spurned Chatterton and thereby 'crush'd young merit in its rising hour'. 'Trade, mighty trade', he contends, so dominates the city that it 'drives the nobler cares of *mind* away'.

Wide spreads the sail from BRISTOL'S busy quay
To Afric's coast directs the eager way,
Their motive avarice, and trade their plan,
Their means oppression, and their commerce man.[15]

In truth, Bristol's share of the British slave trade had, by the time this poem was published, dwindled away to a relatively insignificant level. As Marshall states, the economic crisis of 1793 was undoubtedly the most immediate factor in its decline. Yet many preferred to attribute this change in affairs to the advanced sensibilities of Bristol merchants. Invoking Enlightenment rhetoric in the service of local boosterism, the *Matthews Directory for Bristol 1793–4* declared:

The Ardour for trade to Africa for men and women, our fellow creatures equals is much abated among the humane and benevolent merchants of Bristol. In 1787 there were but 30 ships employed in this melancholy traffick while the people of Liverpool, in their indiscriminate rage for commerce and for getting money at all events have nearly engrossed this Trade, incredibly exceeded London and Bristol in it, employ many thousands tons of shipping for the purpose of buying and enslaving God's rational creatures, and are the vendors (horrifico referens) of the souls and bodies of men and women to almost all the West Indian Islands!!!![16]

Lovell's poem deflates such humbug by reminding his readers that slavery was at the root of the city's West India trade:

Slaves torn and mangled, cultivate the sweet,
That trade may thrive, and luxury may eat.[17]

Coleridge, in an abolitionist lecture delivered in the city in 1795, attacked the 'false and bastard sensibility' by which men claim to be party to fine feelings whilst countenancing slavery. Sensibility and benevolence, Coleridge warns, are not the same, since the latter demands action and some degree of self-denial.[18]

Coleridge's close friend Robert Southey similarly condemned such politically vacuous forms of gentility. Southey wrote six sonnets entitled 'Poems Concerning the Slave Trade'. He also wrote 'The Sailor Who Had Served in the Slave Trade', which was arguably the most powerful of his anti-slavery verses. Unlike his other poems on the subject, this ballad has a passion which derives from its focus on the sufferings not of the enslaved Africans, but on the true story of a Bristol seaman who crewed on a slave ship. According to the poem's brief preface, a Dissenting minister of Bristol (probably John Prior Estlin of the Lewins Mead Congregation) 'discovered a sailor in the neighbourhood of that city, groaning and praying in a cow-house. The circumstance which occasioned his agony of mind is detailed in the annexed ballad, without the slightest addition or alteration.'[19] The sailor, readers are told, had been forced by his captain to flog to death an enslaved woman who had refused to eat. The poem opens with an account of the remorseful sailor's continuing mental torment:

I shut my eyes . . . It matters not.
Still, still the same I see,
And when I lie me down at night
'Tis always day with me!

This sounds to modern ears like an account of post-traumatic stress syndrome and echoes Clarkson's accounts of the cruelties inflicted on British seamen:

we were forced by threats
And blows to make them eat.

The sailor himself, in a scene that recalls Harry Gandy's experience aboard his first slaving voyage, is compelled to violence:

The captain made me tie her up,
And flog while he stood by;
And then he cursed me if I staid
My hand to hear her cry.

She shriek'd she groan'd . . . I could not spare,
For the Captain he stood by;
Dear God! That I might rest one night
From that poor creature's cry!

The sailor exhibits his humanity by his reluctance to do the deed and by his expression of horror against violating a woman in this way:

What woman's child a sight like that
Could bear to look upon!

By contrast, the slaves were described as 'sulky' for refusing their food, and the woman in question, 'sulkier than the rest'. She is a 'poor creature' who 'shriek'd and groan'd' under the whip, a 'poor wretch' who is 'flung overboard' when her moans finally cease. There is no sense of *her* interiority, and the only description of *her* inner feelings is marginalized in relation to those of the sailor:

She could not be more glad than I
When she was taken down:
A blessed minute! . . . 'twas the last
That I have ever known![20]

Only the animal sounds she makes and the horror of her physical condition are portrayed:

Oh Jesus God! I hear her cries!
I see her in her blood![21]

Southey's evident empathy with the seaman manifestly edges out any similar identification with the sailor's victim.

As staunchly abolitionist as he is, Cottle too comes across as more emotionally charged when describing the sufferings of white workers than when describing those of black slaves. Certainly Cottle, Southey and Coleridge all belie the jibe that abolitionists cared more about Africans abroad than about suffering nearer to home. Cottle, in his 'Malvern Hills', likens child labourers in England to slaves and calls their employers 'slave merchants legalized'. As for the maidservants employed in genteel British homes, he asks:

Are not those slaves, and piteous in their plight!
Forced by Task-Masters, often Mistresses
Feeling of heart, who would not hurt a fly!

Who yet exposed their charge, the tender sex
To rigorous exactions, scarced surpass'd
In the abhorr'd Antilles?

Coleridge put a similar point in more revolutionary terms in his 1795 lecture on slavery:

> Now I appeal to common sense whether to affirm that the slaves are as well off as our peasantry be not the same as to assert our peasantry are as bad off as the Negroe Slave? And whether, if our peasantry believed it, they would not be inclined to rebel?[22]

In 1795 Coleridge clearly believed both English peasants and African slaves *were entitled to rebel.* But his pronouncements did not signify a lasting commitment to achieving political equality for the slaves. The Reign of Terror, the unrest and brutalities in St Domingue and the continuing war against France proved too much for the radicalism of both Southey and Coleridge. Though Southey eventually became a Tory, he seems to have remained a liberal on race well into the 1820s. He urged his brother Tom, a naval officer in the Caribbean at this time, to write a history of the West Indies which would not gloss over African culture and the conditions of the slaves.[23] In 1803 he wrote to a friend of his efforts to promote the boycott of slave-grown sugar. He personally lobbied more than 50 persons but was exasperated by his lack of success: 'What', he complained, '. . . can be expected from those, who will not remedy so horrible an iniquity by so easy an exertion?'[24]

Though Southey went on to support the cause of emancipation after abolition was achieved, it was unlikely that he, as a Tory, would have supported full political equality for black people in the colonies.

Sierra Leone and Bristol, 1787–99

In 1786 the Bristol slave-trader James Rogers received a letter from one James Harris, a black man then living in London. We do not know if Harris had once lived in Bristol or whether he was merely the servant of one of James Rogers's London business associates. But Harris knew the Bristol slave-trader well enough to ask for his assistance. In his beautifully penned and eloquent letter, which he appears (to judge from his misspelling of certain words in a particularly 'Caribbean' way') to have written himself, Harris asks Rogers to intervene on his behalf with his former employer, Mr Gibbs. Gibbs had apparently promised Harris his manumission papers but had subsequently refused to supply them, despite Harris's numerous entreaties. Without them Harris and his young family were rendered desperate, as he could find no employment in London, and risked enslavement if he sought it in the Caribbean:

> I am Sir, . . . in the greatest distress immaginable [sic] wanting of bread and cloaths for the quality in general have such an aversion to black servants so that their [sic] is not one in a hundred that will imploy [sic] or take one into their service but for what reason I cannot say.[25]

There is no indication that Rogers ever answered the letter, but it affords us rare first-hand insight into the experience of black people then resident in Britain. Harris seems to have been one of a growing number of Africans who could not find employment in the capital. The white propertied classes, made skittish by the Mansfield judgment and by report after report of slave rebellion, turned out their black servants onto the streets rather than pay them wages.

The new settlement in Sierra Leone was originally conceived by the abolitionist Granville Sharp as a constitutional refuge for just such black people as Harris. Sharp, who had first forced the *Somerset* case on Mansfield's attention, saw a free African colony as a new opportunity for the black English poor. In 1787, over 385 black unemployed people and 70 white women, many of them branded prostitutes, were shipped at Treasury expense over to Sierra Leone.[26] They were under-provisioned and completely unprepared for the conditions there, and all but 60 died before the first year was out. By 1791 the enterprise was reborn as the Sierra Leone Company under the management of such prominent Evangelicals as John Thornton and William Wilberforce, despite the opposition of Bristol's MP Lord Sheffield.[27]

A number of Bristolians had an interest in the territory of Sierra Leone in the last decades of the eighteenth century. These were not simply the slave-traders who had long plied this part of the West African coast, but also various officials, teachers and missionaries and a few destitute women who, for a variety of reasons, came to do service in the new settlement there. During this same period, Africans from Sierra Leone met Bristolians in England and some may even have visited the city itself. The stories of some of these individuals merit our consideration since they shed new light not only on the operations of Bristol slave-traders there but on the political and religious differences within the abolitionist camp.

When the settlement was under its first Governor, the democratically inclined John Clarkson (Thomas Clarkson's brother), it seems to have been regarded as a democratic refuge for all, regardless of rank or colour. British seamen reportedly used it to escape from particularly oppressive captains on the Africa run and one contemporary living there at the time complained of the colony being 'much pestered by renegade seamen'.[28] When a surgeon employed on a Bristol slaver fled his ship for the Sierra Leone settlement, his captain followed in hot pursuit. But, as he disgustedly reported to his Bristol employer, James Rogers, 'The settlers would not suffer me to take him off as they deem'd it a free town.' A few months later, the captain told Rogers:

> 5 of my people as [*sic*] taken the opportunity in running from the ships at Bence island without any Reason but having great encouragement from the settlement of Sierra Leone which has been the cause of many ships in the slave trade disman'd in the river.[29]

The next major influx of black settlers was of so-called 'Nova Scotians'. These people were former American slaves who had sided with the British during the War of Independence. 'Fobbed off' with their freedom and transportation to the uncongenial climes of Nova Scotia in Canada, they never received the land they were promised there and were left to languish in poverty. Many were literate and most seemed to be pious Evangelical Christians, a fact that endeared them, at least at first, to the company. A few years later, Maroons from Jamaica would join them, but in 1792 they seem to be the only colonial blacks in Sierra Leone, despite a resentful charge in the Bristol press that rebels from St Domingue were also being sent there:[30]

> We learn from Kingston Jamaica that on the arrival there of the Negroes who had been sent off the island of St Domigue by the people of colour, after having been extremely useful to them in murdering the white people, and plundering and burning their plantations, it was proposed to the Governor in Council to send them to England . . . in order that they may transport them to Sierra Leone, to assist in the fortune of the new settlement there.[31]

Alexander Falconbridge and his Bristol-born wife, Anna Maria, had travelled out to the settlement in 1791 when Alexander was appointed agent-general of the St George's Bay Company there. Falconbridge was the former ship's surgeon on Bristol slave ships who had testified to the Privy Council about the slave trade. His brief in Sierra Leone was to negotiate with the indigenous rulers of the region for land there. This he did, obtaining it for £30 in trade goods – an agreement which would soon lead to dissension, given the differing perceptions Africans and Europeans had about the nature of landownership.

The Temne people's chief negotiator, King Naimbana, also offered Falconbridge one of his own sons as a pledge of good faith on the condition that the prince (then in his early twenties) be taken by Falconbridge back to England to be educated as a Christian at the company's expense.[32] Anna Maria Falconbridge taught the Prince (also known as Naimbana) to read before his departure for Britain. Her not altogether flattering description of his character indicates that she neither revered him because he was a prince nor despised him because he was an African:

> In his disposition he is surly, but has cunning enough to smother it where he thinks his interest is concerned; he is pettish and implacable, but I think grateful and attached to those he considers his friends; nature has been bountiful in giving him a sound intellect, very capable of improvement, and he also possess a great thirst for knowledge.[33]

The Prince's sojourn in Britain had an impact on abolitionist culture there. When the Prince arrived in England, he stayed with Henry Thornton and met Granville Sharp. Sharp's *Memoirs* describe a bright and volatile young man who was clearly finding it difficult to cope with the attitudes he encountered concerning Africans. Commenting on the 'extreme sensibility' Naimbana felt about the 'honour of his country', Sharp noted that the Prince was particularly

> indisposed to answer questions put to him by strangers concerning the state of his own country, for he was apt to suspect that they meant to draw comparisons unfavourable to its character; and he would therefore, on such occasions often

[remark] . . . that a country so unfavourably circumstanced as Sierra Leone had hitherto been, was not to be supposed capable of having made any attainments worthy of being the subject of conversation in Great Britain.[34]

To read between the lines, it seems obvious that the Prince felt isolated amongst his well-meaning hosts. In one instance he had to justify to them his violent antipathy at the mention of a man who had evidently made degrading public comments in public about the African people. His hosts, Sharp tells us, 'immediately reminded him of the Christian duty of forgiving his enemies'. His spirited and eloquent rejoinder took them, one suspects, rather by surprise:

if a man should sell me and all my family to a slave ship, so that we should pass all the rest of our lives in slavery in the West Indies, I can forgive him; but if a man takes away the character of the people of my country, (added he, rising from his seat with much emotion) I never can forgive him. . . . If a man should try to kill me, or should sell my family for slaves, he would do an injury to as many as he might kill or sell, but if anyone takes away the character of black people, that man injures black people all over the world; and when he has once taken away their character, there is nothing which he may not do to black people ever after.[35]

Whilst at Thornton's Clapham home, Naimbana became friends with another young protégé of Thornton's, Amos Cottle. Cottle was originally from Bristol, the brother of Joseph Cottle the bookseller and modest patron of the romantic poets. A tradesman's son, Amos was considered a promising writer himself and was a friend of Robert Southey. It was Amos Cottle who showed Naimbana around London and it was to Amos Cottle that Naimbana wrote the first letter he ever attempted in English. To someone as sensitively proud as the Prince, this betokens some measure of trust, and Naimbana went on to write two more letters to Cottle before his departure back to Sierra Leone in 1793.[36]

Tragically, Naimbana died from smallpox en route to Sierra Leone. Like his father's two other sons, who had also been sent abroad to be educated, he died before he could reach home.[37] Amos Cottle also died relatively young, and at some point Naimbana's letters to Amos came into the hands of Amos's brother Joseph, whose anti-slavery poem we discussed earlier. Cottle, a Bristol bookseller and publisher,[38] is said to have written the poem 'Lee Boo – of Pelew' in poetic tribute to Naimbana, inspired by George Keane's account of a young Pacific islander, Leeboo, who like Naimbana died of smallpox.[39]

Hannah More would also commemorate Naimbana in her writing, as we shall later see. Throughout the 1790s she took an active interest in Sierra Leone, gleaning much of her information from her correspondence with Zachary Macaulay. Macaulay was a young Evangelical who in 1793 became the second member of the governing council of the Sierra Leone Company and who went on to serve as acting governor of the settlement from 1794 to 1799. During this period many of Macaulay's most revealing letters were written to More's protégé, the Bristolian Selina Mills. A former pupil of Hannah More, Mills came from a Quaker background but was herself an Anglican. Born in 1767, she appears to have been assisting the More sisters run their school on Park Street in Bristol, and by the 1790s had taken over its day-to-day management. (Her pupils by then included the heiress of an immensely rich Jamaican planter.⁴⁰) Selina, the sister of John Mills, the editor of the Whiggish *Bristol Gazette*, was reportedly regarded as the 'sixth sister' of the More entourage.⁴¹ Macaulay, much to the jealous consternation of the More sisters, courted Mills by way of his African letters and married her in Bristol on his return.

As a result of Macaulay's contacts, a steady stream of letters, packages and visitors from Sierra Leone flowed into Bristol. African cloth, sweetmeats, gold pieces, 'curious insects' and even a parrot found their way to the More sisters' Park Street school. Visitors from Sierra Leone were received with particular enthusiasm, and according to the report of one, all at Park Street 'appeared to be extremely anxious to hear of . . . [Sierra Leone]; the minutest particulars were listened to with attention and pleasure'.⁴² It seems that some of the visitors from Sierra Leone to Bristol may have been African. Macaulay wrote to Selina Mills in 1796 about a Methodist missionary and former schoolteacher he was sending to Britain on account of his health:

> A black man of the name of Joseph Brown, one of the most humble Christians I have met with is also going home [i.e. to Britain]. . . . I have mentioned him to Miss Hannah More, Mr. Thornton etc. and when he goes to Bath I have told him to call at Pulteney Street [where the More sisters lived]. As I cannot think of denying you the gratification you will receive from observing the effect of Christianity so strongly manifested, as it is in this poor African, I have put your name down in his pocket book, as . . . he is to call upon [you] when he goes to Bristol.⁴³

We do not know whether Brown ever got to Bristol, but it is clear that Macaulay preferrred his Africans humble. He complained to Selina Mills of the spiritual arrogance of some Africans, especially the Methodists amongst them:

> Methodism has so direct a tendency to exalt animal feelings to an undue empire over the judgement, that with people of weak judgement or little or no knowledge, it may be expected in most cases to produce enthusiasm. This enthusiasm manifests itself among our blacks here, by a proud conceit of their own spiritual gifts and a proportionate undervaluing of . . . submitting themselves to catechitical instruction. Their own visionary and delusive experience comes thus to be substituted by them, as standards of truth . . . fancying themselves wiser than their teachers.⁴⁴

Macaulay's patrician contempt for Africans and their religious enthusiasm, linked as it was to his class position, was not shared by all his white compatriots in Sierra Leone. Melville Horne, a chaplain at Sierra Leone, was sympathetic to the Methodists and had reportedly lectured to 'very great crowds' in Bristol in John Wesley's Room and elsewhere in 1792 about Sierra Leone shortly before going there.[45] John Garvin, who was employed as a schoolmaster at the settlement, was reportedly recommended for the post by John Ryland, the new principal of the Bristol Baptist College. Garvin, a Bristol Evangelical who became a Wesleyan, went out to Sierra Leone as a schoolteacher in 1793 and was soon regarded by Macaulay as a disruptive influence and fomentor of discontent and rebellion.[46] Garvin was charged with 'gross and unfounded attacks' on Macaulay's character and also with telling the (black) colonists that Macaulay 'entertained view inimical to their rights and religious liberties'.[47]

Two graduates of Bristol's Baptist Academy, Jacob Grigg and James Rodway, travelled out to Sierra Leone in 1795 as the Baptist Missionary Society's first missionaries to Africa. One of them, Jacob Grigg, also clashed with Macaulay on the way the colony was run. Fyfe, in his authoritative history of Sierra Leone, represents both Garvin and Grigg as factitious sectarians.[48] This is not surprising since he bases his assessment on the version of events provided by the Sierra Leone Company minutes and Macaulay himself. Garvin and Grigg may have been difficult and tendentious men, but that does not necessarily invalidate all their complaints or prove that both men were of the same ilk. Grigg, as well as Rodway, came highly recommended by the Baptist College in Bristol. John Ryland, the principal of the college, made his own anti-slavery sentiments quite clear when he advised them at a farewell service to be

> [u]nlike the factors of Abaddon, who foment wars among the African chieftans, that they may purchase captives, and regret not the murder of hundreds and thousands, if they can fill their floating hells with a few scores of them . . . and yet gain by selling them, on the other side of the globe into perpetual slavery, [rather] shew that *you* would account it a greater gain to rescue one sable brother from idolatry and sin than to return to Europe with thousands of [pieces] of gold and silver.[49]

It seems clear that both Grigg and Rodway, who kept in touch with Ryland during their stay in Sierra Leone, had a more positive view of the Africans they encountered than Ryland evidently did. Rodway was impressed with the cleanliness and skill with which African women prepared food, pronouncing them as 'decent good cooks', and by the friendliness and civility with which they were generally received. Both men commented on the deference which Africans paid to the opinion of Europeans and to their wish to obtain European education for their children. They interpreted this as an idealistic wish to be 'civilized'. Anna Maria Falconbridge, by contrast, related the views of an African she knew whose reasons for wanting an education were more pragmatic: 'Read book, and learn to be *rogue*, so well as white men.'[50] I think this response explains why the people they encountered were so keen to defer to European knowledge. It was not a matter of intelligence or subtlety of thought which distinguished the African from the European. It was a world-view which offered an effective and practical purchase on their environment and might free them from a dependence on arbitrary magical spirits. Science and technology worked. Literacy was the key to it. It was this, the statement implies, that gave the Europeans their real advantage.

Both Rodway and Grigg were evidently aghast at what they saw of the slave trade in Sierra Leone. Grigg in particular hinted at the problems he had gaining the trust of people who at first assumed his friendliness had economic rather than religious motives behind it.[51] Both stressed their fellowship with the Baptists who led the black settlers' community there, as Rodway told Ryland: 'We soon met with some of our baptist friends: as to their outward hue they are black – by grace they are comely, and brethren in Christ. They were glad to see us, and we to see them.'[52] If Rodway's comments reveal an ambivalence about blackness, they also show how egalitarian his brand of Christian Evangelism was. This helps to explain the disquiet both he and Grigg reportedly felt at the authoritarian conduct of the colony's other superintendent, William Dawes, a former Royal Marine, who alternated in the post with Macaulay. Dawes reportedly treated the black freedmen as he had treated the convicts at his previous posting in Australia. In this way, Dawes alienated the freed American blacks, who had been on much better terms with Clarkson, their former governor, who had been sidelined by the company management.[53]

Certainly, with hindsight it seems that the company did not act in the best interests of the black colonists, in either political or economic terms. Nor did it afford them full religious equality. Though the precise nature of the dispute between Grigg and the Sierra Leone Company awaits further clarification, it seems to have centred, in Grigg's case at least, around his attitude to the slave trade and his relations with both the indigenous Africans and the free black settlers there, most of whom had come via Nova Scotia.[54] For their part, the 'Nova Scotians' also resented Macaulay's cold and socially distant manner. Macaulay's own attitudes towards slavery and race must have seemed contradictory and inconsistent, at times seeming more condemning of African than European slave-traders.[55] Macaulay's encounters with African traders and black settlers at times show humanity and shrewdness, at times high-handed insensitivity. He clearly judged the inhabitants of Sierra Leone according to the extent to which they conformed to his own particular religious doctrines and ideas of political propriety. Unlike Clarkson, he never attended the services run by the freed black pastors, much less those of 'pagan' Africans. He recounts to Selina Mills his refusal to attend a local ruler's housewarming ceremony lest 'he might make a sacrifice to his Demon, to secure protection for the new house'.[56]

Grigg's progress was very different. Grigg, who had soon taught himself to speak the local language of the Temne people of the region, though initially distrusted by the people, reportedly got on well with the local headman, Namina Modo, who was a Muslim. Grigg also took issue with the cosy relationship some officials of the colony had with English slave-traders. As one scholar has described, 'Despite the ideas of the Company, nearly everyone in the colony, Europeans and natives, themselves once slaves, possess their own slaves. . . . Griggs was of a particularly sensitive nature and would weep openly at the sight of the suffering.'[57]

He seems particularly to have disliked the activities of one of these traders, Mr Tilly, a person Anne Maria Falconbridge had found refined and charming.[58] For his part, Tilly could not have been pleased with Grigg's friendship with Namina Modo's wife, Ariana, whose anti-slavery sympathies Grigg, by his own admission, openly encouraged – as this extract from his letter to a friend in England demonstrates:

Ariana, he [*sic*] wife (and headwoman) is also an amiable person. She is possessed of good sense, and very tender feelings which I have had opportunity to discover in her treatment of the slaves who were chained and prepared for sale. She always disowned that she had any part in the trade, and whenever one was brought chained to the house, she would come to me, and, knowing that I was an enemy to the trade, say, 'It is none of me, Mr. Grigg, it is none of me, it is Mr. T[illy]——'s slave.'[59]

Grigg became closely involved with the black Baptist preacher David George, and Thomas Peters, the Nova Scotian who had been elected headman of Freetown and other Africans in the settlement. Grigg's house reportedly 'soon became full of native malcontents, and since he was already unpopular, the rumour spread that he was "going native"'.[60] He openly clashed with Macaulay when the latter imposed an ordinance requiring that all marriages in the colony be officiated by people vetted by his office. Grigg joined with Peters and George in characterizing this policy as an infringement of their religious freedom as non-Anglicans. Grigg's pacifism also led him to oppose Macaulay's attempt to fortify the colony and train its inhabitants against a threatened French incursion,[61] and to object to the imposition of land taxes and rents on the black settlers on the grounds that they did not enjoy proper political representation.[62]

As a result of his criticisms, Grigg, like Garvin, was abruptly expelled from the colony in 1797 and transported at Macaulay's expense to North America, where he became a pastor in the slave colony of Virginia and a very early campaigner against American slavery.[63]

John Ryland, in an attempt to pacify Macaulay, openly repudiated Grigg's conduct. He was moved in part to do so in an attempt to retain the patronage the London Evangelicals had previously extended to Baptist missionaries. He had also been advised to take a cautious stand, both by political conservatives within the Baptist Missionary Society and by his long-standing correspondent and mentor, the Reverend John Newton, who had himself been a slave-trader in Sierra Leone before his conversion to Evangelicalism and abolition.[64] Newton seems to have played a less than helpful role in soothing relations between Macaulay and the Bristol Baptists over Grigg, as a letter from Macaulay to Selina Mills in 1797 reveals:

Dr. Ryland of Bristol has written me a very kind letter, in which he expresses his obligations to me and his disapprobation of Grigg's conduct in a very satisfying way. But a letter from the Rev. John Newton convinces me that no small effect has been produced in the minds of the Baptists by what Grigg has written; and that Dr. Ryland himself, notwithstanding the strain of his letter, is strongly tinctured with prejudice.[65]

Whatever the precise causes of Grigg's expulsion, it demonstrates the existence of deep ideological differences within the Evangelical wing of the abolitionist camp, both in the nation at large and in Bristol itself. Griggs, Rodway and Garvin seem to have regarded their black co-religionists as social equals, something that neither Macaulay nor Newton ever did. Ryland's position is less easy to assess; he was not the firebrand Grigg was, but, as we shall see, Bristol's Baptist College continued, under his regime, to produce highly educated men possessed of deeply held anti-slavery convictions. No further Baptists were afforded the opportunity to replace their departed brethren. Yet the Baptist Missionary Society and Anglican Evangelicals were apparently reluctant, until late in the twentieth century, to acknowledge the racial issues underlying the dispute at Sierra Leone.[66]

As for Macaulay, for all his sanctimonious arrogance and intolerance, he was undoubtedly a committed abolitionist who, on his return to England in 1799, proved an important support to Wilberforce. Macaulay kept More and Mills up to date on the fate of the parliamentary campaign and consulted them both for political advice and support. In May 1799 he informed his fiancée, 'Wilberforce has come in and suggested the adviseability of enquiring whether you know any person in Bristol sufficiently acquainted with the Windward coast of Africa and sufficiently friendly to our cause to give . . . evidence.'[67]

Selina Mills was also kept apprised of the fate of the 25 African children Macaulay had brought from Sierra Leone to London. He had earlier asked her to see if she could raise funds for their education, but she reported difficulties there:

> We have not been able to get one single name for your poor Africans, nor do I expect many from any other quarter, if any. The Bristolians are famous for supporting large public charities . . . and for large turtle dinners; but alas for your Africans. Alas, poor African Education Society![68]

In the event, Macaulay obtained the money from elsewhere and asked her assistance in the recruitment of appropriate schoolmasters for them. Two Bristol-trained Baptists were recruited, namely Ryland's former assistant Joseph Hughes and the young John Foster.[69] Interestingly, Foster lodged in Battersea with the children's domestic manager, Mary Perth. Perth, a black American woman, had been an entrepreneur in both America and Sierra Leone. When employed by Macaulay as his personal servant in Sierra Leone, she took a keen interest in his Bristol fiancée, to whom she sent gifts. Foster described her as 'aged', well-travelled, 'pious and happy', and seemed to get on well with her and her 20-year-old daughter. After his sojourn in Battersea, Foster, who was a friend of Joseph Cottle, went on to become active in the anti-slavery campaign both as a writer and as a Bristol pastor.[70]

Macaulay married Selina Mills in Bristol in August 1799 and the two left the city for London. By this time, however, an Evangelical 'sisterhood' existed of women with similar views who included, according to Selina's sister, the 'misses More, Richards, Tombs, and Campbell'.[71] Nothing is known of Miss Campbell or Miss Richards, but Miss Tombs was probably the daughter or relative of Richard Tombs, the shipbuilder and committed anti-abolitionist. It seems likely that under the Mores' influence, this small coterie kept the interest in the anti-slavery campaign alive, but it was a flame that flickered in the cold winds of political reaction and continuing war. More takes an increasingly authoritarian attitude towards black people as the century ended. In her *Sorrows of Yamba* (1795), slavery is shown to benefit Yamba by exposing her to Christianity, an argument dangerously close to those of some anti-abolitionists.[72] By the turn of the century, More would transmogrify Naimbana into the 'Black Prince', an abolitionist icon acceptable to the most conservative of Evangelicals: baptized, Anglophile, and safely dead.[73]

Black people in Bristol in the age of abolition

How were black people in Bristol faring during these years of abolitionist agitation? We know that the Mansfield judgment had left their legal status dangerously ambivalent and economically unattractive, since they now had to be paid wages.

Those servants who were still employed by their masters risked being forcibly transported back to the plantations, despite the patent illegality of such actions. In a well-known incident described by Hannah More to Walpole in 1790,

> a poor negro girl . . . had run away because she would not return to one of those trafficking islands, whither her master was resolved to send her. To my great grief and indignation, the poor trembling wretch was dragged out from a hole in the top of a house where she had hid her self and forced to go on board ship.[74]

More later wrote to Walpole that the 'poor creature' had managed to escape from the ship some twenty miles upriver from the city and make her way barefoot back to the city. There the Quakers took out a warrant for her protection, and kept her 'in defiance of all human flesh merchants'.[75] It is not known how successful they ultimately were.

Two years later, another 'negro servant girl' who had long resided in the city was forcibly removed back to the Caribbean. This incident aroused public disquiet but apparently no redress for the servant involved: 'A byestander who saw her put on board the boat at Lamplighter's Hall says, "her tears flowed down her face like a shower of rain".' More implied to Walpole with respect to the former case that only the Quakers had the will and organization in the city to take action against these abuses of black workers.[76]

A previously unknown case in 1796 demonstrates that Bristol Quakers continued to look out for abuses of this nature, and that they did so in liaison with abolitionists in London. In this instance Harry Gandy wrote to Granville Sharp for advice on how to help one Harry Harper, 'a young man of colour' currently under arrest and in imminent danger of being shipped back to his master in Dominica. Harper, whom Gandy revealingly characterizes as a 'simple minded and sensible young man, tho' an African born', had escaped his 'severe master' by stowing away aboard the Bristol-bound *Levant*. Gandy relates to Sharp how he and Thomas Mills (probably Selina's father) had visited the young man. Harper told them he had been encouraged to stow away by an acquaintance of his who had served aboard the ship.[77] Evidently, after a few days at sea, Harper had presented himself to the ship's master, one Captain Alleyne, who had ordered him to work as one of the sailors. This Harper insists he did, performing all his duties, 'going aloft day and night' and 'drinking nothing stronger than water' for the next 34 days. Two days after their arrival at Kingroad, the docking point for Bristol, the Captain with some other gentlemen came on board . . . the Captain called him into the cabin, and took a piece of parchment and told him he must sign it, to which Harry Harper said, no Captain, for I can neither read nor write, and therefore he said he could not do it. To this the Captain said he must make his mark, and that he would teach him to write, and thereupon took him by the wrist of his right arm, and forcibly directed his hand to make a cross, on the parchment before the mate and another person [the owner's clerk].[78]

Gandy writes that he and Mills then confronted Captain Alleyne to ask him the cause of Harper's arrest. Alleyne reportedly replied, 'but with a faltering accent', that Harper was an indentured servant to him, and that he had both clothed him (a point Harper expressly denied – probably since the provision of clothing was a common indicator of indenture) and fed him.[79] Alleyne further contended, possibly in a bid to discredit Harper in the eyes of these pious Quakers, that when Harper got on shore, 'he refused to return on board, that he [Alleyne] took him out of a house of Ill fame, where they had corrupted him'.[80] Harper, Alleyne informed them, was a stowaway and suggested that if Gandy and Mills wished to take the matter further, they should meet him at the shipowner's office.

The ship's owner was none other than Walter Jacks, Captain Kimber's former boss and advocate. Jacks may also have been a planter; we know that he mortgaged the Wood Hall plantation in Jamaica to a consortium of Bristol merchants only the year before.[81] The succeeding encounter with Jacks and Alleyne was fresh in Gandy's mind and reported to Sharp the next day. Not only, Alleyne contended, was Harper indentured to him, but, under Dominican law, Alleyne would be liable to a £100 fine if he did not return the escapee. Mills and Gandy remonstrated that as Harper had stowed away, the fine would hardly apply, and pointedly reminded him that as 'the young man had landed here [in England] the Slave was totally lost, in the Liberty of a Subject'.[82] This invocation of the Mansfield judgment evidently alarmed Jacks, who then beckoned Gandy and Mills into a private room and gave them to understand that he had been unaware of this indenture. However, Jacks assured them that the indentures must be above board since '[h]e had such confidence in his clerk as to believe he would not have been a witness to the Indentures, if he had discovered an unwillingness on the party [Harper] that had executed them'. Nor was Jacks willing to compromise on the matter by accepting a sum to recompense the captain for the cost of Harper's passage. As far as Jacks was concerned, Harper was indentured to Alleyne. The prisoner, on the other hand, manifested a 'fixed aversion' to go with Captain Alleyne 'in any capacity whatsoever', saying all such efforts were simply 'a contrivance to carry him to his master again'.

The records do not tell us what Sharp advised or what ultimately happened to Harper. The episode does remind us, though, that the legal status of enslaved Africans in England was still confused and their social status still low enough for them to be open to the rankest exploitation.

Although the African trade was no longer very important to the city's economy, and public opinion in the city was judged, in one contemporary magazine, to have 'nearly brought about its extinction,[83] Bristol ships still managed to ship nearly 11, 000 enslaved Africans to the Americas between 1795 and 1804.[84] Then, too, there were also those Africans who, having gained back their freedom serving with British forces, were abandoned in British ports, where they were soon left friendless and destitute. There was still a brutal underside to a city increasingly congratulating itself on its genteel sensibilities.

Theatrical reactions: Bristol and slavery at a time of war

Harry Gandy, who had risen to become the notary public of the city, died in 1799, his abolitionist activities now acceptable enough for him to be remembered in the press as someone who combined the qualities of 'the scholar, the Christian and the gentleman'.[85] By the time Gandy died, the country had long been at war with France and was in the middle of a government-sponsored backlash against the ideals of the French Revolution. A climate of patriotic reaction can be discerned in the civic celebrations and even in some of the theatrical productions around the turn of the eighteenth century. As Garrick had observed, 'the Stage must float on public favour, as the mirror of a nation's virtue'.[86] Bristol's corporation, which represented so many of the old mercantile elite, was, it is true, becoming increasingly unpopular, especially after a brutal suppression in 1793 of a riot against toll bridge charges (in which some 11 people were shot dead), and because of its continued extravagance in the face of the privation caused by bad harvests in 1795–6 and in 1800. But the patriotism card was repeatedly played in an attempt to guarantee civic unity. Bristol church bells rang for an entire day in April 1794 when the French Caribbean island of Guadeloupe was captured. Three months later the capture of Port-au-Prince in St Domingue was similarly fêted, and the whole city was illuminated when a major victory was scored against the French fleet that summer. In the autumn, a badly damaged Bristol ship limped back home from the West Indies, having successfully fought off a heavily armed French privateer whose crew outnumbered it seven to one. In such a highly charged atmosphere, even the former Quaker Joseph Harford became an enthusiastic supporter of the war, despite the fact that the French revolutionary government had, that very year, outlawed slavery in the French colonies and extended the rights of citizenship to men of all races.

By the late 1790s the Bristol merchant fleet to the West Indies had declined, but many Bristol merchants still had significant investments in the Caribbean and saw British control of the Caribbean as crucial to British interests.[87] In 1796 Lord Sheffield and Charles Bragge (later to assume the name Bathurst) were returned to Parliament. Neither was a friend to abolition. But it is telling that more radical Whigs, taking issue with Sheffield's support of the government's suppression of press freedom and the freedom of assembly, had put forward their own candidate. At first sight, Benjamin Hobhouse, scion of a prominent Bristol slave-trading family and himself a Merchant Venturer, seemed more concerned to champion religious liberty for Dissenters and the provision of bread for the poor than to fight for abolition. Indeed, he campaigned as 'a friend to profitable trade'. Nonetheless, it was public knowledge that his own son was enrolled at the abolitionist Dr Estlin's school, and his later pronouncements indicate a real commitment to the anti-slavery cause.[88] When Hobhouse was squeezed out in favour of Lord Sheffield, an attack was made on Sheffield's political headquarters at the Bush Tavern, as well as on the mayor's mansion house and the council house.[89] This might simply prove Sheffield's unpopularity rather than any groundswell of anti-slavery opinion from the labouring masses. On the other hand, it does indicate the willingness of the unenfranchised to support a candidate friendly to abolition as well as to other reforms.

An abortive French invasion in Pembrokeshire in 1797 and reports of French plans to destroy Bristol fuelled patriotic reaction in the nation. The captured plans of the failed invasion, intended to 'produce the total ruin of the town, the port, the docks, and the vessels and to strike terror and amazement into the very heart of the capital of England', galvanized Bristolians.[90] A Bristol volunteer force was recruited, commanded by the West India trader Evan Baillie, and an astonishing £31,300 was raised locally to finance the force, which was to protect the city from external threat and guard the 2000 French prisoners of war languishing on the city's outskirts at Stapleton. In the meantime, British troops took two years to quell the Jamaican Maroons in 1795–6. The following year they continued to suffer heavy casualties in St Domingue, and were forced to conclude a treaty with Toussaint L'Ouverture, the leader of the rebel slaves, before their withdrawal from the island in 1798.

The French incursions at home and abroad, combined with slave resistance in the colonies, were invoked to justify the ferociously repressive legislation which limited any political activity from the early 1790s. In 1794 Anna Maria Falconbridge had published a swingeing attack on the authoritarian management that had characterized Sierra Leone since the dismissal of her husband for drunkenness. Her writing contained enough radical pronouncements on slavery and race to impress some historians with their egalitarianism. Yet by 1802 even Anna Maria Falconbridge, after a sojourn in the West Indies, reconsidered her stance on abolition. In a new edition of her *Narrative* on her voyages to Sierra Leone, she includes an addendum, 'The present state of the Slave Trade in the West Indies and the Improbability of its Total Abolition': 'I [formerly] viewed the slave Trade with abhorrence . . . but I am not ashamed to confess these sentiments were the effect of ignorance and the prejudice of opinion, imbibed by associating with a circle of acquaintances bigoted for *the abolition*.'[91] Presumably sickened by her experiences in African slaving ports and impressed by the views of some of the West Indian planters she visited, Falconbridge does not wish to be seen as a 'friend to slavery, or wholly as enemy to abolishing the slave trade'; but she did not see the trade as 'inconsistent with any moral or religious law' and remained in favour of it for so long as 'the innate prejudices, ignorance, superstition and savageness overspread Africa'.[92]

Unlike many West Indian planters, Falconbridge did not doubt the intellectual capabilities of Africans, but she felt that the rising generation must be educated in 'morals and manners' by way of seminaries established throughout the African coastal regions. If that were effected, said Falconbridge,

I do not question their geniuses would ripen into ideas congenial with our own and that [they would] . . . emerge . . . from that vortex of disgrace in which they have been overwhelmed since time immemorial, establishing social political and commercial connections throughout the globe, and I even see them blazing among the literati of their age.[93]

Falconbridge here marries the vestiges of Enlightenment egalitarianism with wartime reaction and plantocratic racism. Her resulting ideas prefigure colonialist paternalism.

Theatrical rituals

During wartime, theatre can serve as a blessed diversion and a place where patriotic solidarity can be confirmed. A contemporary Bristol source confirmed the 'very powerful effect which theatrical events have upon public morals and manners'.[94] Mr Weeks of the city's Bush Tavern had 'blacked up' as Mungo, the faithful black servant, in Bickerstaff's *The Padlock*, thus delighting the audience attending a benefit for Bristol's Royal Infirmary in 1796.[95] The Theatre Royal, the only theatre in the city still running at the time, continued to be so popular with the city's elite during the distress caused by bad harvests in 1800 that plans were made to enlarge it.[96] *Inkle and Yarico* had been staged yet again in 1799, and Cumberland's *The West Indian* was staged with a farce called *The Jew and the Doctor* soon afterwards.[97] Cumberland's *The West Indian* had been a favourite with Bristol audiences since its publication in 1771. It centres around the marriage and parentage of a rich young West Indian planter, Belcour, who was reportedly possessed of 'rum and sugar enough to make all the water in the Thames into punch'. The issue of slavery is not raised, and the only reference to Africans in the play is when 'the West Indian' (i.e. Belcour) arrives in London with a retinue of 'several black servants, carrying portmanteaus' which include 'two green monkeys, a pair of grey parrots, a Jamaica sow . . . and a Mangrove dog'. West Indian wealth is at once exoticized and sanitized.[98]

If the audience could take comfort in such disingenuous confections which rendered slave-holding safely innocuous, they may have found a play staged the subsequent year somewhat more unsettling. Sharing the bill with '*The Wonder: A Woman Keeps a Secret!*', *Obi: or, Three-Finger'd Jack* was allegedly based on the real exploits of a robber who terrorized the whites of Jamaica in 1780. The playbill (Figure 17) and the fact of its staging tell us much about the fears and assumptions of the audience who attended it. The play, previously produced in the Theatre Royal in London, features a specially painted 'Display of Views in the Island of Jamaica'. White characters represent the crucial members of a slave regime, i.e. the Planter, the Overseer, a Captain Orford and Rosa (the Planter's daughter). Black characters, aside from the eponymous villain of the piece, include 'Quashee' and 'Sam' and their wives, 'Negro robbers', Obi-Woman and a 'chorus of Negroes and Negresses, Dancing-Negresses and Negro-Children'. All the main actors appear from their names to be white, and the reviews make no mention that anyone in the cast was of African origin.[99]

The story centres around the crimes of Jack and his eventual capture by one of the Maroon Negroes, Quashee, and his unnamed boy assistant. Quashee is the most heroic black character in the play, and significantly he is baptized in the course of the action, eshewing his African name for an English one, James Reeder. Quashee and Sam were said to have hailed from Scots Hall, Maroon Town. The reference to the Maroons was topical, since British troops had just spent two years fighting the Second Maroon War of 1795–6. Maroons were not enslaved, but in 1739 had wrested free status from the government after the First Maroon War, a war in which, incidentally, Henry Bright, one of the Theatre Royal's original founders, had fought.

Symbols of black resistance, the Maroons played an ambiguous role in Jamaican society, sometimes acting on behalf of the British government by returning escaped slaves, and sometimes harbouring them. (It is notable that the other Maroon in the play, Sam, stands back from the fiercely bloody fight in which James Reeder eventually subdues Jack. Jack, by contrast, is described as one of those 'abandoned Exiles' who are neither employed as slaves on a plantation nor enjoy official Maroon status.)

What gives the play its particular drama is that Jack is no ordinary robber, but one of 'a horrible class of negroes' who are skilled in obeah. Obeah is an Akan-derived form of sorcery (as distinct from Haitian voodoo, which is in part based on ritual practices from Dahomey).[100] Jack's own obi or fetish is, the audience is told, particularly grisly, consisting as it did of a goat horn filled with a compound of grave dirt, ashes, the blood of a black cat and human fat. This allusion to human sacrifice is conflated with armed insurrection, since Jack's obi is kept 'along with his guns and sabres' in his obeah bag.

Whilst both James and Jack are credited in the playbill with 'two of the stoutest hearts that were ever hooped with ribs', one suspects that this had more to do with presenting the play's final fight in the most enticing way possible than with presenting Jack in a positive light. The fight of course is symbolic; the baptized free Maroon conquers the criminal and dangerous slave who practises witchcraft. James Reeder might be portrayed as a virtuous black man, but underlying the plot is the image of a malevolent and savage African culture which must be stamped out.

This message is underscored by the local press coverage, which included an account of obeah and of the factual basis of the play. Purportedly based on *Moseley's Treatise on Sugar and Medical Observations*, the article describes the practitioners of obeah in demonic terms. Some whites as well as blacks believed Jack and other obis to be 'possessed of some supernatural powers'. The most venerated obis are the most hideous, 'ugly loathsome creatures' who are 'oracles of woods, caves and unfrequented places'. Some, it was claimed, 'live in spite of the common law of nature, and survive a general mutation of their muscles ligaments and osteology becoming also hideously white in their wooly hair and skins'.[101]

Whatever the truth behind the obi story – and the fact remains that sorcery was practised in the Caribbean along with other elements of traditional African religions – the story of Jack and his obi had a double resonance for the Bristol audience. At one level it alluded to the actual threat of violence posed by a rebellious

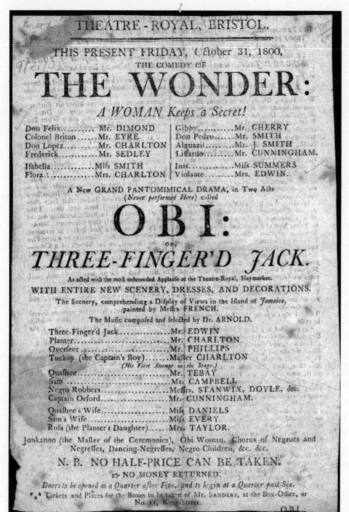

THEATRE - ROYAL, BRISTOL.

THIS PRESENT FRIDAY, October 31, 1800,
THE COMEDY OF

THE WONDER:

A WOMAN Keeps a Secret!

Don Felix............Mr. DIMOND	Gibby.............Mr. CHERRY
Colonel Briton......Mr. EYRE	Don Pedro.......Mr. SMITH
Don Lopez..........Mr. CHARLTON	Alguazil...........Mr. J. SMITH
Frederick............Mr. SEDLEY	Liffardo............Mr. CUNNINGHAM.
Isabella.............Miss SMITH	Inis..............Miss SUMMERS
Flora..............Mrs. CHARLTON	Violante.........Mrs. EDWIN.

A New GRAND PANTOMIMICAL DRAMA, in Two Acts
(Never performed Here) called

O B I:
OR,
THREE-FINGER'D JACK.

As acted with the most unbounded Applause at the Theatre-Royal, Haymarket.

WITH ENTIRE NEW SCENERY, DRESSES, AND DECORATIONS.

The Scenery, comprehending a Display of Views in the Island of *Jamaica*,
painted by Messrs. FRENCH.

The Music composed and selected by Dr. ARNOLD.

Three-Finger'd Jack..............Mr. EDWIN
Planter............................Mr. CHARLTON
Overseer.........................Mr. PHILLIPS
Tuckey (the Captain's Boy).......Master CHARLTON
(His First Attempt on the Stage.)
Quashee...........................Mr. TEBAY
Sam ....Mr. CAMPBELL
Negro Robbers..................Messrs. STANWIX, DOYLE, &c.
Captain Orford...................Mr. CUNNINGHAM.

Quashee's Wife..................Miss DANIELS
Sam's Wife.......................Miss EVERY
Rosa (the Planter's Daughter).....Mrs. TAYLOR.

Jonkanoo (the Master of the Ceremonies), Obi-Woman, Chorus of Negroes and
Negresses, Dancing-Negresses, Negro-Children, &c. &c.

N. B. NO HALF-PRICE CAN BE TAKEN.
☞ NO MONEY RETURNED.

Doors to be opened at a Quarter after Five, and to begin at a Quarter past Six.
✱ Tickets and Places for the Boxes to be taken of Mr. SANDERS, at the Box-Office, or
No. 11, King-Street.
OBI

Figure 17 Playbill

black man in the very year that Toussaint L'Ouverture won control of St Domingue. At another level, the use of sorcery itself, based as it was on an alien world-view, was a symbolic attack on the Christian body politic. For traditional Tories, whose communal culture still contained vestiges of an older, magical mindset, African claims to tap supernatural powers were frightening enough. Anti-slavery Evangelicals would have found such sorcery particularly repugnant, given their hostility to religious ritualism in any form.[102]

At times of war, loyalty to the British Constitution was essential. Loyalty to that Constitution clearly implied a loyalty to Protestant Christianity. In such circumstances, non-Christian slaves were difficult to champion.[103]

Abolition subdued? The Caribbean interest and Bristol politics, 1800–7

Despite the decline of the Bristol merchant fleet to the West Indies,[104] there were still plenty of merchants with interests in the Caribbean. Even amongst those without direct interests in slave plantations, there was a widespread conviction of the importance of Britain's Caribbean interests. When the West Indian fleet from Bristol arrived safely home and fully laden during the food shortage of 1800, despite the depredations of the French, there was joy in the streets.[105]

Generally speaking, the climate of wartime patriotism in the years leading up to 1806 apparently prevented most anti-slavery agitation in Bristol. In 1803 Peter Baillie might record in his diary that he found *John Bull*, staged in Bristol's Theatre Royal in 1803, 'a foolish play not deserving of its great reputation', but the fact that it enjoyed such a reputation is telling enough. Baillie himself epitomized the patriotism the play sought to celebrate, spending, as he did, much of his time supervising the Bristol Volunteers when he could spare the time from attending the meetings of the local Shipowners' Committee and dining at Bristol's West India Club.[106] Yet Robert Hall, in a sermon delivered in Bristol that same year, alludes to an undercurrent of public feeling against the slave trade amongst the unrepresented mass of people. The slave trade, he told the Bridge Street congregation, 'has excited such general indignation among the people', but their 'earnest and unanimous remonstrance, addressed to those who alone could abolish it', had as yet been unsuccessful.[107]

In London the determination of parliamentary campaigners boded ill for those planters who cared to read the signs. In 1804 Evan Baillie, one-time slave-factor, West India merchant and Bristol's Whig MP from 1802 to 1811, wrote despondently to his son Peter in Bristol on the subject of abolition:

> You will see how very feeble our attempts have been to oppose the Abolition of the Slave trade. The Phrensy [*sic*] that has seized all parties on this subject is most unaccountable, I confess it allarms [*sic*] me most seriously, and it will induce me to think of abridging my West India business within very limitted [*sic*] bounds. At all events whatever the measure of abolition [it] must prove a most fatal stab to West India credit as it renders all security on Estates highly precarious, having no promise or engagement to prevent any fanatical Minister from sanctioning even a measure of emancipation.[108]

Locally, though, eyes were focused on the war. A further invasion scare in 1804 led to the setting up of an extensive magazine for 20,000 arms in what is now Armoury Square. The victory at Trafalgar and the death of Nelson were reportedly occasions for 'intense emotion' in the city.[109] A glimpse of such emotions can be discerned in the Theatre Royal's 1806 staging of 'Tars on Shore. Or England's Glory! – a description (in character) of a naval engagement between an English and French frigate in the Chops of the Channel – to conclude with "Rule Britannia" in full chorus.'[110]

In the meantime, abolitionists in Parliament continued to whittle away at the British slave trade by getting through increased regulation of the slave ships and the banning of the slave trade in colonies newly captured from the French. These measures, dressed up in the rhetoric of national interest, amounted to no less than abolition by stealth. By 1806, Anstey tells us, no less than two-thirds of the British slave trade was effectively limited by such legislation.[111] With the continuation of the slave trade increasingly unlikely, labour-saving devices became correspondingly more attractive. One Bristol coppersmith and his partner advertised their newly patented sugar boiler in the local press, stressing that it guaranteed 'the reduction of labour . . . so great that six Negros will be enabled to do the work of a boiling-house that usually employed 22'.[112]

During the November election of 1806, the selected candidates for Bristol were Evan Baillie for the Whigs and Charles Bathurst for the Tories. Neither was a friend to abolition, but press reports indicate that they do not mention the issue during the election. Yet *Felix Farley's Bristol Journal* observes:

> The friends of the oppressed African race will be pleased to learn, that during the course of the election in various parts of the Kingdom, the popular sentiment has been very strongly expressed against the continuance of that traffick in human flesh, which to the disgrace of this enlightened country is still permitted if not occasioned by our laws.[113]

Drescher cites this article as evidence for popular abolitionist pressure in Bristol, but the article itself states that most of the anti-slavery agitation was centred in Yorkshire and the emerging industrial districts. In fact, both *Felix Farley* and the *Bristol Gazette and Public Advertiser* comment on the unprecedentedly quiescent atmosphere which characterized the 1806 election. The editor of *Felix Farley* attributed the 'apparent indifference to politics' to a 'real and unaffected unanimity' which was the sign of a patriotic spirit.[114] Could this be the case? A clue that the answer might be more complex is hinted at by the editor of the *Bristol Gazette*, who tellingly observed:

> There never was a period, since the pestilence of the French Revolution first burst forth, when democratic principles were less in fashion than they are at the present moment. The professors of Jacobinism as well as those who were strongly suspected of partiality to that doctrine have been, or are likely to be universally rejected.[115]

As Drescher sagely notes, to be silenced is not the same thing as to be silent.[116] Was the apparent unanimity a mere chimera, a product of wishful thinking on the part of the propertied classes? Certainly the franchise in Bristol, though relatively extensive by pre-reform standards, hardly reflected the will of the people. Unanimity is hardly indicated by the industrial unrest of the city's carpenters and pipemakers, shipwrights and tailors, between 1799 and 1800, or by the popular disturbances over high food prices and food scarcity in 1801.[117] Nor was unanimity in the minds of the group of Bristol men, women and children who in 1803 attacked a press gang and a party of marine infantry, preventing them from pressing a group of local men into the King's service. Such an attack was one of a long line of violent protests against impressment in Bristol.[118] But radical discontent with conditions at home might not necessarily imply a similar discontent about the slave trade. Pro-abolitionists often, as we have seen, contrasted the 'happy lot' of the African slave with the terrible lot of the English labourer. Did the 'restless and disaffected men', whom Charles Bathurst pledged himself against in his nomination speech, include radical abolitionists from the lower orders? Or was abolitionism still the exclusive preserve of a devout section of the better off? At present, there is simply not the evidence about radical thought in Bristol to answer these questions with complete certainty, but the indications are that those artisans not directly dependent on trades related to the Caribbean were generally abolitionist, especially if they had religious leanings towards Dissent or Methodism.

Bristol had long been disassociating herself from the slave trade. Thus Philip Protheroe could complacently announce that in 1807, when the Act was passed, not a single slaver sailed from the port.[119] Though Bathurst had opposed the bill to the end, such was the groundswell of parliamentary opinion in its favour that Baillie apparently abstained. When the Abolition Act formally took effect the following year, there was little public celebration such as had attended former anti-abolitionist victories. As a friend of Sally Wesley, Charles Wesley's daughter, complained, 'So the slave Trade is at last abolished. . . . For a Victory . . . we should have had illuminations, public rejoicings etc. but nothing of this at the emancipation of our fellow-creatures.'[120]

The Bristol press seemed resigned to abolition. By contrast, West Indian planters called for its repeal and for preferential treatment of Caribbean goods. The gulf between the planters' interests and those of the English consumer were apparent to the editor of *Felix Farley's Bristol Journal*. Clearly conscious that the city's corporation and the Society of Merchant Venturers were still heavily financially involved in the Caribbean, the editor tactfully commiserated with the plight of the West Indian planters but concluded that they were 'much mistaken' in their demands.[121]

Bristol's mercantile elite had failed in their opposition to abolition and were now faced with the challenge of political reform at home and emancipation abroad. For the moment, this challenge could be deflected by an appeal to patriotic unity. But once peace descended, both the enslavement of Africans and the plight of the English working classes would become bitterly contested topics, in both Bristol and the nation at large, in the decades to come.

Notes

1 Since it was customary for the city's church bells to be sounded in support of 'true blue' candidates during elections, this story does have the ring of truth. See 'Philalethes' of Clifton, writing in *The Gentleman's Magazine*, vol. 1, no. 58 (1791), pp. 362–3.

2 Peter Marshall, 'The Anti-Slave Trade Movement in Bristol', in Patrick McGrath (ed.), *Bristol in the Eighteenth Century* (Newton Abbot, 1972), pp. 206–11; John Latimer, *The History of the Society of Merchant Venturers of the City of Bristol* (Bristol, 1903), p. 186. The bombardment is not mentioned by David Richardson, *Bristol, Africa and the*

Eighteenth-Century Slave Trade to America, 4 vols (Bristol: Bristol Record Society, 1986, 1987, 1991 and 1996), vol. 4, pp. 193, 199, 202, in the description of these ships. It is notable that Thomas Jones owned the *Wasp*. Wilberforce's accusation received much newspaper coverage.

3 Alexander Falconbridge, *An Account of the Slave Trade on the Coast of Africa* (London: J. Phillips, 1788), p. 24. The sexual aspect of the case was particularly shocking, given that slave-ship articles routinely enjoined the crew not to interfere with the female slaves. See, for example, the injunction from the owners to the master of the *Africa*, in 1774, 'to treat the negroes with as much lenity as safety will admit and suffer none of your officers or people to beat or abuse them under any pretence whatever', cited in W. E. Minchinton, 'The Voyage of the Snow *Africa*', *The Mariner's Mirror*, vol. 37 (1951), p. 191.

4 M. Robinson (ed.), *Memoirs of Mary Robinson 'Perdita'* (London: Gibbings & Co., 1895); Moira Ferguson, in *Subject to Others: British Women Writers and Colonial Slavery, 1670–1834* (London, 1992), pp. 175–8, 236, 240–2, points out that the heroine of 'The Negro Girl', the enslaved Zelda, decides to attempt to escape when she is threatened with the sexual attentions of her owner: 'My tyrant sought my love . . .'.

5 'The African', in *Mary Robinson: Selected Poems*, ed. Judith Pascoe (Peterborough, Ontario, 2000), pp. 313–14; also quoted 'The Progress of Liberty', *Robinson: Works*, vol. 3, cited in Moira Ferguson, *Subject to Others: British Women Writers and Colonial Slavery, 1670–1834* (London and New York, 1992), p. 178; Janet Todd, *The Sign of Angelica: Women, Writing and Fiction, 1660–1800* (London, 1989), pp. 222–3; Janet Todd (ed.), *A Dictionary of British and American Women Writers, 1660–1800* (London, 1987), pp. 270–2.

6 John Taylor, *A Book about Bristol: Historical Ecclesiastical and Biographical from Original Research* (London and Bristol, 1872), p. 334.

7 Sarah Fox's diary, 13(?) December 1791; see note 16 to Chapter 4.

8 Marshall, 'The Anti-Slave Trade Movement in Bristol', p. 205.

9 Linda Colley, *Britons: Forging the Nation, 1707–1837*, 2nd edition (London, 1994), pp. 351–4; Stephen Poole, 'Popular Politics in Bristol, Somerset and Wiltshire, 1791–1805', Ph.D. dissertation, University of Bristol, 1992, p. 229.

10 Cited in A. Mary Richards, 'The Connection of Bristol with the African Slave Trade with Some Account of the Currents of Public Opinion in the City', MA thesis, University of Bristol, 1923, p. 70.

11 *FFBJ*, 14 April 1792.

12 S. Drescher, *Capitalism and Antislavery: British Mobilization in Comparative Perspective* (New York, 1977), p. 79.

13 PRO, James Rogers Papers, letter from Blacke and Kember to James Rogers, 26 October 1791, C/107/7 part 1.

14 Joseph Cottle, *Early Recollections Chiefly Relating to the Late Samuel Taylor Coleridge during His Long Residence in Bristol*, 2 vols (London: Longman, Rees & Co., 1837), pp. 2–4, 20.

15 *The hapless victim sold to till the soil,*
   Reaps only misery for his lengthened toil;
   To us the grateful plant is freely given,
   A feast unguilty by the hand of heav'n;
   But the sad slave the unblest produce rears,
   'Fans with his sighs, and waters with his tears'.
   Thus man perverts what heav'n intended good,
   And dies [sic] the growing plant with human blood;

(Robert Lovell, 'Bristol: A Satire', in Edward Martin and Bill Pickard (eds), *600 Years of Bristol Poetry* (Bristol, 1973), p. 22).

16 W. Matthews, *The New History . . . of Bristol* (Bristol, 1794), p. 38.

17 Robert Lovell, 'Bristol: A Satire'.

18 Samuel Taylor Coleridge, 'Lecture Concerning the Slave Trade', in Lewis Patten (ed.), *The Watchman* (London, 1970); Kathleen Coburn (gen. ed.), *The Collected Works of Samuel Taylor Coleridge*, pp. 130–40; see also Timothy Morton's 'Blood Sugar', in Tim Fulford and Peter J. Kitson (eds), *Romanticism and Colonialism: Writing and Empire, 1780–1830* (Cambridge, 1998), p. 93.

19 Robert Southey, *Poetical Works* (London, 1837), pp. 100–1. For a similar if more elliptical analysis of this poem, see Alan Richardson, 'Darkness Visible: Race and Representation in Bristol Abolitionist Poetry, 1770–1810', in Fulford and Kitson (eds), *Romanticism and Colonialism*, p. 145. The sonnets can be found in *The Poetical Works of Robert Southey* (London: Longmans Green & Co., 1884), p. 99.

20 Southey, *Poetical Works*.

21 *Ibid.*

22 *Ibid.*

23 *Ibid.*, pp. 309–10; see Thomas Southey, *Chronological History of the West Indies* (London?, 1827, reprinted London, 1968).

24 See 'Southey', in David Patrick and Francis Hindes Groome (eds), *Chambers' Biographical Dictionary* (London and Edinburgh, 1897), pp. 868–9, which dates his conversion to Toryism to the period around 1807; see also Geoffey Carnall, *Robert Southey and His Age: The Development of a Conservative Mind* (Oxford, 1960), and Richard Charles Cuthbert Southey, *The Life and Correspondence of Robert Southey*, 9th edition (London: Longman, Brown, Green & Longman, 1849), vol. 1, p. 318.

25 PRO, letter from James Harris to James Rogers of Bristol, 10 November 1787, James Rogers Papers, C107/9.

26 George Fyfe, *A History of Sierra Leone* (London, 1962), pp. 19–25; F. A. J. Utting, *The Story of Sierra Leone* (London, 1931), p. 81; F. W. Butt Thomason, 'Early Religious Influences in Sierra Leone', *Baptist Quarterly*, vol. 16 (1956), p. 313. There is a debate over whether or not these prostitutes were made drunk and awoke to find themselves en route to Sierra Leone against their wishes, as Anna Maria Falconbridge, in *Narrative of Two Voyages to the River Sierra Leone during the Years 1791–1793* (London, 1967 reprint of second edition, 1802), has attested. Fyfe thinks not, but as even he thinks Falconbridge an honest witness of events, and as she spoke directly to some of the surviving women themselves, I would give credence to her account. According to her version of events, some of the transported women came from Bristol.

27 Fyfe, *A History of Sierra Leone*, p. 26.

28 Falconbridge, *Narrative of Two Voyages*, p. 171.

29 The five men were listed as William Robins, William Eggins, Joshua Tracy, John Duffey and James Hall; PRO, James Rogers Papers, Robert Peake to James Rogers, 18 July 1792 and 10 September 1792, C/107/6.

30 Peter Fryer, *Staying Power: The History of Black People in Britain* (London, 1984), pp. 201–14; F. A. J. Utting, *The Story of Sierra Leone*, pp. 281–96.

31 *FFBJ*, 14 April 1792.

32 Sarah Champion recalls seeing Falconbridge 'just returned from Sierra Leone, whence he brought over a young prince for education, whom he had left at Penzance'; Sarah Champion Fox's diary, n.d., 1791.

33 Falconbridge, *Narrative of Two Voyages*, pp. 126–7, cited in Ferguson, *Subject to Others*, p. 206.

34 *Memoirs of Granville Sharp*, p. 167.

35 *Ibid.* See also Anon. [Hannah More], *The Black Prince, a True Story: Being an Account of the Life and Death of Naimbana, an African King's Son, Who Arrived in England in the Year 1791, and set sail on his return in June 1793* (London, n.d. but *c.* 1801).

36 Basil Cottle, 'The Life (1770–1853), Writings and Literary Relationship of Joseph Cottle of Bristol', unpublished doctoral thesis, University of Bristol, 1958, pp. 5, 20–1.

37 According to Utting in *The Story of Sierra Leone*, p. 67, King Naimbana sent three male members of his family abroad: one to Turkey to study Islam, a second to Portugal to study Roman Catholicism, and a third to England to study Protestantism; all three died young.

38 Basil Cottle and 'Lee Boo – of Pelew: a Poem', in *Poems by Joseph Cottle* (Bristol: Bulgin & Rosser, 1796), pp. 151–96.

39 Cottle, like Yearsley before him, conflated his hero's ethnic identity with those of other 'dark people' and, as More would later do, romanticized his character.

40 John Latimer, *The Annals of Bristol in the Eighteenth Century* (Bristol: privately printed, 1893), p. 493.

41 BRL, Braikenridge Collection, Christ Church, vol. 15, p. 75.

42 Huntington Library, Macaulay Papers (hereafter MP), letter from Thomas Winterbottom to Zachary Macaulay, n.d. but *c.* 1796, Box 4.

43 HL, MP, Zachary Macaulay to Selina Mills, Freetown, Sierra Leone, 29 July 1796, Box 1. Macaulay's servant in Sierra Leone, Mary Perth, also planned to visit England with her daughter and Macaulay told his fiancée that he had no doubt that the Perths 'will find the way to Park Street'. Perth was of African or partial African descent. See HL, MP, Z. Macaulay to S. Mills, 1 December 1797, Box 2.

44 HL, MP, Z. Macaulay to S. Mills, 20 May 1796, Box 4.

45 BULSC, Bristol minister's diary, 7 June 1792, Moravian Collection. According to Fyfe, *History of Sierra Leone*, pp. 51–2, 55, 70, Horne advocated that future ministers live in African villages there rather than in Freetown and set up circuits on the Wesleyan model.

46 See Isaac Mann, 'Calendar of Letters, 1794–1800', *BQ*, vol. 6 (1933), pp. 220–1; Viscountess Knutsford, *Life and Letters of Zachary Macaulay* (London: Edward Arnold, 1900), pp. 23, 60–1. My thanks to David Bruce for his generous loan of this book and other papers concerning the Macaulay family.

47 PRO, Copy of the Resolution of the Court of Inquiry, 22 February 1797, CO270/4.

48 Fyfe, *A History of Sierra Leone*, pp. 69–71.

49 Cited in *Periodical Accounts Relative to the Baptist Missionary Society*, vol. 1 (London: J. Morris, n.d. but *c.* 1799), pp. 108–11.

50 Falconbridge, *Narrative of Two Voyages*, p. 77.

51 See letters of Mr Grigg to 'Dr R.' of Bristol, 1 and 22 April 1796, and Mr Rodway to Dr R. in *Periodical Accounts*, vol. 1, pp. 240–50.

52 *Ibid.*, p. 247.

53 W. T. Whitley, 'The Tune Book of 1791', *BQ*, vol. 10 (October 1941), pp. 438–43.

54 See PRO, letters from Thomas Peters to Henry Dundas (n.d.) and from William Clarkson to Dundas, 21 April 1792 for accounts of the arrival of the settlers; CO267/9. The characterization of Nova Scotians as 'freed slave refugees whom the British had fobbed off with a dead-end resettlement in the Canadian colony', in Jim Hudgens and Richard Trillo, *West Africa: The Rough Guide* (London, 1995 edition), p. 546, is tersely apt.

55 In his journal and his letters to Bristol, he condemned the brutality of English slavers but was resigned to his dependence on some of them for news and letters, and appears to have visited some slave ships and talked to the slaves without interfering with their shipment. It is true that he seemed at times particularly frustrated by his inability to prevent free residents of Sierra Leone from being enslaved by the captain of the Bristol privateer the *General Ord*, whom he calls 'a commissioned robber', but no action seems to have been taken against him. This was probably the former slave ship of the same name owned by none other than Walter Jacks & Co. of Bristol; see Richardson, *Bristol,*

Africa and the Eighteenth-Century Slave Trade, vol. 4, p. 212. Macaulay fumes angrily over the fact that black seamen captured in war were enslaved whilst their white counterparts were made prisoners of war, but his complaints are private rather than formal. At the same time, he loftily condemns the greed of those Africans who 'look with a wishful eye to the slave Trade, as a source of easy profit'; see HL, MP, Z. Macaulay to S. Mills, 1 December 1797, Box 2.

56 HL, MP, Z. Macaulay to S. Mills, 28 June 1797.

57 Kenneth Hyde, 'The Union Church at Launceston, Cornwall (Conti'd)', *BQ*, vol. 14 (1952), pp. 207–8.

58 Bail Amey, 'Baptist Missionary Society Radicals', *BQ*, vol. 26 (1975–6), pp. 368–9; Christopher Fyfe (ed.), *Anna Maria Falconbridge Narrative of Two Voyages to the River Sierrra Leone . . .* (Liverpool, 2000), p. 19. See Deirdre Coleman's excellent introduction to her edition of Falconbridge's *Narrative* in *Maiden Voyages and Infant Colonies: Two Women's Travel Narratives of the 1790s* (Leicester, 1999), esp. p. 24, which came to my attention just before this book went to press.

59 Letter from Grigg to Mr F of Kettering, 16 May 1796, cited in *Periodical Accounts Relative to the Baptist Missionary Society*, p. 253.

60 Hyde, 'The Union Church at Launceston', pp. 207–8.

61 Amey, 'Baptist Missionary Society Radicals', p. 369.

62 Brian Stanley, *The History of the Baptist Missionary Society, 1792–1992* (Edinburgh, 1992), pp. 23–4.

63 Hyde, 'The Union Church at Launceston', pp 209ff. Grigg came from Cornwall and went on to evangelize among slaves in Virginia. He joined an anti-slavery group there in 1804. Hyde relates that some African-American soldiers who visited Launceston during the Second World War asked the Alderman Grigg who was showing them around if he might be related to the Baptist Jacob Grigg, who was still remembered by their people for his services to the slaves.

64 Stanley, in *The History of the Baptist Missionary Society*, pp. 23–4, names Andrew Fuller, the Secretary of the Baptist Missionary Society, as objecting in a letter to Ryland to Grigg's democratic attitudes. The Revd John Newton, who, incidentally, had also been a mentor to Hannah More, corresponded both with Ryland and the Sierra Leone officials over this incident and took the line that Africans should not be exposed to sectarian differences amongst the Europeans in the settlement, Bristol Baptist College Library (henceforth BBCL), letters to John Ryland from John Newton, 28 July 1795 and 26 November 1796, G96 Box N. Like most Anglican Evangelicals, Newton disliked radicalism in any form. In particular, he expressly resented the Baptists' influence over his former protégé, the black preacher David George. 'When David George first arrived [in London], he was often with me. But since he has been published as *Pastor of a Baptist Church* I have lost him. . . . I am sure you mean well. But it would I believe have been better both for him and the [Sierra Leone] colony to have left him under the patronage of Mr. Harry Thornton'; BBCL, letter to John Ryland from John Newton, 2 May 1793, G96 Box N.

65 Knutsford, *Life and Letters of Zachary Macaulay*, pp. 169. See also Macaulay's comments on George and Ryland cited by Newton to Ryland in his letter to Ryland, 20 September 1797; BBCL, G96, Box N.

66 According to Roger Hayden, all references to Sierra Leone and Grigg's accusation regarding the complicity of the colony in slave-trading have been 'studiously avoided'; 'Kettering 1792 and Philadelphia 1814 (I), *BQ*, vol. 21 (1965), pp. 3–20; see also Hyde, 'The Union Church at Launceston'.

67 HL, MP, Z. Macaulay to S. Mills, Battersea Rise, 30 May 1799, Box 2.

68 Letter cited in Knutsford, *Life and Letters of Zachary Macaulay*, pp. 249–50.

69 HL, MP, Z. Macaulay to S. Mills, 30 May 1799, 3 June 1799, 5 June 1799, 2 July 1799 and 7 July 1799. Hughes had been appointed to a pastorate in Battersea, where the children were located. Foster was by then involved with the Religious Tract Society and would later go on to become secretary of the British and Foreign Bible Society; Norman Moon, *Education for Ministry: Bristol Baptist College, 1679–1979* (Bristol: Bristol Baptist College, 1979), p. 28.

70 J. E. Ryland (ed.), *Life and Correspondence of John Foster*, 2 vols (London, 1848), pp. 68–9. Foster lodged with Mary Perth and her daughter. He does not name her but her identity is confirmed in HL, letter from Z. Macaulay to S. Mills, 8 June 1797, Macaulay Papers, Box 2.

71 The couple were married in St Augustine's Church, Bristol, on 26 August 1799. For the reference to the 'sisterhood', see HL, MP, V. Mills to Z. Macaulay, 30 August 1799.

72 Moira Ferguson, *Subject to Others*, p. 219.

73 Anon. [Hannah More], *The Black Prince, a True Story: Being an Account of the Life and Death of Naimbana, an African King's Son, Who Arrived in England in the Year 1791, and set sail on his return in June 1793* (London: Cheap Repository Tracts, n.d. but c. 1801).

74 Latimer, *The Annals of Bristol in the Eighteenth Century*, p. 492.

75 W. S. Lewis, *The Yale Edition of Horace Walpole's Correspondence* (New Haven, CT, and London, 1961), vol. 31, pp. 340, 349.

76 Latimer, *The Annals of Bristol in the Eighteenth Century*, p. 492. A 'gentleman from Clifton' writes in 1791 that Dissenters would do well to follow the example of the Quakers in supporting the anti-slavery cause, thus implying that the Quakers were the most active group in this regard; *The Gentleman's Magazine*, vol. 1, no. 58 (1791), pp. 362–3.

77 GRO, letter from Harry Gandy to Granville Sharp, 4 August 1796, Granville Sharp Collection, D3549, 13/1/G2. This reminds one of the way the Old Calabar princes had been encouraged to get to Bristol; it offers a glimpse of an unofficial support network amongst seamen (possibly themselves of African origin) and slaves wishing to escape.

78 *Ibid.* See the relatively short list of Bristol subscribers to the 1794 edition of Olaudah Equiano's *The Interesting Narrative . . .* in the Penguin edition of this work: Vincent Caretta (ed.) (London, 1995), pp. 21–2.

79 GRO, letter from Gandy to Sharp, 4 August 1796.

80 *Ibid.*

81 NatWest Archives, deed transferring the Jamaican plantation of Walter Jacks, Bristol merchant, to a number of his creditors, 1795, 4961.

82 *Ibid.*

83 Cited in John Latimer, *The Annals of Bristol in the Nineteenth Century* (Bristol: privately printed, 1893), p. 29.

84 These figures are derived from a statement to the House of Commons, 5 April 1805, reported in the *Bristol Gazette and Public Advertiser* (henceforth *BGPA*), 13 November 1806.

85 *FFBJ*, 22 June 1799. Earlier that year, a new poetic version of *Inkle and Yarico* was published in the *Bristol Gazette* which concluded that readers
    . . . soon would find
    Man has no License to enslave Mankind.

86 Cited in John Brewer, *The Pleasures of the Imagination: English Culture in the Eighteenth Century* (London, 1997), p. 422.

87 According to Latimer, *The Annals of Bristol in the Eighteenth Century* (Bristol: privately printed, 1893), pp. 519–22. Only seven Bristol vessels were found in a fleet of a hundred Jamaica merchantmen convoyed by the Royal Navy in 1796, but the Bristol Volunteers attracted many of Bristol's most influential West India merchants.

88 Sir Charles Parry Hobhouse, *Some Account of the Family of Hobhouse and Reminiscences* (Leicester: Johnson Wykes & Co., n.d.), pp. 13–14.

89 Latimer, *The Annals of Bristol in the Eighteenth Century*, p. 518; Stephen Poole, 'Popular Politics in Bristol', pp. 90–1.

90 Cited in Stephen Poole, 'Popular Politics in Bristol', p. 246.

91 Falconbridge, *Narrative of Two Voyages*, p. 238.

92 *Ibid.*

93 *Ibid.*

94 *FFBJ*, 8 January 1803.

95 Mr Weeks owned the Bush Tavern, 'which appears to be the general slaughterhouse for the demolition of turtles'; Rowland Watson, *A Scrapbook of Inns* (London, 1949), p. 134.

96 Latimer, *The Annals of Bristol in the Eighteenth Century*, p. 532; Kathleen Barker, *The Theatre Royal Bristol, 1766–1966: Two Centuries of Stage History* (London: Society for Theatre Research, 1974), pp. 61–6.

97 BRO, Playbills, 8982 (23) and (24).

98 [Cumberland], *The West Indian: A Comedy* (London: W. Griffin, 1771); Kathleen Barker, *The Theatre Royal*, p. 26.

99 Given the fuss that was made when a group of Lascars came to the Theatre Royal to see Mrs Siddons in *The Fair Circassian* in 1782, it seems unlikely that the presence of black actors would have passed unmentioned. See University of Bristol Theatre Collection, Kathleen Barker Collection, February 1782.

100 I am grateful to my colleague Dr Diana Jeater for this information.

101 *Bonner and Middleton's Bristol Journal*, 1 November 1800; see also University of Bristol Theatre Collection, *Bristol Journal*, 1 November 1800 and 8 November 1800, Kathleen Barker Collection.

102 Mary Douglas, *Purity and Danger: An Analysis of the Concepts of Pollution and Taboo* (London, 1966, reprinted London, 1984), pp. 61–2; John and Jean Romaroff, *Ethnography and the Historical Imagination* (Boulder, CO, 1992), pp. 3–48, 184–90, 239.

103 The case of 'Obeah Jack' was used in anti-abolitionist propaganda as late as the 1820s; see *The Anti-Slavery Monthly Reporter* (London: Printed for the London Society for the Mitigation and Abolition of Slavery in the British Dominions), vol. 1 (1827), pp. 173–4 text and note.

104 According to Latimer, *The Annals of Bristol in the Eighteenth Century*, p. 519, only seven Bristol vessels were found in a fleet of a hundred Jamaica merchantmen convoyed by the Royal Navy in 1796.

105 *Ibid.*, p. 417.

106 BULSC, Pinney Papers, diary entries for 4 and 25 July, 14 September, and 5, 14 and 25 December 1803 in unnamed diary in the Baillie Papers, Box 33. We do not know whether Baillie saw *Inkle and Yarico* or *The West Indian*, which were staged in Bath's Theatre Royal that same year, or if they also were staged in Bristol, BCRL, Jefferies Collection, vol. 16.

107 R. Hall, 'Sentiments Proper to the Present Crisis', cited in Richards, 'The Connection of Bristol with the African Slave Trade', p. 86.

108 BLSC, Pinney Papers, Evan Baillie to Peter Baillie, 13 June 1804, Baillie Papers, Box 1810 [*sic*]–1861. An extract of this passage is also cited in R. G. Thorne, *The House of Commons, 1790–1820* (London: History of Parliament Trust, 1986), vol. 3, p. 108.

109 Latimer, *The Annals of Bristol in the Nineteenth Century*, p. 27.

110 *FFBJ*, 12 July 1806.

111 Anstey makes the point that once French democracy gave way to 'despotism', 'the damaging taunt that abolition was founded on French democratic principles now fell

wide of the mark'; Roger Anstey, *The Atlantic Slave Trade and British Abolition, 1760–1810* (London, 1975), pp. 342–3.

112 *BGPA*, 11 December 1806. The high price of slaves also spurred planter interest in the use of steam power, and Thomas Daniel of Bristol and Barbados was amongst those who used it on his slave estates; see Jennifer Tann, 'Steam and Sugar: The Diffusion of the Stationary Steam Engine to the Caribbean Sugar Industry, 1770–1840', *History of Technology*, vol. 19 (1997), pp. 63–83. Thanks to Stephen Price for drawing this article to my attention.

113 *FFBJ*, 22 November 1806; also cited in Seymour Drescher, 'Whose Abolition? Popular Pressure and the Ending of the British Slave Trade', *Past and Present*, vol. 143 (1994), p. 145.

114 *FFBJ*, 29 November 1806.

115 *BGPA*, 13 November 1806.

116 Drescher, 'Whose Abolition?', p. 140.

117 Poole, 'Popular Politics', pp. 380, 418, 465, 469, 471, 476, 504–5, 515–16.

118 Latimer, *The Annals of Bristol in the Nineteenth Century*, pp. 20–1.

119 *Ibid.*, p. 29.

120 JRL, letter from Marianne F—— to Sally Wesley, n.d. but *c.* 1806, Wesley Family Correspondence, DDWF 26/36.

121 *FFBJ*, 2 January 1808.

6

THE STRUGGLE FOR EMANCIPATION

[C]ompulsory manumission . . . is incompatible with the well being of the slaves . . . with the safety of the colonies and with a fair and equitable consideration of vested private interests. (Resolution made at a meeting of Bristol planters interested in the colonies of Demerara and Berbice, Bristol Merchants Hall, 24 November 1826)

Ye who Britain's freedom love,
Ye who boast her equal laws,
Now your love of freedom praise.
Plead. Oh! Plead the Negro's cause.

Whilst you talk of charter'd rights,
See your sable brethren mourn,
By the hands of cruel whites
Heaven's own charter from them torn.

('Edina', in the *Bristol Mercury*, 11 August 1832)

How different were attitudes towards Africans and the question of slavery after abolition? One historian has already explored the *politics* of Bristol's emancipation campaign, but what was its subtext?[1] What can we learn from an investigation of the general political culture between 1807 and 1834? Who were involved in agitating for and against emancipation and in what terms did they perceive the issues? Can an examination of the ritual and rhetoric of Bristol's electoral politics yield new insights into the ways in which anxieties around race and class were connected?

Slavery does not seem to have featured as an issue in the parliamentary elections immediately after abolition. But abolition and the prospect of slave emancipation helped to forge a new, contradictory discourse around the theme of liberty. 'Britons never would be slaves', but what, some wondered, about the Africans they governed?

Others begrudged the attention paid to colonial injustice when there were white 'wage slaves' nearer to home. Dislocated artisans, exploited industrial workers, honest people imprisoned for debt, were beginning to chafe against a system which gave them little political voice. In other words, the theme of slavery, long a trope in political rhetoric, was reinvigorated by new concerns about industrial distress and political reform at home.

Political radicals and the issue of colonial slavery

What did political radicals in Bristol think about the issue of colonial slavery? Surviving records do not yield much on this point. The nationally prominent political campaigner Henry Hunt owned a brewery in the Hotwells area of Bristol at the time of the 1807 parliamentary elections, and agitated for reform there. A champion of universal suffrage and annual parliaments, he could rally large, enthusiastic and sometimes violent crowds in the city. Hunt was no apologist for the slave trade. The standing Whig and Tory candidates whom he opposed on behalf of a reform candidate both represented the West India interest. Yet while Hunt later characterized the Abolition Act, in his *Memoirs*, as the one good thing the Whigs had ever done, he clearly thought it was used to divert attention away from more pressing reforms at home. His position on slave emancipation is less clear. Hunt clearly disliked Evangelical anti-slavery campaigners, particularly Hannah More, whose views he characterized as 'fanatick' and whose sexual reputation he impugned.[2] For many years his fellow radical William Cobbett, notoriously hostile to black people, was his political ally.[3]

In 1812 Hunt stood as a reform candidate for Bristol and was actively endorsed in Cobbett's *Political Register*. Though apparently not as hostile to 'Negro emancipation' as Cobbett, both men clearly prioritized the distress of English workers as an election theme. In Hunt's rhetorical universe it was the Englishman, not the African, who was most threatened by slavery. As one of his election handbills proclaimed,

> We come to reason not to fight
> To let the greedy locusts see
> We are not slaves and ne'er will we
> Cringe to a sordid troop
> Of well-fed Pensioners in power
> Who all our hard-earned gains devour.[4]

When Hunt asked his Bristol constituents, 'what has any Englishman now left that he can call his own but his bare life; and what is Life without Liberty?'[5] he implied that they suffered the same disadvantages as colonial slaves.

The election of 1812 and the West India interest

During the 1812 election, Hunt's opponents included not only the West India merchants Richard Hart Davis for the blues and Edward Protheroe for the 'Old

Whigs', but also Sir Samuel Romilly (1757–1818), a Progressive Whig reformer who was a committed anti-slavery campaigner. In the event, Romilly was edged out by a coalition between the Whig and Tory wings of Bristol's West India interest, which according to Latimer 'heartily concurred in detesting the anti-slavery principle of Romilly'.[6]

'Orator' Hunt, accused of inciting the mob to smash the doors and windows of the council house and Hart Davis's home on the first day of polling, was regarded by the Bristol political establishment as a dangerous gadfly. A man of Romilly's experience and calibre was, however, less easily dismissed. The Tories in particular seemed somewhat rattled by Romilly's candidacy. The corruption which attended the campaign was exceptional, even for Bristol. Hart Davis spent an extraordinary amount of money to guarantee his victory. But it would be misleading to represent the radicals as violent and their opponents merely as corrupt.[7] Such a gloss on events plays down the extent to which the West India interest used violence and threats to prevent an anti-slavery candidate from reaching Parliament. A large number of Hart Davis's less genteel supporters, supplied with blue jackets, white trousers and glazed blue hats, were also, it was alleged, supplied with 'tremendous' blue bludgeons which they 'exercise in the most wanton and brutal manner'.[8] Such 'bludgeon men' were variously identified as Kingswood colliers, press gang recruits and shipwrights.[9] Hunt charged that one such group, acting under the leadership of a well-known local prizefighter, threatened Romilly's supporters as they were about to vote for their candidate.[10]

For their part, Protheroe's supporters were reported to have moved two hefty cannons into the Exchange and aimed them directly at Romilly's headquarters. It says much about the political culture of the time that this was represented as a mere 'prank'. Hunt, however, pointed out that this gesture had a sinister and frightening aspect, and although Romilly's supporters later discovered that the cannons were unloaded, the symbolic message was unmistakable.[11]

Though it is to Hunt's credit that he testified that Romilly's supporters had been violently intimidated by both Davis and Protheroe, it is equally true that his insistence on standing for election split the progressive vote. But the very fact that he noticeably toned down his rhetorical attacks on Romilly after intimidation had allegedly begun makes his account more credible, though Romilly himself attributes this to Hunt's opportunism.[12] Romilly was ultimately forced to withdraw after a series of 'dirty tricks' by Davis and Protheroe, though he still, thanks to the tenacity of his supporters, mustered over 1600 votes compared to the 2485 Protheroe garnered.[13] Romilly's vote was further depressed by another range of intimidating tactics. It is reasonable to suppose that in the days before secret ballots, voters supporting radical or progressive candidates might find themselves blacklisted. Those who had shops might find they were no longer patronized by the city's elite; freemen employed in workshops might find themselves out of a job. There is certainly evidence for this in the 1830 and 1831 Bristol elections, and Romilly confirms that some of his supporters dared not vote for him lest they be 'ruined'.[14] Another form of intimidation, that of denying freemen and their families grants from the city's various endowed charities, also seems to have been deployed in 1812. The wife of John Richards, a brazier, claimed she received no money from the Peloquin Trust on the birth of her child because her husband had voted for Romilly.[15]

The colourful customs of pre-reform elections were a way of involving the wider population in the city's political life. In 1812, Bristol's political establishment had effectively confirmed the Tory ascendancy by utilizing a wide range of symbolic gestures and rites. Churches were draped in blue ribbons and their bells rung as the victorious Davis processed in his 'Triumphal Car' through the city, attended by 150 carriers and sidemen, 1200 constables and nearly 2000 gentlemen.[16] Election ritual here is a symbolic affirmation of the existing social order, an order that was increasingly under threat.

The election of 1812 clearly demonstrated that Bristol's Tories and traditional Whigs were more united by their West Indian interests than divided by party loyalties. Subsequent elections featured 'West Indian' candidates from both parties. The issue of slavery would not surface as an election issue until nearly two decades later.

Changing public attitudes towards slavery, 1814–30

At first sight it seemed startling that in 1814, Bristol's Whig MP, Edward Protheroe, would support Wilberforce's efforts to ensure the abolition of the French slave trade. Certainly one of Protheroe's fellow MPs professed that such a turnaround from the members for Liverpool and Bristol was 'too extraordinary ever to have been prophesied or expected'.[17] Protheroe clearly seems to have been responding to his constituents, some of whom staged a widely publicized meeting in Bristol lobbying for the inclusion of an abolitionist clause in any peace treaty with France.[18] But there were clear limits to his reforming instincts. For although, in the following year, he professed himself anxious to end the illegal importation of slaves into the British West Indies, he did not support Wilberforce's bill to prevent it, advising that an inquiry alone into the practice would suffice. Protheroe, himself a slave-owner, was worried about alienating the West Indian plantocracy, of which he was an absentee member. In any case, a directive from the West India Association, the organized West Indian lobby in Britain, requested that their provincial members 'use their influence' to obtain their opposition to Mr Wilberforce's bill.[19]

Contemporaries in Britain as a whole, and in Bristol in particular, attest to a shift in public opinion regarding slavery. Even this shift was part of a wider transformation in cultural values. The early nineteenth century saw an explosion of charitable groups in the city and the ascendancy of Evangelical values amongst local Protestants. Mistreated animals, fallen women, displaced seamen and the increasingly restive working classes more and more engaged the attentions of Bristol's growing middle class. *Matthew's Annual Bristol Directory* for 1823 lists no fewer than 27 charities, and this list does not include those in the gift of the corporation.[20] This period sees the beginning of the era of female philanthropy, and, significantly, the slave-trader Isaac Hobhouse's fine house on Cornwallis Cresent in Clifton was by 1825 the residence of a secular order of women devoted to charitable works.[21]

The conversion of the slaves, Jews and 'Hindoos' was a popular cause and Hannah More, now living in Clifton, turned her attention to the enslaved workers in east India. In 1813 a local branch of the Church of England Missionary Society for Africa and the East was established.[22] There was increasing emphasis, too, on improving the conditions of the West Indian slaves, particularly with respect to ensuring that they received a religious education. Local studies make no mention of Bristol's contribution to the massive anti-slavery petitions that were nationally circulated in 1815, but it seems likely there were Bristol signatories to them. The Reverend Dr John Ryland[23] had long been in touch with black American Baptists, the former slaves George Liele (c. 1750–1828) and his protégé Moses Baker. They had been evangelizing slaves in Jamaica since 1783, and had relied to some extent on Ryland's support in the face of violent planter hostility and little money. It was they who asked the Baptist Missionary Society to send them trained ministers to help spread the Baptist word in the Caribbean.[24] In response to their entreaties, the first European Baptist missionary to the West Indies, John Rowe, began his duties in Jamaica in 1813. Rowe was a product of the Bristol Baptist College, and shortly before Rowe's premature death in 1816, John Ryland also began an extended correspondence with Wilberforce about sending more Baptist missionaries to the West Indies, though it is clear that Wilberforce thought sending in non-Anglican missionaries was politically risky.[25]

By this era, most planters resident in England had inherited their estates, and a few seem embarrassed by the source of their wealth. Mr Samuel Gist, who had been schooled in Bristol, left £10,000 on his death in 1815 to two Bristol schools (his alma mater, Queen Elizabeth Hospital, and Red Maids School for Girls). He also freed his 300 slaves and provided for their subsistence and education and for those of their descendants.[26] Four years later, Ann Morgan Foulkes of Redland, near Bristol, instructed her brother Arthur to free Mary Ellis, a slave resident on his Jamaican estate.[27]

When, however, Clarkson and a few others began to organize a campaign for slave emancipation in 1822, they found their goal had to be couched in the least alarming terms possible. Bristol's abolition committee had been disbanded in 1806, and so had most of the other 60-odd provincial committees throughout the nation. Nor did it follow that members of the old committees would necessarily join the new one. There were many, said Clarkson, 'who thought the abolition of the slave Trade practicable and its consequences beneficial, who were less sanguine as to the abolition of slavery'.[28]

Catholic emancipation and the Corn Laws rather than slavery excited the passions of the Bristol electorate in that year, according to one contemporary. Out of the 519 people Clarkson listed as supporters of his campaign in 1823, only six were listed as being from Bristol (Table 10). Nevertheless, a meeting was set up in October of that year at the Savings Bank at Bristol supporting 'the mitigation and gradual abolition' of slavery.

Table 10   Bristol supporters of Thomas Clarkson, 1823

Joseph and James Wright	Quakers	Timber merchants?
Joseph Storrs Fry	Quaker	Chocolate Manufacturer
Revd T. Biddulph	Anglican	Minister
George Ashmead	Baptist	Land surveyor, map-maker
Thomas Sanders	Anglican?	Seed and corn merchant

The West India Association saw that 'melioration' might be sold as an alternative to emancipation.[29] By their definition, 'melioration' meant affording slaves the time and opportunity for religious instruction and granting them 'more security against unnecessary severity of punishment and more facility in purchasing their freedom'. Privately, the association worked hard to sell this idea to its more intractable counterparts in the colonial assemblies governing the British West Indian islands. In 1823 the standing committee reported to the assemblies that British public opinion had a 'deep and general though undoubtedly most unjust and unmerited impression' that the colonial assemblies were dragging their heels on these issues of slave welfare. The Association warned that it was vital to the stability of the slave colonies that 'Negroes should look up to those who were in immediate authority over them and not to the British Parliament, British Government, or British Public as their protectors'.[30] However, the colonial assemblies were generally angry, and resistant to any suggestion of reform. As the new Governor of Barbados complained in confidence to the Colonial Secretary, Lord Bathurst, in 1824, 'The slightest breath of the Slave Emancipation Question produces such a Flame, as to render my situation most uncomfortably warm.'[31]

In order to set an example to colleagues in the colonies, the West India Association donated £1000 to the National Society for the Conversion and Education of Negro Slaves, a charity designed to supply tractable Anglican missionaries to the plantations. Members of the West India Association were also urged to subscribe as individuals, and by 1824 some of Bristol's most prominent planters, including Thomas Daniel, Charles Pinney, Philip Protheroe and Robert Bright, did just that.[32]

In tandem with these measures, the West India lobby began to mount an aggressive propaganda campaign against emancipation. According to Clarkson,

> They circulated the most furious scurrilous and false publications through the whole kingdom, and they had done their work so well, that I found their books in the libraries, reading rooms and coffee houses and at some of the Inns as I went along. These books had been sent free of all cost . . . [and] stated that the slaves were totally unfit for Emancipation. They foreboded insurrections of the most fearful kind, destructions to the planters and even ruin of the Mother Country, and they painted these ends in such strong colours that some people thought they actually saw them in the distance all approaching rapidly. All such persons would not only not hear us, but considered us as traitors to our country. They poisoned too the minds of others, with whom I came into contact, so that I was obliged to be exceedingly circumspect both in my words and conduct.[33]

Nevertheless, provincial abolitionist committees were organized. Shortly afterwards, in 1824, two Baptist missionaries, Thomas Burchell, from the Bristol Baptist College, and Thomas Knibb, a member of Ryland's Broadmead congregation, were placed in Jamaica.[34] Mindful of the debacle at Sierra Leone, Ryland and the Baptist Missionary Society enjoined the men in no uncertain terms to keep out of politics and not to antagonize the planters by any expression of their anti-slavery views. Their letters home, however, helped to fuel distaste for the brutalities of the Jamaican regime, and in 1825 the Baptist minister John Foster urged in a sermon to his Bristol congregation of the need to organize in order to conquer the 'palpable and horrid iniquity' of slavery.[35]

Anxious about the growing influence of the emancipation campaign, the West India Association's management committee met deputations from Bristol, Liverpool and Glasgow early in 1826. There it was admitted that 'to the Question abstractly put, "Are you a Friend to Slavery?" no Englishman will answer in the affirmative – To obtain Petitions against Slavery therefore, cannot be a work of Difficulty'.[36] A special meeting of Bristol planters interested in the colonies of Demerara and Berbice on 14 November 1826 formally condemned 'compulsory manumission . . . [as being] incompatible with the well being of the slaves themselves, with the safety of the colonies and with a fair and equitable consideration of vested private interests'.[37]

Despite this formidable lobby, public meetings were called in Bristol in 1825 and 1826 to petition Parliament for the gradual abolition of slavery in the British colonies.[38] Evidently four petitions from Bristol were sent to Parliament between 1826 and 1830. The published proceedings of the 1826 meeting survive, and report that the Guildhall was 'crowded with a very respectable company in which members of the Society of Friends formed a conspicuous part [and] the galleries were filled with Ladies'.[39] Women were increasingly attending public meetings, mainly concerning religious issues, albeit 'in the galleries'. Readers of the meeting's published account were urged to read an anti-slavery pamphlet, anonymous but written by Marianne Schimmelpenninck, a former Moravian of Quaker parentage who was now a member of Bristol's Unitarian congregation at Lewins Mead. Her pamphlet debunked in great and learned detail the notion that the Bible condoned modern slave regimes.[40]

Only men were reported to have spoken at the 1826 meeting, and most were Dissenting clergy or connected with Evangelical organizations. Its published proceedings reveal a deep ambivalence about slave emancipation. Though resolutions passed at the meeting lamented the lot of the slaves, there was much emphasis on the importance of acting in the interests of all parties concerned, including the planters; of steering between the 'whirlwind of passion' and the 'debasing power of self-interest', as T. C. Cowan of the Bible Missionary and Peace Societies put it. No one at the meeting appeared to advocate immediate emancipation. The Unitarian minister Dr Lant Carpenter sounded both cautious and conciliatory, agreeing with a gradualist approach and attesting to the 'high character and respectability' of many of 'our planters here', though he could not say the same of 'all those who resided abroad'.[41] The Baptist minister the Reverend Thomas Roberts,[42] celebrated as a champion of anti-slavery by modern Baptist writers, appeared to be willing to dispense with emancipation altogether, so convinced was he that 'Negroes could be managed without cruelty'. He cited with warm approval the example of plantations managed by the Moravians (United Brethren) where 'the whip was never used and the Sabbath never profaned by the market'.[43] The Congregationalist minister Robert Thorpe, famous for his virulently anti-Catholic writing, boomed in with eloquent denunciations of the evils of owning another human being, pronounced on society's collective guilt, but called for little more than 'a day of general Fasting'.[44]

Even the former secretary and treasurer of the old Abolition Committee, J. E. Lunnell, stressed the necessity of gradualism:

> Sudden emancipation would be cruel as well as absurd, nothing qualifies a man of low birth for the confidence, comfort and enjoyments of civil life more than property saved from industry by prudence. . . . I think slaves might be allowed to purchase their freedom, and when able to do it, they might on the whole be considered as qualified for it; for there is no describing the difference in the civil characters of men, who never had any property but consume everything, and those who create property by honest industry and prudence.[45]

Lunnell's arguments could have been applied with equal facility by those opposing universal male suffrage in Britain. Extending full civil rights to Dissenting Protestants (a reform which would be achieved two years later in 1828) was one thing, but extending freedom to slaves or votes to those whites possessed of neither education nor property was evidently a more daunting prospect, especially in the light of riots at home and rebellion in the colonies.[46]

The gradualism was typical of these early anti-slavery societies. In Bristol there was a particular concern amongst the speakers to stress the good character of Bristol planters, an indication of their deference towards the Bristol West India interest.[47] The minister of Bristol's Moravian congregation refused to lend public support to the anti-slavery meetings of 1825 and 1826: 'However desirable we deem the object we do not think it consistent with our calling and especially with the prosperity of our missions in the West Indies to make a public show in the attainment of that object.'[48] The Moravians were, it is true, forbidden by their synod to take part in politics, but Bristol's Moravian minister of the day, the Reverend Ramftler, appears to have been much less wedded to the anti-slavery cause than some of his predecessors, or indeed much of his congregation. Ramftler had been happy enough to welcome, in 1826, a free 'Negro-Brother' from a Moravian settlement in Antigua who visited Bristol when serving as a ship's steward, but he did not wish to alienate planters who might fund Moravian mission settlements. His reference to the 'prosperity of our missions' is particularly revealing on this point, for the following year the minister reported that Charles Pinney, 'a West India proprietor of the city', communicated with the Moravians regarding a 'very benevolent and generous proposal for a missionary Establishment by the Brn. [Moravians]'.[49] This probably refers to the school which Pinney and his sister Mary Ames had funded in Nevis by 1827.

Were Pinney's gestures simply a straightforward attempt to pre-empt abolitionist criticisms? Certainly his ideas about 'Negro education' had more to do with inculcating ideals of 'obedience, duty and order' into the 'Negro mind' than about preparing his charges for political empowerment.[50] And the general thrust of anti-emancipationist propaganda makes much of the establishment of missions and schools by benevolent planters.

A political engagement?

Pinney's motives, however, seem to have been complicated by personal circumstances. For sometime early in 1827, Charles Pinney had proposed marriage to none other than the daughter of William Wilberforce, the parliamentary grand master of the abolitionist campaign. Astonishingly, Wilberforce was initially inclined to approve the match, though Pinney had informed him that he was a West India merchant and had asked if that would be an insuperable objection. As he later explained to Pinney,

> Tho' a suitor being a West Indian merchant was an objection, it was not an insuperable one . . . always taking for granted that the gentleman should possess, secure from mercantile or West Indian risk, so much property, as when combined with the Ladies Fortune, might suffice for their comfortable maintainance.[51]

However, Wilberforce soon withdrew his approval, and though he did not explicitly forbid his daughter to marry Pinney, his disapproval was enough to end their courtship.[52] Pinney, after consulting with his friend the former abolitionist J. S. Harford, ended his suit. Why did Wilberforce change his mind so suddenly; why did he not object from the outset to his daughter's relationship with a West Indian suitor? Was there more than romance motivating Pinney's approach?

The answers to the first two questions are contained in an apologetic letter written by Wilberforce's wife, Barbara, to Pinney's sister, Mrs Mary Ames. Her husband, she explains, had originally thought Charles Pinney was only a West India merchant in the sense that he was in the 'carrying trade' – that is, that he shipped goods to the island. He changed his mind only when he realized that his prospective son-in-law was also involved in granting mortgages to planters in need of funds, since

> these mortgages lead to the labour of the Negroes being employed in a greater or less degree according to the sum lent, *for his use* on the various estates to which he lends money. While *He* [i.e. Pinney] however humane and good, has no part in the management of those Negroes [he] cannot, like a Proprietor, who has both capital of his own and negroes, employ his influence, authority and Revenue – and so prov[e] . . . for the benefit of those who work for Him.[53]

Since even a humane proprietor, Mrs Wilberforce continues, could have a 'divided duty' between 'Humanity to his slaves on the one hand' and the 'necessity of producing produce to satisfy the mortgagee on the other', the whole mortgage system upholds and reinforces many of the worst parts of the slavery system. Barbara Wilberforce tactfully suggests Pinney was a victim rather than a villain since he was 'entangled in these affairs by birth':

> I am sure your Brother would be amongst the first to rejoice if no such system [as slavery] existed. I merely glance at these points to account for that change of opinion which Mr. Wilberforce has expressed in his letter to Mr. Pinney.

This exchange nicely illustrates just how complex was the web of West Indian interests in which many Bristol families found themselves enmeshed. As Marshall reminds us, ownership of West Indian plantations 'was often a mere façade' concealing the reality of mortgaged property.[54] According to George Stephen, the colonial interest resided in 'London, Liverpool, . . . Glasgow [and] Bristol', not the colonies, since 'The slaves were scarcely more the property of the planters, than the planters themselves were the property of the consignees and creditors on this side of the Atlantic.'[55]

Yet one wonders whether Pinney was quite as sincere as he pretended to be. He was, after all, a member of the West India Association, which was in the midst of conducting an empire-wide campaign to subvert emancipation through a programme of melioration. Had not Pinney shown himself aware of the match's political implications when he told his prospective father-in-law that the match between the Wilberforce and Pinney families would be 'most likely to produce beneficial results to the improvement of the slave population'?[56] Since such a marriage would have done much to conflate the principle of emancipation with the expedient of melioration in the public mind, one is tempted to wonder whether Pinney's engagement was not in part undertaken for political purposes. In any case, the rejected suitor departed for Nevis later that same year, convincing the Reverend Ramftler, at least, that his visit was 'for the express purpose of ameliorating the condition of his Negroes'.[57]

It seems clear, though, that few planters followed even Pinney's modest example of melioration. The Society for the Conversion and Religious Instruction of the Negro Slaves in the West Indies admitted in its annual report for 1828 that it had made little progress. The reasons for this can be found in the complaint of the Lord Bishop of the Jamaican dioceses that the planters would not allow clergymen to teach slaves to read.[58]

The West Indian interest did not confine itself to exercises in public philanthropy in pursuing its case against emancipation. The national West India Association regularly received local deputations from Bristol and other outports at its strategy meetings in London. In 1829, for example, a meeting held at the Commercial Rooms in Bristol appointed a deputation consisting of the MP for Bristol, Henry Bright, along with Philip John Miles, James Lewis, James Evan Baillie, George Gibb and Charles Pope, to attend London meetings, along with any other local members who might be 'in Town' at the relevant times.[59]

Women and the anti-slavery campaign

Readers of Marshall's account of the emancipation campaign might be forgiven for assuming that women had no active role in the anti-slavery campaign. Yet by around 1827, local women had established the Bristol and Clifton Female Anti-Slavery Society. A report from 1829 shows that over 66 local women subscribed to the society, drawn from Anglican and Nonconformist groups. This compares with the 87 or so members in Bristol's main Anti-Slavery Society, and even in that overwhelmingly male group, six of the thirteen largest subscribers were female.[60]

The Female Anti-Slavery Society stated that its aims included the producing of anti-slavery propaganda and the spreading of the boycott of West Indian sugar. Members were pledged to '[d]iligence in disseminating information, to abstinence from the great staple article of slave cultivation, and above all, . . . to spread before the footstool of mercy, the cause of our oppressed and degraded African Brethren'.[61]

The largely male Anti-Slavery Society in Bristol was overwhelmingly middle class in composition, with a striking preponderance of professionals and manufacturers. The Female Anti-Slavery Society had, by contrast, a small but influential contingent from the gentry. Lady Isabella King, who headed the lay order of women at Isaac Hobhouse's old house in Cornwallis Crescent, Clifton, was one of three titled women included in the membership of 66. Marianne Schimmelpenninck and Hannah More also numbered among the more prominent members. But others, though devout, were not necessarily rich. In this period there was a significant constituency of Bristol women, mainly spinsters, who could be classed as the 'genteel poor'.

The society's budget was small (just under £50 in 1829), but members managed to donate money to the London Anti-Slavery Society. They also contributed money to Baptist schools in Jamaica, at a time when Baptists were seen as stirring up 'insolence' and political sedition amongst the slaves. On occasion they provided practical help to individual black people. They financed clothing 'for a negro at Bristol, going out to service' and asked individual members to contribute to a fund 'which is now being raised in Bristol, for the manumission of a peculiarly interesting pious female Slave, under 15 years of age'.[62]

It was, however, their promotion of the boycott of West Indian sugar which caused the West Indian Association the most anxiety. A pamphlet printed in Bristol around this time may well have been one of the 2000 the Female Anti-Slavery Society printed and distributed in 1829. Its title, *Consumers of West Indian Sugar, the Supporters of West Indian Slavery*, conveys its argument well. At 3s. per 1000, these pamphlets were meant for mass distribution. In passionate language, the pamphlet put the moral onus firmly on consumers, arguing that slaves were 'driven by the lash to uncompensated toil' not as a result 'of their crimes, but of *our own*'.[63] Above all, its attack on the bounties and tariffs protecting West Indian sugar and its urging of the public to buy Bengal sugar alarmed the West Indians, who had argued that the current depression of sugar prices was causing severe distress in the sugar colonies and were pressing the government for more protective duties on sugar and rum. By early 1830 the society had circulated its annual report to clergymen in the city, requesting their public backing for the emancipation in general and the boycott in particular.

The West Indian Association could not let this pass. In the archives of the Bristol Merchant Venturers is a handwritten draft of an anonymous letter to an unnamed newspaper editor attacking the arguments posed by the Bristol and Clifton Female Anti-Slavery Society as ill-informed 'puff':

If Puff were living in these days, he would admire the ingenuity with which his art is exercised in puffing East India sugar. This is a report emanating from the Ladies anti-slavery society, it is . . . recommended by the puff direct and puff oblique to promote in families the use of 'the free or Bengal sugar.' But the Ladies seem ignorant that . . . slave labour exist[s] in our East Indian settlements.[64]

The letter conflates sugar grown in Malabar in India with the 'free' sugar grown in Bengal, but such 'confusions' were part of the cut and thrust of the political struggle. Though Bristol plantation owners were known to shield female visitors from witnessing the punishment of slaves, they saw no contradiction in feeling outraged when abolitionists publicized 'exceptional' abuses of the slave regime. If the abolitionists used self-righteous piety as their not-so-secret weapon, the West Indians were increasingly reduced to bombastic pronouncements rooted in panic, desperation and fear.

The 'slavery election' of 1830

The 1830 election for Bristol's parliamentary representatives was popularly known as the 'slavery election'. Though its political intricacies have been ably discussed elsewhere,[65] our intention here is to examine some of its wider social dimensions and to consider what these tell us about commonly held attitudes towards race and slavery amongst the city's various constituencies.

The parliamentary elections after 1812 had consistently returned one Whig and one Tory member, both of whom had West Indian connections. It was thus generally assumed that the same custom would continue in 1830. So it was that after Hart Davis's retirement, Charles Bragge Bathurst was proposed by Charles Pinney, recently returned from the West Indies. Bathurst was also supported by John Scandrett Harford, whose conversion from Quaker abolitionism to Tory reaction now seemed complete. Evan Baillie was nominated to represent the Whigs.

However, Edward Protheroe Jr contested the Whig candidacy on an anti-slavery and general reform ticket. Given his family background, Protheroe seemed at first glance an unlikely champion of emancipation. His grandfather, Philip, was a Bristol West India merchant and shipowner in partnership with Robert Claxton. The Protheroes were related by marriage to the Claxtons, and his father, Edward Sr (1774–1856), had, as we have seen, successfully opposed Sir Samuel Romilly on the Whig ticket, serving as Bristol MP from 1812 to 1820.[66]

Edward Jr seems already to have been serving as an MP, for when he stepped forward to second Brougham's Commons motion pledging the House in the next session to adopt a measure for the abolition of slavery, this, according to one sympathetic contemporary source, aroused the ire of Bristol's West India interest:

> The disappointment and resentment of the powerful body of West India Planters and Merchants in this city knew no bounds at the very thought of the presumption of a man daring to offer himself on such principle as Representative of the very City where the Slave Trade had its Principal seat.[67]

Yet the climate of public opinion had changed to such an extent by 1830 that neither Davis nor Baillie rushed forward to declare himself a friend of slavery. Thus, when Charles Pinney proposed Baillie at a meeting of Whigs, he was noticeably reticent about the subject. He was immediately challenged by a Protheroe supporter on this issue:

Mr. Tripp, carpenter, said that Mr. Pinney had not been sufficiently explicit on the subject of the slave trade, a subject which half the people in the country did not understand, though everyone knew what humanity was. Mr. Pinney had not stated his views on religious liberty. . . . (Mr. Tripp proceeded to read a pamphlet on the slave trade but his voice was for some time drowned in the clamour.)[68]

Tripp's reference questioning Pinney's stand on religious liberty probably refers to the repressive measures Caribbean planters adopted towards Baptist and Methodist missionaries there, whom they accused of fomenting rebellions amongst the slaves. It reminds us that before 1835, parish vestries were almost wholly under the control of the Tories and could be expected to toe the party line on the issues of emancipation and reform.

It is significant that it was a carpenter who first spoke up on behalf of Protheroe, since other sources confirm that his candidacy was supported by the lower and middling classes of the town, although sailors were reportedly 'made absolutely frantic' at the threat Protheroe was said to pose to their livelihood.[69]

Protheroe's campaign sought to present itself as all things to all men, making, according to one admittedly hostile source, wild promises of a huge compensation package for planters on the emancipation of their slaves.[70] Nonetheless, Protheroe's campaign attracted Nonconformist support precisely because of its focus on the slavery question. Even some Moravians, whose religion forbade direct political involvement, had reportedly been impressed with some free black Brethren who visited Bristol in the late 1820s, and

> not withstanding a serious admonition which was given on that subject in the chapel, some of the B[rethren] engaged too deeply in the contest, on behalf of Mr. E. Protheroe who was brought forward on the ground of favouring the effectual amelioration of slavery with a means to its final extinction.[71]

One eyewitness, writing decades after the event, recalls seeing Edward Protheroe Jr brought up in a carriage and four to his headquarters at the Bush Tavern, accompanied by his agent, the Congregationalist manufacturer John Hare,[72] and 'Parson' Roberts (probably the Baptist minister Thomas Roberts). They were, he recollects, surrounded by an enormous mob:

> A poor black beggar was standing near the corner of the Council-house, little dreaming of the honours awaiting him, when all of a sudden he was seized by the mob, carried in triumph to the carriage, and presented to the candidate, who grasped his hand in token of his being 'a man and a brother,' whilst his companion showered blessings on the poor black, to the inexpressible delight of the mob. I shall never forget the expression of wonder and fear in the countenance of the beggar when the mob first pounced upon him, and indeed almost crushed him to death in their zeal for 'the liberty of the slave.'[73]

This account of a black beggar being crushed nearly to death by his overzealous abolitionist 'friends' has an apocryphal feel about it, implying as it does the foolish emotionality of the supporters of abolition. If true, it does indicate the continued black presence in the city and grass-roots support for the slaves, as symbols if not as individual human beings. Protheroe's reputed greeting, 'Are you not a man and a brother?' theatrically mimics the slogan inscribed on Wedgwood's popular anti-slavery medallions.

Protheroe's supporters claimed that 'almost every Female in the city espouses his cause with enthusiasm'. The authors of that observation were not referring exclusively to the wives and mothers of electors, for the elections involved the civic community as a whole in the processions, rituals and gatherings they spawned. We know, from accounts of people complaining about the violence at the election, that women and children joined the pro-Protheroe crowds witnessing the candidates as they made their way into the city at the outset of the elections.[74] At a time when most married women could not own their own property and most single middle-class women were dependent on their fathers for support, just over 10 per cent of the 193 individuals listed as subscribers to Protheroe's campaign were female.[75] Certainly the women of the Bristol and Clifton Female Anti-Slavery Society supported him, and at least five of the twenty or so women subscribing to Protheroe's campaign were society members. The wife of Protheroe's agent, John Hare, subscribed to the Society, as did the pamphleteer Marianne Schimmelpenninck, who wrote supportive letters to Mrs Hare when Hare's husband was threatened with violence during the electoral campaign. Schimmelpenninck also requested copies of a song extolling Protheroe's virtues and Baillie's vices on the slavery question (Figure 18) which she undertook to distribute.

Yet Schimmelpenninck, as a devout Evangelical, conceived of women's political role as purely supportive, casting them as the spiritual handmaidens to their warrior husbands:

> May you and all of us females lift up our hands in continual prayer whilst our champions are engaged in the conflict and never let us forget that to us appointed by God as their helpers especially belongs the honourable privilege to strengthen, to cheer and to refresh them in the labours of their day.[76]

Of course, such a role had its uses. Abolitionists generally did believe that their cause was a holy one, and this gave them an assurance and energy which is singularly lacking in most of the literature from the anti-abolitionist camp. The very fact that some election propaganda was specifically addressed to women demonstrates the influence they were felt to have. Take, for example, *The Negro Mother's Petition to the Ladies of Bristol; That, in Pity to Poor Slaves, They Would Entreat Their Fathers, Husbands, Brothers, and Sons, to Vote for Edwd. Protheroe, Esq.* (Figure 18).

According to one private account, many of the 'Principal Females' in Bristol were canvassed on Protheroe's behalf.[77] Given the violence and intimidation attending the campaign, such female support and exhortation was probably crucial to keeping up morale. It was charged before and after the election that tradesmen supporting Protheroe were told they would lose their customers. A draft election bill which seems to have been written by an anonymous woman exhorted electors to act with courage:

You may lose[,] if you are determined to act upon principle[,] some orders for hats and shoes and ship biscuits and perhaps for *whips*, but let it be seen that your votes are not equally vendible with our poor fellow men in bondage.[78]

The evangelical mode of some of Protheroe's campaign literature hardly champions political equality for blacks but represents them as objects of pity who need the assistance of their English champions. The cloying maternalism of 'The Negro Mother's Petition' is a case in point. Couched in what purports to be West Indian patois, the effect demeans the moral authority of the fictitious petitioner and flatteringly appeals to its intended audience:

Massa Proderoe – he good man!
Send him, Missey – SURE YOU CAN!
Den you fill poor Neger eye
Wid de tear brimful of joy!

Two other surviving broadsides pruriently exploit for political effect the mistreatment of female slaves by one Mrs Earnshaw, a slave-owner in Jamaica. The more sensationalist of the two, addressed to 'Brother Freemen!', asks where was Mrs Earnshaw's 'humanity and delicacy' in ordering

the clothes of a woman to be taken up in her presence and in the presence of negro men. . . . And where was her modesty, when she refused her slave to pull down her clothes, and when she walked behind her in a state of nudity with a bleeding body from the house to the bilboes?

Another rhetorical theme, also aimed at male freeholders, is invoked in those broadsides which identify the freedom of slaves with the freedom of Bristol's electorate. One Protheroe supporter writing in this mode debunks Baillie's own protestations that he too is for 'the Mitigation and Gradual Abolition of Slavery' as completely unconvincing:

The word 'GRADUAL' will cover a period of 500 years. . . . Depend upon It, Fellow citizens, SLAVE-HOLDERS NEVER WILL EXTINGUISH SLAVERY. The Imperial Parliament must take this matter into their own hands, and enact measure that shall lead directly to the *Speedy Extinction* of SLAVERY.

Marshall points out that Protheroe's literature 'time and time again' told the electorate that they had to choose between 'submission to slavery or assertion of freedom', and, by linking the fortunes of the freemen of Bristol with those of the slaves, fed the demand for both reform at home and emancipation in the West Indies[79] (Figure 19). That is true, but it also led the popular imagination to assume a spurious equality between the position of British workers and that of the slaves. Though there were some real parallels between the plight of the Irish peasantry and those of the colonial slave, the legal fact of slavery put the experience of the slaves on an altogether different footing. In England, Scotland and Wales, pauper apprentices, who comprised

THE
Negro Mother's Petition
TO

THE LADIES OF BRISTOL;

That, in Pity to Poor

SLAVES,

THEY WOULD ENTREAT THEIR

Fathers, Husbands, Brothers, and Sons,

TO VOTE FOR

EDW^D· PROTHEROE, ESQ.

MISSEY, MISSEY, tink on we,
Toder side de big blue sea—
How we flogg'd, and how we cry—
How we sometimes wish to die.

When we old, and when we weak,
Massa flog—we no dare 'peak—
If we 'peak, or murmur sigh,
Massa flog till almost die.

Den he clap on heaby chain,
Gib poor Neger body pain:
But, *dat* pain no *near* so deep
As de *memory* make we weep.

Oh! we 'memory well de day,
Piccaninny round we play!
Oh! we 'memory well de night,
Piccaninny 'tolen quite!

How we poor heart t'rob and ache!
How we cry! Dey almost break!
How we head swim round and round!
How we wish we underground!

Do Missey say—"*How* tink on we,
Toder side de big blue sea?"
Missey pray her *Massa* dear,
Wipe away de Neger tear.

When de Buckra 'peaker sent
To de House call Parliament,
Send *such* Buckra 'peaker dere
As regard poor Neger prayer.

Massa PRODEROE—*he* good man!
Send *him*, Missey - SURE YOU CAN!
Den you fill poor Neger eye
Wid de tear brimful of joy!

Toder man—call Massa *Baillie*,
He no care what Neger ail 'e!
Massa PRODEROE—*he* de man!
Send *him*, Missey—SURE YOU CAN!

Den Neger for dear Missey pray;
For Massa too, de lib-long day—
For Fader, Broder, ebery Friend—
For ebery blessing widout end!

Printed and Sold by J. G. FULLER, St. Stephen's Avenue.

Figure 18 'The Negro Mother's Petition'. Bristol Central Reference Library

perhaps one of the most downtrodden groups of workers, might suffer the horrors of sexual and physical abuse; handloom weavers might starve to death or face degradation in the workhouse; child textile workers might be deformed by long hours crouched over dangerous machinery; farmworkers might be evicted from their homes when work was scarce; sailors might still be flogged and bullied; chimney sweeps smothered to death and maidservants 'seduced' and turned out without a reference; but when all is said and done, the plight of the slaves was made incomparably worse by the legal fact of their enslavement. Their very status as human beings was contested, their legal rights virtually non-existent. One bold anti-abolitionist broadside[80] celebrated the fact that slaves of a few islands were belatedly given the right to marry and that in some islands it was no longer legal to force a slave to flog or torture a family member. Discerning readers might have asked why these basic decencies took so long to be awarded, or why they were still denied in some colonies.

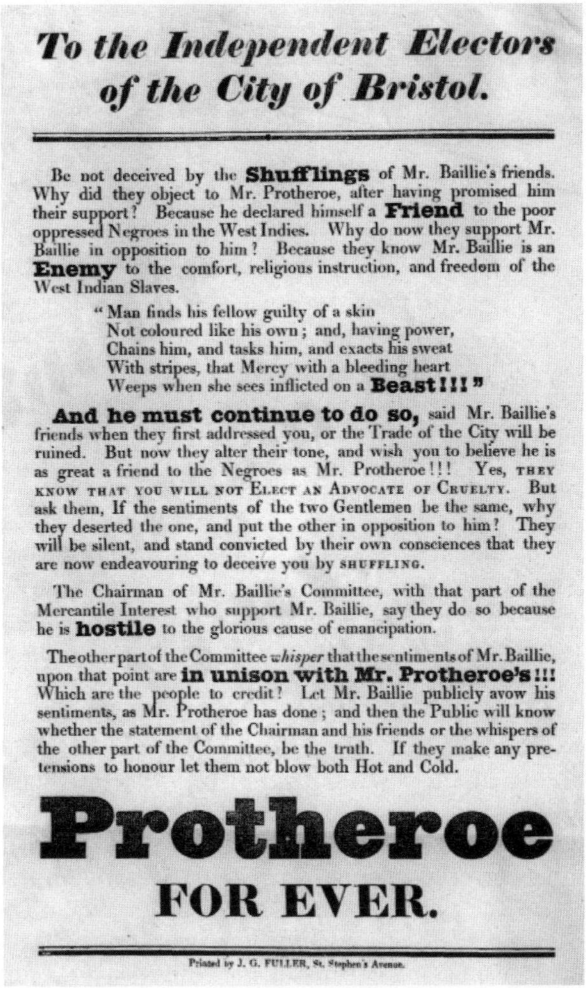

To the Independent Electors of the City of Bristol.

Be not deceived by the **Shufflings** of Mr. Baillie's friends. Why did they object to Mr. Protheroe, after having promised him their support? Because he declared himself a **Friend** to the poor oppressed Negroes in the West Indies. Why do now they support Mr. Baillie in opposition to him? Because they know Mr. Baillie is an **Enemy** to the comfort, religious instruction, and freedom of the West Indian Slaves.

> "Man finds his fellow guilty of a skin
> Not coloured like his own; and, having power,
> Chains him, and tasks him, and exacts his sweat
> With stripes, that Mercy with a bleeding heart
> Weeps when she sees inflicted on a **Beast!!!**"

And he must continue to do so, said Mr. Baillie's friends when they first addressed you, or the Trade of the City will be ruined. But now they alter their tone, and wish you to believe he is as great a friend to the Negroes as Mr. Protheroe!!! Yes, THEY KNOW THAT YOU WILL NOT ELECT AN ADVOCATE OF CRUELTY. But ask them, If the sentiments of the two Gentlemen be the same, why they deserted the one, and put the other in opposition to him! They will be silent, and stand convicted by their own consciences that they are now endeavouring to deceive you by SHUFFLING.

The Chairman of Mr. Baillie's Committee, with that part of the Mercantile Interest who support Mr. Baillie, say they do so because he is **hostile** to the glorious cause of emancipation.

The other part of the Committee *whisper* that the sentiments of Mr. Baillie, upon that point are **in unison with Mr. Protheroe's**!!! Which are the people to credit? Let Mr. Baillie publicly avow his sentiments, as Mr. Protheroe has done; and then the Public will know whether the statement of the Chairman and his friends or the whispers of the other part of the Committee, be the truth. If they make any pretensions to honour let them not blow both Hot and Cold.

Protheroe
FOR EVER.

Printed by J. G. FULLER, St. Stephen's Avenue.

Figure 19   Protheroe handbill. Bristol Central Reference Library

The election campaign of 1830 was legendary for its violence. During the course of it, Protheroe's headquarters were wrecked and people assaulted. Protheroe was struck on the head by a missile and Hare threatened by violence and challenged to a duel by Baillie's agent, Christopher Claxton.

The exchange of letters between Hare and Claxton on this subject epitomizes two different world-views and two correspondingly contrasting models of masculine behaviour. The volatile Claxton, a naval lieutenant and long-time West Indian agent, was a traditional man of action and he was apoplectic with rage at an allegation Hare had reportedly made. Feeling that his honour had been impugned, he sent a tersely worded challenge to Hare via a naval colleague deputed to be his second.

By contrast, Hare epitomized a new Evangelical model of masculinity, refusing Claxton's challenge on the grounds that he was neither schooled in using weapons nor willing to jeopardize the security of his employees and that of his family by risking his own life.

Claxton and slavery

If Charles Pinney and James Evan Baillie represented the urbane face of the slave-owning plantocracy, Claxton was its unselfconscious wild man. Yet Claxton was no outcast. He came from a well-established Bristol family which settled in St Kitts in the early seventeenth century. The wealthy West India merchant Robert Claxton was his father and he was, in 1830, brother-in-law to the mayor.[81] In his speeches, pamphlets and letters he appears to articulate many of the unspoken assumptions his more polite counterparts had about slavery as an institution and about the slaves themselves. It is for this reason that we should pause to consider in some depth his attitudes to slavery and race.

It was Claxton who was accused of inflaming Baillie's supporters to personal violence against Protheroe. Although Baillie was an old-fashioned Whig,[82] his agent, Claxton, is best understood as an English nationalist in the old Tory tradition. He is anti-reform in general and is contemptuous of the liberalizing process which effected such a reformation of manners and morals in the early nineteenth century. Claxton scoffed at such 'Progress': 'the Walk of Mind, the March of Intellect, the Trot of Reason and the Canter of New Light, will in the end be found [to be] nothing but the Gallop of Humbug'.[83]

Whilst Baillie was desperately trying to appear as an opponent of slavery, Claxton was happy to circulate a petition in Bristol defending the institution of slavery.[84] Slavery, he wrote, was ordained in the Bible, and though certainly susceptible to 'melioration', was part and parcel of a hierarchical social order in which the rights of property were deemed more acceptable than notions of the universal 'rights of man'.

In one of his pamphlets, *A Letter to Lord Combermere*, Claxton indignantly accused army officers in Bristol of inciting the masses to 'rise en masse' if they did not get reform. He condemned what he saw as the subversive tendencies of the Methodist missionaries in the Caribbean and warned in one pamphlet that if the government further supported such 'sectarians', the Church of England itself, 'its towers its steeple, [were] all in a fair way of being crumpled into the dust'. He likens the anti-slavery Anglicans to Roundheads and sees himself as a loyal imitator of the 'ancient cavaliers'.[85] Claxton's self-characterization is most apt. The very image of the Church of England being trampled into dust, his characterizations of the populace as barbarians without the gates, his horror at the idea of army officers daring to subvert the established order, are all motifs which feature in royalist political caricature of the seventeenth century.

Seeing themselves as the honest enemies of pious 'humbug', Claxton and his allies made much of their discovery that some Protheroe supporters owned shares in a Brazilian mine which employed slave labour. An embarrassed Hare quickly responded to reassure him and the public that this underwriting of slave labour had been unintentional and that the status of the miners had been immediately improved.[86]

A particularly scurrilous broadside against the Protheroe camp, very much in Claxton's robust style, reveals some deeper prejudices which he judged would appeal to the electorate. Proclaiming that Protheroe had been nominated by the 'Jew Sir Manassee Lopes', a fictional composite of two Jewish merchants,[87] the broadside goes on to impugn Protheroe's pedigree by questioning his legitimacy and his Englishness. It questions his masculinity and political integrity by implying that he is a circumcised (i.e. unchristian) alien.

> Is he [Protheroe Jr] really the son of the person the Quakers pretend he is? Or is he some CIRCUMCISED pencil or orange-boy from Change Alley; and this by one of the most impudent sects in existence thrust on the People of Bristol, is the son of Protheroe?

Having cast Jews and Quakers as low-born political manipulators, it goes on to make an outrageous suggestion to Protheroe's female supporters: 'I think that the Quaker women ought to sit in Committee and examine if he be really an Israelite indeed – and the cry from mouth to mouth ought to run – Is he Circumcised?'[88]

However undesirable Claxton deemed Jews, Quakers and politically active women, he reserved his most profound contempt for Africans. Like many planters opposing emancipation, Claxton did not think Africans would work once they were freed. Claxton had been prevented from addressing the large audience of men and women attending a tumultuous anti-slavery meeting in October 1830. Undeterred, he published the resolutions he 'would have made' had he been allowed to address the audience. These urged that Parliament be petitioned to purchase one of the 'small Caribbean islands' for an experimental pilot scheme in 'Free Cultivation'. Claxton insisted that such an experiment would be the best way of determining whether 'the agricultural Negro, when freed, will overcome his objection to field labour'.[89]

Though professing to be an enemy of 'heartless cruelty', Claxton reveals, in another publication, his conviction that 'the Negroe gives ample occasion for the greatest trial of temper. Hasty emancipation will ensure that the negro race, a barbarian in grain . . . will as surely retrograde . . . as his master will be ruined'. The result of such emancipation would be dangerous to the 'well being' of thousands 'of all colours'. He stresses his patriotic motives by wondering how the loss of colonies would affect England's status in the 'scale of nations'. However, his very notion of 'the Negroe' 'retrograding' introduces the language of breeding, which implies that Africans are at some profound level intrinsically inferior to whites. In other words, Claxton is importing from the West Indies a newer strain of a specifically racialist terminology into British political discourse. This may well explain why some of the election literature from the Claxton/Baillie camp saw fit to nickname Edward Protheroe Jr 'Nigger Ned'.

In order to prove the essentially barbarian nature of the enslaved Africans, Claxton cited in his 1830 address to Lord Combermere the instances of sabotage which discontented slaves had carried out in various West Indian colonies. One group of slaves, not liking a new manager of the Lodge Plantation in St Kitts, reportedly killed 99 cattle. The manner of killing, he reveals, was 'to stick a wire up the animal's nostrils into its brain so that the animal pined for 48 hours and died'. Claxton goes on to detail other instances of animal mutilation by discontented slaves: the cutting of mules' gums from their lips so that they starved, the inoculation of mules with fatal diseases, and the placing of nails in the hooves of valuable horses. Slaves, he continues, also resorted to the slow poisoning of 'their human masters', as a result of which many had died and many had had 'their constitutions utterly ruined'.

Such is the heart of darkness which Claxton seeks to expose, yet in so doing it is the dark fears of the planter class which he unwittingly lays bare. Such revelations were designed to horrify well-meaning Evangelicals who, aside from slavery, campaigned in this period against cruelty to animals.[90] The point is that Claxton *racializes* such barbarous behaviour. If one accepts that such cruelties were practised by slaves, they were hardly exclusive to them. Though the climate of opinion was changing, the torture of animals was, as Robert Darnton observes, 'a popular amusement throughout early modern Europe. You have only to look at Hogarth's *Stages of Cruelty* to see its importance, and once you start looking you see people torturing animals everywhere.'[91]

Indeed, the brutal mutilation of farm animals by disaffected English farmworkers is well documented for much of the nineteenth century. One study shows striking similarities between the actions and motivations of East Anglian farmworkers and the slaves at the Lodge Plantation. Just as the English protesters were not revolutionaries, so the slaves do not seem to be attempting to revolt against the institution of slavery per se. In the case of the English farmworkers, it was the worsening conditions they suffered at the hands of their employers which triggered their assaults; in the case of the slaves, it was the behaviour of an unpopular manager. Both groups resented the food and affection lavished on animals when their own welfare was neglected. Both acts had a ritual, and possibly even magical, element to them. Both were, at one level at least, a social protest, a dramatic statement against what its players saw as an unjust state of affairs.

Mary Douglas's seminal book *Purity and Danger: An Analysis of the Concepts of Pollution and Taboo* is particularly germane to this discussion. Douglas, an anthropologist, argues that people in all societies, at all levels of scientific and technological development, 'think of their own social environment as consisting of other people joined or separated by lines which must be obeyed'.[92] Whenever it is thought that these social lines or boundaries are being transgressed, there is anger and fear because social order is being challenged and because such a challenge poses danger to those who champion the order. The physical crossing of the social barrier is, Douglas argues, 'treated as a dangerous pollution'.[93]

When the slaves at Lodge Plantation resorted to the destruction of property to make their point, they were seen by the planters to have done something far more portentous than commit a simple crime. In the British slave societies of the Caribbean, the boundaries governing relations between people were both precarious and blurred. Africans and their descendants were never comfortably accommodated in the social order because they were deemed to be commodities and yet were demonstrably human beings.[94] The intrinsically contradictory status of the slave, made more unstable by the prospect of emancipation, rendered the slave a dangerous element in the social order. Slaves who did not obey their owners and who harmed the property of those owners 'crossed the line' as far as planter society was concerned – they polluted that society, they posed a danger to social stability. Douglas argues that it is because of their subaltern status that they are 'demonized' by those in power, and vested with uncontrollable and unconscious powers of disruption. Intriguingly, the mutilation discussed by Claxton involved the literal piercing of boundaries – of nostrils, hooves and skin. This 'mixing of bodily fluids' also betokens pollution, as does the act of poisoning, which pollutes the body and subverts the social order.

The fact that many slaves had a magical view of the universe common to traditional societies, and that some resorted to sorcery to exert some control over their lives, seemed to confirm their infernal status. Attitudes towards Africans themselves had been both challenged and reinforced by the publication of the descriptions of African culture provided by travellers and, increasingly, explorers, as for example the Bristolian Thomas Bowdich's studies of African culture in his *Mission from Cape Coast Castle to Ashantee*, first published in 1819.[95] Bowdich (1793–1824), the son of a Bristol hat manufacturer, was engaged by his uncle, the then governor of Cape Coast Castle, to go on the mission to the Ashanti. Bowditch represented the Ashanti culture as sensationally brutal, portraying some hair-raising descriptions of human sacrifice and authoritarian brutality. He argued that the Ashanti were in need of a civilizing influence through commercial relations with England, and maintained that England's anti-slavery stance was harmful to her own trading interests so long as the Spanish slave trade furnished the Ashanti with incentives to continue slave-trading. On the other hand, Bowdich portrayed the Ashanti culture as highly sophisticated in many respects and celebrated Ashanti people's expertise in textiles, pottery and metallurgy.[96]

Bowdich's local origins were celebrated in the local press and histories, and his work provided ammunition for both sides of the slavery debate.[97] Nevertheless, the stories of sorcery and fetish worship were disturbing, especially when they had to do with Africans transported to the Caribbean. Such 'outlandish' magical beliefs contrasted disturbingly with the physical proximity of the slaves themselves.

Abolition and reform

Protheroe narrowly lost the 1830 election to his Whig rival, and the close result encouraged, Marshall tells us, the anti-slavery faction. Certainly the Bristol Anti-Slavery Society was now, under the influence of the national society, and like its female sister society, pressing for immediate rather than gradual emancipation.[98]

By the time of the 1831 election, such was the surge in pro-reform sentiment that Baillie and Protheroe submerged their differences under a Whig banner and successfully edged out the Tory candidate. This was an uneasy alliance, and the West India Association must have been anxious that Baillie's ownership of West Indian plantations (his firm owned some 2000 slaves) did not alienate voters. Virtually all its members took out two-year subscriptions to support the Society for Promoting Religious Instruction to the Negroes, whilst Claxton told readers of the Whig paper the *Bristol Mirror* that he had personally witnessed 'a striking scene' of Christian devotion on Baillie's Camden Estate in Trinidad: 'on a Sunday morning all the gang assembled in a dwelling house and devoutly prayed . . . one of the Negroes preaching the word of God in their own language'.[99]

The ideal of well-treated slaves seemed to appeal to the 'eminent' Bristol physician William Porter Esq. (d. 1850), who is buried in Bristol Cathedral along with the rest of his literary family. In 1831 he published his fictional account *Sir Edward Seward's Narrative of His Shipwreck and Consequent Discovery of Certain Islands in the Caribbean Sea*, which was edited by his sister Jane (d. 1856), a well-known novelist. Its preface, which his sister apparently wrote, commends the meliorative slave regime portrayed in his book for the consideration of 'all sincere friends in England', since, she writes, it meets the demands of 'the right of property . . . and the brotherly pleadings of a general humanity'.[100] The Porters lived in Brunswick Square, as did a number of members of the Anti-Slavery committee.

Baillie's and Protheroe's victory on a Reform ticket did not prevent public anger over the slow progress of the Reform Bill. The labouring classes hoped the bill would enfranchise them and thereby afford them the power to improve their lives. When the Bristol riots occurred that autumn, rioters attacked visible symbols of the old order: the cathedral, the Lord Mayor's home and the Customs House. Many of the homes and business premises of the members of the West Indian interest, including those of Pinney and Claxton, were also destroyed or damaged.

More often than not, subsequent accounts of the riots include the story of the Claxton's black manservant, who reportedly defended his absent employer's Queen Square home from rioters.[101] Like the anecdote about Protheroe's embrace of the bemused black beggar, this story has a symbolic appeal independent of its actual veracity. In this case, the thought of a faithful black servant literally throwing out male and female radicals from his master's home was reassuring at a time of increasing slave unrest.

Missionaries and revolt

On Christmas Day 1831 some 20,000–30,000 slaves rose up against their planters in western Jamaica. The angry ferocity and brutality exhibited by the slaves in revolt, though more than matched by the planters' response, contrasted uncomfortably with the image of the loyal and contented slave repeatedly put forward by the anti-emancipationists.

Planters who resented the egalitarian version of Christianity which Noncon-formist missionaries preached, blamed these missionaries for spreading discontent. Baillie's Bristol supporters seemed genuinely to believe that Anglican activities in Westmorland, Jamaica, where one schoolteacher had been provided for 60 slave children in one part of the parish, disproved the charge that planters neglected the religious improvement of slaves.[102] Not surprisingly, it was Westmorland where the Baptists were strongest.

After the revolt, planters and their allies cited atrocity stories of the slaves' behaviour to argue the slaves' essential savagery. The very language of their accounts indicates that the actual facts of the events are laden with symbolic meaning. Take, for example, a description of an incident in the 1831 uprising which was published in *Felix Farley's Bristol Journal* in the spring of 1832. Purporting to be from a letter from Jamaica sent to a Bristol gentleman, it charges the Moravians as well as the Baptists and Methodists for stirring up insurrection: 'the minds of the negroes are poisoned by these Sectaries'.

In some ways they had a point. The egalitarian way Baptist missionaries treated slaves was in such sharp distinction to the treatment meted out to them by the planters that it was bound to be unsettling. Thomas Burchell, in a letter to his brother, recounts a telling incident about a time when he and his wife were travelling alone in Jamaica shortly after their arrival. Lost at a crossroads, Burchell addressed a passing slave with 'Friend, which is the way to Kingston?' The slave pointed the way but started to laugh. On being asked what he found so amusing, the man said he had just misdirected another white man in the opposite direction. Perplexed, Burchell asked him why he did not also misdirect him. The man laughingly replied that he would never misdirect a missionary and that he knew Burchell was a missionary because 'You say *friend*! Busha [white man] say "*rascal*! Which is the way to Kingston? Tell me in a minute or I'll flog you." I say, dat and him gone, massa, gone miles before now; him gone like mad!'[103] To the planters, Burchell's respectful demeanour towards slaves amounted to betrayal. So too did his adaptation of some of the practices instituted by the black Baptist churches on the island, practices seen by the planters as instilling fanaticism and an inflated sense of self-importance in the slaves.[104] Both Thomas Burchell and his fellow Baptist William Knibb had in their private correspondence made no secret of their revulsion against slavery, but Burchell's views had been made public in 1827, when his brother published one of his letters home in a Baptist periodical.

William Knibb's influence was, in the planters' eyes, just as malign. Knibb had lived in Bristol from the age of 13 to 19, where he also worked as a missionary in the 'toughest slums' of the city and surrounding villages before leaving for Jamaica in 1824.[105] He was inspired to go there by his brother Thomas's reports of 'the eagerness of the poor Negroes to hear the word of God'. William Knibb left for the Caribbean with his new wife, Mary, to further his brother's missionary work amongst 'the swarthy sons of Africa'.[106] He was sincere and pure-minded, and his manuscript diary shows him to be shocked to the core by a discussion he had had with a slave-owner on the voyage to Jamaica. The views of this man clearly demonstrated to him the 'brutalising and immoral tendency of this execrable system' of slavery:

> He informed me . . . that he personally knows overseers who employ an old woman to bring them all the young females when they arrive at maturity, for the purpose of debauchery . . . and in order to divest them of every feeling of modesty usually compels them to work in a state of complete nudity, and it is no uncommon practice for them to cohabit with female slaves for the purpose of *increasing their Stock!!!* I pray God that I may never view with indifference a system of such infernal a nature.[107]

William's vivid and warm-hearted letters to friends in Bristol, including Fuller and two Bristol women, Misses Griffiths and Spurrier, were doubtless shared with others. He directly involved his 'dear Bristol friends' in his efforts to establish schools for the slave and free black children of Kingston and Port Royal. A picture of John Ryland stared down at him in his Kingston home as he penned letters extolling the intellectual potential of some of his students: 'Their writing is excellent and they improve vastly . . . some of them have excellent capacities and retentive memories. One slave girl has repeated my chapter and the whole of Divine Song at one time and can write remarkably well.'[108] He forwarded them a touching appeal for funds painstakingly written by his 14-year-old school monitor, William Sutcliffe, 'a slave'.[109] Knibb stressed the sacrifices slaves would make, walking miles in the hot sun without food or drink, in order to hear a sermon, adding in another letter: 'You may tell the Broad Mead children [from his Bristol congregation] that the poor slaves behave ten times better than I have ever seen them behave in a place of worship.'[110]

One senses an overly bright tone in these missives. Knibb was less flattering about his charges when he was not attempting to raise funds for them. He spoke despairingly of the moral state of the older children, implying that they found the opposite sex more engaging than the classroom. He referred to the uneducated mass of slaves as 'poor ignorant creatures' and confessed to one Bristol friend that he found, in his increasingly exhausted state, 'the climate oppressive and the children depraved'.[111]

Moreover, Knibb had absorbed some of the racialist attitudes of his day. He and his wife confessed in one letter to feeling distaste at having to have a black wet-nurse for their new twins.[112] Nevertheless, his professions of 'love' for his black pupils – he refers to them and his own twins as his 'little dears' – still convince. More to the point, Knibb's unpretentious informality and warmth, his close involvement with the slaves and black freemen, and his unceasing efforts to build schools earned him the increasing hostility of the planters.

In a number of indirect ways, then, Knibb and Burchell had 'crossed the line', challenging the increasingly fragile hegemony of the planter regime in Jamaica. Such betrayal, planters propagandists implied, was the root cause of the murder and anarchy which boiled over in 1831.

The slave revolt in Jamaica of 1831, which, as we have seen, was concentrated in the parishes in which Baptist influence was strongest, resulted in the execution of Samuel Sharp, a black Baptist deacon, one of the 312 people formally executed after the revolt. There was some sympathy for Sharp amongst Bristol anti-slavery campaigners, though all were appalled at the violence of the uprising. But concern turned to fury when the self-styled 'Colonial Church Union' (a planters' body) burned down nine Baptist and six Methodist chapels, tarred and feathered at least one missionary, and jailed the two Bristol Baptists William Knibb and Thomas Burchell.

Knibb's arrest in 1831 for helping to foment the rebellion and his subsequent acquittal in Jamaica were of particular interest to Bristol Baptists.[113] Knibb left Jamaica in 1832 to tour Britain on behalf of emancipation, and by all accounts proved an eloquent spokesman. Most of the British press, however, according to the *Bristol Mercury*, opposed the Anti-Slavery committee and 'studiously avoided'

Figure 20   F. Bacon
after H. Pickersgill,
Thomas Daniel, c. 1843.
Engraving. Bristol City
Museum and Art
Gallery

'all mention of slavery'.[114] This was not wholly true, for though unforthcoming about the cruel treatment of slaves, and the harassment of missionaries, the editor of *Felix Farley's Bristol Journal* ensured that his paper included detailed descriptions of slave violence.

In one outrage connected to the 1831 revolt, Bristol readers were told, 'A number of white ladies were rescued from these wretches in Westmorland in time to save them from pollution.'[115] In another, the 'blood thirsty and savage cruelties' of the slaves knew no bounds, and whilst white men were horribly murdered, their 'unfortunate females were reserved in their [the slaves'] caves and fastnesses often witnessing the mangling of their fathers, husbands and brothers, for the more brutal purposes not to be described'.[116] Horrible atrocities did occur, but the language in which they are described is revealing, and it is also pertinent that the Planters blamed everyone but themselves. Planters of Demerara and Essequibo (British Guiana, now Guyana), a group which included the powerful Bristol alderman Thomas Daniel (Figure 20), also cited outside influences for the growing unrest. Talk of emancipation, they felt, had occasioned a very feverish and dangerous excitement in the minds of the slaves, and have produced a very extensive and deep rooted insubordination and resistance to authority – they in many instances refusing to work and in others persisting in not doing the fourth of the regulated, moderate task assigned.[117]

Despite the torrent of unrest and resistance which characterized this period, and despite the legacy of slave resistance which stretched back to the fifteenth century, *Felix Farley*'s Tory editor, J. M. Gutch, persisted in stating his belief that 'The slaves, until disastrously meddled with, were comfortable, happy and contented.'[118]

What does seem to be true is that slave resistance took on a new political potency as public opinion in Britain turned in favour of emancipation.[119] In such a context, it is little wonder that the idea of Claxton's loyal black servant, ready to defend his master's property against radical and disruptive elements, was attractive not only to Bristol's West India interest, but to Tory opponents of domestic political reform.

Emancipation and reform in 1832

In the first half of 1832 two remarkable spectacles occurred in Bristol. The first, in January 1832, was the performance as Othello by Ira Aldridge, a free black actor from America who was touring England and the Continent. But the event, 'a novelty for one night only', did not attract any press comment in the newspapers obsessed by the trial of Bristol rioters and the threat of cholera. It was, after all, the third time Aldridge had trodden the boards in Bristol since 1826, and only the short-lived *Bristol Liberal* bothered to review his performance, which it damned with faint praise.[120]

The second spectacle, which was far more widely publicized, occurred in June, only weeks after the Reform Act was passed, an Act which, incidentally, did not seem to have significantly enlarged Bristol's electorate.[121] Then the General Union organized a huge procession of 'Trades Reformers'. Some 12,000 or so operatives and artisans from Bristol trades defied the wishes of some of their employers to march for five hours through the city with banners, flags and the emblems of their trade aloft. Most of the procession seemed very traditional: tinplaters marched with a huge tin tray on which was placed a joint of sirloin beef (representing the roast beef of Old England); coppersmiths featured a 'champion' dressed in fine copper armour; and cabinetmakers held aloft an 'anatomical figure' carved in mahogany. Of all the groups reported in admiring detail by the radical *Bristol Mercury*, the printers, with their series of gold-embossed banners sporting such slogans as 'Equal Rights', 'Prosperity for Bristol' and 'Liberty to the Slave', were the only one reported to have expressed any specifically anti-slavery sentiments. Though printers have a well-deserved reputation for radicalism, there may have been those amongst the Bristol procession who remembered or had even worshipped with William Knibb, who after all had served as an apprentice printer in Bristol only eight years before.

It seems clear, nonetheless, that slavery was not at the top of most workers' list of concerns. At a meeting of the Bristol Trades that autumn, a glass-stainer listed his immediate preoccupations as the abolition of the Corn Laws, of the East India monopoly and 'the infernal Six Acts'.[122] The fact that the gaily dressed workers of

Hare's floorcloth factory were later accused of stealing trade emblems for the procession, a charge they earnestly denied, indicates the division of interests that could obtain between middle-class anti-slavery campaigners and their working-class counterparts.

By contrast, members of the largely middle-class constituency of Bristol's emancipationist lobby were becoming increasingly exercised by what was happening to Baptist and Methodist missionaries at the hands of West Indian planters. As the prospect of a parliamentary election approached, Bristol's Tories moved in to lure the still-disenfranchised workers away from Protheroe and anti-slavery. The evidence suggests that many operatives and small tradesmen were threatened or bribed by their employers and patrons into professing 'true blue' loyalties.[123] Protheroe publicly regretted that some workers had decided to 'prostitute the name of reform' and join the conservative Operatives' Association. Now that the Reform Bill had passed, the coalition between Bristol's West India lobby and the pro-emancipationist Protheroe broke down. Evan Baillie linked up with the new Tory candidate, Sir Richard Vyvyan, and both were elected to Parliament.

In the meantime, radicalized by the persecution of Baptist and Methodist missionaries by Jamaican planters, the Anti-Slavery Society pushed more energetically than ever for immediate emancipation. The *Bristol Mercury* noted in May 1833 that 179,000 females had signed a petition to this end.[124] The rhetoric employed in such campaigns was high-minded but ethnocentric. On 25 May 1833 the *Mercury* reprinted a poem from the *Examiner* entitled 'Negro Rhymes', purportedly written by 'Sambo' in imitation patois. By ascribing its authorship to a stock slave name and by gently poking fun at slave dialect, the poem's often well-observed critique of pro-slavery propaganda was rendered unthreateningly comic:

> *Some say how Goramity*
> *Hab nothing made in vain*
> *An nigger fit for oder ting*
> *'sides plant 'm sugar cane,*
> *But oders say, he only brute,*
> *By Goramity's plan,*
> *An 'sides he great deal better off*
> *Dan English working man.*
>
> *Him easy for Believe*
> *Dere be poor English men,*
> *But not bad off like nigger*
> *Ah, that believe no can.*
> *For ib him so bad off*
> *As massa sometime say,*
> *Him fight, him scratch, him debil pay*
> *Or else him run away.*

Can overseer him daughter force
Away to naughty place,
And flog him pickininny
Before him fader face.
And ib him fader grumble,
Or look a little blue,
As many lash him giv him sum
Him giv his father too.

Hab working man a driver
Wid great large big cart whip
To give him now and den a cut
An make him jump and skip?
An when in busy crop time
Him little stop in work
Call out – 'You bloody nigger
I'll score you down like pork.'

Cun massa part him from him wife
An send her far away
An sell him pickininny
For all out he can say?
An tak him pig and plaintain
Off an yam and yarden ground;
And ib him to the mountains go
Hunt him with big blood hound?

Gor bless you Massa Buxton
Gor bless Lord Suffield too
Pray no believe what massa say.
Indeed it be no true
For Goramity's sake
Protect us ib you can,
For none on earth's so wretched
As de poor Negro man.[125]

Nevertheless, when its condemnation of the vitriolic anti-Catholicism of the Tory-supported Reformation Society, and its early support of the unsuccessful bill for Jewish emancipation, are taken into account, the *Mercury*'s relative liberalism is apparent.

When the Act for the emancipation of the slaves in the British colonies was finally passed in August 1833, Bristol's main newspapers responded according to form. The *Bristol Mercury* was contemptuous of the conservative nature of the reform, calling it the 'Bill for Continuing slavery in the British Colonies for a period of 7 Years under the designation of apprenticeship'. It denounced – with, one suspects, even more fervour – the fact that British taxpayers would have to shoulder a £20 million compensation bill to British slave-owners, no doubt cognizant of the fact that the tax burden fell heaviest on the middle and labouring classes.

> . . . Oh! Is this all
> the poor fruit of hope long deferred;
> all we have won from those who keep in part
> The promise to the ear, but break it to the heart?[126]

At the other end of the political spectrum was the coverage, or rather lack of it, by *Felix Farley*. When its editor deigned to mention the Act at all, he sputtered with obfuscating indignation about the way the legislation was rushed through Parliament. Gutch larded his paper with letters and extracts from Jamaican and Liverpool papers predicting the dire effects of emancipation and retelling atrocity stories of 'negro violence'.[127] A week after the Act's passage, the *Journal* articulated the sentiments of the colonial planters:

> Now that slavery is virtually abolished in the colonies, and the negroes consequently free from those restraints which were deemed necessary for the welfare both of the proprietors and the blacks, the colonists naturally entertain great anxiety for the future.[128]

English agricultural labourers were enjoined to come as role models for the newly emancipated slaves, to 'infuse a new spirit' amongst them, by showing that agricultural labour should no longer be 'considered (as it is now in the West Indies) a degrading employment'.[129]

The *Bristol Gazette*, by contrast, welcomed the Act. Its jubilation says much about the way the more Whiggish West India merchants and planters, such as Baillie, saw the issue. Relieved that Parliament had refused to allow 'clamour to dictate the terms of injustice', it saw the debate over emancipation as one between 'the undoubted rights of property on the one side and the undoubted mass of public feeling on the other'.[130] Such a characterization of the debate renders slaves themselves altogether invisible, except, of course, as property or as the implied and passive objects of British public feeling. This may account for why apprenticeship is accepted without question by the paper's editor.

Ever mindful of its readership amongst the more progressive members of the West India Association and the Merchant Venturers, the *Gazette* justified the £20 million compensation package on the grounds that it would have been unjust 'to inflict upon a part only of the British subjects those pecuniary losses which on every principle of fairness and equity ought to be shared by all'.[131] Well into the twentieth century, the settlement was seen as the moderate third way between 'extremist' abolitionists and intransigent planters.[132] Of all the Bristol planters, Thomas Daniel, known as 'the King of Bristol' (Figure 20), received the most compensation, some £120,000. Danielstown in Essequibo (later British Guiana) bore his family name.[133]

Many Bristol West India traders and agents were relieved to divert their investments from troublesome plantations and Bristol's declining port into new industrial projects such as the railway. Certainly, as Marshall succinctly puts it, most were happy 'to replace slaves by sleepers'.[134] The transmogrification of Christopher Claxton into a modern pioneer of the transatlantic steamship is a case in point. Claxton is now best remembered as a managing director of the Great Western Steam Ship Company and for his involvement with the SS *Great Britain*, the famous ship designed by his friend and business partner Isambard Kingdom Brunel.[135] It is hard, however, to believe that such a turnaround in his business activities was paralleled by a turnaround in his racial attitudes. The same might be said of some of Bristol's commercial institutions. Bristol's West Indian Association survived until 1872, and more research is needed to determine its impact on racial attitudes.

So far as the emancipation settlement itself was concerned, at least one historian of Bristol maintained that 'substantial justice had been done'.[136] But such a judgement fails completely to consider how just the settlement was with regard to the former slaves themselves. It was left to the West Country-born Quaker Joseph Sturge to outline the oppressive mistreatment inflicted until 1838 on those 'emancipated' under the apprenticeship system.[137]

Notes

1 Peter Marshall, *Bristol and the Abolition of Slavery: The Politics of Emancipation* (Bristol: Bristol Historical Association, 1975, reprinted 1998).

2 Henry Hunt, *Memoirs* (London, 1821), pp. 206–7.

3 Cobbett, a true champion of the English labouring poor, denigrated the plight of the West Indian slave. See G. D. H. Cole, *The Life of William Cobbett* (London, 1924), pp. 59–60; Peter Fryer, *Staying Power* (London, 1984), pp. 234–5; Robin Blackburn, *The Overthrow of Colonial Slavery, 1776–1848* (London and New York, 1988), p. 471n.

4 BCRL, 'The Invasion of Bristol. Mr. Hunt's Attempt to Take Bristol By Storm!' (n.d. but *c.* 1812), BL 4H.

5 BRO, Election Proceedings, 1806, 12144.

6 John Latimer, *Annals of Bristol in the Eighteenth Century* (Bristol: privately printed, 1893), p. 51. Interestingly, there seems to be no mention of the slavery issue in William Cobbett's coverage of the Bristol election in his *Political Register* of 1812.

7 Rioters attacked Hart Davis's house in Clifton on the closing of the poll, and Hunt is accused of fomenting the disorder.

8 BRO, record taken from L. B. Simmons sent 1 July 1812, recorded 3 July 1812, Election Proceedings 1806–12, 12144.

9 *Ibid.*; BCRL, *An Authentic Report of the Evidence and Proceedings before the Committee of the Honourable House of Commons Appointed to Try the Merits of the Bristol Elections of 1812* (Bristol: Philip Rose, 1813), pp. 1–9.

10 This was corroborated years later by an eyewitness of the events at the Guildhall, who recollected that Hunt himself physically seized the prizefighter leading the bludgeon men and delivered him up to the sheriffs, who had earlier professed themselves too outnumbered to intervene; BCRL, 'Old Bristol Elections (From the *Bristol Times*)' (n.d. but late nineteenth century), Jefferies Collection, vol. 12.

11 *Ibid.*

12 Romilly accused Cobbett of misrepresenting him during the election and felt that Hunt was only friendly to him once he realized how popular Romilly was with the Bristol electorate. See Sir Samuel Romilly, *Memoirs* (London: John Murray, 1860), vol. 3, pp. 28–9, 57–8.

13 The final figures were:

Richard Hart Davis (T)   2910
Edward Protheroe (W)   2435
Samuel Romilly (W)   1685
Henry Hunt   446

Spencer Jordan, Keith Ramsey and Matthew Woollard, *Abstract of Bristol Historical Statistics: Part 3, Political Representation and Bristol's Elections, 1700–1997* (Bristol Historical Databases Project, University of the West of England, Bristol, 1997), p. 196. See also Romilly, *Memoirs*, vol. 3, pp. 58–60.

14 Romilly, *Memoirs*, vol. 3, p. 61n.

15 The Peloquin Trust had a fund specifically for freemen's wives who had recently given birth; *Report from the Select Committee on Bribery at Elections, Minutes of Evidence and Appendix, Parliamentary Papers (1835)*, vol. 8, pp. 379–401.

16 Election Proceedings 1806–12, 12144.

17 T. C. Hansard (ed.), *Parliamentary Debates*, vol. 27, November 1813–June 1814, p. 647.

18 C. M. MacInnes, *Bristol: A Gateway of Empire* (Bristol, 1939; Newton Abbot, 1968 edn), p. 344.

19 R. G. Thorne (ed.), *The House of Commons, 1790–1820* (London: History of Parliament Trust, 1988), vol. 4, pp. 898–900.

20 *Matthew's Annual Bristol Directory and Commercial List* (Bristol: Joseph Matthews, 1823).

21 Sir Charles Parry Hobhouse, *Some Account of the Family of Hobhouse and Reminiscences* (Leicester: Johnson Wykes & Co., n.d.), p. 30.

22 MacInnes, *Bristol: A Gateway of Empire*, p. 343.

23 Ryland, referred to in the previous chapter, was then the President of the Bristol Baptist College and Caleb Evans's successor as minister to Bristol's Broadmead Baptist congregation.

24 See, for example, the letter from George Liele, 18 May 1792, in John Rippon (ed.), *The Baptist Annual Register, 1790–1792*, p. 343. See also Edward A. Holms, 'George Liele: Negro Slavery's Prophet of Deliverance', *BQ*, vol. 20 (1964–5), esp. pp. 345–8, and G. A. Catherall, 'The Native Baptist Church', *BQ*, vol. 24 (1971–2), pp. 65–73.

25 BBCL, William Wilberforce to Revd Dr John Ryland, 29 June 1816; letters from Wilberforce to John Ryland, G97a. In this letter Wilberforce reminds Ryland how planters 'set themselves against all improvements . . . [in the religious instruction of their slaves] for fear of contagion' and thinks it advisable that all missionaries be vetted by a commission composed of planters and missionaries to ascertain that they be 'competent and safe instructors'. Ryland also pressed Wilberforce to get permission from Emperor Christopher of Haiti – a monarch with whom Clarkson and Wilberforce had a warm correspondence – to send Protestant missionaries. Again Wilberforce demurred, not wishing to offend Catholic authorities operating on the island.

26 John Latimer, *Annals of Bristol in the Nineteenth Century* (Bristol, 1893), pp. 61–2.

27 It appears that Ann Morgan Foulkes was the legal owner of Mary Ellis as the deed of manumission was to be made in her name; BCRL, letter from A. Foulkes to A. Palmer, 2 November 1819, and deed of manumission, Jefferies Collection, vol. 13, p. 167.

28 Huntington Library, San Marino, California, Clarkson Papers, CN33.

29 David Brion Davis, *Slavery and Human Progress* (New York and Oxford, 1984, 1986 edn), pp. 192–5.

30 BSMV, 'Report to be transmitted to the Colonial Assemblies by the Sub-Committee appointed by the Standing Committee of West Indian Planters and Merchants', 25 April 1823, West India Association Papers 1813–26/28. The association was correct to imply that the government was not entirely at one with the planters on the issue of slavery and emancipation. One official wrote to Bathurst, the Colonial Secretary, in the aftermath of the Demerara revolt, implying that the situation was rapidly becoming

untenable, with only four to five proprietors of some 20,000 slaves in the west of the colony under the control of some badly selected managers. As for the slaves themselves, he confided that though they 'no longer expect their freedom as they once did, . . . disappointed expectation still rankles, and discontent, and impatience . . . are the natural consequence'. PRO, letter to Bathurst from B.D.?, 30 September 1824, CO323/142P.

31 PRO, Henry Warde to Earl Bathurst, 1 December 1824, CO323/142P.

32 BSMV, West Indian Association Papers, 1813–1826/31, Bodleian Library, Oxford, 'Society for the Conversion and Education of Negroe Slaves', under 'Slavery' in the John Johnson Collection. The society was founded in 1793 from a bequest from Sir Robert Boyle. Other Bristol subscribers included G. Ames, John and Philip Vaughan, Charles Payne and George Gibbs.

33 HL, Clarkson Papers, CN33.

34 Knibb went to Jamaica in 1822 to teach at a free school there and to join his brother Thomas, who was there working as a Baptist missionary. When Thomas died in Jamaica in 1824, William took over his brother's missionary work; William Burchell, *Memoir of Thomas Burchell: Twenty-two Years a Missionary in Jamaica* (London: Benjamin Green, 1849), p. 43; R. A. L. Knight, *William Knibb: Missionary and Emancipator* (London: The Carey Press, 1924), pp. 7–9. See also Catherine Hall's pertinent discussion of Knibb in chapter 9 of her *White, Male and Middle Class: Explorations in Feminism and History* (London, 1992).

35 A. Mary Richards, 'The Connection of Bristol with the African Slave Trade, with Some Account of the Currents of Public Opinion in the City', MA thesis, University of Bristol, 1923, pp. 86–7.

36 BSMV, resolution at a meeting of the standing committee of the West India Association . . . 10 February 1826, West Indian Association Papers 1813–26.

37 BSMV, meeting of Bristol planters interested in the colonies of Demerary and Berbice, 24 November 1826, West Indian Association Papers, 1813–26.

38 BULSC, Moravian Collection, Bristol minister's diary, 1 February 1825. The Revd Ramftler, then the minister, wrote that 'however desirable we deem the object, we do not think it consistent with our calling and especially with the prosperity of our missions in the West Indies, to take a public stand in the attainment of that object'.

39 BL, *Proceedings of the Anti-Slavery Meeting held at the Guildhall Bristol Thursday 2 February 1826* (Bristol, 1826), pp. 1–7.

40 BULSC, Anon., *Twenty-Six Points of Comparison between Hebrew Slavery under the Mosaic, and British Colonial and American Slavery under the Christian Dispensation* (Bristol: Wright & Bagnall, n.d.), Pinney Papers S.4/5.

41 BL, *Proceedings of the Anti-Slavery Meeting . . . 1826*, p. 26.

42 Roberts (1780–1841), extolled for his advocacy of 'the cause of the slave', was born in Chester and spent much of his early life in London before becoming pastor at Pithay Church in Broadmead, Bristol, and later pastor of a larger chapel in the city in King Street. See J. G. Fuller, *A Memoir of the Rev. Thomas Roberts* (London and Bristol, 1842), pp. 32–4, p. 45. Thanks to Stephen Price for drawing my attention to this source.

43 *Ibid.*, p. 34. Roberts actually states that 'The only thing to be adopted was amelioration.'

44 *Ibid.*, p. 23.

45 *Ibid.*, p. 12.

46 The 1823 rebellion in Demerara must have been fresh in their minds. English individualism was, as Lunnell himself pointed out, based on the belief in the sanctity of private property, and even when it was accepted that it was wrong to have property in another human being, it was still believed that the prudent management of property was an essential precondition for political empowerment.

47 BL, *Proceedings of the Anti-Slavery Meeting . . . 1826*, pp. 12–26; Henry Richard, *Memoirs of Joseph Sturge* (London: A. W. Partridge, 1864), pp. 78–9.

48 BULSC, Moravian Collection, Bristol minister's diary, 1 February 1825 and 2 February 1826. Although there were only around 200 Moravians in the city, their missionary work was seen to be of vital importance by Evangelicals, and planters viewed this quietistic group as less politically troublesome than their Methodist and Baptist counterparts.

49 BULSC, Moravian Collection, minister's diary, 26 February 1826.

50 BULSC, Pinney Papers.

51 BULSC, Pinney Papers, letter from W. Wilberforce to Charles Pinney, 26 April 1827, S/4/21.

52 Richard H. Pares, *A West India Fortune* (London, 1950), p. 295.

53 BULSC, Pinney Papers, B. A. Wilberforce to Mrs Ames, 28 April 1827, S/4/21.

54 Marshall, *Bristol and the Abolition of Slavery*, p. 2.

55 George Stephen, *Antislavery Recollections* (London, 1854), p. 113, cited in Marshall, *Bristol and the Abolition of Slavery*, p. 3.

56 BULSC, Charles Pinney to William Wilberforce, 30 April 1827, Pinney Papers, Bristol, 5/4/21.

57 BULSC, Moravian Collection, elder committee minutes, 1827.

58 The Bristol abolitionist W. T. Blair of Cotham Lodge cited extracts from the annual report of the Society for the Conversion and Religious Instruction of the Negro Slaves in the West Indies and from the Lord Bishop of Jamaica Dioceses in a letter to the *Bristol Mercury*, 14 July 1832. Robin Blackburn states that slave exploitation intensified after 1815 'as planters and managers strove to increase output from a static or declining work-force' and that most planters neglected to organize opportunities for religious worship (let alone education); R. Blackburn, *The Overthrow of Colonial Slavery, 1776–1848* (London and New York, 1988), pp. 428–9.

59 BSMV, West Indian Association Papers, 1825–30/26.

60 Mrs Towell, Mrs Foote, Mrs Bonville, Miss F. Wright, Mrs M. Wright and Miss L. Wright, BCRL, Report of the Bristol Auxiliary Anti-Slavery Society to 31 December 1830.

61 BSMV, *Report of the Bristol and Clifton Female Anti-Slavery society, 1829* (Bristol: Wright & Bangle, n.d. but *c.* 1829), West Indian Association Papers, 1825–1830.

62 *Ibid.*

63 JRL, *The Consumers of West Indian Sugar, the Supporters of West Indian Slavery* (Bristol: Wright & Bagnall, n.d. but *c.* 1830), Collection of Printed Anti-Slavery Tracts, R107337/21/13.

64 BSMV, West Indian Association Papers, 1825–30/27. Of course the 'ladies' did know about slave labour in East India since some of its members led the campaign against it, but evidently concluded that Bengal sugar was grown by free labour as opposed to sugar grown in Malabar, which is what the letter's case was based on.

65 *Ibid.* See Marshall, *Bristol and the Abolition of Slavery*.

66 Edward Sr had, it is true, publicly supported Wilberforce's 1814 address, which urged the British government to ensure that the restored monarchy in France ended the slave trade, but that did not make him a friend to emancipation. See R. G. Thorne (ed.), *The House of Commons, 1790–1820* (London: History of Parliament Trust, 1988), vol. 4, pp. 898–901.

67 BRO, Bristol election: extract from a letter dated Bristol, 26 July [1830?], 8033(a).

68 *FFBJ*, 17 July 1830.

69 'It must be confessed they [Protheroe's supporters] were chiefly of the middle and lower classes, and that notwithstanding Mr. Protheroe's connections in that city, not

one great merchant or Banker sent his carriage or came himself to meet him, so close do they hang together'; BRO, Bristol Election, Hare Manuscripts, 8033(2).

70 Protheroe was accused by one correspondent to the press of offering £100 million in compensation, which was allegedly twice the amount of all the tax revenue! See *FFBJ*, 21 January 1831.

71 UBLSC, Elders' Conference, 28 July 1830, Moravian Collection.

72 John Hare & Co. was a floorcloth, linoleum, white lead and colour manufacturer at Temple Gate, Bristol. It was founded by John Hare (b. 1753), a Taunton man who moved to Bristol. It was probably his son or grandson of the same name who was Protheroe's agent and who, in June 1830, opened the Zion Congregational Chapel in Bedminster which he had built at his own and sole expense. BRO, 1830 Election, Schedule 40785.

73 BCRL, 'Old Bristol Elections' (from *The Bristol Times*, n.d. but *c.* 1860), Jefferies Collection, vol. 12.

74 BRO, letter to Thomas Hare from William Owen, 28 July 1830, Hare MSS, 8033(1).

75 BRO, book listing subscribers to the Protheroe campaign; Hare MSS, 8033(4). Regarding the distribution of papers, see BRO, letter from M. A. Schimmelpenninck to Mrs Hare, n.d. but *c.* July/August 1830, Hare MSS, 8033(16a).

76 BRO, letter to Mrs Hare from Wm. Millard on behalf of Mrs. Schimmelpenninck, n.d. but *c.* July 1830, in the Hare MSS, 8033(16c).

77 BRO, letter from Mrs Hare (?) to Mrs Schimmelpenninck (?), n.d., Hare MSS, 8033(35).

78 BRO, draft bill sent by Della (?) to J. Hare, 31 July 1830, Hare MSS, 8033(20). 'Della' may have alluded to 'Della Crusca', literally 'of the cross', an epithet associated with floridly romantic writing and one used more than once by female anti-slavery writers.

79 Marshall, *Bristol and the Abolition of Slavery*, pp. 10–11.

80 Bodleian Library, 'A Plain Man', *A Few Plain Answers to Plain Questions* ([London?]: King, Printer, College Hill, n.d. but *c.* 1830), John Johnson Collection.

81 Kenneth Morgan, 'Bristol West India Merchants in the Eighteenth Century', *Transactions of the Royal Historical Society*, sixth series, no. 3 (1993), pp. 190, 202; V. Olivier (ed.), *Caribbeana: Being Miscellaneous Papers Relating to the History, Genealogy, Topography and Antiquities of the British West Indies*, 6 vols (London, 1910), vol. 6, pp. 41–3.

82 Generally speaking, Merchant Venturers were identified with the old Whig interest – that is, relatively liberal on notions of religious liberty and free trade compared to their Tory counterparts – but they were willing to liaise with the Tories when it came to defending their colonial interests. It is during this period that anti-reform Whigs increasingly came to identify with the Tories whilst pro-reform Whigs saw themselves increasingly as 'Liberals'.

83 Reformers spoke warmly of the changing intellectual and moral climate, which, as G. M. Young once observed, was the product of an alliance between once incompatible traditions of Utilitarianism and Evangelicalism. The Bristol Institution for the Advancement of Science, Literature and the Arts was established in 1823 in a fine building in Park Street; BCRL, 'Anti-Slavery Meeting', 1830, 34473.

84 BSMV, West India Correspondence, 'Petition of the undersigned inhabitants of the City of Bristol and its vicinity, adopted in consequence of some assertions respecting the existing state of Slavery in the British colonies . . . which your Petitioners do not consider founded in truth', n.d.

85 BULSC, C. Claxton, 'A Letter to Lord Combermere . . . 1830 . . . including some remarks on the measures of Government with Regard to the Colonies', Pinney Papers, S/3/5.

86 Hare wrote to the press informing them that unbeknown to his colleagues, some 200 slaves were indeed employed in the mine, but that a programme of freeing and maintaining the enslaved children and paying wages to the adults with a view to their

eventual emancipation had been immediately instated. See *FFBJ*, 21 July 1830; BCRL, Braikenridge Collection, 'Election of 1830'. The charge that Quakers owned shares in Brazilian mines employing slave labour was repeated as late as 1833 in W. Lloyd Caldecot, *The Immediate Abolition of Slavery Proved to be Inconsistent with Humanity, and Tending to Perpetuate the African Slave Trade in Foreign States* (Bath: M. Meyler Printer, January 1833).

87 Most probably 'Manassee' refers to Manessah ben Israel, who had successfully petitioned Oliver Cromwell to readmit Jews into England, and 'Lopes' to a wealthy Jewish merchant of that name who bought West Country estates with money earned from investments in slave plantations.

88 BCRL, Anon., *Replication to the Parson* (Bristol: J. Smith, n.d. but 1830). Weare Collection of Broadsides.

89 BCRL, 'Anti-Slavery Meeting [date?]', 34473.

90 See, for example, the advertisement offering a five-guinea reward for information regarding the identity of the person responsible for the brutal mistreatment of a donkey in the *Bristol Mirror*, 25 July 1829.

91 Robert Darnton, *The Great Cat Massacre and Other Episodes in French Cultural History* (London, 1991 edn), p. 92; John Archer, *By a Flash and a Scare: Incendiarism, Animal Maiming and Poaching: East Anglia 1815–1870* (Oxford, 1990), pp. 7, 198–221.

92 People in traditional societies may think of physical forces as interwoven with people in a way which those in scientific societies do not (e.g. as in astrology or feng shui?); they may not distinguish people from their natural environment as we do now; they may believe that the universe responds to speech and ritual behaviour in a way 'modern' people do not. But all people, Douglas holds, are concerned to order their relations with other people and with the environment in what they deem to be within satisfactory boundaries; Mary Douglas, *Purity and Danger: An Analysis of the Concepts of Pollution and Taboo*, 2nd edition (London, 1984), p. 138.

93 *Ibid.*, p. 139.

94 *Ibid.*, p. 101. The unavailability of the option of classifying them as property was most deeply challenged by the existence of people of mixed race. Race mixing challenged social stability at a profound level precisely because it blurred social boundaries. No wonder it was charged with notions of pollution and taboo.

95 T. Edward Bowdich, *Mission from Cape Coast Castle to Ashantee*, 3rd edition (London, 1966).

96 *Ibid.*, pp. 275, 304–31; BCRL, Anon., 'Mr. Bowdich the African Traveller', *Literary Gazette*, 20 March in Braikenridge Collection, vol. 19 (St Stephen's parish), p. 313.

97 John Evans, *A Chronological Outline of the History of Bristol and the Strangers' Guide through Its Streets and Neighbourhood* (Bristol, 1824), p. 328.

98 BCRL, *Report of the Bristol Auxiliary Anti-Slavery Society to 31 December 1830*, B3218.

99 *Bristol Mirror*, 31 July 1831.

100 [William Porter], *Sir Edward Seaward's narrative of his Shipwreck and Consequent Discovery of Certain islands in the Caribbean Sea; with a detail of many Extraordinary and Highly Interesting Events in his Life for the Year 1733 to 1749 as Written in his own Diary*, 2nd edition, 3 vols (London: Longman & Co., 1832); see also the entry on Jane Porter in David Patrick and Francis Hindes Groome (eds), *Chambers' Biographical Dictionary* (London and Edinburgh, 1897), p. 759, and the memorial tablet in Bristol Cathedral.

101 Marshall, *Bristol and the Abolition of Slavery*, p. 23.

102 See Robert Bright's speech at a public dinner for Mr Baillie in *FFBJ*, 14 August 1831.

103 W. Burchell, *Memoir of Thomas Burchell*, p. 84.

104 The ticket system, whereby congregation members accepted for instruction by a pastor received a personalized ticket, was open to abuse: it could be sold or used to exert influence and may also have had a fetish status amongst some believers. The planters

mainly objected to it because it gave the slaves what they deemed to be an undue sense of self-importance, and probably too helped to create a network of like-minded slaves beyond particular estates. See Catherall, 'The Native Baptist Church', pp. 69–70.

105 *Bristol Mercury*, 23 June 1832.

106 Angus Library, Regent's Park College, Oxford, William Knibb to Thomas Knibb, 2 and 10 April 1823, W1/3.

107 Angus Library, Memorandum Book of William Knibb, W1/3.

108 Angus Library, letter from William Knibb to J. G. Fuller, 19 February 1825, W1/3.

109 William Sutcliffe's note read thus:

> You could not show your love to the poor children in Kingston in a better manner than by trying to help pay for the New School Room in which so many of them are taught to read the Bible.
>
> [signed]William Sutcliffe [aged] 14 a slave

Angus Library, William and Mary Knibb to Miss B. J. Spurrier, 13 September 1825, Knibb/Spurrier file.

110 Angus Library, extract of a letter from William Knibb, February 1826, in W1/3 'file to various people'.

111 Angus Library, W. Knibb to B. J. Spurrier, 19 February [1826?] and W. Knibb to Margaret Williams, 20 May 1827.

112 Angus Library, William on behalf of Mary Knibb to Sarah Griffith, of Cotham House, Bristol, 9 August 1825, W1/3.

113 See *BM*, 22 September 1832, 20 October 1832, 3 November 1833, and BSMV, letter from E. Irving, 18 July 1832, West India Association Letters, 1832.

114 'The most atrocious instances of cruelty occurring in the West Indies are rarely noticed, excepting in a few of the weekly papers'; *BM*, 8 September 1832.

115 This account was gleaned from what was purportedly a private letter from Jamaica to a Bristol 'gentleman'; *FFBJ*, 21 April 1832.

116 *FFBJ*, 21 April 1832.

117 BSMV, 'Petition to the Rt Hon. Viscount Goderich, His Majesty's Principal Secretary of State for the Colonies' (1832); 'Letters, petitions etc. regarding the plight of the colonists of Demerary and Esseqebo [*sic*]', 1832–1851.

118 *FFBJ*, 22 September 1832.

119 Seymour Drescher, *Capitalism and Antislavery: British Mobilization in Comparative Perspective* (New York, 1977), p. 109.

120 *FFBJ* and *Bristol Mirror*, 14 January 1832; BL, Drama Collection, Kathleen Wilson Collection, *Bristol Liberal*, 1 and 21 January 1832. Kathleen Barker, *The Theatre Royal Bristol, 1766–1966: Two Centuries of Stage History* (London: Society for Theatre Research, 1974), p. 236, lists Aldridge as appearing at the Theatre Royal on 3 February 1826, and from 23 March to 1 April 1830. He also appeared in 1846, 1847 and 1850. See also the introduction and brief biography listed on the Web site of the Herbert Marshal collection of Ira Aldridge at http://www.lib.siu.edu/spcol/SC139.html and a less academic short piece at http://library.thinkquest.org/3337/aldridge.html. My thanks to my colleague Dr James Gibbs for drawing my attention to these sites.

121 According to Jordan *et al.*, *Abstract of Bristol Historical Statistics*, p. 196, the electorate in 1830 numbered 11,254 and in 1832 was 10,315. Even allowing for the eradication of plural voting, this does not indicate a large increase in terms of one man one vote. The *Bristol Mercury*, 3 December 1832, estimated that there were 8000 voters in a city of 100,000.

122 *BM*, 13 October 1832.

123 For allegations of such malpractice, see *BM*, 15 and 22 December 1832.

124 *BM*, 18 May 1833.

125 *BM*, 25 May 1833.

126 *BM*, 27 July 1833.

127 *FFBJ*, 24 and 31 August 1833.

128 *FFBJ*, 7 September 1833. For a full dicussion of the impact of compensation on planters and merchants, see Kathleen Mary Butler, *The Economics of Emancipation: Jamaica and Barbados, 1823–1843* (Chapel Hill, NC, and London, 1995).

129 *FFBJ*, 7 September 1833.

130 *Bristol Gazette*, 29 August 1833, and letter from C. Bethell Codrington on slave emancipation in 12 September 1833.

131 *Bristol Gazette*, 29 August 1833.

132 MacInnes, *Bristol: A Gateway to Empire*, p. 355.

133 Marshall, *Bristol and the Abolition of Slavery*, Appendix I; for Danielstown, see Henry W. Case, *On Sea and Land, On Creek and River: Being an Account of Experiences in the Visitation of Assemblies of Christians in the West Indies and British Guinea; With Reminiscences of Pioneer Missionaries and of the Slave Trade Formerly Carried on from Bristol* (London, 1910), p. 33 and map; Butler, *The Economics of Emancipation* pp. 56–7, 164 n. 25.

134 Marshall, *Bristol and the Abolition of Slavery*, p. 27.

135 BL, 'Formula Requested to be Filled up for Mr. O'Byrnes's *Biographical Dictionary of All Living Naval Officers*', n.d. but *c.* 1845, in Add. MSS 38041, ff. 234–7.

136 More accurately MacInnes characterizes those who thought justice had been done as those of 'moderate opinion' whilst those who condemned the settlement as too favourable to the planters he calls 'extremists'. See MacInnes, *Bristol: A Gateway to Empire*, p. 355.

137 Joseph Sturge, *Memoirs of Joseph Sturge*, ed. Henry Richard (London: S. W. Partridge, 1864), pp. 157–201.

CONCLUSION

THRESHOLDS OF RECOLLECTION

An African youth aged 13 was charged with sleeping in the Grove, and having no place of residence. 'The darkie stated he was brought from Jamaica by the Captain of the Monmouth Brig, who put him ashore at Bristol.' The Captain was sent for and at first 'declined to be pestered by the urchin any more' but upon the solicitation of His Worship consented to take him at the same time observing to the young Imp of Darkness 'If you don't behave yourself or if you steal tobacco, sugar or any of dem tings I'll hang you up at de yard arm, Mr. Nigger.' The boy received the caution with a grin and he was sent on board in the custody of a policeman. (*Felix Farley's Bristol Journal*, 29 September 1850)[1]

What is so striking about the report quoted above (apart from its apparent lack of sympathy for the child portrayed) is the aggressively racialist language it employs. It is this which distinguishes it from reports of the previous century. The account articulates its contempt for the young black 'urchin' in a light-heartedly humorous way that deflects any critical inquiry. It implicitly conflates black people with impoverishment in a way that allows no possibility of blacks having a higher status, and reassures readers by way of a grinning victim that all is well with such a racial hierarchy.

There is something new about the tone of the article. Within one paragraph it manages to employ two abusive descriptors to characterize its subject, and cite two more with patrician amusement. True, the epithet 'Imp of Darkness' draws on ancient and medieval iconography which associated the darkness of night with spiritual darkness, but here it is given a specifically racial and comic twist. The terms 'nigger' and 'darkie' incontrovertibly bespeak the influence of colonial slavery. Though the term 'nigger' occasionally surfaces in Georgian government documents, it was used much more commonly as a term of abuse in the United States and the Caribbean. The term 'darkie' seems also to have been American (it appears in *Uncle*

Tom's Cabin by Harriet Beecher Stowe). It survived as late as the 1970s in popular parlance in Bristol.

In any case, the language used in this article, aimed as it was for a Bristol audience, illustrates how slavery had helped to shape racialist discourse in Britain. Such discourse became increasingly virulent during the last half of the nineteenth century, spurred by reactions to the Morant Bay Uprising in Jamaica in 1865.[2] As James Walvin observes, it was in

> that crucial period between the ending of British slavery and the major British imperial incursions into Africa in the 1880's, the groundwork was laid for a racial view of the world, reinforced by disappointment with the results of black freedom.[3]

The predicament of the young boy decanted into a foreign port apparently penniless was not a new one. White sailors on the slaving run had sometimes found themselves left in the West Indies, particularly if they were ill or their services were not needed on the journey home. Black sailors who had won their freedom fighting on Britain's side in the French wars were unceremoniously dumped in foreign ports, where they were often ruthlessly exploited. There were many white 'urchins' in mid-Victorian Bristol. Nevertheless, the destitution of the lad described in the report reminds us of slavery's particular economic impact in the British Caribbean. After emancipation, a legacy of economic under-development was established there and it persisted for longer than is popularly assumed. Well into the twentieth century, absentee landowners siphoned off what profits they could still make from their declining plantations. (The first banana boat came from the Caribbean into Bristol's new port at Avonmouth in 1904.) As late as 1938 a Royal Commission reported that field workers in the Caribbean were earning in real terms what their ancestors had earned as newly emancipated slaves a century before.[4] The dearth of secondary schools, the absence of industry and a poor housing stock (some people were still living in the old slave quarters) would guarantee a ready supply of migrants to England immediately after the Second World War. The Afro-Caribbean population in Bristol today (largely of Jamaican and Barbadian descent) was first established in this immediate post-war period as a direct result of the islands' impoverishment. (The city's black population from the days of slavery had long disappeared. It had been absorbed into the resident white population.[5])

Bristol's trading relations with Africa also continued long after 1807. In an evocative eyewitness account, another mid-Victorian reporter tells of a ship coming into the city's port on its return from Africa. The cargo is now palm oil, not slaves, and the straw-hatted sailors on board are bringing home, we are told, rude wood carvings, goats and parrots which they had exchanged for beads and knives with the 'shining negroes' of the West African coast.[6] This picturesque scene contrasts with the persistent rumours that for some years after the abolition of the slave trade, an illegal trade in slaves persisted. According to one report, this trade, under the aegis of Thomas Daniel, brought Africans to Hungroad near Bristol and clandestinely transferred them to West Indian ships to supply the labour-starved plantations of the British Caribbean until 1811.[7] Be that as it may, the British Navy, applauded by the anti-slavery lobby, soon became the scourge of European and African slave-traders. Ironically, it was this very intervention which helped to set the scene for Britain's subsequent colonization of Africa.

What else, besides a new detachment of migrant workers, did slavery bequeath to Bristol? This study has challenged traditional accounts in emphasizing the role some Bristolians played in the colonization of the Caribbean and in arguing that this role was instrumental in the establishment and proliferation of slave regimes. It stresses too the fact that it was black labour that was overwhelmingly behind the prosperity engendered by Bristol's plantation trade, a trade established well before the city's legal entry into the slave trade. The city's architectural heritage and early financial institutions clearly owed much to the wealth generated by the slave and slave plantation trades.[8] Some very prominent planters and West India merchants in Bristol managed to diversify their wealth into enterprises more compatible with an industrial age. The owners of that most Smilesian of Bristol institutions, the Bristol Prudent Men's Savings Bank, included Thomas Daniel, who was also a partner in the Great Western Cotton Factory, along with Charles Pinney and Robert Bright. Charles Pinney's forebears had invested in the Dorset and Somersetshire Canal Company and Levi Ames in the Somersetshire Coal Canal. Scions of the Bright, Cave, Gibbs and Harford families were all on the Bristol committee of the Great Western Railway, whose bankers included Messrs Elton, Baillie, Ames & Co.[9] Though more work remains to be done on the subject, it is clear that many of the merchants discussed in this book owned valuable urban properties in Bristol and were ground landlords of sizeable areas of the city as well as owning land further afield.

I have argued that the very prosperity which slavery brought to the city helped to engender the refinement of manners and mind which made the idea of enslavement unpalatable to more and more of its residents. Yet the political struggles over slavery in the 1820s and 1830s mobilized a conservative element within the city which retained quite a powerful place in Bristol society for a century to come. More work needs to be done on the development of racial attitudes in Bristol after 1833, but it appears that the racial attitudes commonly ascribed to this elite were shared by some other sections of the population, particularly by some of those who had served in the British colonies.

By the same token, opposition to slavery, largely Evangelical in origin, had mobilized a liberal and mainly middle-class and artisan constituency in the city. To speak very broadly, the growing professional element within the city served as an articulate counterbalance to the views of the merchants.[10] However, social deference and ethnocentrism (along with economic interests) meant that opposition to slavery did not always guarantee an absence of racialist attitudes. Nevertheless, in terms of both ideology and personnel, the abolitionist and emancipation campaigns in Bristol fed into future campaigns for radical reform. Most notable amongst these were the campaigns for the emancipation of American slaves and for British women's emancipation. (There were direct links between Bristol campaigners and the American abolitionists William Lloyd Garrison and Frederick Douglass.)[11] There is a direct continuity between these campaigns and the campaign against racial discrimination that surfaced in the 1960s in the city. Yet even in such campaigns, ambivalent racial attitudes were in evidence.[12]

A few years ago, Bristol chose to celebrate a grand 'Festival of the Sea' which featured a replica of John Cabot's ship the *Matthew* and Brunel's SS *Great Britain* as the touchstones of the city's maritime history. This book has by contrast looked at other ships. These include the ships commanded by Admiral Penn during the conquest of Jamaica; the gaily decorated slavers whose fetid holds were the scene of so much suffering; the privateers with their human booty; the naval vessels taking settlers to Sierra Leone; and the West India merchantmen. The image of the ship is, as Paul Gilroy has observed, an apt metaphor for the transfer of peoples, values and attitudes which were at the heart of the emerging Atlantic economy.[13] It is with this in mind that the term 'ship-shape and Bristol fashion' begins to take on a wider meaning.

Notes

1 My thanks to Doreen Lindegaard for bringing this entry to my attention.

2 Douglas A. Lorimer, *Colour, Class and the Victorians: English Attitudes to the Negro in the Mid-Nineteenth Century* (New York and Leicester, 1978), pp. 21–45, 179–86, 200–6.

3 James Walvin, *Black Ivory: A History of British Slavery* (London, 1992), p. 333.

4 This was the Moyne Commission; see Ron Ramdin, *The Making of the Black English Working Class* (Aldershot, Hants., 1987), pp. 95, 117, 119, 128, 136, 170, 172.

5 There is a curious oral tradition that a birthmark popularly known as 'Mongolian blue spot' was exceptionally common amongst Bristol's indigenous white population and was a genetic marker of a racially mixed ancestry.

6 BCRL, Anon., *The Land We Live In: A Pictorial and Literary Sketch-book of the British Empire. Part 12: Bristol* (London: Charles Knight, n.d. [1848]), pp. 197–8.

7 BCRL, John C. Whitting, 'Report on Pill' (typescript MS, 14 December 1969), B27993.

8 Imports of slave-produced tobacco from the USA would still continue to supply the Bristol tobacco-processing industry until the 1860s.

9 BRO, Great Western Cotton Company Partnership Articles, 12142 (1); Certificate of the Somersetshire Coal Canal Lock fund, 1803, kindly supplied to me by Derrick Hunt of Bradford-on-Avon, Wilts, who also gave me the other information about canal investments in the West Country. See also Geoffrey Channon, *Bristol and the Promotion of the Great Western Railway* (Bristol: Bristol Historical Association, 1985), p. 22.

10 Manufacturing interests played a more ambiguous role, given the interests of some of their group in the processing of slave-produced commodities.

11 It is interesting how Catholic, Jewish and female emancipation campaigns sought to gain full political rights and privileges whilst slave emancipation focused simply on securing free legal status.

12 Madge Dresser, *Black and White on the Buses: The 1963 Colour Bar Dispute in Bristol* (Bristol, 1986).

13 Paul Gilroy, *The Black Atlantic: Modernity and Double Consciousness* (London and New York, 1993).

SELECT BIBLIOGRAPHY

OF UNPUBLISHED PRIMARY SOURCES

Angus Library, Regent's College, Oxford
Thomas Knibb Correspondence
William Knibb Correspondence

Bodleian Library, University of Oxford
John Johnson Collection
Slavery file

Bristol Baptist College Library, Bristol
John Ryland Correspondence
John Newton letters
William Wilberforce letters

Bristol Central Reference Library
Richard Arding's Letter Book
Braikenridge Collection
Caleb Dickinson's Letter Book
Dyer Diary
Jefferies Collection
Southwell Papers
Weare Collection

Bristol City Museum and Art Gallery
Braikenridge Collection Catalogues
Portrait Collection

Bristol Record Office
Family and individual collections:
Baker Family Papers
Charles Bell Papers
Bright Papers
Creswick Papers
Day Family accounts
Freke Family Papers
Hare Papers
Harford Papers
Holder Papers
Munckley Papers
Miles Papers
Pedler/Wheeler Papers
Vanderhorst and Duncombe
Families Papers
Vigor Papers
Woolnough Papers
Worrall Family Papers
Solicitors' and Surveyors' Collections:
Clarke, Gwyn & Press
Harley & Duval
Loman, Chapman & Harrison
Lawrence & Co.
Meade-King & Co.
Osborne, War & Vassal, Abbot & Co.
Rider, Heaton, Meredith & Mills

Stanley Wasbrough
Religious groups' records:
  Records of the Bristol Quakers'
    Monthly Meetings
  Records of the Lewins Mead
    [Presbyterian/Unitarian]
    Congregation
  Records of the Broadmead Baptist
    Congregation
  Corporation records:
    Bristol Bargain Book, 1694–1712
      Bristol Ratebooks (selected
        parishes), 1712–60
      Scavenging Books
      Deposition Books, 1654–7

Miscellaneous
  I. V. Hall Papers
  Anti-Slavery Collection

British Library
  Liverpool Papers (Add. 38373 f. 68–69)
  Additional MSS 34181 (Abstracts of
    Jamaican Wills)
  Additional MSS 38714
  Additional MSS 38041 ff. 234–237

Friends' House Library, London
  Anti-Slavery Collection for the
    Eighteenth and Nineteenth
    Centuries – microfilm

Gloucestershire County Record Office
(Gloucester)
  Granville Sharp Correspondence D3549

Huntington Library, San Marino,
California
  Manuscript Autobiography of Joseph
    Banfield
  Stowe Papers
  Clarkson
  Brydges Papers
  Macaulay Papers

Leeds District Archives, West Yorkshire
  Wilmer Gossip Correspondence

Metropolitan Archives (London)
  Duckinfield Estate Papers

National Westminster Bank
  Bristol Old Bank and Related Records

Private Papers
  The Becher Papers

Public Record Office, Kew
  BOARD OF TRADE
    Correspondence CO388/47
  CHANCERY PAPERS
    James Rogers Papers C107/1–15
    Masters' Exhibits C105/27;
      C106/223; C107/1–15 (James
      Rogers Papers) C108/4
    Court of Chancery Proceedings:
      C11/524/25; C11/861/32;
      C11/2246/14
  COLONIAL OFFICE
  CORRESPONDENCE
    Earl of Bathurst's private
      correspondence 1824: CO323/142
    Sierra Leone Correspondence:
      CO270/3 and CO270/4;
      CO267/10
  KING'S BENCH COURT
    King's Bench Papers: KB1/19/3
  PREROGATIVE COURT OF
  CANTERBURY
    Prob. 5: Misc. Inventories, Accounts
      and Associated Documents:
      5/1149; 5/11705; 5/2725.
    Prob. 9: Limited Probate Account
      Books: PROB 9/4/152
    Prob. 11: Wills: 11/338/34; 11/350/32;
      11/358/135; 11/380/38; 11/380/101;
      11/548/214; 11/606/249;
      11/609/147; 11/612/233;
      11/644/157; 11/696/141;
      11/699/230; 11/699/233;
      11/711/225; 11/728/264;
      11/1374/352
    Prob. 20: Supplementary Wills:
      20/2238

STATE PAPER OFFICE RECORDS
  SP36/14 and 36/40
TREASURY PAPERS
  African Company Papers:
    T/70/1/70/80; 70/85; 70/188;
    70/1454; 70/1456

John Rylands Library, University of Manchester
  Charles Wesley Correspondence
  DDCW
  Tracts

Society of Merchant Venturers of the City of Bristol Archives
  African Trade
    Letters; bundles C–G: 1730–97
  Book of Trade, 1598–1693
  Miscellaneous Letters, 1830–4
  Papers of the West India Association
    Proceedings, Misc. Papers, 1813–26
    and 1825–30
  Seamen's Hospital Fund
    Ships' Muster Rolls, 1754–94
    Accounts for the relief of merchant
    seamen
  Miscellaneous Papers
  Steadfast Society Papers
  Wharfage Books, 1654–94; 1711–12

Somerset County Record Office (Taunton)
  Helyar MSS (Bybrook Plantation,
    Jamaica) DD/WHh 1089

Wiltshire County Record Office (Trowbridge)
  Thomas Goldney's Account Book
    473/295
  Dickinson Family Papers 282/1 and
    282/2
  Jamaica Correspondence 776/650
  Tonge Family Bible 226/2

Woodbrook College Library
  Bevan-Naish Collection
    Manuscript extracts from the diary of
    Sarah Fox of Bristol, 1745–1802

University of Bristol
  Special Collections
    Moravian Collection: Papers relating
    to the Bristol congregation,
    1755–1833
    Pinney Papers
  Drama Department Library
    Kathleen Barker Collection

University of Melbourne, Australia
  Bright Family Papers
    Boxes 7 and 8 (microfilm)

York Minster Library
  Granville Sharp Letter Book

INDEX

Page references in italics refer to illustrations.